Programming in Objective-C 2.0

Developer's Library

ESSENTIAL REFERENCES FOR PROGRAMMING PROFESSIONALS

Developer's Library books are designed to provide practicing programmers with unique, high-quality references and tutorials on the programming languages and technologies they use in their daily work.

All books in the *Developer's Library* are written by expert technology practitioners who are especially skilled at organizing and presenting information in a way that's useful for other programmers.

Key titles include some of the best, most widely acclaimed books within their topic areas:

PHP & MySQL Web Development
Luke Welling & Laura Thomson
ISBN 978-0-672-32916-6

MySQL
Paul DuBois
ISBN-13: 978-0-672-32938-8

Linux Kernel Development
Robert Love
ISBN-13: 978-0-672-32946-3

Python Essential Reference
David Beazley
ISBN-13: 978-0-672-32862-6

PostgreSQL
Korry Douglas
ISBN-13: 978-0-672-33015-5

Developer's Library books are available at most retail and online bookstores, as well as by subscription from Safari Books Online at **safari.informit.com**

**Developer's
Library**
informit.com/devlibrary

Programming in Objective-C 2.0

Stephen G. Kochan

♦♦ Addison-Wesley

Upper Saddle River, NJ • Boston • Indianapolis • San Francisco
New York • Toronto • Montreal • London • Munich • Paris • Madrid
Cape Town • Sydney • Tokyo • Singapore • Mexico City

Programming in Objective-C 2.0

Copyright © 2009 by Pearson Education, Inc.

ISBN-13: 978-0-321-56615-7
ISBN-10: 0-321-56615-7

Library of Congress Cataloging-in-Publication Data:
Kochan, Stephen G.
  Programming in Objective-C 2.0 / Stephen G. Kochan. – 2nd ed.
    p. cm.
  ISBN 978-0-321-56615-7 (pbk.)
  1. Objective-C (Computer program language) 2. Object-oriented programming (Computer science) 3. Macintosh (Computer)–Programming.
I. Title.
  QA76.73.O115K63 2009
  005.1'17–dc22

                        2008049771

Printed in the United States of America

Seventh Printing, March 2010

Trademarks

All terms mentioned in this book that are known to be trademarks or service marks have been appropriately capitalized. Pearson cannot attest to the accuracy of this information. Use of a term in this book should not be regarded as affecting the validity of any trademark or service mark.

Warning and Disclaimer

Every effort has been made to make this book as complete and as accurate as possible, but no warranty or fitness is implied. The information provided is on an "as is" basis. The author and the publisher shall have neither liability nor responsibility to any person or entity with respect to any loss or damages arising from the information contained in this book.

Bulk Sales

Pearson offers excellent discounts on this book when ordered in quantity for bulk purchases or special sales. For more information, please contact

U.S. Corporate and Government Sales
1-800-382-3419
corpsales@pearsontechgroup.com

For sales outside of the U.S., please contact

International Sales
international@pearsoned.com

Acquisitions Editor
Mark Taber

Development Editor
Michael Thurston

Managing Editor
Patrick Kanouse

Project Editor
Mandie Frank

Copy Editor
Krista Hansing Editorial Services, Inc.

Indexer
Ken Johnson

Proofreader
Arle Writing and Editing

Technical Editor
Michael Trent

Publishing Coordinator
Vanessa Evans

Designer
Gary Adair

Compositor
Mark Shirar

❖

To Roy and Ve, two people whom I dearly miss

❖

Contents at a Glance

Table of Contents

About the Author

Stephen Kochan is the author and coauthor of several bestselling titles on the C language, including *Programming in C* (Sams, 2004), *Programming in ANSI C* (Sams, 1994), and *Topics in C Programming* (Wiley, 1991), and several Unix titles, including *Exploring the Unix System* (Sams, 1992) and *Unix Shell Programming* (Sams 2003). He has been programming on Macintosh computers since the introduction of the first Mac in 1984, and he wrote *Programming C* for the Mac as part of the Apple Press Library. In 2003 Kochan wrote *Programming in Objective-C* (Sams, 2003), and followed that with another Mac-related title, *Beginning AppleScript* (Wiley, 2004).

About the Technical Reviewer

Michael Trent has been programming in Objective-C since 1997—and programming Macs since well before that. He is a regular contributor to Steven Frank's www.cocoadev.com Web site, a technical reviewer for numerous books and magazine articles, and an occasional dabbler in Mac OS X open source projects. Currently, he is using Objective-C and Apple Computer's Cocoa frameworks to build professional video applications for Mac OS X. Michael holds a Bachelor of Science degree in computer science and a Bachelor of Arts degree in music from Beloit College of Beloit, Wisconsin. He lives in Santa Clara, California, with his lovely wife, Angela.

We Want to Hear from You!

As the reader of this book, *you* are our most important critic and commentator. We value your opinion and want to know what we're doing right, what we could do better, what areas you'd like to see us publish in, and any other words of wisdom you're willing to pass our way.

You can email or write me directly to let me know what you did or didn't like about this book—as well as what we can do to make our books stronger.

Please note that I cannot help you with technical problems related to the topic of this book, and that due to the high volume of mail I receive, I might not be able to reply to every message.

When you write, please be sure to include this book's title and author, as well as your name and phone or email address. I will carefully review your comments and share them with the author and editors who worked on the book.

E-mail: feedback@developers-library.info
Mail: Mark Taber
           Associate Publisher
           Pearson Education
           800 East 96th Street
           Indianapolis, IN 46240 USA

Reader Services

Visit our website and register this book at www.informit.com/register for convenient access to any updates, downloads, or errata that might be available for this book.

1

Introduction

Dennis Ritchie at AT&T Bell Laboratories pioneered the C programming language in the early 1970s. However, this programming language did not begin to gain widespread popularity and support until the late 1970s. This was because, until that time, C compilers were not readily available for commercial use outside of Bell Laboratories. Initially, this growth in popularity was also partly spurred by the equal, if not faster, growth in popularity of the UNIX operating system, which was written almost entirely in C.

Brad J. Cox designed the Objective-C language in the early 1980s. The language was based on a language called SmallTalk-80. Objective-C was *layered* on top of the C language, meaning that extensions were added to C to create a new programming language that enabled *objects* to be created and manipulated.

NeXT Software licensed the Objective-C language in 1988 and developed its libraries and a development environment called NEXTSTEP. In 1992, Objective-C support was added to the Free Software Foundation's GNU development environment. The copyrights for all Free Software Foundation (FSF) products are owned by the FSF. It is released under the GNU General Public License.

In 1994, NeXT Computer and Sun Microsystems released a standardized specification of the NEXTSTEP system, called OPENSTEP. The Free Software Foundation's implementation of OPENSTEP is called GNUStep. A Linux version, which also includes the Linux kernel and the GNUStep development environment, is called, appropriately enough, LinuxSTEP.

On December 20, 1996, Apple Computer announced that it was acquiring NeXT Software, and the NEXTSTEP/OPENSTEP environment became the basis for the next major release of Apple's operating system, OS X. Apple's version of this development environment was called Cocoa. With built-in support for the Objective-C language, coupled with development tools such as Project Builder (or its successor Xcode) and Interface Builder, Apple created a powerful development environment for application development on Mac OS X.

In 2007, Apple released an update to the Objective-C language and labeled it Objective-C 2.0. That version of the language is covered in this second edition of the book.

When the iPhone was released in 2007, developers clamored for the opportunity to develop applications for this revolutionary device. At first, Apple did not welcome third-party application development. The company's way of placating wannabe iPhone developers was to allow them to develop web-based applications. A web-based application runs under the iPhone's built-in Safari web browser and requires the user to connect to the website that hosts the application in order to run it. Developers were not satisfied with the many inherent limitations of web-based applications, and Apple shortly thereafter announced that developers would be able to develop so-called *native* applications for the iPhone.

A native application is one that resides on the iPhone and runs under the iPhone's operating system, in the same way that the iPhone's built-in applications (such as Contacts, iPod, and Weather) run on the device. The iPhone's OS is actually a version of Mac OS X, which meant that applications could be developed and debugged on a MacBook Pro, for example. In fact, Apple soon provided a powerful Software Development Kit (SDK) that allowed for rapid iPhone application development and debugging. The availability of an iPhone simulator made it possible for developers to debug their applications directly on their development system, obviating the need to download and test the program on an actual iPhone or iPod Touch device.

What You Will Learn from This Book

When I contemplated writing a tutorial on Objective-C, I had to make a fundamental decision. As with other texts on Objective-C, I could write mine to assume that the reader already knew how to write C programs. I could also teach the language from the perspective of using the rich library of routines, such as the Foundation and Application Kit frameworks. Some texts also take the approach of teaching how to use the development tools, such as the Mac's Xcode and Interface Builder.

I had several problems adopting this approach. First, learning the entire C language before learning Objective-C is wrong. C is a *procedural* language containing many features that are not necessary for programming in Objective-C, especially at the novice level. In fact, resorting to some of these features goes against the grain of adhering to a good object-oriented programming methodology. It's also not a good idea to learn all the details of a procedural language before learning an object-oriented one. This starts the programmer in the wrong direction, and gives the wrong orientation and mindset for fostering a good object-oriented programming style. Just because Objective-C is an extension to the C language doesn't mean you have to learn C first.

So I decided neither to teach C first nor to assume prior knowledge of the language. Instead, I decided to take the unconventional approach of teaching Objective-C and the underlying C language as a single integrated language, from an object-oriented programming perspective. The purpose of this book is as its name implies: to teach you how to program in Objective-C 2.0. It does not profess to teach you in detail how to use the development tools that are available for entering and debugging programs, or to provide in-depth instructions on how to develop interactive graphical applications with Cocoa. You can learn all that material in greater detail elsewhere, after you've learned how to write programs in Objective-C. In fact, mastering that material will be much easier when you have a solid foundation of how to program in Objective-C. This book does not assume much, if any, previous programming experience. In fact, if you're a novice programmer, you should be able to learn Objective-C as your first programming language.

This book teaches Objective-C by example. As I present each new feature of the language, I usually provide a small complete program example to illustrate the feature. Just as a picture is worth a thousand words, so is a properly chosen program example. You are strongly encouraged to run each program (all of which are available online) and compare the results obtained on your system to those shown in the text. By doing so, you will learn the language and its syntax, but you will also become familiar with the process of compiling and running Objective-C programs.

How This Book Is Organized

This book is divided into three logical parts. Part I, "The Objective-C 2.0 Language," teaches the essentials of the language. Part II, "The Foundation Framework," teaches how to use the rich assortment of predefined classes that form the Foundation framework. Part III, "Cocoa Programming and the iPhone SDK," gives you an overview of Cocoa's Application Kit framework and then walks you through the process of developing a simple iPhone application using the UIKit framework, and developing and debugging the code with Xcode and Interface Builder.

A *framework* is a set of classes and routines that have been logically grouped together to make developing programs easier. Much of the power of programming in Objective-C rests on the extensive frameworks that are available.

Chapter 2, "Programming in Objective-C," begins by teaching you how to write your first program in Objective-C.

Because this is not a book on Cocoa programming, graphical user interfaces (GUIs) are not extensively taught and are hardly even mentioned until Part III. So an approach was needed to get input into a program and produce output. Most of the examples in this text take input from the keyboard and produce their output in a window: a Terminal window if you're using gcc from the command line, or a Console window if you're using Xcode.

Chapter 3, "Classes, Objects, and Methods," covers the fundamentals of object-oriented programming. This chapter introduces some terminology, but it's kept to a minimum. I also introduce the mechanism for defining a class and the means for sending messages to instances or objects. Instructors and seasoned Objective-C programmers will notice that I use *static* typing for declaring objects. I think this is the best way for the student to get started because the compiler can catch more errors, making the programs more self-documenting and encouraging the new programmer to explicitly declare the data types when they are known. As a result, the notion of the id type and its power is not fully explored until Chapter 9, "Polymorphism, Dynamic Typing, and Dynamic Binding."

Chapter 4, "Data Types and Expressions," describes the basic Objective-C data types and how to use them in your programs.

Chapter 5, "Program Looping," introduces the three looping statements you can use in your programs: `for`, `while`, and `do`.

Making decisions is fundamental to any computer programming language. Chapter 6, "Making Decisions," covers the Objective-C language's `if` and `switch` statements in detail.

Chapter 7, "More on Classes," delves more deeply into working with classes and objects. Details about methods, multiple arguments to methods, and local variables are discussed here.

Chapter 8, "Inheritance," introduces the key concept of inheritance. This feature makes the development of programs easier because you can take advantage of what comes from above. Inheritance and the notion of subclasses make modifying and extending existing class definitions easy.

Chapter 9 discusses three fundamental characteristics of the Objective-C language. Polymorphism, dynamic typing, and dynamic binding are the key concepts covered here.

Chapters 10–13 round out the discussion of the Objective-C language, covering issues such as initialization of objects, protocols, categories, the preprocessor, and some of the underlying C features, including functions, arrays, structures, and pointers. These underlying features are often unnecessary (and often best avoided) when first developing object-oriented applications. It's recommended that you skim Chapter 13, "Underlying C Features," the first time through the text and return to it only as necessary to learn more about a particular feature of the language.

Part II begins with Chapter 14, "Introduction to the Foundation Framework," which gives an introduction to the Foundation framework and how to access its documentation.

Chapters 15–19 cover important features of the Foundation framework. These include number and string objects, collections, the file system, memory management, and the process of copying and archiving objects.

By the time you're done with Part II, you will be able to develop fairly sophisticated programs in Objective-C that work with the Foundation framework.

Part III starts with Chapter 20, "Introduction to Cocoa." Here you'll get a quick overview of the Application Kit that provides the classes you need to develop sophisticated graphical applications on the Mac.

Chapter 21, "Writing iPhone Applications," introduces the iPhone SDK and the UIKit framework. This chapter illustrates a step-by-step approach to writing a simple iPhone (or iTouch) application, followed by a calculator application that enables you to use your iPhone to perform simple arithmetic calculations with fractions.

Because object-oriented parlance involves a fair amount of terminology, Appendix A, "Glossary," provides definitions of some common terms.

Appendix B, "Objective-C Language Summary," gives a summary of the Objective-C language, for your quick reference.

Appendix C, "Address Book Source Code," gives the source code listing for two classes that are developed and used extensively in Part II of this text. These classes define address card and address book classes. Methods enable you to perform simple operations such as adding and removing address cards from the address book, looking up someone, listing the contents of the address book, and so on.

After you've learned how to write Objective-C programs, you can go in several directions. You might want to lean more about the underlying C programming language—or you might want to start writing Cocoa programs to run on Mac OS X, or develop more sophisticated iPhone applications. In any case, Appendix D, "Resources," will guide you in the right direction.

Acknowledgments

I would like to acknowledge several people for their help in the preparation of the first edition of this text. First, I want to thank Tony Iannino and Steven Levy for reviewing the manuscript. I am also grateful to Mike Gaines for providing his input.

I'd also like to thank my technical editors, Jack Purdum (first edition) and Mike Trent. I was lucky enough to have Mike review both editions of this text. He provided the most thorough review of any book I've ever written. Not only did he point out weaknesses, but he was also generous enough to offer his suggestions. Because of Mike's comments in the first edition, I changed my approach to teaching memory management and tried to make sure that every program example in this book was "leak free." Mike also provided invaluable input for my chapter on iPhone programming.

From the first edition, Catherine Babin supplied the cover photograph and provided me with many wonderful pictures to choose from. Having the cover art from a friend made the book even more special.

I am so grateful to Mark Taber from Pearson for putting up with all delays and for being kind enough to work around my schedule and to tolerate my consistent missing of deadlines while working on this second edition. From Pearson I'd also like to thank my development editor, Michael Thurston, my copy editor, Krista Hansing, and my project editor, Mandie Frank, who expertly managed the mad dash to the finish line.

I am extremely grateful to Michael de Haan and Wendy Mui for doing an incredible, unsolicited job proofreading this second edition. Their meticulous attention to detail has resulted in a list of both typographical and substantive errors that have been addressed in the second printing. Publishers take note: these two pairs of eyes are priceless!

As always, my children showed an incredible amount of maturity and patience while I pulled this book together over the summer (and then into the fall)! To Gregory, Linda, and Julia, I love you!

Stephen G. Kochan
October 2008

Part I

The Objective-C 2.0 Language

2

Programming in Objective-C

In this chapter, we dive right in and show you how to write your first Objective-C program. You won't work with objects just yet; that's the topic of the next chapter. We want you to understand the steps involved in keying in a program and compiling and running it. We give special attention to this process both under Windows and on a Macintosh computer.

To begin, let's pick a rather simple example: a program that displays the phrase "Programming is fun!" on your screen. Without further ado, Program 2.1 shows an Objective-C program to accomplish this task:

Program 2.1

```
// First program example

#import <Foundation/Foundation.h>

int main (int argc, const char * argv[])
{
    NSAutoreleasePool * pool = [[NSAutoreleasePool alloc] init];
    NSLog (@"Programming is fun!");

    [pool drain];
    return 0;
}
```

Compiling and Running Programs

Before we go into a detailed explanation of this program, we need to cover the steps involved in compiling and running it. You can both compile and run your program using Xcode, or you can use the GNU Objective-C compiler in a Terminal window. Let's go through the sequence of steps using both methods. Then you can decide how you want to work with your programs throughout the rest of this book.

> **Note**
>
> These tools should be preinstalled on all Macs that came with OS X. If you separately in-
> stalled OS X, make sure you install the Developer Tools as well.

Using Xcode

Xcode is a sophisticated application that enables you to easily type in, compile, debug, and execute programs. If you plan on doing serious application development on the Mac, learning how to use this powerful tool is worthwhile. We just get you started here. Later we return to Xcode and take you through the steps involved in developing a graphical application with it.

First, Xcode is located in the `Developer` folder inside a subfolder called `Applications`. Figure 2.1 shows its icon.

Start Xcode. Under the File menu, select New Project (see Figure 2.2).

Xcode

Figure 2.1   Xcode Icon

A window appears, as shown in Figure 2.3.

New Project...	⇧⌘N
New File...	⌘N
Open...	⌘O
Open Quickly...	⇧⌘D
Open Recent File	▶
Open Recent Project	▶
Get Info	⌘I
Close Window	⌘W
Close Current File	⇧⌘W
Save	⌘S
Save As...	⇧⌘S
Revert to Saved	⌘U
Make Snapshot	^⌘S
Snapshots	
Print...	⌘P

Figure 2.2   Starting a new project

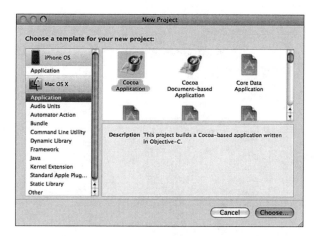

Figure 2.3   Starting a new project: selecting the application type

Scroll down the left pane until you get to Command Line Utility. In the upper-right pane, highlight Foundation Tool. Your window should now appear as shown in Figure 2.4.

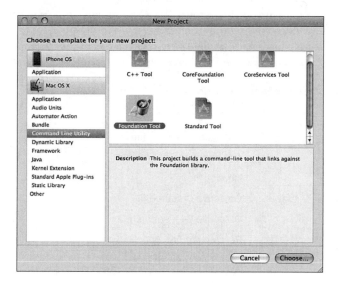

Figure 2.4   Starting a new project: creating a Foundation tool

Click Choose. This brings up a new window, shown in Figure 2.5.

Figure 2.5   Xcode file list window

We'll call the first program prog1, so type that into the Save As field. You may want to create a separate folder to store all your projects in. On my system, I keep the projects for this book in a folder called ObjC Progs.

Click the Save button to create your new project. This gives you a project window such as the one shown in Figure 2.6. Note that your window might display differently if you've used Xcode before or have changed any of its options.

Now it's time to type in your first program. Select the file prog1.m in the upper-right pane. Your Xcode window should now appear as shown in Figure 2.7.

Objective-C source files use .m as the last two characters of the filename (known as its *extension*). Table 2.1 lists other commonly used filename extensions.

Table 2.1   **Common Filename Extensions**

Extension	Meaning
.c	C language source file
.cc, .cpp	C++ language source file
.h	Header file
.m	Objective-C source file
.mm	Objective-C++ source file
.pl	Perl source file
.o	Object (compiled) file

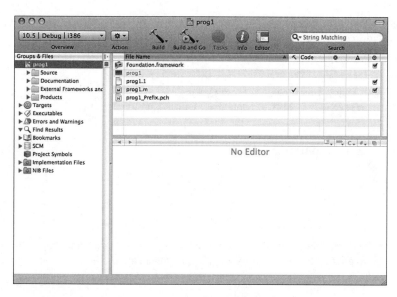

Figure 2.6   Xcode **prog1** project window

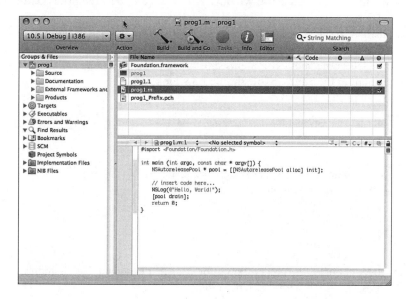

Figure 2.7   File **prog1.m** and **edit window**

Returning to your Xcode project window, the bottom-right side of the window shows the file called `prog1.m` and contains the following lines:

```
#import <Foundation/Foundation.h>

int main (int argc, const char * argv[]) {
    NSAutoreleasePool * pool = [[NSAutoreleasePool alloc] init];

    // insert code here...
    NSLog (@"Hello World!");
    [pool drain];
    return 0;
}
```

> **Note**
>
> If you can't see the file's contents displayed, you might have to click and drag up the bottom-right pane to get the edit window to appear. Again, this might be the case if you've previously used Xcode.

You can edit your file inside this window. Xcode has created a template file for you to use.

Make changes to the program shown in the Edit window to match Program 2.1. The line you add at the beginning of `prog1.m` that starts with two slash characters (`//`) is called a *comment*; we talk more about comments shortly.

Your program in the edit window should now look like this:

```
// First program example

#import <Foundation/Foundation.h>

int main (int argc, const char * argv[])
{
    NSAutoreleasePool * pool = [[NSAutoreleasePool alloc] init];
    NSLog (@"Programming is fun!");

    [pool drain];
    return 0;
}
```

Don't worry about all the colors shown for your text onscreen. Xcode indicates values, reserved words, and so on with different colors.

Now it's time to compile and run your first program—in Xcode terminology, it's called *build and run*. You need to save your program first, however, by selecting Save from the File menu. If you try to compile and run your program without first saving your file, Xcode asks whether you want to save it.

Under the Build menu, you can select either Build or Build and Run. Select the latter because that automatically runs the program if it builds without any errors. You can also click the Build and Go icon that appears in the toolbar.

> **Note**
>
> Build and Go means "Build and then do the last thing I asked you to do," which might be Run, Debug, Run with Shark or Instruments, and so on. The first time you use this for a project, Build and Go means to build and run the program, so you should be fine using this option. However, just be aware of the distinction between "Build and Go" and "Build and Run."

If you made mistakes in your program, you'll see error messages listed during this step. In this case, go back, fix the errors, and repeat the process. After all the errors have been removed from the program, a new window appears, labeled prog1 - Debugger Console. This window contains the output from your program and should look similar to Figure 2.8. If this window doesn't automatically appear, go to the main menu bar and select Console from the Run menu. We discuss the actual contents of the Console window shortly.

Figure 2.8   Xcode Debugger Console window

You're now done with the procedural part of compiling and running your first program with Xcode (whew!). The following summarizes the steps involved in creating a new program with Xcode:

1. Start the Xcode application.

2. If this is a new project, select File, New Project.

3. For the type of application, select Command Line Utility, Foundation Tool, and click Choose.

4. Select a name for your project, and optionally a directory to store your project files in. Click Save.

5. In the top-right pane, you will see the file `prog1.m` (or whatever name you assigned to your project, followed by `.m`. Highlight that file. Type your program into the edit window that appears directly below that pane.

6. Save the changes you've entered by selecting File, Save.

7. Build and run your application by selecting Build, Build and Run, or by clicking the Build and Go Button.

8. If you get any compiler errors or the output is not what you expected, make your changes to the program and repeat steps 6 and 7.

Using Terminal

Some people might want to avoid having to learn Xcode to get started programming with Objective-C. If you're used to using the UNIX shell and command-line tools, you might want to edit, compile, and run your programs using the Terminal application. Here we examine how to go about doing that.

The first step is to start the Terminal application on your Mac. The Terminal application is located in the `Applications` folder, stored under Utilities. Figure 2.9 shows its icon.

Start the Terminal application. You'll see a window that looks like Figure 2.10.

Terminal

Figure 2.9   Terminal program icon

You type commands after the `$` (or `%`, depending on how your Terminal application is configured) on each line. If you're familiar with using UNIX, you'll find this straightforward.

First, you need to enter the lines from Program 2.1 into a file. You can begin by creating a directory in which to store your program examples. Then you must run a text editor, such as vi or emacs, to enter your program:

```
sh-2.05a$ mkdir Progs    Create a directory to store programs in
sh-2.05a$ cd Progs       Change to the new directory
sh-2.05a$ vi prog1.m     Start up a text editor to enter program
    . .
```

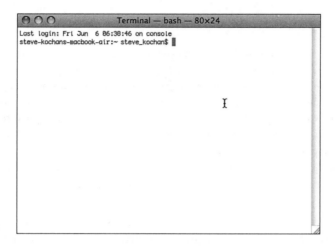

Figure 2.10   Terminal window

Note

In the previous example and throughout the remainder of this text, commands that you, the user, enter are indicated in boldface.

For Objective-C files, you can choose any name you want; just make sure the last two characters are .m. This indicates to the compiler that you have an Objective-C program.

After you've entered your program into a file, you can use the GNU Objective-C compiler, which is called gcc, to compile and link your program. This is the general format of the gcc command:

```
gcc -framework Foundation files -o progname
```

This option says to use information about the Foundation framework:

```
-framework Foundation
```

Just remember to use this option on your command line. *files* is the list of files to be compiled. In our example, we have only one such file, and we're calling it prog1.m. *progname* is the name of the file that will contain the executable if the program compiles without any errors.

We'll call the program prog1; here, then, is the command line to compile your first Objective-C program:

```
$ gcc -framework Foundation prog1.m -o prog1   Compile prog1.m & call it prog1
$
```

The return of the command prompt without any messages means that no errors were found in the program. Now you can subsequently execute the program by typing the name prog1 at the command prompt:

```
$ prog1        Execute prog1
```

```
sh: prog1: command not found
$
```

This is the result you'll probably get unless you've used Terminal before. The UNIX shell (which is the application running your program) doesn't know where `prog1` is located (we don't go into all the details of this here), so you have two options: One is to precede the name of the program with the characters `./` so that the shell knows to look in the current directory for the program to execute. The other is to add the directory in which your programs are stored (or just simply the current directory) to the shell's `PATH` variable. Let's take the first approach here:

```
$ ./prog1        Execute prog1
2008-06-08 18:48:44.210 prog1[7985:10b] Programming is fun!
$
```

You should note that writing and debugging Objective-C programs from the terminal is a valid approach. However, it's not a good long-term strategy. If you want to build Mac OS X or iPhone applications, there's more to just the executable file that needs to be "packaged" into an application bundle. It's not easy to do that from the Terminal application, and it's one of Xcode's specialties. Therefore, I suggest you start learning to use Xcode to develop your programs. There is a learning curve to do this, but the effort will be well worth it in the end.

Explanation of Your First Program

Now that you are familiar with the steps involved in compiling and running Objective-C programs, let's take a closer look at this first program. Here it is again:

```
// First program example

#import <Foundation/Foundation.h>

int main (int argc, const char * argv[])
{
    NSAutoreleasePool * pool = [[NSAutoreleasePool alloc] init];

    NSLog (@"Programming is fun!");
    [pool drain];
    return 0;
}
```

In Objective-C, lowercase and uppercase letters are distinct. Also, Objective-C doesn't care where on the line you begin typing—you can begin typing your statement at any position on the line. You can use this to your advantage in developing programs that are easier to read.

The first line of the program introduces the concept of the *comment*:

```
// First program example
```

A comment statement is used in a program to document a program and enhance its readability. Comments tell the reader of the program—whether it's the programmer or someone else whose responsibility it is to maintain the program—just what the programmer had in mind when writing a particular program or a particular sequence of statements.

You can insert comments into an Objective-C program in two ways. One is by using two consecutive slash characters (//). The compiler ignores any characters that follow these slashes, up to the end of the line.

You can also initiate a comment with the two characters / and *. This marks the beginning of the comment. These types of comments have to be terminated. To end the comment, you use the characters * and /, again without any embedded spaces. All characters included between the opening /* and the closing */ are treated as part of the comment statement and are ignored by the Objective-C compiler. This form of comment is often used when comments span many lines of code, as in the following:

```
/*
This file implements a class called Fraction, which
represents fractional numbers. Methods allow manipulation of
fractions, such as addition, subtraction, etc.

For more information, consult the document:
   /usr/docs/classes/fractions.pdf
*/
```

Which style of comment you use is entirely up to you. Just note that you can't nest the /* style comments.

Get into the habit of inserting comment statements in the program as you write it or type it into the computer, for three good reasons. First, documenting the program while the particular program logic is still fresh in your mind is far easier than going back and rethinking the logic after the program has been completed. Second, by inserting comments into the program at such an early stage of the game, you can reap the benefits of the comments during the debug phase, when program logic errors are isolated and debugged. Not only can a comment help you (and others) read through the program, but it also can help point the way to the source of the logic mistake. Finally, I haven't yet discovered a programmer who actually enjoys documenting a program. In fact, after you've finished debugging your program, you will probably not relish the idea of going back to the program to insert comments. Inserting comments while developing the program makes this sometimes tedious task a bit easier to handle.

This next line of Program 2.1 tells the compiler to locate and process a file named Foundation.h:

```
#import <Foundation/Foundation.h>
```

This is a system file—that is, not a file that you created. #import says to import or include the information from that file into the program, exactly as if the contents of the file were typed into the program at that point. You imported the file Foundation.h because it has information about other classes and functions that are used later in the program.

In Program 2.1, this line specifies that the name of the program is `main`:

```
int main (int argc, const char *argv[])
```

`main` is a special name that indicates precisely where the program is to begin execution. The reserved word `int` that precedes `main` specifies the type of value `main` returns, which is an integer (more about that soon). We ignore what appears between the open and closed parentheses for now; these have to do with *command-line arguments*, a topic we address in Chapter 13, "Underlying C Language Features."

Now that you have identified `main` to the system, you are ready to specify precisely what this routine is to perform. This is done by enclosing all the program *statements* of the routine within a pair of curly braces. In the simplest case, a statement is just an expression that is terminated with a semicolon. The system treats all the program statements included between the braces as part of the `main` routine. Program 2.1 has four statements.

The first statement in Program 2.1 reads

```
NSAutoreleasePool * pool = [[NSAutoreleasePool alloc] init];
```

It reserves space in memory for an *autorelease pool*. We discuss this thoroughly in Chapter 17, "Memory Management." Xcode puts this line into your program automatically as part of the template, so just leave it there for now.

The next statement specifies that a routine named `NSLog` is to be invoked, or *called*. The parameter, or *argument*, to be passed or handed to the `NSLog` routine is the following string of characters:

```
@"Programming is fun!"
```

Here, the `@` sign immediately precedes a string of characters enclosed in a pair of double quotes. Collectively, this is known as a constant `NSString` object.

Note

If you have C programming experience, you might be puzzled by the leading `@` character. Without that leading `@` character, you are writing a constant C-style string; with it, you are writing an `NSString` string object.

The `NSLog` routine is a function in the Objective-C library that simply displays or logs its argument (or arguments, as you will see shortly). Before doing so, however, it displays the date and time the routine is executed, the program name, and some other numbers we don't describe here. Throughout the rest of this book, we don't bother to show this text that `NSLog` inserts before your output.

You must terminate all program statements in Objective-C with a semicolon (;). This is why a semicolon appears immediately after the closed parenthesis of the NSLog call.

Before you exit your program, you should release the allocated memory pool (and objects that are associated with it) with a line such as the following:

```
[pool drain];
```

Again, Xcode automatically inserts this line into your program for you. Again, we defer detailed explanation of what this does until later.

The final program statement in main looks like this:

```
return 0;
```

It says to terminate execution of main and to send back, or *return*, a status value of 0. By convention, 0 means that the program ended normally. Any nonzero value typically means some problem occurred—for example, perhaps the program couldn't locate a file that it needed.

If you're using Xcode and you glance back to your Debug Console window (refer to Figure 2.8), you'll recall that the following displayed after the line of output from NSLog:

```
The Debugger has exited with status 0.
```

You should understand what that message means now.

Now that we have finished discussing your first program, let's modify it to also display the phrase "And programming in Objective-C is even more fun!" You can do this by simply adding another call to the NSLog routine, as shown in Program 2.2. Remember that every Objective-C program statement must be terminated by a semicolon.

Program 2.2

```
#import <Foundation/Foundation.h>

int main (int argc, const char *argv[])
{
    NSAutoreleasePool * pool = [[NSAutoreleasePool alloc] init];

    NSLog (@"Programming is fun!");
    NSLog (@"Programming in Objective-C is even more fun!");

    [pool drain];
    return 0;
}
```

If you type in Program 2.2 and then compile and execute it, you can expect the following output (again, without showing the text that NSLog normally prepends to the output):

Program 2.2 Output

```
Programming is fun!
Programming in Objective-C is even more fun!
```

As you will see from the next program example, you don't need to make a separate call to the NSLog routine for each line of output.

First, let's talk about a special two-character sequence. The backslash (\) and the letter n are known collectively as the *newline* character. A newline character tells the system to do precisely what its name implies: go to a new line. Any characters to be printed after the newline character then appear on the next line of the display. In fact, the newline character is very similar in concept to the carriage return key on a typewriter (remember those?).

Study the program listed in Program 2.3 and try to predict the results before you examine the output (no cheating, now!).

Program 2.3

```
#import <Foundation/Foundation.h>

int main (int argc, const char *argv[])
{
    NSAutoreleasePool * pool = [[NSAutoreleasePool alloc] init];

    NSLog (@"Testing...\n..1\n...2\n....3");
    [pool drain];
    return 0;
}
```

Program 2.3 Output

```
Testing...
..1
...2
....3
```

Displaying the Values of Variables

Not only can simple phrases be displayed with NSLog, but the values of *variables* and the results of computations can be displayed as well. Program 2.4 uses the NSLog routine to display the results of adding two numbers, 50 and 25.

Program 2.4

```
#import <Foundation/Foundation.h>

int main (int argc, const char *argv[])
{
    NSAutoreleasePool * pool = [[NSAutoreleasePool alloc] init];

    int sum;

    sum = 50 + 25;
    NSLog (@"The sum of 50 and 25 is %i", sum);
    [pool drain];

    return 0;
}
```

Program 2.4 Output

The sum of 50 and 25 is 75

The first program statement inside main after the autorelease pool is set up defines the variable sum to be of type integer. You must define all program variables before you can use them in a program. The definition of a variable specifies to the Objective-C compiler how the program should use it. The compiler needs this information to generate the correct instructions to store and retrieve values into and out of the variable. A variable defined as type int can be used to hold only integral values—that is, values without decimal places. Examples of integral values are 3, 5, -20, and 0. Numbers with decimal places, such as 2.14, 2.455, and 27.0, are known as *floating-point* numbers and are real numbers.

The integer variable sum stores the result of the addition of the two integers 50 and 25. We have intentionally left a blank line following the definition of this variable to visually separate the variable declarations of the routine from the program statements; this is strictly a matter of style. Sometimes adding a single blank line in a program can make the program more readable.

The program statement reads as it would in most other programming languages:

```
sum = 50 + 25;
```

The number 50 is added (as indicated by the plus sign) to the number 25, and the result is stored (as indicated by the assignment operator, the equals sign) in the variable sum.

The NSLog routine call in Program 2.4 now has two arguments enclosed within the parentheses. These arguments are separated by a comma. The first argument to the NSLog routine is always the character string to be displayed. However, along with the display of the character string, you often want to have the value of certain program variables displayed as well. In this case, you want to have the value of the variable sum displayed after these characters are displayed:

```
The sum of 50 and 25 is
```

The percent character inside the first argument is a special character recognized by the NSLog function. The character that immediately follows the percent sign specifies what type of value is to be displayed at that point. In the previous program, the NSLog routine recognizes the letter i as signifying that an integer value is to be displayed.

Whenever the NSLog routine finds the %i characters inside a character string, it automatically displays the value of the next argument to the routine. Because sum is the next argument to NSLog, its value is automatically displayed after "The sum of 50 and 25 is".

Now try to predict the output from Program 2.5.

Program 2.5

```
#import <Foundation/Foundation.h>

int main (int argc, const char *argv[])
{
    NSAutoreleasePool * pool = [[NSAutoreleasePool alloc] init];
    int value1, value2, sum;

    value1 = 50;
    value2 = 25;
    sum = value1 + value2;

    NSLog (@"The sum of %i and %i is %i", value1, value2, sum);

    [pool drain];
    return 0;
}
```

Program 2.5 Output

The sum of 50 and 25 is 75

The second program statement inside main defines three variables called value1, value2, and sum, all of type int. This statement could have equivalently been expressed using three separate statements, as follows:

```
int value1;
int value2;
int sum;
```

After the three variables have been defined, the program assigns the value 50 to the variable value1 and then the value 25 to value2. The sum of these two variables is then computed and the result assigned to the variable sum.

The call to the NSLog routine now contains four arguments. Once again, the first argument, commonly called the *format string*, describes to the system how the remaining arguments are to be displayed. The value of value1 is to be displayed immediately following the phrase "The sum of." Similarly, the values of value2 and sum are to be printed at the points indicated by the next two occurrences of the %i characters in the format string.

Summary

After reading this introductory chapter on developing programs in Objective-C, you should have a good feel of what is involved in writing a program in Objective-C—and you should be able to develop a small program on your own. In the next chapter, you begin to examine some of the intricacies of this powerful and flexible programming language. But first, try your hand at the exercises that follow, to make sure you understand the concepts presented in this chapter.

Exercises

1. Type in and run the five programs presented in this chapter. Compare the output produced by each program with the output presented after each program.

2. Write a program that displays the following text:

    ```
    In Objective-C, lowercase letters are significant.
    main is where program execution begins.
    Open and closed braces enclose program statements in a routine.
    All program statements must be terminated by a semicolon.
    ```

3. What output would you expect from the following program?

    ```
    #import <Foundation/Foundation.h>

    int main (int argc, const char *argv[])
    {
        NSAutoreleasePool * pool = [[NSAutoreleasePool alloc] init];
        int i;

        i = 1;
        NSLog (@"Testing...");
        NSLog (@"....%i", i);
        NSLog (@"...%i",  i + 1);
        NSLog (@"..%i", i + 2);

        [pool drain];
        return 0;
    }
    ```

4. Write a program that subtracts the value 15 from 87 and displays the result, together with an appropriate message.

5. Identify the syntactic errors in the following program. Then type in and run the corrected program to make sure you have identified all the mistakes:

```
#import <Foundation/Foundation.h>

int main (int argc, const char *argv[]);
(
    NSAutoreleasePool * pool = [[NSAutoreleasePool alloc] init];

    int
    INT sum;
    /* COMPUTE RESULT */
    sum = 25 + 37 - 19 ;
    // DISPLAY RESULTS //
    NSLog (@"The answer is %i", sum);

    [pool drain];
    return 0;
}
```

6. What output would you expect from the following program?

```
#import <Foundation/Foundation.h>

int main (int argc, const char *argv[])
{
    NSAutoreleasePool * pool = [[NSAutoreleasePool alloc] init];

    int answer, result;

    answer = 100;
    result = answer - 10;

    NSLog (@"The result is %i\n", result + 5);

    [pool drain];
    return 0;
}
```

3

Classes, Objects, and Methods

In this chapter, you'll learn about some key concepts in object-oriented programming and start working with classes in Objective-C. You'll need to learn a little bit of terminology, but we keep it fairly informal. We also cover only some of the basic terms here because you can easily get overwhelmed. Refer to Appendix A, "Glossary," at the end of this book, for more precise definitions of these terms.

What Is an Object, Anyway?

An *object* is a thing. Think about object-oriented programming as a thing and something you want to do to that thing. This is in contrast to a programming language such as C, known as a procedural programming language. In C, you typically think about what you want to do first and then you worry about the objects, almost the opposite of object orientation.

Consider an example from everyday life. Let's assume that you own a car, which is obviously an object, and one that you own. You don't have just any car; you have a particular car that was manufactured in a factory, maybe in Detroit, maybe in Japan, or maybe someplace else. Your car has a vehicle identification number (VIN) that uniquely identifies that car.

In object-oriented parlance, your car is an *instance* of a car. Continuing with the terminology, car is the name of the class from which this instance was created. So each time a new car is manufactured, a new instance from the class of cars is created, and each instance of the car is referred to as an object.

Your car might be silver, have a black interior, be a convertible or hardtop, and so on. Additionally, you perform certain actions with your car. For example, you drive your car, fill it with gas, (hopefully) wash it, take it in for service, and so on. Table 3.1 depicts this.

The actions listed in Table 3.1 can be done with you car, and they can be done with other cars as well. For example, your sister drives her car, washes it, fills it with gas, and so on.

Table 3.1   **Actions on Objects**

Object	What You Do with It
Your car	Drive it
	Fill it with gas
	Wash it
	Service it

Instances and Methods

A unique occurrence of a class is an instance, and the actions that are performed on the instance are called *methods*. In some cases, a method can be applied to an instance of the class or to the class itself. For example, washing your car applies to an instance (in fact, all the methods listed in Table 3.1 can be considered instance methods). Finding out how many types of cars a manufacturer makes would apply to the class, so it would be a class method.

Suppose you have two cars that came off the assembly line and are seemingly identical: They both have the same interior, same paint color, and so on. They might start out the same, but as each car is used by its respective owner, it acquires its own unique characteristics. For example, one car might end up with a scratch on it and the other might have more miles on it. Each instance or object contains not only information about its initial characteristics acquired from the factory, but also its current characteristics. Those characteristics can change dynamically. As you drive your car, the gas tank becomes depleted, the car gets dirtier, and the tires get a little more worn.

Applying a method to an object can affect the *state* of that object. If your method is to "fill up my car with gas," after that method is performed, your car's gas tank will be full. The method then will have affected the state of the car's gas tank.

The key concepts here are that objects are unique representations from a class, and each object contains some information (data) that is typically private to that object. The methods provide the means of accessing and changing that data.

The Objective-C programming language has the following particular syntax for applying methods to classes and instances:

```
[ ClassOrInstance method ];
```

In this syntax, a left bracket is followed by the name of a class or instance of that class, which is followed by one or more spaces, which is followed by the method you want to perform. Finally, it is closed off with a right bracket and a terminating semicolon. When you ask a class or an instance to perform some action, you say that you are sending it a *message*; the recipient of that message is called the *receiver*. So another way to look at the general format described previously is as follows:

```
[ receiver message ] ;
```

Let's go back to the previous list and write everything in this new syntax. Before you do that, though, you need to get your new car. Go to the factory for that, like so:

```
yourCar = [Car new];      get a new car
```

You send a message to the `Car` class (the receiver of the message) asking it to give you a new car. The resulting object (which represents your unique car) is then stored in the variable `yourCar`. From now on, `yourCar` can be used to refer to your instance of the car, which you got from the factory.

Because you went to the factory to get the car, the method new is called a *factory* or *class* method. The rest of the actions on your new car will be instance methods because they apply to your car. Here are some sample message expressions you might write for your car:

```
[yourCar prep];          get it ready for first-time use
[yourCar drive];         drive your car
[yourCar wash];          wash your car
[yourCar getGas];        put gas in your car if you need it
[yourCar service];       service your car

[yourCar topDown];       if it's a convertible
[yourCar topUp];
currentMileage = [yourCar currentOdometer];
```

This last example shows an instance method that returns information—presumably, the current mileage, as indicated on the odometer. Here we store that information inside a variable in our program called `currentMileage`.

Your sister, Sue, can use the same methods for her own instance of a car:

```
[suesCar drive];
[suesCar wash];
[suesCar getGas];
```

Applying the same methods to different objects is one of the key concepts of object-oriented programming, and you'll learn more about it later.

You probably won't need to work with cars in your programs. Your objects will likely be computer-oriented things, such as windows, rectangles, pieces of text, or maybe even a calculator or a playlist of songs. And just like the methods used for your cars, your methods might look similar, as in the following:

```
[myWindow erase];               Clear the window

[myRect getArea];               Calculate the area of the rectangle

[userText spellCheck];          Spell-check some text

[deskCalculator clearEntry];    Clear the last entry

[favoritePlaylist showSongs];   Show the songs in a playlist of favorites

[phoneNumber dial];             Dial a phone number
```

An Objective-C Class for Working with Fractions

Now it's time to define an actual class in Objective-C and learn how to work with instances of the class.

Once again, you'll learn procedure first. As a result, the actual program examples might not seem very practical. We get into more practical stuff later.

Suppose you need to write a program to work with fractions. Maybe you need to deal with adding, subtracting, multiplying, and so on. If you didn't know about classes, you might start with a simple program that looked like this:

Program 3.1

```
// Simple program to work with fractions
#import <Foundation/Foundation.h>

int main (int argc, char *argv[])
{
    NSAutoreleasePool * pool = [[NSAutoreleasePool alloc] init];
    int   numerator = 1;
    int   denominator = 3;
    NSLog (@"The fraction is %i/%i", numerator, denominator);

    [pool drain];
    return 0;
}
```

Program 3.1 Output

```
The fraction is 1/3
```

In Program 3.1 the fraction is represented in terms of its numerator and denominator. After the autorelease pool is created, the two lines in main both declare the variables numerator and denominator as integers and assign them initial values of 1 and 3, respectively. This is equivalent to the following lines:

```
int numerator, denominator;

numerator = 1;
denominator = 3;
```

We represented the fraction 1/3 by storing 1 in the variable numerator and 3 in the variable denominator. If you needed to store a lot of fractions in your program, this could be cumbersome. Each time you wanted to refer to the fraction, you'd have to refer to the corresponding numerator and denominator. And performing operations on these fractions would be just as awkward.

It would be better if you could define a fraction as a single entity and collectively refer to its numerator and denominator with a single name, such as myFraction. You can do that in Objective-C, and it starts by defining a new class.

Program 3.2 duplicates the functionality of Program 3.1 using a new class called Fraction. Here, then, is the program, followed by a detailed explanation of how it works.

Program 3.2

```
// Program to work with fractions - class version

#import <Foundation/Foundation.h>

//---- @interface section ----

@interface Fraction: NSObject
{
    int   numerator;
    int   denominator;
}

-(void)   print;
-(void)   setNumerator: (int) n;
-(void)   setDenominator: (int) d;

@end

//---- @implementation section ----


@implementation Fraction
-(void) print
{
    NSLog (@"%i/%i", numerator, denominator);
}

-(void) setNumerator: (int) n
{
    numerator = n;
}

-(void) setDenominator: (int) d
{
    denominator = d;
}
```

```
@end

//---- program section ----


int main (int argc, char *argv[])
{
    NSAutoreleasePool * pool = [[NSAutoreleasePool alloc] init];
    Fraction  *myFraction;

    // Create an instance of a Fraction

    myFraction = [Fraction alloc];
    myFraction = [myFraction init];

    // Set fraction to 1/3

    [myFraction setNumerator: 1];
    [myFraction setDenominator: 3];

    // Display the fraction using the print method

    NSLog (@"The value of myFraction is:");
    [myFraction print];
    [myFraction release];

    [pool drain];
    return 0;
}
```

Program 3.2 Output

```
The value of myFraction is:
1/3
```

As you can see from the comments in Program 3.2, the program is logically divided into three sections:

- @interface section
- @implementation section
- program section

The @interface section describes the class, its data components, and its methods, whereas the @implementation section contains the actual code that implements these methods. Finally, the program section contains the program code to carry out the intended purpose of the program.

Each of these sections is a part of every Objective-C program, even though you might not need to write each section yourself. As you'll see, each section is typically put in its own file. For now, however, we keep it all together in a single file.

The @interface Section

When you define a new class, you have to do a few things. First, you have to tell the Objective-C compiler where the class came from. That is, you have to name its *parent* class. Second, you have to specify what type of data is to be stored in the objects of this class. That is, you have to describe the data that members of the class will contain. These members are called the *instance variables*. Finally, you need to define the type of operations, or *methods*, that can be used when working with objects from this class. This is all done in a special section of the program called the @interface section. The general format of this section looks like this:

```
@interface NewClassName: ParentClassName
{
    memberDeclarations;
}

methodDeclarations;
@end
```

By convention, class names begin with an uppercase letter, even though it's not required. This enables someone reading your program to distinguish class names from other types of variables by simply looking at the first character of the name. Let's take a short diversion to talk a little about forming names in Objective-C.

Choosing Names

In Chapter 2, "Programming in Objective-C," you used several variables to store integer values. For example, you used the variable sum in Program 2.4 to store the result of the addition of the two integers 50 and 25.

The Objective-C language allows you to store data types other than just integers in variables as well, as long as the proper declaration for the variable is made before it is used in the program. Variables can be used to store floating-point numbers, characters, and even objects (or, more precisely, references to objects).

The rules for forming names are quite simple: They must begin with a letter or underscore (_), and they can be followed by any combination of letters (upper- or lowercase), underscores, or the digits 0–9. The following is a list of valid names:

- sum
- pieceFlag

- i
- myLocation
- numberOfMoves
- _sysFlag
- ChessBoard

On the other hand, the following names are not valid for the stated reasons:

- sum$value $—is not a valid character.
- piece flag—Embedded spaces are not permitted.
- 3Spencer—Names can't start with a number.
- int—This is a reserved word.

int cannot be used as a variable name because its use has a special meaning to the Objective-C compiler. This use is known as a *reserved name* or *reserved word*. In general, any name that has special significance to the Objective-C compiler cannot be used as a variable name. Appendix B, "Objective-C 2.0 Language Summary," provides a complete list of such reserved names.

Always remember that upper- and lowercase letters are distinct in Objective-C. Therefore, the variable names sum, Sum, and SUM each refer to a different variable. As noted, when naming a class, start it with a capital letter. Instance variables, objects, and method names, on the other hand, typically begin with lowercase letters. To aid readability, capital letters are used inside names to indicate the start of a new word, as in the following examples:

- AddressBook—This could be a class name.
- currentEntry—This could be an object.
- current_entry—Some programmers use underscores as word separators.
- addNewEntry—This could be a method name.

When deciding on a name, keep one recommendation in mind: Don't be lazy. Pick names that reflect the intended use of the variable or object. The reasons are obvious. Just as with the comment statement, meaningful names can dramatically increase the readability of a program and will pay off in the debug and documentation phases. In fact, the documentation task will probably be much easier because the program will be more self-explanatory.

Here, again, is the @interface section from Program 3.2:

```
//---- @interface section ----

@interface Fraction: NSObject
{
    int   numerator;
```

```
    int   denominator;
}

-(void) print;
-(void) setNumerator: (int) n;
-(void) setDenominator: (int) d;

@end
```

The name of the new class (*NewClassName*) is Fraction, and its parent class is NSObject. (We talk in greater detail about parent classes in Chapter 8, "Inheritance.") The NSObject class is defined in the file NSObject.h, which is automatically included in your program whenever you import Foundation.h.

Instance Variables

The *memberDeclarations* section specifies what types of data are stored in a Fraction, along with the names of those data types. As you can see, this section is enclosed inside its own set of curly braces. For your Fraction class, these declarations say that a Fraction object has two integer members, called numerator and denominator:

```
int   numerator;
int   denominator;
```

The members declared in this section are known as the instance variables. As you'll see, each time you create a new object, a new and unique set of instance variables also is created. Therefore, if you have two Fractions, one called fracA and another called fracB, each will have its own set of instance variables. That is, fracA and fracB each will have its own separate numerator and denominator. The Objective-C system automatically keeps track of this for you, which is one of the nicer things about working with objects.

Class and Instance Methods

You have to define methods to work with your Fractions. You need to be able to set the value of a fraction to a particular value. Because you won't have direct access to the internal representation of a fraction (in other words, direct access to its instance variables), you must write methods to set the numerator and denominator. You'll also write a method called print that will display the value of a fraction. Here's what the declaration for the print method looks like in the interface file:

```
-(void) print;
```

The leading minus sign (-) tells the Objective-C compiler that the method is an instance method. The only other option is a plus sign (+), which indicates a class method. A class method is one that performs some operation on the class itself, such as creating a new instance of the class. This is similar to manufacturing a new car, in that the car is the class and you want to create a new one, which would be a class method.

An instance method performs some operation on a particular instance of a class, such as setting its value, retrieving its value, displaying its value, and so on. Referring to the car example, after you have manufactured the car, you might need to fill it with gas. The operation of filling it with gas is performed on a particular car, so it is analogous to an instance method.

Return Values

When you declare a new method, you have to tell the Objective-C compiler whether the method returns a value and, if it does, what type of value it returns. You do this by enclosing the return type in parentheses after the leading minus or plus sign. So this declaration specifies that the instance method called retrieveNumerator returns an integer value:

```
-(int) retrieveNumerator;
```

Similarly, this line declares a method that returns a double precision value. (You'll learn more about this data type in Chapter 4, "Data Types and Expressions.")

```
-(double) retrieveDoubleValue;
```

A value is returned from a method using the Objective-C return statement, similar to the way in which we returned a value from main in previous program examples.

If the method returns no value, you indicate that using the type void, as in the following:

```
-(void) print;
```

This declares an instance method called print that returns no value. In such a case, you do not need to execute a return statement at the end of your method. Alternatively, you can execute a return without any specified value, as in the following:

```
return;
```

You don't need to specify a return type for your methods, although it's better programming practice if you do. If you don't specify a type, id is the default. You'll learn more about the id data type in Chapter 9, "Polymorphism, Dynamic Typing, and Dynamic Binding." Basically, you can use the id type to refer to any type of object.

Method Arguments

Two other methods are declared in the @interface section from Program 3.2:

```
-(void) setNumerator: (int) n;
-(void) setDenominator: (int) d;
```

These are both instance methods that return no value. Each method takes an integer argument, which is indicated by the (int) in front of the argument name. In the case of setNumerator, the name of the argument is n. This name is arbitrary and is the name the method uses to refer to the argument. Therefore, the declaration of setNumerator specifies that one integer argument, called n, will be passed to the method and that no value will be returned. This is similar for setDenominator, except that the name of its argument is d.

Notice the syntax of the declaration for these methods. Each method name ends with a colon, which tells the Objective-C compiler that the method expects to see an argument. Next, the type of the argument is specified, enclosed in a set of parentheses, in much the same way the return type is specified for the method itself. Finally, the symbolic name to be used to identify that argument in the method is specified. The entire declaration is terminated with a semicolon. Figure 3.1 depicts this syntax.

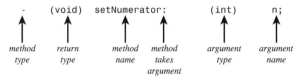

Figure 3.1   Declaring a method

When a method takes an argument, you also append a colon to the method name when referring to the method. Therefore, setNumerator: and setDenominator: is the correct way to identify these two methods, each of which takes a single argument. Also, identifying the print method without a trailing colon indicates that this method does not take any arguments. In Chapter 7, "More on Classes," you'll see how methods that take more than one argument are identified.

The @implementation Section

As noted, the @implementation section contains the actual code for the methods you declared in the @interface section. Just as a point of terminology, you say that you *declare* the methods in the @interface section and that you *define* them (that is, give the actual code) in the @implementation section.

The general format for the @implementation section is as follows:

```
@implementation NewClassName
    methodDefinitions;
@end
```

NewClassName is the same name that was used for the class in the @interface section. You can use the trailing colon followed by the parent class name, as we did in the @interface section:

```
@implementation Fraction: NSObject
```

However, this is optional and typically not done.

The *methodDefinitions* part of the @implementation section contains the code for each method specified in the @interface section. Similar to the @interface section, each method's definition starts by identifying the type of method (class or instance), its return type, and its arguments and their types. However, instead of the line ending with a semicolon, the code for the method follows, enclosed inside a set of curly braces.

Consider the `@implementation` section from Program 3.2:

```
//---- @implementation section ----
@implementation Fraction
-(void) print
{
    NSLog (@"%i/%i", numerator, denominator);
}

-(void) setNumerator: (int) n
{
    numerator = n;
}

-(void) setDenominator: (int) d
{
    denominator = d;
}

@end
```

The `print` method uses `NSLog` to display the values of the instance variables `numerator` and `denominator`. But to which numerator and denominator does this method refer? It refers to the instance variables contained in the object that is the receiver of the message. That's an important concept, and we return to it shortly.

The `setNumerator:` method stores the integer argument you called `n` in the instance variable `numerator`. Similarly, `setDenominator:` stores the value of its argument `d` in the instance variable `denominator`.

The program Section

The `program` section contains the code to solve your particular problem, which can be spread out across many files, if necessary. Somewhere you must have a routine called `main`, as we've previously noted. That's where your program always begins execution. Here's the program section from Program 3.2:

```
//---- program section ----

int main (int argc, char *argv[])
{
    NSAutoreleasePool * pool = [[NSAutoreleasePool alloc] init];
```

```
    Fraction  *myFraction;

    // Create an instance of a Fraction

    myFraction = [Fraction alloc];
    myFraction = [myFraction init];

    // Set fraction to 1/3

    [myFraction setNumerator: 1];
    [myFraction setDenominator: 3];

    // Display the fraction using the print method

    NSLog (@"The value of myFraction is:");
    [myFraction print];

    [myFraction release];
    [pool drain];

    return 0;
}
```

Inside main, you define a variable called myFraction with the following line:

```
Fraction *myFraction;
```

This line says that myFraction is an object of type Fraction; that is, myFraction is used to store values from your new Fraction class. The asterisk (*) in front of myFraction is required, but don't worry about its purpose now. Technically, it says that myFraction is actually a reference (or *pointer*) to a Fraction.

Now that you have an object to store a Fraction, you need to create one, just as you ask the factory to build you a new car. This is done with the following line:

```
myFraction = [Fraction alloc];
```

alloc is short for *allocate*. You want to allocate memory storage space for a new fraction. This expression sends a message to your newly created Fraction class:

```
[Fraction alloc]
```

You are asking the Fraction class to apply the alloc method, but you never defined an alloc method, so where did it come from? The method was inherited from a parent class. Chapter 8, "Inheritance" deals with this topic in detail.

When you send the alloc message to a class, you get back a new instance of that class. In Program 3.2, the returned value is stored inside your variable myFraction. The alloc method is guaranteed to zero out all of an object's instance variables. However, that doesn't mean that the object has been properly initialized for use. You need to initialize an object after you allocate it.

This is done with the next statement in Program 3.2, which reads as follows:

```
myFraction = [myFraction init];
```

Again, you are using a method here that you didn't write yourself. The init method initializes the instance of a class. Note that you are sending the init message to myFraction. That is, you want to initialize a specific Fraction object here, so you don't send it to the class—you send it to an instance of the class. Make sure you understand this point before continuing.

The init method also returns a value—namely, the initialized object. You store the return value in your Fraction variable myFraction.

The two-line sequence of allocating a new instance of class and then initializing it is done so often in Objective-C that the two messages are typically combined, as follows:

```
myFraction = [[Fraction alloc] init];
```

This inner message expression is evaluated first:

```
[Fraction alloc]
```

As you know, the result of this message expression is the actual Fraction that is allocated. Instead of storing the result of the allocation in a variable, as you did before, you directly apply the init method to it. So, again, first you allocate a new Fraction and then you initialize it. The result of the initialization is then assigned to the myFraction variable.

As a final shorthand technique, the allocation and initialization is often incorporated directly into the declaration line, as in the following:

```
Fraction *myFraction = [[Fraction alloc] init];
```

We use this coding style often throughout the remainder of this book, so it's important that you understand it. You've seen in every program up to this point with the allocation of the autorelease pool:

```
NSAutoreleasePool * pool = [[NSAutoreleasePool alloc] init];
```

Here an alloc message is sent to the NSAutoreleasePool class requesting that a new instance be created. The init message then is sent to the newly created object to get it initialized.

Returning to Program 3.2, you are now ready to set the value of your fraction. These program lines do just that:

```
// Set fraction to 1/3

[myFraction setNumerator: 1];
[myFraction setDenominator: 3];
```

The first message statement sends the `setNumerator:` message to `myFraction`. The argument that is supplied is the value `1`. Control is then sent to the `setNumerator:` method you defined for your `Fraction` class. The Objective-C system knows that it is the method from this class to use because it knows that `myFraction` is an object from the `Fraction` class.

Inside the `setNumerator:` method, the passed value of `1` is stored inside the variable n. The single program line in that method stores that value in the instance variable `numerator`. So you have effectively set the numerator of `myFraction` to `1`.

The message that invokes the `setDenominator:` method on `myFraction` follows next. The argument of `3` is assigned to the variable d inside the `setDenominator:` method. This value is then stored inside the `denominator` instance variable, thus completing the assignment of the value `1/3` to `myFraction`. Now you're ready to display the value of your fraction, which you do with the following lines of code from Program 3.2:

```
// display the fraction using the print method
```

```
NSLog (@"The value of myFraction is:");
[myFraction print];
```

The `NSLog` call simply displays the following text:

```
The value of myFraction is:
```

The following message expression invokes the `print` method:

```
[myFraction print];
```

Inside the `print` method, the values of the instance variables `numerator` and `denominator` are displayed, separated by a slash character.

The message in the program releases or frees the memory that was used for the `Fraction` object:

```
[myFraction release];
```

This is a critical part of good programming style. Whenever you create a new object, you are asking for memory to be allocated for that object. Also, when you're done with the object, you are responsible for releasing the memory it uses. Although it's true that the memory will be released when your program terminates anyway, after you start developing more sophisticated applications, you can end up working with hundreds (or thousands) of objects that consume a lot of memory. Waiting for the program to terminate for the memory to be released is wasteful of memory, can slow your program's execution, and is not good programming style. So get into the habit of releasing memory when you can right now.

The Apple runtime system provides a mechanism known as *garbage collection* that facilitates automatic cleanup of memory. However, it's best to learn how to manage your memory usage yourself instead of relying on this automated mechanism. In fact, you can't rely on garbage collection when programming for certain platforms on which garbage collection is not supported, such as the iPhone. For that reason, we don't talk about garbage collection until much later in this book.

It seems as if you had to write a lot more code to duplicate in Program 3.2 what you did in Program 3.1. That's true for this simple example here; however, the ultimate goal in working with objects is to make your programs easier to write, maintain, and extend. You'll realize that later.

The last example in this chapter shows how you can work with more than one fraction in your program. In Program 3.3, you set one fraction to 2/3, set another to 3/7, and display them both.

Program 3.3

```
// Program to work with fractions - cont'd

#import <Foundation/Foundation.h>

//---- @interface section ----

@interface Fraction: NSObject
{
    int  numerator;
    int  denominator;
}

-(void) print;
-(void) setNumerator: (int) n;
-(void) setDenominator: (int) d;

@end

//---- @implementation section ----


@implementation Fraction
-(void) print
{
    NSLog (@"%i/%i", numerator, denominator);
}

-(void) setNumerator: (int) n
{
    numerator = n;
}

-(void) setDenominator: (int) d
{
```

```
    denominator = d;
}

@end

//---- program section ----

int main (int argc, char *argv[])
{
    NSAutoreleasePool * pool = [[NSAutoreleasePool alloc] init];

    Fraction  *frac1 = [[Fraction alloc] init];
    Fraction  *frac2 = [[Fraction alloc] init];

    // Set 1st fraction to 2/3

    [frac1 setNumerator: 2];
    [frac1 setDenominator: 3];

    // Set 2nd fraction to 3/7

    [frac2 setNumerator: 3];
    [frac2 setDenominator: 7];

    // Display the fractions

    NSLog (@"First fraction is:");
    [frac1 print];

    NSLog (@"Second fraction is:");
    [frac2 print];

    [frac1 release];
    [frac2 release];

    [pool drain];
    return 0;
}
```

Program 3.3 Output

```
First fraction is:
2/3
Second fraction is:
3/7
```

The @interface and @implementation sections remain unchanged from Program 3.2. The program creates two Fraction objects, called frac1 and frac2, and then assigns the value 2/3 to the first fraction and 3/7 to the second. Realize that when the setNumerator: method is applied to frac1 to set its numerator to 2, the instance variable frac1 gets its instance variable numerator set to 2. Also, when frac2 uses the same method to set its numerator to 3, its distinct instance variable numerator is set to the value 3. Each time you create a new object, it gets its own distinct set of instance variables. Figure 3.2 depicts this.

Based on which object is getting sent the message, the correct instance variables are referenced. Therefore, here frac1's numerator is referenced whenever setNumerator: uses the name numerator inside the method:

```
[frac1 setNumerator: 2];
```

That's because frac1 is the receiver of the message.

Figure 3.2   Unique instance variables

Accessing Instance Variables and Data Encapsulation

You've seen how the methods that deal with fractions can access the two instance variables numerator and denominator directly by name. In fact, an instance method can always directly access its instance variables. A class method can't, however, because it's dealing only with the class itself, not with any instances of the class (think about that for a second). But what if you wanted to access your instance variables from someplace else—for example, from inside your main routine? You can't do that directly because they are hidden. The fact that they are hidden from you is a key concept called *data encapsulation*. It enables someone writing class definitions to extend and modify the class definitions, without worrying about whether programmers (that is, users of the class) are tinkering with the internal details of the class. Data encapsulation provides a nice layer of insulation between the programmer and the class developer.

You can access your instance variables in a clean way by writing special methods to retrieve their values. For example, you'll create two new methods called, appropriately enough, numerator and denominator to access the corresponding instance variables of the Fraction that is the receiver of the message. The result is the corresponding integer value, which you return. Here are the declarations for your two new methods:

```
-(int) numerator;
-(int) denominator;
```

And here are the definitions:

```
-(int) numerator
{
    return numerator;
}
```

```
-(int) denominator
{
   return denominator;
}
```

Note that the names of the methods and the instance variables they access are the same. There's no problem doing this; in fact, it is common practice. Program 3.4 tests your two new methods.

Program 3.4

```
// Program to access instance variables - cont'd

#import <Foundation/Foundation.h>
//---- @interface section ----

@interface Fraction: NSObject
{
   int  numerator;
   int  denominator;
}

-(void) print;
-(void) setNumerator: (int) n;
-(void) setDenominator: (int) d;
-(int) numerator;
-(int) denominator;

@end

//---- @implementation section ----


@implementation Fraction
-(void) print
{
   NSLog (@"%i/%i", numerator, denominator);
}

-(void) setNumerator: (int) n
{
    numerator = n;
}

-(void) setDenominator: (int) d
{
    denominator = d;
}

-(int) numerator
{
    return numerator;
}
```

```
-(int) denominator
{
    return denominator;
}

@end


//---- program section ----

int main (int argc, char *argv[])
{
    NSAutoreleasePool * pool = [[NSAutoreleasePool alloc] init];
    Fraction  *myFraction = [[Fraction alloc] init];

    // Set fraction to 1/3

    [myFraction setNumerator: 1];
    [myFraction setDenominator: 3];

    // Display the fraction using our two new methods

    NSLog (@"The value of myFraction is: %i/%i",
        [myFraction numerator], [myFraction denominator]);
    [myFraction release];
    [pool drain];

    return 0;
}
```

Program 3.4 Output

```
The value of myFraction is 1/3
```

This NSLog statement displays the results of sending two messages to myFraction: the first to retrieve the value of its numerator, and the second the value of its denominator:

```
NSLog (@"The value of myFraction is: %i/%i",
    [myFraction numerator], [myFraction denominator]);
```

Incidentally, methods that set the values of instance variables are often collectively referred to as *setters*, and methods used to retrieve the values of instance variables are called *getters*. For the Fraction class, setNumerator: and setDenominator: are the setters, and numerator and denominator are the getters.

> **Note**
> Soon you'll learn a convenient feature of Objective-C 2.0 that allows for the automatic creation of getter and setter methods.

We should also point out that there's also a method called new that combines the actions of an alloc and init. So this line could be used to allocate and initialize a new Fraction:

```
Fraction *myFraction = [Fraction new];
```

It's generally better to use the two-step allocation and initialization approach so you conceptually understand that two distinct events are occurring: You're first creating a new object and then you're initializing it.

Summary

Now you know how to define your own class, create objects or instances of that class, and send messages to those objects. We return to the Fraction class in later chapters. You'll learn how to pass multiple arguments to your methods, how to divide your class definitions into separate files, and also how to use key concepts such as inheritance and dynamic binding. However, now it's time to learn more about data types and writing expressions in Objective-C. First, try the exercises that follow to test your understanding of the important points covered in this chapter.

Exercises

1. Which of the following are invalid names? Why?

Int	playNextSong	6_05
_calloc	Xx	alphaBetaRoutine
clearScreen	_1312	z
ReInitialize	_	A$

2. Based on the example of the car in this chapter, think of an object you use every day. Identify a class for that object and write five actions you do with that object.

3. Given the list in exercise 2, use the following syntax to rewrite your list in this format:
   ```
   [instance method];
   ```

4. Imagine that you owned a boat and a motorcycle in addition to a car. List the actions you would perform with each of these. Do you have any overlap between these actions?

5. Based on question 4, imagine that you had a class called Vehicle and an object called myVehicle that could be either Car, Motorcycle, or Boat. Imagine that you wrote the following:
   ```
   [myVehicle prep];
   [myVehicle getGas];
   [myVehicle service];
   ```
   Do you see any advantages of being able to apply an action to an object that could be from one of several classes?

6. In a procedural language such as C, you think about actions and then write code to perform the action on various objects. Referring to the car example, you might write a procedure in C to wash a vehicle and then inside that procedure write code to handle washing a car, washing a boat, washing a motorcycle, and so on. If you took that approach and then wanted to add a new vehicle type (see the previous exercise), do you see advantages or disadvantages to using this procedural approach over an object-oriented approach?

7. Define a class called XYPoint that will hold a Cartesian coordinate (x, y), where x and y are integers. Define methods to individually set the x and y coordinates of a point and retrieve their values. Write an Objective-C program to implement your new class and test it.

Data Types and Expressions

In this chapter, we take a look at the basic data types and describe some fundamental rules for forming arithmetic expressions in Objective-C.

Data Types and Constants

You have already been exposed to the Objective-C basic data type int. As you will recall, a variable declared to be of type int can be used to contain integral values only—that is, values that do not contain decimal places.

The Objective-C programming language provides three other basic data types: float, double, and char. A variable declared to be of type float can be used for storing floating-point numbers (values containing decimal places). The double type is the same as type float, only with roughly twice the accuracy. Finally, the char data type can be used to store a single character, such as the letter a, the digit character 6, or a semicolon (more on this later).

In Objective-C, any number, single character, or character string is known as a *constant*. For example, the number 58 represents a constant integer value. The string @"Programming in Objective-C is fun.\n" is an example of a constant character string object. Expressions consisting entirely of constant values are called *constant expressions*. So this expression is a constant expression because each of the terms of the expression is a constant value:

```
128 + 7 - 17
```

But if i were declared to be an integer variable, this expression would not represent a constant expression:

```
128 + 7 - i
```

Type int

In Objective-C, an integer constant consists of a sequence of one or more digits. A minus sign preceding the sequence indicates that the value is negative. The values 158, -10, and 0 are all valid examples of integer constants. No embedded spaces are permitted between the digits, and values larger than 999 cannot be expressed using commas. (So the value 12,000 is not a valid integer constant and must be written as 12000.)

Two special formats in Objective-C enable integer constants to be expressed in a base other than decimal (base 10). If the first digit of the integer value is 0, the integer is considered to be expressed in *octal* notation—that is, in base 8. In this case, the remaining digits of the value must be valid base 8 digits and, therefore, must be 0–7. So to express the value 50 in base 8 in Objective-C, which is equivalent to the value 40 in decimal, the notation 050 is used. Similarly, the octal constant 0177 represents the decimal value 127 (1 × 64 + 7 × 8 + 7). An integer value can be displayed in octal notation by using the format characters %o in the format string of an NSLog call. In such a case, the value is displayed in octal without a leading zero. The format character %#o does cause a leading zero to be displayed before an octal value.

If an integer constant is preceded by a 0 and a letter *x* (either lower case or upper case), the value is considered to be expressed in hexadecimal (base 16) notation. Immediately following the x are the digits of the hexadecimal value, which can be composed of the digits 0–9 and the letters a–f (or A–F). The letters represent the values 10–15, respectively. So to assign the hexadecimal value FFEF0D to an integer variable called rgbColor, you can use this statement:

```
rgbColor = 0xFFEF0D;
```

The format characters %x display a value in hexadecimal format without the leading 0x and using lowercase letters a–f for hexadecimal digits. To display the value with the leading 0x, you use the format characters %#x, as in the following:

```
NSLog ("Color is %#x\n", rgbColor);
```

An uppercase X, as in %X or %#X, can be used to display the leading x and hexidecimal digits that follow using uppercase letters.

Every value, whether it's a character, an integer, or a floating-point number, has a *range* of values associated with it. This range has to do with the amount of storage allocated to store a particular type of data. In general, that amount is not defined in the language; it typically depends on the computer you're running on and is therefore called *implementation* or *machine dependent*. For example, an integer can take 32 bits on your computer, or perhaps it might be stored in 64.

You should never write programs that make assumptions about the size of your data types. However, you are guaranteed that a minimum amount of storage will be set aside for each basic data type. For example, it's guaranteed that an integer value will be stored in a minimum of 32 bits of storage. See Table B.3 in Appendix B, "Objective-C Language Summary," for more information about data type sizes.

Type `float`

You can use a variable declared to be of type `float` to store values containing decimal places. A floating-point constant is distinguished by the presence of a decimal point. You can omit digits before the decimal point or digits after the decimal point, but, obviously, you can't omit both. The values `3.`, `125.8`, and `-.0001` are all valid examples of floating-point constants. To display a floating-point value, the `NSLog` conversion characters `%f` are used.

Floating-point constants can also be expressed in so-called *scientific notation*. The value `1.7e4` is a floating-point value expressed in this notation that represents the value 1.7×10^4. The value before the letter `e` is known as the *mantissa*, whereas the value that follows is called the *exponent*. This exponent, which can be preceded by an optional plus or minus sign, represents the power of 10 by which the mantissa is to be multiplied. So in the constant `2.25e-3`, the `2.25` is the value of the mantissa and `-3` is the value of the exponent. This constant represents the value 2.25×10^{-3}, or `0.00225`. Incidentally, the letter `e`, which separates the mantissa from the exponent, can be written in either lower case or upper case.

To display a value in scientific notation, the format characters `%e` should be specified in the `NSLog` format string. The format characters `%g` can be used to let `NSLog` decide whether to display the floating-point value in normal floating-point notation or in scientific notation. This decision is based on the value of the exponent: If it's less than −4 or greater than 5, `%e` (scientific notation) format is used; otherwise, `%f` format is used.

A *hexadecimal* floating constant consists of a leading `0x` or `0X`, followed by one or more decimal or hexadecimal digits, followed by a `p` or `P`, followed by an optionally signed binary exponent. For example, `0x0.3p10` represents the value $3/16 \times 2^{10} = 192$.

Type `double`

The type `double` is similar to the type `float`, but it is used whenever the range provided by a `float` variable is not sufficient. Variables declared to be of type `double` can store roughly twice as many significant digits as can a variable of type `float`. Most computers represent `double` values using 64 bits.

Unless told otherwise, the Objective-C compiler considers all floating-point constants to be `double` values. To explicitly express a `float` constant, append either `f` or `F` to the end of the number, like so:

```
12.5f
```

To display a `double` value, you can use the format characters `%f`, `%e`, or `%g`, which are the same format characters used to display a `float` value.

Type `char`

You can use a `char` variable to store a single character. A character constant is formed by enclosing the character within a pair of single quotation marks. So `'a'`, `';'`, and `'0'` are all valid examples of character constants. The first constant represents the letter *a*, the second is a semicolon, and the third is the character zero—which is not the same as the number zero. Do not confuse a character constant, which is a single character enclosed in single quotes, with a C-style character string, which is any number of characters enclosed in double quotes. As mentioned in the last chapter, a string of characters enclosed in a pair of double quotes that is preceded by an @ character is an NSString character string object.

> **Note**
>
> Appendix B discusses methods for storing characters from extended character sets, through special escape sequences, universal characters, and wide characters.

The character constant '\n', the newline character, is a valid character constant even though it seems to contradict the rule cited previously. The reason for this is that the backslash character is a special character in the Objective-C system and does not actually count as a character. In other words, the Objective-C compiler treats the character '\n' as a single character, even though it is actually formed by two characters. Other special characters are initiated with the backslash character. See Appendix B for a complete list. The format characters %c can be used in an NSLog call to display the value of a char variable.

Program 4.1 uses the basic Objective-C data types.

Program 4.1

```
#import <Foundation/Foundation.h>

int main (int argc, char *argv[])
{
    NSAutoreleasePool * pool = [[NSAutoreleasePool alloc] init];

    int    integerVar = 100;
    float  floatingVar = 331.79;
    double doubleVar = 8.44e+11;
    char   charVar = 'W';

    NSLog (@"integerVar = %i", integerVar);
    NSLog (@"floatingVar = %f", floatingVar);
    NSLog (@"doubleVar = %e", doubleVar);
    NSLog (@"doubleVar = %g", doubleVar);
    NSLog (@"charVar = %c", charVar);

    [pool drain];
    return 0;
}
```

Program 4.1 Output

```
integerVar = 100
floatingVar = 331.790009
```

```
doubleVar = 8.440000e+11
doubleVar = 8.44e+11
charVar = W
```

In the second line of the program's output, notice that the value of 331.79, which is assigned to floatingVar, is actually displayed as 331.790009. The reason for this inaccuracy is the particular way in which numbers are internally represented inside the computer. You have probably come across the same type of inaccuracy when dealing with numbers on your calculator. If you divide 1 by 3 on your calculator, you get the result .33333333, with perhaps some additional 3s tacked on at the end. The string of 3s is the calculator's approximation to one third. Theoretically, there should be an infinite number of 3s. But the calculator can hold only so many digits, thus the inherent inaccuracy of the machine. The same type of inaccuracy applies here: Certain floating-point values cannot be exactly represented inside the computer's memory.

Qualifiers: `long`, `long long`, `short`, `unsigned`, and `signed`

If the qualifier long is placed directly before the int declaration, the declared integer variable is of extended range on some computer systems. An example of a long int declaration might be this:

```
long int factorial;
```

This declares the variable factorial to be a long integer variable. As with floats and doubles, the particular accuracy of a long variable depends on your particular computer system. On many systems, an int and a long int both have the same range and can be used to store integer values up to 32 bits wide ($2^{31} - 1$, or 2,147,483,647).

A constant value of type long int is formed by optionally appending the letter *L* (in upper or lower case) onto the end of an integer constant. No spaces are permitted between the number and the L. So the declaration declares the variable numberOfPoints to be of type long int with an initial value of 131,071,100:

```
long int numberOfPoints = 131071100L;
```

To display the value of a long int using NSLog, the letter *l* is used as a modifier before the integer format characters i, o, and x. This means that the format characters %li can be used to display the value of a long int in decimal format, the characters %lo can display the value in octal format, and the characters %lx can display the value in hexadecimal format.

A long long integer data type can be used like this:

```
long long int maxAllowedStorage;
```

This declares the indicated variable to be of the specified extended accuracy, which is guaranteed to be at least 64 bits wide. Instead of using a single letter *l*, two *l*s are used in the NSLog string to display long long integers, as in "%lli".

The long qualifier is also allowed in front of a double declaration, like so:

```
long double US_deficit_2004;
```

A `long double` constant is written as a floating constant with an `1` or `L` immediately following, like so:

`1.234e+7L`

To display a `long double`, you use the `L` modifier. So `%Lf` would display a `long double` value in floating-point notation, `%Le` would display the same value in scientific notation, and `%Lg` would tell `NSLog` to choose between `%Lf` and `%Le`.

The qualifier `short`, when placed in front of the `int` declaration, tells the Objective-C compiler that the particular variable being declared is used to store fairly small integer values. The motivation for using `short` variables is primarily one of conserving memory space, which can be an issue when the program needs a lot of memory and the amount of available memory is limited.

On some machines, a `short int` takes up half the amount of storage as a regular `int` variable does. In any case, you are guaranteed that the amount of space allocated for a `short int` will not be less than 16 bits.

No way exists to explicitly write a constant of type `short int` in Objective-C. To display a `short int` variable, place the letter `h` in front of any of the normal integer-conversion characters: `%hi`, `%ho`, or `%hx`. Alternatively, you can use any of the integer-conversion characters to display `short ints` because they can be converted into integers when they are passed as arguments to the `NSLog` routine.

The final qualifier that can be placed in front of an `int` variable is used when an integer variable will be used to store only positive numbers. The following declares to the compiler that the variable `counter` is used to contain only positive values:

`unsigned int counter;`

Restricting the use of an integer variable to the exclusive storage of positive integers extends the accuracy of the integer variable.

An `unsigned int` constant is formed by placing a `u` or `U` after the constant, like so:

`0x00ffU`

You can combine the `u` (or `U`) and `1` (or `L`) when writing an integer constant, so this tells the compiler to treat the constant `20000` as `unsigned long`:

`20000UL`

An integer constant that's not followed by any of the letters `u`, `U`, `1`, or `L` and that is too large to fit into a normal-sized `int` is treated as an `unsigned int` by the compiler. If it's too small to fit into an `unsigned int`, the compiler treats it as a `long int`. If it still can't fit inside a `long int`, the compiler makes it an `unsigned long int`.

When declaring variables to be of type `long int`, `short int`, or `unsigned int`, you can omit the keyword `int`. Therefore, the `unsigned` variable `counter` could have been equivalently declared as follows:

`unsigned counter;`

You can also declare `char` variables to be `unsigned`.

The signed qualifier can be used to explicitly tell the compiler that a particular variable is a signed quantity. Its use is primarily in front of the char declaration, and further discussion is beyond the scope of this book.

Type id

The id data type is used to store an object of any type. In a sense, it is a generic object type. For example, this line declares number to be a variable of type id:

```
id    number;
```

Methods can be declared to return values of type id, like so:

```
-(id) newObject: (int) type;
```

This declares an instance method called newObject that takes a single integer argument called type and returns a value of type id. Note that id is the default type for return and argument type declarations. So, the following declares a class method that returns a value of type id:

```
+allocInit;
```

The id data type is an important data type used often in this book. We mention it in passing here for the sake of completeness. The id type is the basis for very important features in Objective-C know as *polymorphism* and *dynamic binding*, which Chapter 9, "Polymorphism, Dynamic Typing, and Dynamic Binding," discusses extensively.

Table 4.1 summarizes the basic data types and qualifiers.

Table 4.1   **Basic Data Types**

Type	Constant Examples	NSLog chars
char	'a', '\n'	%c
short int	—	%hi, %hx, %ho
unsigned short int	—	%hu, %hx, %ho
int	12, -97, 0xFFE0, 0177	%i, %x, %o
unsigned int	12u, 100U, 0XFFu	%u, %x, %o
long int	12L, -2001, 0xffffL	%li, %lx, %lo
unsigned long int	12UL, 100ul, 0xffeeUL	%lu, %lx, %lo
long long int	0xe5e5e5e5LL, 500ll	%lli, %llx, &llo
unsigned long long int	12ull, 0xffeeULL	%llu, %llx, %llo
float	12.34f, 3.1e-5f, 0x1.5p10, 0x1P-1	%f, %e, %g, %a
double	12.34, 3.1e-5, 0x.1p3	%f, %e, %g, %a
long double	12.341, 3.1e-5l	%Lf, $Le, %Lg
id	nil	%p

Arithmetic Expressions

In Objective-C, just as in virtually all programming languages, the plus sign (+) is used to add two values, the minus sign (-) is used to subtract two values, the asterisk (*) is used to multiply two values, and the slash (/) is used to divide two values. These operators are known as *binary* arithmetic operators because they operate on two values or terms.

Operator Precedence

You have seen how a simple operation such as addition can be performed in Objective-C. The following program further illustrates the operations of subtraction, multiplication, and division. The last two operations performed in the program introduce the notion that one operator can have a higher priority, or *precedence*, over another operator. In fact, each operator in Objective-C has a precedence associated with it.

This precedence is used to determine how an expression that has more than one operator is evaluated: The operator with the higher precedence is evaluated first. Expressions containing operators of the same precedence are evaluated either from left to right or from right to left, depending on the operator. This is known as the *associative* property of an operator. Appendix B provides a complete list of operator precedences and their rules of association.

Program 4.2

```
// Illustrate the use of various arithmetic operators

#import <Foundation/Foundation.h>

int main (int argc, char *argv[])
{
   NSAutoreleasePool * pool = [[NSAutoreleasePool alloc] init];

   int    a = 100;
   int    b = 2;
   int    c = 25;
   int    d = 4;
   int    result;

   result = a - b;   //subtraction
   NSLog (@"a - b = %i", result);

   result = b * c;   //multiplication
   NSLog (@"b * c = %i", result);

   result = a / c;   //division
   NSLog (@"a / c = %i", result);
```

```
result = a + b * c;    //precedence
NSLog (@"a + b * c = %i", result);

NSLog (@"a * b + c * d = %i", a * b + c * d);

[pool drain];
return 0;
}
```

Program 4.2 Output

```
a - b = 98
b * c = 50
a / c = 4
a + b * c = 150
a * b + c * d = 300
```

After declaring the integer variables a, b, c, d, and result, the program assigns the result of subtracting b from a to result and then displays its value with an appropriate NSLog call.

The next statement has the effect of multiplying the value of b by the value of c and storing the product in result:

```
result = b * c;
```

The result of the multiplication is then displayed using a NSLog call that should be familiar to you by now.

The next program statement introduces the division operator, the slash. The NSLog statement displays the result of 4, obtained by dividing 100 by 25, immediately following the division of a by c.

Attempting to divide a number by zero results in abnormal termination or an exception when the division is attempted. Even if the program does not terminate abnormally, the results obtained by such a division will be meaningless. In Chapter 6, "Making Decisions," you will see how you can check for division by zero before the division operation is performed. If the divisor is determined to be zero, an appropriate action can be taken and the division operation can be averted.

This expression does not produce the result of 2550 (102 × 25); instead, the result displayed by the corresponding NSLog statement is shown as 150:

```
a + b * c
```

This is because Objective-C, like most other programming languages, has rules for the order of evaluating multiple operations or terms in an expression. Evaluation of an expression generally proceeds from left to right. However, the operations of multiplication and division are given precedence over the operations of addition and subtraction. Therefore, the system evaluates the expression

```
a + b * c
```

as follows:

```
a + (b * c)
```

(This is the same way this expression would be evaluated if you applied the basic rules of algebra.)

If you want to alter the order of evaluation of terms inside an expression, you can use parentheses. In fact, the expression listed previously is a perfectly valid Objective-C expression. Thus, the following statement could have been substituted in Program 4.2 to achieve identical results:

```
result = a + (b * c);
```

However, if this expression were used instead, the value assigned to `result` would be 2550:

```
result = (a + b) * c;
```

This is because the value of `a` (100) would be added to the value of `b` (2) before multiplication by the value of `c` (25) would take place. Parentheses can also be nested, in which case evaluation of the expression proceeds outward from the innermost set of parentheses. Just be sure to have as many closed parentheses as you have open ones.

Notice from the last statement in Program 4.2 that it is perfectly valid to give an expression as an argument to `NSLog` without having to first assign the result of the expression evaluation to a variable. The expression

```
a * b + c * d
```

is evaluated according to the rules stated previously as

```
(a * b) + (c * d)
```

or

```
(100 * 2) + (25 * 4)
```

The result of 300 is handed to the `NSLog` routine.

Integer Arithmetic and the Unary Minus Operator

Program 4.3 reinforces what we have just discussed and introduces the concept of integer arithmetic.

Program 4.3

```
// More arithmetic expressions

#import <Foundation/Foundation.h>

int main (int argc, char *argv[])
{
```

```
NSAutoreleasePool * pool = [[NSAutoreleasePool alloc] init];

int   a = 25;
int   b = 2;
float c = 25.0;
float d = 2.0;

NSLog (@"6 + a / 5 * b = %i", 6 + a / 5 * b);
NSLog (@"a / b * b = %i", a / b * b);
NSLog (@"c / d * d = %f", c / d * d);
NSLog (@"-a = %i", -a);

[pool drain];
return 0;
}
```

Program 4.3 Output

```
6 + a / 5 * b = 16
a / b * b = 24
c / d * d = 25.000000
-a = -25
```

We inserted extra blank spaces between int and the declaration of a, b, and result in the first three statements to align the declaration of each variable. This helps make the program more readable. You also might have noticed in each program presented thus far that a blank space was placed around each operator. This, too, is not required and is done solely for aesthetic reasons. In general, you can add extra blank spaces just about anywhere that a single blank space is allowed. A few extra presses of the spacebar will prove worthwhile if the resulting program is easier to read.

The expression in the first NSLog call of Program 4.3 reinforces the notion of operator precedence. Evaluation of this expression proceeds as follows:

1. Because division has higher precedence than addition, the value of a (25) is divided by 5 first. This gives the intermediate result of 5.

2. Because multiplication also has higher precedence than addition, the intermediate result of 5 is next multiplied by 2, the value of b, giving a new intermediate result of 10.

3. Finally, the addition of 6 and 10 is performed, giving a final result of 16.

The second NSLog statement introduces a new twist. You would expect that dividing a by b and then multiplying by b would return the value of a, which has been set to 25. But this does not seem to be the case, as shown by the output display of 24. Did the computer lose a bit somewhere along the way? Very unlikely. The fact of the matter is that this expression was evaluated using integer arithmetic.

If you glance back at the declarations for the variables a and b, you will recall that both were declared to be of type int. Whenever a term to be evaluated in an expression consists of two integers, the Objective-C system performs the operation using integer arithmetic. In such a case, all decimal portions of numbers are lost. Therefore, when the value of a is divided by the value of b, or 25 is divided by 2, you get an intermediate result of 12, and *not* 12.5, as you might expect. Multiplying this intermediate result by 2 gives the final result of 24, thus explaining the "lost" digit.

As you can see from the next-to-last NSLog statement in Program 4.3, if you perform the same operation using floating-point values instead of integers, you obtain the expected result.

The decision of whether to use a float variable or an int variable should be made based on the variable's intended use. If you don't need any decimal places, use an integer variable. The resulting program will be more efficient—that is, it will execute more quickly on many computers. On the other hand, if you need the decimal place accuracy, the choice is clear. The only question you then must answer is whether to use a float or a double. The answer to this question depends on the desired accuracy of the numbers you are dealing with, as well as their magnitude.

In the last NSLog statement, the value of the variable a is negated by use of the unary minus operator. A *unary* operator is one that operates on a single value, as opposed to a binary operator, which operates on two values. The minus sign actually has a dual role: As a binary operator, it is used for subtracting two values; as a unary operator, it is used to negate a value.

The unary minus operator has higher precedence than all other arithmetic operators, except for the unary plus operator (+), which has the same precedence. So the following expression results in the multiplication of -a by b:

```
c = -a * b;
```

Once again, you will find a table in Appendix B summarizing the various operators and their precedences.

The Modulus Operator

The last arithmetic operator to be presented in this chapter is the modulus operator, which is symbolized by the percent sign (%). Try to determine how this operator works by analyzing the output from Program 4.4.

Program 4.4

```
// The modulus operator

#import <Foundation/Foundation.h>

int main (int argc, char *argv[])
{
    NSAutoreleasePool * pool = [[NSAutoreleasePool alloc] init];
```

```
int a = 25, b = 5, c = 10, d = 7;

NSLog (@"a %% b = %i", a % b);
NSLog (@"a %% c = %i", a % c);
NSLog (@"a %% d = %i", a % d);
NSLog (@"a / d * d + a %% d = %i", a / d * d + a % d);

[pool drain];
return 0;
}
```

Program 4.4 Output

```
a % b = 0
a % c = 5
a % d = 4
a / d * d + a % d = 25
```

Note the statement inside main that defines and initializes the variables a, b, c, and d in a single statement.

As you know, NSLog uses the character that immediately follows the percent sign to determine how to print its next argument. However, if it is another percent sign that follows, the NSLog routine takes this as an indication that you really intend to display a percent sign and inserts one at the appropriate place in the program's output.

You are correct if you concluded that the function of the modulus operator % is to give the remainder of the first value divided by the second value. In the first example, the remainder, after 25 is divided by 5, is displayed as 0. If you divide 25 by 10, you get a remainder of 5, as verified by the second line of output. Dividing 25 by 7 gives a remainder of 4, as shown in the third output line.

Let's now turn our attention to the last arithmetic expression evaluated in the last statement. You will recall that any operations between two integer values in Objective-C are performed with integer arithmetic. Therefore, any remainder resulting from the division of two integer values is simply discarded. Dividing 25 by 7, as indicated by the expression a / d, gives an intermediate result of 3. Multiplying this value by the value of d, which is 7, produces the intermediate result of 21. Finally, adding the remainder of dividing a by d, as indicated by the expression a % d, leads to the final result of 25. It is no coincidence that this value is the same as the value of the variable a. In general, this expression will always equal the value of a, assuming, of course, that a and b are both integer values:

```
a / b * b + a % b
```

In fact, the modulus operator % is defined to work only with integer values.

As far as precedence is concerned, the modulus operator has equal precedence to the multiplication and division operators. This implies, of course, that an expression such as

```
table + value % TABLE_SIZE
```

will be evaluated as

```
table + (value % TABLE_SIZE)
```

Integer and Floating-Point Conversions

To effectively develop Objective-C programs, you must understand the rules used for the implicit conversion of floating-point and integer values in Objective-C. Program 4.5 demonstrates some of the simple conversions between numeric data types.

Program 4.5

```
// Basic conversions in Objective-C

#import <Foundation/Foundation.h>

int main (int argc, char *argv[])
{
   NSAutoreleasePool * pool = [[NSAutoreleasePool alloc] init];
   float  f1 = 123.125, f2;
   int    i1, i2 = -150;

   i1 = f1;   // floating to integer conversion
   NSLog (@"%f assigned to an int produces %i", f1, i1);

   f1 = i2;   // integer to floating conversion
   NSLog (@"%i assigned to a float produces %f", i2, f1);

   f1 = i2 / 100;   // integer divided by integer
   NSLog (@"%i divided by 100 produces %f", i2, f1);

   f2 = i2 / 100.0;   // integer divided by a float
   NSLog (@"%i divided by 100.0 produces %f", i2, f2);

   f2 = (float) i2 / 100;   // type cast operator
   NSLog (@"(float) %i divided by 100 produces %f", i2, f2);

   [pool drain];
   return 0;
}
```

Program 4.5 Output

```
123.125000 assigned to an int produces 123
-150 assigned to a float produces -150.000000
-150 divided by 100 produces -1.000000
-150 divided by 100.0 produces -1.500000
(float) -150 divided by 100 produces -1.500000
```

Whenever a floating-point value is assigned to an integer variable in Objective-C, the decimal portion of the number gets truncated. So when the value of f1 is assigned to i1 in the previous program, the number 123.125 is *truncated*, which means that only its integer portion, or 123, is stored in i1. The first line of the program's output verifies that this is the case.

Assigning an integer variable to a floating variable does not cause any change in the value of the number; the system simply converts the value and stores it in the floating variable. The second line of the program's output verifies that the value of i2 (−150) was correctly converted and stored in the float variable f1.

The next two lines of the program's output illustrate two points to remember when forming arithmetic expressions. The first has to do with integer arithmetic, which we have already discussed in this chapter. Whenever two operands in an expression are integers (and this applies to short, unsigned, and long integers as well), the operation is carried out under the rules of integer arithmetic. Therefore, any decimal portion resulting from a division operation is discarded, even if the result is assigned to a floating variable (as we did in the program). When the integer variable i2 is divided by the integer constant 100, the system performs the division as an integer division. The result of dividing −150 by 100, which is −1, is, therefore, the value that is stored in the float variable f1.

The next division performed in the previous program involves an integer variable and a floating-point constant. Any operation between two values in Objective-C is performed as a floating-point operation if either value is a floating-point variable or constant. Therefore, when the value of i2 is divided by 100.0, the system treats the division as a floating-point division and produces the result of −1.5, which is assigned to the float variable f1.

The Type Cast Operator

You've already seen how enclosing a type inside a set of parentheses is used to declare the return and argument types when declaring and defining methods. It serves a different purpose when used inside expressions.

The last division operation from Program 4.5 that reads as follows introduces the type cast operator:

```
f2 = (float) i2 / 100;   // type cast operator
```

The type cast operator has the effect of converting the value of the variable i2 to type float for purposes of evaluating the expression. In no way does this operator permanently affect the value of the variable i2; it is a unary operator that behaves like other unary operators. Just as the expression −a has no permanent effect on the value of a, neither does the expression (float) a.

The type cast operator has a higher precedence than all the arithmetic operators except the unary minus and unary plus. Of course, if necessary, you can always use parentheses in an expression to force the terms to be evaluated in any desired order.

As another example of the use of the type cast operator, the expression

```
(int) 29.55 + (int) 21.99
```

is evaluated in Objective-C as

```
29 + 21
```

because the effect of casting a floating value to an integer is one of truncating the floating-point value. The expression

```
(float) 6 / (float) 4
```

produces a result of 1.5, as does the following expression:

```
(float) 6 / 4
```

The type cast operator is often used to coerce an object that is a generic id type into an object of a particular class. For example, the following lines convert the value of the id variable myNumber to a Fraction object:

```
id    myNumber;
Fraction *myFraction;
   . . .
myFraction = (Fraction *) myNumber;
```

The result of the conversion is assigned to the Fraction variable myFraction.

Assignment Operators

The Objective-C language permits you to combine the arithmetic operators with the assignment operator using the following general format:

```
op=
```

In this format, op is any of the arithmetic operators, including +, -, *, /, or %. In addition, *op* can be any of the bit operators for shifting and masking, discussed later.

Consider this statement:

```
count += 10;
```

The effect of the so-called "plus equals" operator += is to add the expression on the right side of the operator to the expression on the left side of the operator, and to store the result back into the variable on the left side of the operator. So the previous statement is equivalent to this statement:

```
count = count + 10;
```

The following expression uses the "minus equals" assignment operator to subtract 5 from the value of counter:

```
counter -= 5
```

It is equivalent to this expression:

```
counter = counter - 5
```

This is a slightly more involved expression:

```
a /= b + c
```

It divides a by whatever appears to the right of the equals sign—or by the sum of b and c—and stores the result in a. The addition is performed first because the addition operator has higher precedence than the assignment operator. In fact, all operators but the comma operator have higher precedence than the assignment operators, which all have the same precedence.

In this case, this expression is identical to the following:

```
a = a / (b + c)
```

The motivation for using assignment operators is threefold. First, the program statement becomes easier to write because what appears on the left side of the operator does not have to be repeated on the right side. Second, the resulting expression is usually easier to read. Third, the use of these operators can result in programs that execute more quickly because the compiler can sometimes generate less code to evaluate an expression.

A Calculator Class

It's time now to define a new class. We're going to make a `Calculator` class, which will be a simple four-function calculator you can use to add, multiply, subtract, and divide numbers. Similar to a regular calculator, this one must keep track of the running total, or what's usually called the *accumulator*. So methods must let you set the accumulator to a specific value, clear it (or set it to zero), and retrieve its value when you're done. Program 4.6 includes the new class definition and a test program to try your calculator.

Program 4.6

```
// Implement a Calculator class

#import <Foundation/Foundation.h>

@interface Calculator: NSObject
{
    double accumulator;
}

// accumulator methods
-(void)    setAccumulator: (double) value;
-(void)    clear;
-(double) accumulator;

// arithmetic methods
-(void) add: (double) value;
-(void) subtract: (double) value;
-(void) multiply: (double) value;
-(void) divide: (double) value;
@end

@implementation Calculator
-(void) setAccumulator: (double) value
{
```

```
        accumulator = value;
}

-(void) clear
{
    accumulator = 0;
}

-(double) accumulator
{
    return accumulator;
}

-(void) add: (double) value
{
    accumulator += value;
}

-(void) subtract: (double) value
{
    accumulator -= value;
}

-(void) multiply: (double) value
{
    accumulator *= value;
}

-(void) divide: (double) value
{
    accumulator /= value;
}
@end

int main (int argc, char *argv[])
{
    NSAutoreleasePool * pool = [[NSAutoreleasePool alloc] init];
    Calculator *deskCalc;

    deskCalc = [[Calculator alloc] init];

    [deskCalc clear];
    [deskCalc setAccumulator: 100.0];
    [deskCalc add: 200.];
    [deskCalc divide: 15.0];
    [deskCalc subtract: 10.0];
    [deskCalc multiply: 5];
    NSLog (@"The result is %g", [deskCalc accumulator]);
    [deskCalc release];

    [pool drain];
    return 0;
}
```

Program 4.6 Output
```
The result is 50
```

The `Calculator` class has only one instance variable, a `double` value that holds the value of the accumulator. The method definitions themselves are quite straightforward.

Notice the message that invokes the `multiply` method:

```
[deskCalc multiply: 5];
```

The argument to the method is an integer, yet the method expects a `double`. No problem arises here because numeric arguments to methods are automatically converted to match the type expected. A `double` is expected by `multiply:`, so the integer value 5 automatically is converted to a double precision floating value when the function is called. Even though this automatic conversion takes place, it's better programming practice to supply the correct argument types when invoking methods.

Realize that, unlike the `Fraction` class, in which you might work with many different fractions, you might want to work with only a single `Calculator` object in your program. Yet it still makes sense to define a new class to make working with this object easy. At some point, you might want to add a graphical front end to your calculator so the user can actually click buttons on the screen, such as the calculator application you probably have installed on your system or phone.

In several of the exercises that follow, you'll see that one additional benefit of defining a `Calculator` class has to do with the ease of extending it.

Bit Operators

Various operators in the Objective-C language work with the particular bits inside a number. Table 4.2 presents these operators.

> **Note**
>
> You won't use bitwise operators much, if at all, in your Objective-C programs. As this material may be a little dense for new programmers, you can just skim this section and refer back to it later, if necessary.

Table 4.2   **Bit Operators**

Symbol	Operation
&	Bitwise AND
|	Bitwise inclusive-OR
^	Bitwise OR
~	Ones complement
<<	Left shift
>>	Right shift

All the operators listed in Table 4.2, with the exception of the ones complement operator (~), are binary operators and, as such, take two operands. Bit operations can be performed on any type of integer value but cannot be performed on floating-point values.

The Bitwise AND Operator

When two values are ANDed, the binary representations of the values are compared bit by
bit. Each corresponding bit that is a 1 in the first value *and* a 1 in the second value produce a 1 in the corresponding bit position of the result; anything else produces a 0. If b1
and b2 represent corresponding bits of the two operands, the following table, called a *truth
table*, shows the result of b1 ANDed with b2 for all possible values of b1 and b2.

b1	b2	b1 & b2
0	0	0
0	1	0
1	0	0
1	1	1

For example, if w1 and w2 are defined as short ints, and w1 is set equal to hexadecimal
15 and w2 is set equal to hexadecimal 0c, then the following C statement assigns the value
0x04 to w3:

```
w3 = w1 & w2;
```

You can see this more easily by treating the values of w1, w2, and w3 as binary numbers.
Assume that you are dealing with a short int size of 16 bits:

```
w1    0000 0000 0001 0101    0x15
w2    0000 0000 0000 1100  & 0x0c

w3    0000 0000 0000 0100    0x04
```

Bitwise ANDing is frequently used for masking operations. That is, this operator can be
used to easily set specific bits of a data item to 0. For example, the following statement assigns to w3 the value of w1 bitwise ANDed with the constant 3.

```
w3 = w1 & 3;
```

This has the effect of setting all the bits in w3, other than the rightmost 2 bits, to 0, and
of preserving the rightmost 2 bits from w1.

As with all binary arithmetic operators in Objective-C, the binary bit operators can
also be used as assignment operators by tacking on an equals sign. So the statement

```
word &= 15;
```

will perform the same function as

```
word = word & 15;
```

and will have the effect of setting all but the rightmost 4 bits of word to 0.

The Bitwise Inclusive-OR Operator

When two values are bitwise Inclusive-ORed in Objective-C, the binary representation of the two values is once again compared bit by bit. This time, each bit that is a 1 in the first value *or* a 1 in the second value will produce a 1 in the corresponding bit of the result. The truth table for the Inclusive-OR operator is shown next.

b1	b2	b1 | b2
0	0	0
0	1	1
1	0	1
1	1	1

So if w1 is a `short int` equal to hexadecimal 19 and w2 is a `short int` equal to hexadecimal 6a, then a bitwise Inclusive-OR of w1 and w2 will produce a result of hexadecimal 7b, as shown:

```
w1    0000 0000 0001  1001          0x19
w2    0000 0000 0110  1010     |    0x6a
      ─────────────────────────────────
      0000 0000 0111  1011          0x7b
```

Bitwise Inclusive-ORing, frequently called just bitwise ORing, is used to set some specified bits of a word to 1. For example, the following statement sets the three rightmost bits of w1 to 1, regardless of the state of these bits before the operation was performed.

```
w1 = w1 | 07;
```

Of course, you could have used a special assignment operator in the statement, as in this statement:

```
w1 |= 07;
```

We defer a program example that illustrates the use of the Inclusive-OR operator until later.

The Bitwise Exclusive-OR Operator

The bitwise Exclusive-OR operator, which is often called the XOR operator, works as follows: For corresponding bits of the two operands, if either bit is a 1—but not both bits—the corresponding bit of the result is a 1; otherwise, it is a 0. The truth table for this operator is as shown.

b1	b2	b1 ^ b2
0	0	0
0	1	1
1	0	1
1	1	0

If w1 and w2, were set equal to hexadecimal 5e and d6, respectively, the result of w1 Exclusive-ORed with w2 would be hexadecimal e8, as illustrated:

```
w1    0000 0000 0101  1110      0x5e
w2    0000 0000 1011  0110   ^  0xd6
```
```
      0000 0000 1110  1000      0xe8
```

The Ones Complement Operator

The ones complement operator is a unary operator, and its effect is to simply "flip" the bits of its operand. Each bit of the operand that is a 1 is changed to a 0, and each bit that is a 0 is changed to a 1. The truth table is provided here simply for the sake of completeness.

```
b1    ~b1
```
```
0     1
1     0
```

If w1 is a short int that is 16 bits long and is set equal to hexadecimal a52f, then taking the ones complement of this value produces a result of hexadecimal 5ab0:

```
 w1   1010  0101  0010  1111     0xa52f
~w1   0101  1010  1101  0000     0x5ad0
```

The ones complement operator is useful when you don't know the precise bit size of the quantity that you are dealing with in an operation, and its use can help make a program less dependent on the particular size of an integer data type. For example, to set the low-order bit of an int called w1 to 0, you can AND w1 with an int consisting of all 1s except for a single 0 in the rightmost bit. So a statement in C such as this one works fine on machines on which an integer is represented by 32 bits:

```
w1 &= 0xFFFFFFFE;
```

If you replace the preceding statement with this one, w1 will be ANDed with the correct value on any machine:

```
w1 &= ~1;
```

This is because the ones complement of 1 will be calculated and will consist of as many leftmost 1 bits as necessary to fill the size of an int (31 leftmost bits on a 32-bit integer system).

Now it is time to show an actual program example that illustrates the use of the various bit operators (see Program 4.7).

Program 4.7

```
// Bitwise operators illustrated

#import <Foundation/Foundation.h>

int main (int argc, char *argv[])
```

```
{
    NSAutoreleasePool * pool = [[NSAutoreleasePool alloc] init];

    unsigned int w1 = 0xA0A0A0A0, w2 = 0xFFFF0000,
                 w3 = 0x00007777;

    NSLog (@"%x %x %x", w1 & w2, w1 | w2, w1 ^ w2);
    NSLog (@"%x %x %x", ~w1, ~w2, ~w3);
    NSLog (@"%x %x %x", w1 ^ w1, w1 & ~w2, w1 | w2 | w3);
    NSLog (@"%x %x", w1 | w2 & w3, w1 | w2 & ~w3);
    NSLog (@"%x %x", ~(~w1 & ~w2), ~(~w1 | ~w2));

    [pool drain];
    return 0;
}
```

Program 4.7 Output

```
a0a00000 ffffa0a0 5f5fa0a0
5f5f5f5f ffff ffff8888
0 a0a0 fffff7f7
a0a0a0a0 ffffa0a0
ffffa0a0 a0a00000
```

Work out each of the operations from Program 4.7 to verify that you understand how the results were obtained.

In the fourth NSLog call, it is important to note that the bitwise AND operator has higher precedence than the bitwise OR because this fact influences the resulting value of the expression. For a summary of operator precedence, see Appendix B.

The fifth NSLog call illustrates DeMorgan's rule: ~(~a & ~b) is equal to a | b, and ~(~a | ~b) is equal to a & b.

The Left Shift Operator

When a left shift operation is performed on a value, the bits contained in the value are literally shifted to the left. Associated with this operation is the number of places (bits) that the value is to be shifted. Bits that are shifted out through the high-order bit of the data item are lost, and 0s are always shifted in through the low-order bit of the value. So if w1 is equal to 3, then the expression

```
w1 = w1 << 1;
```

which can also be expressed as

```
w1 <<= 1;
```

will result in 3 being shifted one place to the left, which will result in 6 being assigned to w1:

```
w1          ... 0000 0011    0x03
w1 << 1     ... 0000 0110    0x06
```

The operand on the left of the << operator is the value to be shifted, while the operand on the right is the number of bit positions the value is to be shifted by. If we were to shift w1 one more place to the left, we would end up with hexadecimal 0c:

```
w1          ... 0000 0110    0x06
w1 << 1     ... 0000 1100    0x0c
```

The Right Shift Operator

As implied from its name, the right shift operator >> shifts the bits of a value to the right. Bits shifted out of the low-order bit of the value are lost. Right-shifting an unsigned value always results in 0s being shifted in on the left—that is, through the high-order bits. What is shifted in on the left for signed values depends on the sign of the value that is being shifted and also on how this operation is implemented on your computer system. If the sign bit is 0 (meaning the value is positive), 0s will be shifted in no matter what machine is used. However, if the sign bit is 1, on some machines 1s will be shifted in, and on others 0s will be shifted in. This former type of operation is known as an *arithmetic* right shift, while the latter is known as a *logical* right shift.

Caution

Never make any assumptions about whether a system implements an arithmetic or a logical right shift. A program that shifts signed values right might work correctly on one system and then fail on another due to this type of assumption.

If w1 is an unsigned int, which is represented in 32 bits, and w1 is set equal to hexadecimal F777EE22, then shifting w1 one place to the right with the statement

```
w1 >>= 1;
```

will set w1 equal to hexadecimal 7BBBF711, as shown:

```
w1        1111 0111 0111 0111 1110 1110 0010 0010    0xF777EE22
w1 >> 1   0111 1011 1011 1011 1111 0111 0001 0001    0x7BBBF711
```

If w1 were declared to be a (signed) short int, the same result would be produced on some computers; on others, the result would be FBBBF711 if the operation were performed as an arithmetic right shift.

It should be noted that the Objective-C language does not produce a defined result if an attempt is made to shift a value to the left or right by an amount that is greater than or equal to the number of bits in the size of the data item. So on a machine that represents integers in 32 bits, for example, shifting an integer to the left or right by 32 or more bits is not guaranteed to produce a defined result in your program. You should also note that if you shift a value by a negative amount, the result is similarly undefined.

Types: _Bool, _Complex, and _Imaginary

Before leaving this chapter, we should mention three other types in the language: _Bool, for working with Boolean (that is, 0 or 1) values, and _Complex and _Imaginary, for working with complex and imaginary numbers, respectively.

Objective-C programmers tend to use the BOOL data type instead of _Bool for working with Boolean values in their programs. This "data type" is actually not a data type unto itself, but is another name for the char data type. This is done with the language's special typedef keyword, which is described in Chapter 10, "More on Variables and Data Types."

Exercises

1. Which of the following are invalid constants. Why?

```
123.456     0x10.5    0X0G1
0001        0xFFFF    123L
0Xab05      0L        -597.25
123.5e2     .0001     +12
98.6F       98.7U     17777s
0996        -12E-12   07777
1234uL      1.2Fe-7   15,000
1.234L      197u      100U
0XABCDEFL   0xabcu    +123
```

2. Write a program that converts 27° from degrees Fahrenheit (F) to degrees Celsius (C) using the following formula:

   C = (F - 32) / 1.8

3. What output would you expect from the following program?

```
#import <Foundation/Foundation.h>

int main (int argc, char *argv[])
{
   NSAutoreleasePool * pool = [[NSAutoreleasePool alloc] init];
   char c, d;

   c = 'd';
   d = c;
   NSLog (@"d = %c", d);

   [pool drain];
   return 0;
}
```

4. Write a program to evaluate the polynomial shown here:

$3x^3 - 5x^2 + 6$
for $x = 2.55$

5. Write a program that evaluates the following expression and displays the results (remember to use exponential format to display the result):

$$(3.31 \times 10^{-8} + 2.01 \times 10^{-7}) / (7.16 \times 10^{-6} + 2.01 \times 10^{-8})$$

6. *Complex* numbers are numbers that contain two components: a *real* part and an *imaginary* part. If `a` is the real component and `b` is the imaginary component, this notation is used to represent the number:

```
a + b i
```

Write an Objective-C program that defines a new class called `Complex`. Following the paradigm established for the `Fraction` class, define the following methods for your new class:

```
-(void) setReal: (double) a;
-(void) setImaginary: (double) b;
-(void) print;      // display as a + bi
-(double) real;
-(double) imaginary;
```

Write a test program to test your new class and methods.

7. Suppose you are developing a library of routines to manipulate graphical objects. Start by defining a new class called `Rectangle`. For now, just keep track of the rectangle's width and height. Develop methods to set the rectangle's width and height, retrieve these values, and calculate the rectangle's area and perimeter. Assume that these rectangle objects describe rectangles on an integral grid, such as a computer screen. In that case, assume that the width and height of the rectangle are integer values.

Here is the `@interface` section for the `Rectangle` class:

```
@interface Rectangle: NSObject
{
    int  width;
    int  height;
}

-(void) setWidth: (int) w;
-(void) setHeight: (int) h;
-(int)  width;
-(int)  height;
-(int)  area;
-(int)  perimeter;
@end
```

Write the `implementation` section and a test program to test your new class and methods.

8. Modify the `add:`, `subtract:`, `multiply:`, and `divide:` methods from Program 4.6 to return the resulting value of the accumulator. Test the new methods.

9. After completing exercise 8, add the following methods to the `Calculator` class and test them:

```
-(double) changeSign;   // change sign of accumulator
-(double) reciprocal;   // 1/accumulator
-(double) xSquared;     // accumulator squared
```

10. Add a memory capability to the `Calculator` class from Program 4.6. Implement the following method declarations and test them:

```
-(double) memoryClear;     // clear memory
-(double) memoryStore;     // set memory to accumulator
-(double) memoryRecall;    // set accumulator to memory
-(double) memoryAdd;       // add accumulator to memory
-(double) memorySubtract;  // subtract accumulator from memory
```

Have each method return the value of the accumulator.

Program Looping

In Objective-C, you can repeatedly execute a sequence of code in several ways. These looping capabilities are the subject of this chapter, and they consist of the following:

- The `for` statement
- The `while` statement
- The `do` statement

We start with a simple example: counting numbers.

If you were to arrange 15 marbles into the shape of a triangle, you would end up with an arrangement that might look something like Figure 5.1.

Figure 5.1   Triangle arrangement example

The first row of the triangle contains one marble, the second row contains two marbles, and so on. In general, the number of marbles required to form a triangle containing *n* rows would be the sum of the integers from 1 through *n*. This sum is known as a *triangular number*.

If you started at 1, the fourth triangular number would be the sum of the consecutive integers 1–4 (1 + 2 + 3 + 4), or 10.

Suppose you wanted to write a program that calculated and displayed the value of the eighth triangular number at the terminal. Obviously, you could easily calculate this number in your head, but for the sake of argument, let's assume you wanted to write a program in Objective-C to perform this task. Program 5.1 illustrates such a program.

Program 5.1

```
#import <Foundation/Foundation.h>


// Program to calculate the eighth triangular number

int main (int argc, char *argv[])
{
    NSAutoreleasePool * pool = [[NSAutoreleasePool alloc] init];
    int triangularNumber;

    triangularNumber = 1 + 2 + 3 + 4 + 5 + 6 + 7 + 8;

    NSLog (@"The eighth triangular number is %i", triangularNumber);

    [pool drain];
    return 0;
}
```

Program 5.1 Output

```
The eighth triangular number is 36
```

The technique of Program 5.1 works fine for calculating relatively small triangular numbers, but what would happen if you needed to find the value of the 200th triangular number, for example? It certainly would be tedious to have to modify Program 5.1 to explicitly add up all the integers from 1 to 200. Luckily, there is an easier way.

One of the fundamental properties of a computer is its capability to repetitively execute a set of statements. These looping capabilities enable programmers to develop concise programs containing repetitive processes that could otherwise require thousands or even millions of program statements to perform. The Objective-C language contains three program statements for program looping.

The for Statement

Let's take a look at a program that uses the for statement. The purpose of Program 5.2 is to calculate the 200th triangular number. See whether you can determine how the for statement works.

Program 5.2

```
// Program to calculate the 200th triangular number
// Introduction of the for statement

#import <Foundation/Foundation.h>

int main (int argc, char *argv[])
```

```
{
    NSAutoreleasePool * pool = [[NSAutoreleasePool alloc] init];
    int n, triangularNumber;

    triangularNumber = 0;

    for ( n = 1; n <= 200; n = n + 1 )
        triangularNumber += n;

    NSLog (@"The 200th triangular number is %i", triangularNumber);

    [pool drain];
    return 0;
}
```

Program 5.2 Output

```
The 200th triangular number is 20100
```

Some explanation is needed for Program 5.2. The method employed to calculate the 200th triangular number is really the same as that used to calculate the 8th triangular number in the previous program: The integers from 1 to 200 are summed.

The variable `triangularNumber` is set equal to 0 before the `for` statement is reached. In general, you need to initialize all variables to some value (just like your objects) before you use them in your program. As you'll learn later, certain types of variables are given default initial values, but it's safer not to rely on those and you should set them anyway.

The `for` statement enables you to avoid having to explicitly write each integer from 1 to 200. In a sense, this statement generates these numbers for you.

The general format of the `for` statement is as follows:

```
for ( init_expression; loop_condition; loop_expression )
    program statement
```

The three expressions enclosed within the parentheses—*init_expression*, *loop_condition*, and *loop_expression*—set up the environment for the program loop. The *program statement* that immediately follows (which is, of course, terminated by a semi-colon) can be any valid Objective-C program statement and constitutes the body of the loop. This statement is executed as many times as specified by the parameters set up in the `for` statement.

The first component of the `for` statement, labeled *init_expression*, is used to set the initial values before the loop begins. In Program 5.2, this portion of the `for` statement is used to set the initial value of n to 1. As you can see, an assignment is a valid form of an expression.

The second component of the `for` statement specifies the condition(s) necessary for the loop to continue. In other words, looping continues as long as this condition is satisfied. Again referring to Program 5.2, the *loop_condition* of the `for` is specified by the following relational expression:

```
n <= 200
```

This expression can be read as "n less than or equal to 200." The "less than or equal to" operator (which is the less than character [<] followed immediately by the equals sign [=]) is only one of several relational operators provided in the Objective-C programming language. These operators are used to test specific conditions. The answer to the test is yes (or TRUE) if the condition is satisfied and no (or FALSE) if the condition is not satisfied.

Table 5.1 lists all the relational operators available in Objective-C.

Table 5.1   **Relational Operators**

Operator	Meaning	Example
==	Equal to	count == 10
!=	Not equal to	flag != DONE
<	Less than	a < b
<=	Less than or equal to	low <= high
>	Greater than	points > POINT_MAX
>=	Greater than or equal to	j >= 0

The relational operators have lower precedence than all arithmetic operators. This means, for example, that an expression such as

```
a < b + c
```

is evaluated as

```
a < (b + c)
```

This is as you would expect. It would be TRUE if the value of a were less than the value of b + c, and FALSE otherwise.

Pay particular attention to the "is equal to" operator (==) and do not confuse its use with the assignment operator (=). The expression

```
a == 2
```

tests whether the value of a is equal to 2, whereas the expression

```
a = 2
```

assigns the number 2 to the variable a.

The choice of which relational operator to use depends on the particular test being made and, in some instances, on your particular preferences. For example, the relational expression

```
n <= 200
```

can be equivalently expressed as

```
n < 201
```

Returning to the previous example, the program statement that forms the body of the `for` loop—`triangularNumber += n;`—is repetitively executed *as long as* the result of the relational test is TRUE, or, in this case, as long as the value of n is less than or equal to 200. This program statement has the effect of adding the value of n to the value of `triangularNumber`.

When the *loop_condition* is no longer satisfied, execution of the program continues with the program statement immediately following the `for` loop. In this program, execution continues with the NSLog statement after the loop has terminated.

The final component of the `for` statement contains an expression that is evaluated each time after the body of the loop is executed. In Program 5.2, this *loop_expression* adds 1 to the value of n. Therefore, the value of n is incremented by 1 each time after its value has been added into the value of `triangularNumber`, and it ranges in value from 1 through 201.

It is worth noting that the last value that n attains, 201, is not added into the value of `triangularNumber` because the loop is terminated as soon as the looping condition is no longer satisfied, or as soon as n equals 201.

In summary, execution of the `for` statement proceeds as follows:

1. The initial expression is evaluated first. This expression usually sets a variable that is used inside the loop, generally referred to as an *index* variable, to some initial value (such as 0 or 1).

2. The looping condition is evaluated. If the condition is not satisfied (the expression is FALSE), the loop immediately terminates. Execution continues with the program statement that immediately follows the loop.

3. The program statement that constitutes the body of the loop is executed.

4. The looping expression is evaluated. This expression is generally used to change the value of the index variable, frequently by adding 1 to it or subtracting 1 from it.

5. Return to step 2.

Remember that the looping condition is evaluated immediately on entry into the loop, before the body of the loop has executed one time. Also remember not to put a semicolon after the closed parenthesis at the end of the loop because this immediately ends the loop.

Program 5.2 actually generates all the first 200 triangular numbers on its way to its final goal, so it might be nice to generate a table of these numbers. To save space, however, let's assume that you want to print a table of just the first 10 triangular numbers. Program 5.3 performs this task.

Program 5.3

```
// Program to generate a table of triangular numbers

#import <Foundation/Foundation.h>
```

```
int main (int argc, char *argv[])
{
   NSAutoreleasePool * pool = [[NSAutoreleasePool alloc] init];
   int n, triangularNumber;

   NSLog (@"TABLE OF TRIANGULAR NUMBERS");
   NSLog (@" n  Sum from 1 to n");
   NSLog (@"-- --------");

   triangularNumber = 0;

   for ( n = 1; n <= 10; ++n ) {
        triangularNumber += n;
        NSLog (@" %i          %i", n, triangularNumber);
   }

   [pool drain];
   return 0;
}
```

Program 5.3 Output

```
TABLE OF TRIANGULAR NUMBERS
 n   Sum from 1 to n
--  ------------------
 1       1
 2       3
 3       6
 4       10
 5       15
 6       21
 7       28
 8       36
 9       45
10       55
```

In Program 5.3, the purpose of the first three NSLog statements is simply to provide a general heading and to label the columns of the output.

After the appropriate headings have been displayed, the program calculates the first 10 triangular numbers. The variable n is used to count the current number whose sum from 1 to n you are computing, and the variable triangularNumber is used to store the value of triangular number n.

Execution of the for statement commences by setting the value of the variable n to 1. As mentioned earlier, the program statement immediately following the for statement constitutes the body of the program loop. But what happens if you want to repetitively execute not just a single program statement, but a group of program statements? This can be accomplished by enclosing all such program statements within a pair of braces. The system then treats this group, or *block*, of statements as a single entity. In general, any place in a Objective-C program that a single statement is permitted, a block of statements can be used, provided that you remember to enclose the block within a pair of braces.

Therefore, in Program 5.3, both the expression that adds n into the value of triangularNumber and the NSLog statement that immediately follows constitute the body of the program loop. Pay particular attention to the way the program statements are indented. At a quick glance, you can easily determine which statements form part of the for loop. You should also note that programmers use different coding styles; some prefer to type the loop this way:

```
for ( n = 1; n <= 10; ++n )
{
  triangularNumber += n;
  NSLog (@" %i %i", n, triangularNumber);
}
```

Here, the opening brace is placed on the line following the for. This is strictly a matter of taste and has no effect on the program.

The next triangular number is calculated by simply adding the value of n to the previous triangular number. The first time through the for loop, the previous triangular number is 0, so the new value of triangularNumber when n is equal to 1 is simply the value of n, or 1. The values of n and triangularNumber are then displayed, with an appropriate number of blank spaces inserted into the format string to ensure that the values of the two variables line up under the appropriate column headings.

Because the body of the loop has now been executed, the looping expression is evaluated next. The expression in this for statement appears a bit strange, however. Surely you must have made a typographical mistake and meant to insert n = n + 1 instead of this funny-looking expression:

```
++n
```

But ++n is actually a perfectly valid Objective-C expression. It introduces a new (and rather unique) operator in the Objective-C programming language: the *increment operator*. The function of the double plus sign, or the increment operator, is to add 1 to its operand. Addition by 1 is such a common operation in programs that a special operator was created solely for this purpose. Therefore, the expression ++n is equivalent to the expression n = n + 1. At first glance, it might appear that n = n + 1 is more readable, but you will soon get used to the function of this operator and even learn to appreciate its succinctness.

Of course, no programming language that offers an increment operator to add 1 would be complete without a corresponding operator to subtract 1. As you would guess, the name of this operator is the *decrement operator*, and it is symbolized by the double minus sign. So an expression in Objective-C that reads

```
bean_counter = bean_counter - 1
```

can be equivalently expressed using the decrement operator, like so:

```
--bean_counter
```

Some programmers prefer to put the ++ or -- after the variable name, as in n++ or bean_counter--. This is acceptable and is a matter of personal preference.

You might have noticed that the last line of output from Program 5.3 doesn't line up. You can correct this minor annoyance by substituting the following NSLog statement in place of the corresponding statement from Program 5.3:

```
NSLog ("%2i %i", n, triangularNumber);
```

To verify that this change solves the problem, here's the output from the modified program (called Program 5.3A).

Program 5.3A Output

```
TABLE OF TRIANGULAR NUMBERS


 n   Sum from 1 to n
--   _____
 1        1
 2        3
 3        6
 4        10
 5        15
 6        21
 7        28
 8        36
 9        45
10        55
```

The primary change made to the NSLog statement is the inclusion of a field width specification. The characters %2i tell the NSLog routine not only that you want to display the value of an integer at that particular point, but also that the size of the integer to be displayed should take up at least two columns in the display. Any integer that would normally take up less than two columns (that is, the integers 0–9) will be displayed with a leading space. This is known as *right justification*.

Thus, by using a field width specification of %2i, you guarantee that at least two columns will be used for displaying the value of n; you also ensure that the values of triangularNumber will be aligned.

Keyboard Input

Program 5.2 calculates the 200th triangular number, and nothing more. What if you wanted to calculate the 50th or the 100th triangular number instead? Well, if that were the case, you would have to change the program so that the for loop would be executed the correct number of times. You would also have to change the NSLog statement to display the correct message.

An easier solution might be to somehow have the program ask you which triangular number you want to calculate. Then, after you had given your answer, the program could calculate the desired triangular number. You can effect such a solution by using a routine called scanf. The scanf routine is similar in concept to the NSLog routine. Whereas the NSLog routine is used to display values, the purpose of the scanf routine is to enable the programmer to type values into the program. Of course, if you're writing an Objective-C program that uses a graphical User Interface (UI), such as a Cocoa or iPhone application, you likely won't be using NSLog or scanf at all in your program.

Program 5.4 asks the user which triangular number should be calculated, calculates that number, and then displays the results.

Program 5.4

```
#import <Foundation/Foundation.h>

int main (int argc, char *argv[])
{
    NSAutoreleasePool * pool = [[NSAutoreleasePool alloc] init];
    int n, number, triangularNumber;

    NSLog (@"What triangular number do you want?");
    scanf ("%i", &number);

    triangularNumber = 0;

    for ( n = 1; n <= number; ++n )
        triangularNumber += n;

    NSLog (@"Triangular number %i is %i\n", number, triangularNumber);

    [pool drain];
    return 0;
}
```

In the program output that follows, the number typed in by the user (100) is set in bold type, to distinguish it from the output displayed by the program.

Program 5.4 Output

```
What triangular number do you want?
100
Triangular number 100 is 5050
```

According to the output, the user typed the number 100. The program then calculated the 100th triangular number and displayed the result of 5050 at the terminal. The user could have just as easily typed in the number 10 or 30, for example, if he or she wanted to calculate those particular triangular numbers.

The first NSLog statement in Program 5.4 is used to prompt the user to type in a number. Of course, it is always nice to remind the user of what you want entered. After the message is printed, the scanf routine is called. The first argument to scanf is the format string, which *does not* begin with the @ character. Unlike NSLog, whose first argument is always an NSString object, the first argument to scanf is a C-style string. As noted earlier in this text, C-style character strings are not preceded by the @ character.

The format string tells scanf what types of values are to be read in from the console (or terminal window, if you're compiling your programs using the Terminal application). As with NSLog, the %i characters are used to specify an integer value.

The second argument to the scanf routine specifies where the value that the user types in is to be stored. The & character before the variable number is necessary in this case. Don't worry about its function here, though. We discuss this character, which is actually an operator, in great detail when we talk about pointers in Chapter 13, "Underlying C Language Features."

Given the preceding discussion, you can now see that the scanf call from Program 5.4 specifies that an integer value is to be read and stored into the variable number. This value represents the particular triangular number the user wants to have calculated.

After the user has typed in this number (and pressed the Enter key on the keyboard to signal that typing of the number is completed), the program calculates the requested triangular number. This is done in the same way as in Program 5.2; the only difference is that, instead of using 200 as the limit, number is used as the limit.

After the desired triangular number has been calculated, the results are displayed. Execution of the program is then complete.

Nested for Loops

Program 5.4 gives the user the flexibility to have the program calculate any triangular number that is desired. But suppose the user had a list of five triangular numbers to be calculated? In such a case, the user could simply execute the program five times, each time typing in the next triangular number from the list to be calculated.

Another way to accomplish the same goal, and a far more interesting method, as far as learning about Objective-C is concerned, is to have the program handle the situation. This can best be accomplished by inserting a loop into the program to repeat the entire series of calculations five times. You can use the for statement to set up such a loop. Program 5.5 and its associated output illustrate this technique.

Program 5.5

```
#import <Foundation/Foundation.h>

int main (int argc, char *argv[])
{
    NSAutoreleasePool * pool = [[NSAutoreleasePool alloc] init];
```

```
    int n, number, triangularNumber, counter;

    for ( counter = 1; counter <= 5; ++counter ) {
        NSLog (@"What triangular number do you want?");
        scanf ("%i", &number);

        triangularNumber = 0;

        for ( n = 1; n <= number; ++n )
            triangularNumber += n;

        NSLog (@"Triangular number %i is %i", number, triangularNumber);

    }

    [pool drain];
    return 0;
}
```

Program 5.5 Output

```
What triangular number do you want?
12
Triangular number 12 is 78

What triangular number do you want?
25
Triangular number 25 is 325

What triangular number do you want?
50
Triangular number 50 is 1275

What triangular number do you want?
75
Triangular number 75 is 2850

What triangular number do you want?
83
Triangular number 83 is 3486
```

The program consists of two levels of for statements. The outermost for statement is as follows:

```
for ( counter = 1; counter <= 5; ++counter )
```

This specifies that the program loop is to be executed precisely five times. The value of counter is initially set to 1 and is incremented by 1 until it is no longer less than or equal to 5 (in other words, until it reaches 6).

Unlike the previous program examples, the variable counter is not used anywhere else within the program. Its function is solely as a loop counter in the for statement. Nevertheless, because it is a variable, you must declare it in the program.

The program loop actually consists of all the remaining program statements, as indicated by the braces. You might be able to more easily comprehend the way this program operates if you conceptualize it as follows:

```
For 5 times
{
    Get the number from the user.
    Calculate the requested triangular number.
    Display the results.
}
```

The portion of the loop referred to in the preceding as *Calculate the requested triangular number* actually consists of setting the value of the variable triangularNumber to 0 *plus the for loop that calculates the triangular number.* Thus, a for statement is actually contained within another for statement. This is perfectly valid in Objective-C, and nesting can continue even further to any desired level.

The proper use of indentation becomes even more critical when dealing with more sophisticated program constructs, such as nested for statements. At a quick glance, you can easily determine which statements are contained within each for statement.

for Loop Variants

Before leaving this discussion of the for loop, we should mention some of the syntactic variations that are permitted in forming this loop. When writing a for loop, you might discover that you want to initialize more than one variable before the loop begins, or perhaps you want to evaluate more than one expression each time through the loop. You can include multiple expressions in any of the fields of the for loop, as long as you separate such expressions by commas. For example, in the for statement that begins

```
for ( i = 0, j = 0; i < 10; ++i )
    ...
```

the value of i is set to 0 and the value of j is set to 0 before the loop begins. The two expressions i = 0 and j = 0 are separated from each other by a comma, and both expressions are considered part of the *init_expression* field of the loop. As another example, the for loop that starts

```
for ( i = 0, j = 100; i < 10; ++i, j -= 10 )
    ...
```

sets up two index variables: i and j, which initialize to 0 and 100, respectively, before the loop begins. Each time after the body of the loop is executed, the value of i is incremented by 1 and the value of j is decremented by 10.

Just as you might need to include more than one expression in a particular field of the for statement, you also might need to omit one or more fields from the statement. You can do this simply by omitting the desired field and marking its place with a semicolon. The most common application for the omission of a field in the for statement occurs when no initial expression needs to be evaluated. You can simply leave the *init_expression* field blank in such a case, as long as you still include the semicolon:

```
for ( ; j != 100; ++j )
   ...
```

This statement might be used if j were already set to some initial value before the loop was entered.

A for loop that has its *looping_condition* field omitted effectively sets up an infinite loop—that is, a loop that theoretically will be executed forever. Such a loop can be used as long as some other means is used to exit from the loop (such as executing a return, break, or goto statement, as discussed later in this book).

You can also define variables as part of your initial expression inside a for loop. This is done using the typical ways we've defined variables in the past. For example, the following can be used to set up a for loop with an integer variable counter both defined and initialized to the value 1, like so:

```
for ( int counter = 1; counter <= 5; ++counter )
```

The variable counter is known only throughout the execution of the for loop (it's called a *local* variable) and cannot be accessed outside the loop. As another example, the following for loop defines two integer variables and sets their values accordingly:

```
for ( int n = 1, triangularNumber = 0; n <= 200; ++n )
    triangularNumber += n;
```

A final for loop variant, for performing what's known as *fast enumerations* on collections of objects is described in detail in Chapter 15, "Numbers, Strings, and Collections."

The while Statement

The while statement further extends the Objective-C language's repertoire of looping capabilities. The syntax of this frequently used construct is as follows:

```
while ( expression )
   program statement
```

The *expression* specified inside the parentheses is evaluated. If the result of the *expression* evaluation is TRUE, the *program statement* that immediately follows is executed. After execution of this statement (or statements, if enclosed in braces), *expression* is again evaluated. If the result of the evaluation is TRUE, the *program statement* is again executed. This process continues until *expression* finally evaluates FALSE, at which point the loop is terminated. Execution of the program then continues with the statement that follows *program statement*.

As an example of its use, the following program sets up a while loop, which merely counts from 1 to 5.

Program 5.6

```
// This program introduces the while statement

#import <Foundation/Foundation.h>

#import <stdio.h>

int main (int argc, char *argv[])
{
    NSAutoreleasePool * pool = [[NSAutoreleasePool alloc] init];
    int count = 1;

    while ( count <= 5 ) {
        NSLog (@"%i", count);
        ++count;
    }

    [pool drain];

    return 0;
}
```

Program 5.6 Output

```
1
2
3
4
5
```

The program initially sets the value of count to 1; execution of the while loop then begins. Because the value of count is less than or equal to 5, the statement that immediately follows is executed. The braces define both the NSLog statement and the statement that increments count as the body of the while loop. From the output of the program, you can see that this loop is executed five times or until the value of count reaches 5.

You might have realized from this program that you could have readily accomplished the same task by using a for statement. In fact, a for statement can always be translated into an equivalent while statement, and vice versa. For example, the general for statement

```
for ( init_expression; loop_condition; loop_expression )
    program statement
```

can be equivalently expressed in the form of a while statement, like so:

```
init_expression;
while ( loop_condition )
{
    program statement
    loop_expression;
}
```

When you become familiar with the use of the while statement, you will gain a better feel for when it seems more logical to use a while statement and when you should use a for statement. In general, a loop executed a predetermined number of times is a prime candidate for implementation as a for statement. Also, if the initial expression, looping expression, and looping condition all involve the same variable, the for statement is probably the right choice.

The next program provides another example of the use of the while statement. The program computes the greatest common divisor of two integer values. The greatest common divisor (we abbreviate it hereafter as gcd) of two integers is the largest integer value that evenly divides the two integers. For example, the gcd of 10 and 15 is 5 because 5 is the largest integer that evenly divides both 10 and 15.

A procedure, or algorithm, that can be followed to arrive at the gcd of two arbitrary integers is based on a procedure originally developed by Euclid around 300 B.C. It can be stated as follows:

Problem: Find the greatest common divisor of two nonnegative integers u and v.

Step 1: If v equals 0, then we are done and the gcd is equal to u.

Step 2: Calculate temp = u % v, u = v, v = temp and go back to step 1.

Don't concern yourself with the details of how the previous algorithm works—simply take it on faith. We are more concerned here with developing a program to find the greatest common divisor than in performing an analysis of how the algorithm works.

After expressing the solution to the problem of finding the greatest common divisor in terms of an algorithm, developing the computer program becomes a much simpler task. An analysis of the steps of the algorithm reveals that step 2 is repetitively executed as long as the value of v is not equal to 0. This realization leads to the natural implementation of this algorithm in Objective-C with the use of a while statement.

Program 5.7 finds the gcd of two nonnegative integer values typed in by the user.

Program 5.7

```
// This program finds the greatest common divisor
// of two nonnegative integer values

#import <Foundation/Foundation.h>

int main (int argc, char *argv[])
```

```
{
    NSAutoreleasePool * pool = [[NSAutoreleasePool alloc] init];
    unsigned int u, v, temp;

    NSLog (@"Please type in two nonnegative integers.");
    scanf ("%u%u", &u, &v);

    while ( v != 0 ) {
        temp = u % v;
        u = v;
        v = temp;
    }

    NSLog (@"Their greatest common divisor is %u", u);

    [pool drain];

    return 0;
}
```

Program 5.7 Output

```
Please type in two nonnegative integers.
150 35
Their greatest common divisor is 5
```

Program 5.7 Output (Rerun)

```
Please type in two nonnegative integers.
1026 540
Their greatest common divisor is 54
```

After the two integer values have been entered and stored in the variables u and v (using the %u format characters to read in an unsigned integer value), the program enters a while loop to calculate their greatest common divisor. After the while loop is exited, the value of u, which represents the gcd of v and of the original value of u, is displayed with an appropriate message.

You will use the algorithm for finding the greatest common divisor again in Chapter 7, "More on Classes," when you return to working with fractions.

For the next program that illustrates the use of the while statement, let's consider the task of reversing the digits of an integer that is entered from the terminal. For example, if the user types in the number 1234, the program should reverse the digits of this number and display the result of 4321.

> ### Note
>
> Using NSLog calls will cause each digit to appear on a separate line of the output. C programmers who are familiar with the printf function can use that routine instead to get the digits to appear consecutively.

To write such a program, you first must come up with an algorithm that accomplishes the stated task. Frequently, analyzing your own method for solving the problem leads to an algorithm. For the task of reversing the digits of a number, the solution can be simply stated as "successively read the digits of the number from right to left." You can have a computer program successively read the digits of the number by developing a procedure to successively isolate or extract each digit of the number, beginning with the rightmost digit. The extracted digit can be subsequently displayed at the terminal as the next digit of the reversed number.

You can extract the rightmost digit from an integer number by taking the remainder of the integer after it is divided by 10. For example, 1234 % 10 gives the value 4, which is the rightmost digit of 1234 and is also the first digit of the reversed number. (Remember that the modulus operator gives the remainder of one integer divided by another.) You can get the next digit of the number by using the same process if you first divide the number by 10, bearing in mind the way integer division works. Thus, 1234 / 10 gives a result of 123, and 123 % 10 gives you 3, which is the next digit of the reversed number.

You can continue this procedure until you've extracted the last digit. In the general case, you know that the last digit of the number has been extracted when the result of the last integer division by 10 is 0.

Program 5.8 prompts the user to enter a number and then proceeds to display the digits from that number from the rightmost to leftmost digit.

Program 5.8

```
// Program to reverse the digits of a number

#import <Foundation/Foundation.h>

int main (int argc, char *argv[])
{
    NSAutoreleasePool * pool = [[NSAutoreleasePool alloc] init];
    int number, right_digit;

    NSLog (@"Enter your number.");
    scanf ("%i", &number);

    while ( number != 0 ) {
        right_digit = number % 10;
        NSLog (@"%i", right_digit);
        number /= 10;
    }

    [pool drain];
    return 0;
}
```

Program 5.8 Output

```
Enter your number.
13579
9
7
5
3
1
```

The do Statement

The two looping constructs discussed thus far in this chapter both test the conditions before the loop is executed. Therefore, the body of the loop might never be executed if the conditions are not satisfied. When developing programs, you sometimes want to have the test made at the end of the loop instead of at the beginning. Naturally, the Objective-C language provides a special language construct to handle such a situation, known as the do statement. The syntax of this statement is as follows:

```
do
    program statement
while ( expression );
```

Execution of the do statement proceeds as follows: *program statement* is executed first. Next, the *expression* inside the parentheses is evaluated. If the result of evaluating *expression* is TRUE, the loop continues and *program statement* is again executed. As long as the evaluation of *expression* continues to be TRUE, *program statement* is repeatedly executed. When the evaluation of the expression proves FALSE, the loop is terminated and the next statement in the program is executed in the normal sequential manner.

The do statement is simply a transposition of the while statement, with the looping conditions placed at the end of the loop instead of at the beginning.

Program 5.8 used a while statement to reverse the digits of a number. Go back to that program and try to determine what would happen if the user had typed in the number 0 instead of 13579. The loop of the while statement would never have been executed, and nothing would have been displayed for output. If you were to use a do statement instead of a while statement, you would be assured that the program loop would be executed at least once, thus guaranteeing the display of at least one digit in all cases. Program 5.9 illustrates the use of the do statement.

```
// Program to reverse the digits of a number

#import <Foundation/Foundation.h>

int main (int argc, char *argv[])
{
    NSAutoreleasePool * pool = [[NSAutoreleasePool alloc] init];

    int number, right_digit;
```

```
    NSLog (@"Enter your number.");
    scanf ("%i", &number);

    do {
        right_digit = number % 10;
        NSLog (@"%i", right_digit);
        number /= 10;
    }
    while ( number != 0 );

    [pool drain];
    return 0;
}
```

Program 5.9 Output

```
Enter your number.
135
5
3
1
```

Program 5.9 Output (Rerun)

```
Enter your number.
0
0
```

As you can see from the program's output, when 0 is keyed into the program, the program correctly displays the digit 0.

The `break` Statement

Sometimes when executing a loop, you'll want to leave the loop as soon as a certain condition occurs—for instance, maybe you detect an error condition or reach the end of your data prematurely. You can use the `break` statement for this purpose. Execution of the `break` statement causes the program to immediately exit from the loop it is executing, whether it's a `for`, `while`, or `do` loop. Subsequent statements in the loop are skipped and execution of the loop is terminated. Execution continues with whatever statement follows the loop.

If a `break` is executed from within a set of nested loops, only the innermost loop in which the `break` is executed is terminated.

The format of the break statement is simply the keyword break followed by a semi-colon, like so:

```
break;
```

The continue Statement

The continue statement is similar to the break statement, except that it doesn't cause the loop to terminate. At the point that the continue statement is executed, any statements that appear after the continue statement up to the end of the loop are skipped. Execution of the loop otherwise continues as normal.

The continue statement is most often used to bypass a group of statements inside a loop based on some condition, but then to otherwise continue executing the loop. The format of the continue statement is as follows:

```
continue;
```

Don't use the break or continue statements until you become very familiar with writing program loops and gracefully exiting from them. These statements are too easy to abuse and can result in programs that are hard to follow.

Summary

Now that you are familiar with all the basic looping constructs the Objective-C language provides, you're ready to learn about another class of language statements that enables you to make decisions during the execution of a program. The next chapter describes these decision-making capabilities in detail.

Exercises

1. Write a program to generate and display a table of n and n^2, for integer values of n ranging from 1 through 10. Be sure to print the appropriate column headings.

2. A triangular number can also be generated for any integer value of n by this formula:
   ```
   triangularNumber = n (n + 1) / 2
   ```

   For example, the 10th triangular number, 55, can be calculated by substituting 10 as the value for n into the previous formula. Write a program that generates a table of triangular numbers using the previous formula. Have the program generate every fifth triangular number between 5 and 50 (that is, 5, 10, 15, ..., 50).

3. The factorial of an integer n, written n!, is the product of the consecutive integers 1 through n. For example, 5 factorial is calculated as follows:
   ```
   5! = 5 x 4 x 3 x 2 x 1 = 120
   ```
   Write a program to generate and print a table of the first 10 factorials.

4. A minus sign placed in front of a field width specification causes the field to be displayed left-justified. Substitute the following **NSLog** statement for the corresponding statement in Program 5.3, run the program, and compare the outputs produced by both programs:

```
NSLog (@"%-2i %i", n, triangularNumber);
```

5. Program 5.5 allows the user to type in only five different numbers. Modify that program so that the user can type in the number of triangular numbers to be calculated.

6. Rewrite Programs 5.2 through 5.5, replacing all uses of the **for** statement with equivalent **while** statements. Run each program to verify that both versions are identical.

7. What would happen if you typed a negative number into Program 5.8? Try it and see.

8. Write a program that calculates the sum of the digits of an integer. For example, the sum of the digits of the number **2155** is **2 + 1 + 5 + 5**, or **13**. The program should accept any arbitrary integer the user types.

6

Making Decisions

A fundamental feature of any programming language is its capability to make decisions.
Decisions were made when executing the looping statements to determine when to terminate a loop. The Objective-C programming language also provides several other decision-making constructs, which are covered in this chapter:

- The `if` statement
- The `switch` statement
- The `conditional` operator

The `if` Statement

The Objective-C programming language provides a general decision-making capability in
the form of a language construct known as the `if` statement. The general format of this
statement is shown here:

```
if ( expression )
    program statement
```

Imagine that you could translate a statement such as "If it is not raining, then I will go
swimming" into the Objective-C language. Using the previous format for the `if` statement, this might be "written" in Objective-C as follows:

```
if ( it is not raining )
    I will go swimming
```

The `if` statement is used to stipulate execution of a program statement (or statements,
if enclosed in braces) based on specified conditions. I will go swimming if it is not raining. Similarly, in the program statement

```
if ( count > MAXIMUM_SONGS )
    [playlist maxExceeded];
```

the `maxExceeded` message is sent to `playlist` *only* if the value of `count` is greater
than the value of `MAXIMUM_SONGS`; otherwise, it is ignored.

An actual program example will help drive the point home. Suppose you want to write a program that accepts an integer entered from the keyboard and then displays the absolute value of that integer. A straightforward way to calculate the absolute value of an integer is to simply negate the number if it is less than zero. The phrase "if it is less than zero" in the previous sentence signals that the program must make a decision. This decision can be affected by the use of an `if` statement, as shown in the program that follows.

Program 6.1

```
// Calculate the absolute value of an integer

#import <Foundation/Foundation.h>

int main (int argc, char *argv[])
{
    NSAutoreleasePool * pool = [[NSAutoreleasePool alloc] init];

    int number;

    NSLog (@"Type in your number: ");
    scanf ("%i", &number);

    if ( number < 0 )
        number = -number;

    NSLog (@"The absolute value is %i", number);

    [pool drain];
    return 0;
}
```

Program 6.1 Output

```
Type in your number:
-100
The absolute value is 100
```

Program 6.1 Output (Rerun)

```
Type in your number:
2000
The absolute value is 2000
```

The program was run twice to verify that it is functioning properly. Of course, it might be desirable to run the program several more times to get a higher level of confidence so that you know it is indeed working correctly, but at least you know that you have checked both possible outcomes of the program's decision.

After a message is displayed to the user and the integer value that is entered is stored in `number`, the program tests the value of `number` to see whether it is less than zero. If it is, the following program statement, which negates the value of `number`, is executed. If the value of `number` is not less than zero, this program statement is automatically skipped. (If it is already positive, you don't want to negate it.) The absolute value of `number` is then displayed by the program, and program execution ends.

Let's look at another program that uses the `if` statement. We'll add one more method to the `Fraction` class, called `convertToNum`. This method will provide the value of a fraction expressed as a real number. In other words, it will divide the numerator by the denominator and return the result as a double precision value. So if you have the fraction `1/2`, you want the method to return the value `0.5`.

The declaration for such a method might look like this:

```
-(double) convertToNum;
```

This is how you could write its definition:

```
-(double) convertToNum
{
    return numerator / denominator;
}
```

Well, not quite. As it's defined, this method actually has two serious problems. Can you spot them? The first has to do with arithmetic conversions. Recall that `numerator` and `denominator` are both integer instance variables. So what happens when you divide two integers? Correct, it is done as an integer division! If you wanted to convert the fraction `1/2`, the previous code would give you zero! This is easily corrected by using the type cast operator to convert one or both of the operands to a floating-point value before the division takes place:

```
(double) numerator / denominator
```

Recalling the relatively high precedence of this operator, the value of `numerator` is first converted to `double` before the division occurs. Furthermore, you don't need to convert the `denominator` because the rules of arithmetic conversion take care of that for you.

The second problem with this method is that you should check for division by zero (you should always check for that!). The invoker of this method could inadvertently have forgotten to set the denominator of the fraction or might have set the denominator of the fraction to zero, and you don't want your program to terminate abnormally.

The modified version of the `convertToNum` method appears here:

```
-(double) convertToNum
{
    if (denominator != 0)
        return (double) numerator / denominator;
    else
        return 0.0;
}
```

We arbitrarily decided to return 0.0 if the denominator of the fraction is zero. Other options are available (such as printing an error message, throwing an exception, and so on), but we won't go into them here.

Let's put this new method to use in Program 6.2.

Program 6.2

```
#import <Foundation/Foundation.h>

@interface Fraction: NSObject
{
  int   numerator;
  int   denominator;
}

-(void)   print;
-(void)   setNumerator: (int) n;
-(void)   setDenominator: (int) d;
-(int)    numerator;
-(int)    denominator;
-(double) convertToNum;
@end


@implementation Fraction
-(void) print
{
    NSLog (@" %i/%i ", numerator, denominator);
}

-(void) setNumerator: (int) n
{
    numerator = n;
}

-(void) setDenominator: (int) d
{
    denominator = d;
}

-(int) numerator
{
    return numerator;
}

-(int) denominator
{
```

```
        return denominator;
}

-(double) convertToNum
{
    if (denominator != 0)
        return (double) numerator / denominator;
    else
        return 0.0;
}
@end

int main (int argc, char *argv[])
{
    NSAutoreleasePool * pool = [[NSAutoreleasePool alloc] init];

    Fraction *aFraction = [[Fraction alloc] init];
    Fraction *bFraction = [[Fraction alloc] init];

    [aFraction setNumerator: 1];  // 1st fraction is 1/4
    [aFraction setDenominator: 4];

    [aFraction print];
    NSLog (@" =");
    NSLog (@"%g", [aFraction convertToNum]);

    [bFraction print];      // never assigned a value
    NSLog (@" =");
    NSLog (@"%g", [bFraction convertToNum]);
    [aFraction release];
    [bFraction release];

    [pool drain];
    return 0;
}
```

Program 6.2 Output

```
1/4
 =
0.25
0/0
 =
0
```

After setting aFraction to 1/4, the program uses the convertToNum method to convert the fraction to a decimal value. This value is then displayed as 0.25.

In the second case, the value of bFraction is not explicitly set, so its numerator and denominator are initialized to zero, which is the default for instance variables. This explains the result from the print method. It also causes the if statement inside the convertToNum method to return the value 0, as verified from the output.

The if-else Construct

If someone asks you whether a particular number is even or odd, you will most likely make the determination by examining the last digit of the number. If this digit is 0, 2, 4, 6, or 8, you will readily state that the number is even. Otherwise, you will claim that the number is odd.

An easier way for a computer to determine whether a particular number is even or odd is effected not by examining the last digit of the number to see whether it is 0, 2, 4, 6, or 8, but by simply determining whether the number is evenly divisible by 2. If it is, the number is even; otherwise, it is odd.

You have already seen how the modulus operator % is used to compute the remainder of one integer divided by another. This makes it the perfect operator to use in determining whether an integer is evenly divisible by 2. If the remainder after division by 2 is 0, it is even; otherwise, it is odd.

Now let's write a program that determines whether an integer value that the user types in is even or odd and then displays an appropriate message at the terminal—see Program 6.3.

Program 6.3

```
// Program to determine if a number is even or odd

#import <Foundation/Foundation.h>

int main (int argc, char *argv[])

{
    NSAutoreleasePool * pool = [[NSAutoreleasePool alloc] init];

    int number_to_test, remainder;

    NSLog (@"Enter your number to be tested: ");
    scanf ("%i", &number_to_test);

    remainder = number_to_test % 2;

    if ( remainder == 0 )
        NSLog (@"The number is even.");
```

```
    if ( remainder != 0 )
        NSLog (@"The number is odd.");

    [pool drain];
    return 0;
}
```

Program 6.3 Output

```
Enter your number to be tested:
2455
The number is odd.
```

Program 6.3 Output (Rerun)

```
Enter your number to be tested:
1210
The number is even.
```

After the number is typed in, the remainder after division by 2 is calculated. The first if statement tests the value of this remainder to see whether it is equal to zero. If it is, the message "The number is even." displays.

The second if statement tests the remainder to see if it's *not* equal to zero and, if that's the case, displays a message stating that the number is odd.

Whenever the first if statement succeeds, the second one must fail, and vice versa. If you recall from our discussions of even/odd numbers at the beginning of this section, we said that if the number is evenly divisible by 2, it is even; otherwise, it is odd.

When writing programs, this "else" concept is so frequently required that almost all modern programming languages provide a special construct to handle this situation. In Objective-C, this is known as the if-else construct, and the general format is as follows:

```
if ( expression )
    program statement 1
else
    program statement 2
```

The if-else is actually just an extension of the general format of the if statement. If the result of the expression's evaluation is TRUE, then *program statement 1*, which immediately follows, is executed; otherwise, *program statement 2* is executed. In either case, either *program statement 1* or *program statement 2* will be executed, but not both.

You can incorporate the if-else statement into the previous program, replacing the two if statements by a single if-else statement. You will see how this new program construct actually helps reduce the program's complexity somewhat and also improves its readability.

Program 6.4

```
// Determine if a number is even or odd (Ver. 2)


#import <Foundation/Foundation.h>

int main (int argc, char *argv[])
{
    NSAutoreleasePool * pool = [[NSAutoreleasePool alloc] init];

    int number_to_test, remainder;

    NSLog (@"Enter your number to be tested:");
    scanf ("%i", &number_to_test);

    remainder = number_to_test % 2;

    if ( remainder == 0 )
        NSLog (@"The number is even.");
    else
        NSLog (@"The number is odd.");

    [pool drain];
    return 0;
}
```

Program 6.4 Output

```
Enter your number to be tested:
1234
The number is even.
```

Program 6.4 Output (Rerun)

```
Enter your number to be tested:
6551
The number is odd.
```

Don't forget that the double equals sign (==) is the equality test, and the single equals sign is the assignment operator. Forgetting this and inadvertently using the assignment operator inside the if statement can lead to a lot of headaches.

Compound Relational Tests

The if statements you've used so far in this chapter set up simple relational tests between two numbers. Program 6.1 compared the value of number against zero, whereas Program 6.2 compared the denominator of the fraction to zero. Sometimes it becomes desirable, if not necessary, to set up more sophisticated tests. Suppose, for example, that you want to count the number of grades from an exam that were between 70 and 79, inclusive. In such a case, you would want to compare the value of a grade not merely against one limit, but against the two limits 70 and 79 to ensure that it fell within the specified range.

The Objective-C language provides the mechanisms necessary to perform these types of compound relational tests. A *compound relational test* is simply one or more simple relational tests joined by either the logical AND or the logical OR operator. These operators are represented by the character pairs && and || (two vertical bar characters), respectively. As an example, the following Objective-C statement increments the value of grades_70_to_79 only if the value of grade is greater than or equal to 70 and less than or equal to 79:

```
if ( grade >= 70 && grade <= 79 )
    ++grades_70_to_79;
```

In a similar manner, the following statement causes execution of the NSLog statement if index is less than 0 *or* greater than 99:

```
if ( index < 0 || index > 99 )
    NSLog (@"Error - index out of range");
```

The compound operators can be used to form extremely complex expressions in Objective-C. The Objective-C language grants the programmer the ultimate flexibility in forming expressions, but this flexibility is a capability that programmers often abuse. Simpler expressions are almost always easier to read and debug.

When forming compound relational expressions, liberally use parentheses to aid readability of the expression and avoid getting into trouble because of a mistaken assumption about the precedence of the operators in the or expression. (The && operator has lower precedence than any arithmetic or relational operator but higher precedence than the || operator.) Blank spaces also can aid in the expression's readability. An extra blank space around the && and || operators visually sets these operators apart from the expressions they are joining.

To illustrate the use of a compound relational test in an actual program example, let's write a program that tests whether a year is a leap year. We all know that a year is a leap year if it is evenly divisible by 4. What you might not realize, however, is that a year that is divisible by 100 is not a leap year unless it is also divisible by 400.

Try to think how you would go about setting up a test for such a condition. First, you could compute the remainders of the year after division by 4, 100, and 400, and assign these values to appropriately named variables, such as rem_4, rem_100, and rem_400, respectively. Then you could test these remainders to determine whether the desired criteria for a leap year were met.

If we rephrase our previous definition of a leap year, we can say that a year is a leap year if it is evenly divisible by 4 and not by 100 or if it is evenly divisible by 400. Stop for a moment to reflect on this last sentence and to verify to yourself that it is equivalent to the previously stated definition. Now that we have reformulated our definition in these terms, it becomes a relatively straightforward task to translate it into a program statement, as follows:

```
if ( (rem_4 == 0 && rem_100 != 0) || rem_400 == 0 )
    NSLog (@"It's a leap year.");
```

The parentheses around the following subexpression are not required:

```
rem_4 == 0 && rem_100 != 0
```

This is because the expression will be evaluated that way anyway: Remember that && has higher precedence than ||.

In fact, in this particular example, the following test would work just as well:

```
if ( rem_4 == 0 && ( rem_100 != 0 || rem_400 == 0 ) )
```

If you add a few statements in front of the test to declare the variables and to enable the user to key in the year from the terminal, you end up with a program that determines whether a year is a leap year, as shown in Program 6.5.

Program 6.5

```
// This program determines if a year is a leap year


#import <Foundation/Foundation.h>

int main (int argc, char *argv[])
{
    NSAutoreleasePool * pool = [[NSAutoreleasePool alloc] init];

    int year, rem_4, rem_100, rem_400;

    NSLog (@"Enter the year to be tested: ");
    scanf ("%i", &year);

    rem_4 = year % 4;
    rem_100 = year % 100;
    rem_400 = year % 400;

    if ( (rem_4 == 0 && rem_100 != 0) || rem_400 == 0 )
        NSLog (@"It's a leap year.");
    else
        NSLog (@"Nope, it's not a leap year.");

    [pool drain];
    return 0;
}
```

Program 6.5 Output

```
Enter the year to be tested:
1955
Nope, it's not a leap year.
```

Program 6.5 Output (Rerun)

```
Enter the year to be tested:
2000
It's a leap year.
```

Program 6.5 Output (Rerun)

```
Enter the year to be tested:
1800
Nope, it's not a leap year.
```

The previous examples use a year that is not a leap year because it isn't evenly divisible by 4 (1955), a year that is a leap year because it is evenly divisible by 400 (2000), and a year that isn't a leap year because it is evenly divisible by 100 but not by 400 (1800). To complete the run of test cases, you should also try a year that is evenly divisible by 4 and not by 100. This is left as an exercise for you.

We mentioned that Objective-C gives the programmer a tremendous amount of flexibility in forming expressions. For instance, in the previous program, you did not have to calculate the intermediate results `rem_4`, `rem_100`, and `rem_400`—you could have performed the calculation directly inside the `if` statement, as follows:

```
if ( ( year % 4 == 0 && year % 100 != 0 ) || year % 400 == 0 )
```

Using blank spaces to set off the various operators still makes the previous expression readable. If you decided to ignore this and removed the unnecessary set of parentheses, you could end up with an expression that looked like this:

```
if(year%4==0&&year%100!=0||year%400==0)
```

This expression is perfectly valid and, believe it or not, executes identically to the expression shown immediately before it. Obviously, those extra blanks go a long way toward aiding our understanding of complex expressions.

Nested if Statements

In discussions of the general format of the `if` statement, we indicated that if the result of evaluating the expression inside the parentheses is TRUE, the statement that immediately follows is executed. It is perfectly valid for this program statement to be another `if` statement, as in the following statement:

```
if ( [chessGame isOver] == NO )
    if ( [chessGame whoseTurn] == YOU )
        [chessGame yourMove];
```

If the value returned by sending the `isOver` message to `chessGame` is NO, the following statement is executed; this statement, in turn, is another `if` statement. This `if` statement compares the value returned from the `whoseTurn` method against YOU. If the two values are equal, the `yourMove` message is sent to the `chessGame` object. Therefore, the `yourMove` message is sent only if both the game is not done and it's your turn. In fact, this statement could have been equivalently formulated using compound relationals, like so:

```
if ( [chessGame isOver] == NO && [chessGame whoseTurn] == YOU )
    [chessGame yourMove];
```

A more practical example of nested `if` statements might involve adding an `else` clause to the previous example, as shown here:

```
if ( [chessGame isOver] == NO )
    if ( [chessGame whoseTurn] == YOU )
        [chessGame yourMove];
    else
        [chessGame myMove];
```

Executing this statement proceeds as described previously. However, if the game is not over and it's not your move, the `else` clause is executed. This sends the message `myMove` to `chessGame`. If the game is over, the entire `if` statement that follows, including its associated `else` clause, is skipped.

Notice how the `else` clause is associated with the `if` statement that tests the value returned from the `whoseTurn` method, not with the `if` statement that tests whether the game is over. The general rule is that an `else` clause is always associated with the last `if` statement that doesn't contain an `else`.

You can go one step further and add an `else` clause to the outermost `if` statement in the preceding example. This `else` clause is executed if the game is over:

```
if ( [chessGame isOver] == NO )
    if ( [chessGame whoseTurn] == YOU )
        [chessGame yourMove];
    else
        [chessGame myMove];
else
    [chessGame finish];
```

Of course, even if you use indentation to indicate the way you think a statement will be interpreted in the Objective-C language, it might not always coincide with the way the system actually interprets the statement. For instance, removing the first `else` clause from the previous example will *not* result in the statement being interpreted as its format indicates:

```
if ( [chessGame isOver] == NO )
    if ( [chessGame whoseTurn] == YOU )
        [chessGame yourMove];
else
    [chessGame finish];
```

Instead, this statement will be interpreted as follows:

```
if ( [chessGame isOver] == NO )
```

```
if ( [chessGame whoseTurn] == YOU )
    [chessGame yourMove];
else
    [chessGame finish];
```

This is because the `else` clause is associated with the last un-`else`d `if`. You can use braces to force a different association when an innermost `if` does not contain an `else` but an outer `if` does. The braces have the effect of closing off the `if` statement. Thus, the following statement achieves the desired effect:

```
if ( [chessGame isOver] == NO ) {
    if ( [chessGame whoseTurn] == YOU )
        [chessGame yourMove];
}
else
    [chessGame finish];
```

The `else if` Construct

You have seen how the `else` statement comes into play when you have a test against two possible conditions—either the number is even or it is odd; either the year is a leap year or it is not. However, programming decisions you have to make are not always so black and white. Consider the task of writing a program that displays -1 if a number the user types is less than zero, 0 if the number is equal to zero, and 1 if the number is greater than zero. (This is actually an implementation of what is commonly called the *sign* function.) Obviously, you must make three tests in this case to determine whether the number that is keyed in is negative, zero, or positive. The simple `if-else` construct will not work. Of course, in this case, you can always resort to three separate `if` statements, but this solution does not always work—especially if the tests are not mutually exclusive.

You can handle the situation just described by adding an `if` statement to your `else` clause. We mentioned that the statement that follows an `else` could be any valid Objective-C program statement, so why not another `if`? Thus, in the general case, you could write the following:

```
if ( expression 1 )
    program statement 1
else
    if ( expression 2 )
        program statement 2
    else
        program statement 3
```

This effectively extends the `if` statement from a two-valued logic decision to a three-valued logic decision. You can continue to add `if` statements to the `else` clauses, in the manner just shown, to effectively extend the decision to an n-valued logic decision.

The preceding construct is so frequently used that it is generally referred to as an `else if` construct and is usually formatted differently from that shown previously:

```
if ( expression 1 )
    program statement 1
else if ( expression 2 )
    program statement 2
else
    program statement 3
```

This latter method of formatting improves the readability of the statement and makes it clearer that a three-way decision is being made.

The next program illustrates the use of the `else if` construct by implementing the sign function discussed earlier.

Program 6.6

```
// Program to implement the sign function

#import <Foundation/Foundation.h>

int main (int argc, char *argv[])
{
    NSAutoreleasePool * pool = [[NSAutoreleasePool alloc] init];

    int number, sign;

    NSLog (@"Please type in a number: ");
    scanf ("%i", &number);

    if ( number < 0 )
        sign = -1;
    else if ( number == 0 )
        sign = 0;
    else        // Must be positive
        sign = 1;

    NSLog (@"Sign = %i", sign);
    [pool drain];
    return 0;
}
```

Program 6.6 Output

```
Please type in a number:
1121
Sign = 1
```

Program 6.6 Output (Rerun)

```
Please type in a number:
-158
Sign = -1
```

Program 6.6 Output (Rerun)

```
Please type in a number:
0
Sign = 0
```

If the number that is entered is less than zero, sign is assigned the value -1; if the number is equal to zero, sign is assigned the value 0; otherwise, the number must be greater than zero, so sign is assigned the value 1.

The next program analyzes a character that is typed in from the terminal and classifies it as either an alphabetic character (a–z or A–Z), a digit (0–9), or a special character (anything else). To read a single character from the terminal, the format characters %c are used in the scanf call.

Program 6.7

```
// This program categorizes a single character
//       that is entered from the keyboard

#import <Foundation/Foundation.h>

int main (int argc, char *argv[])
{
    NSAutoreleasePool * pool = [[NSAutoreleasePool alloc] init];
    char c;

    NSLog (@"Enter a single character:");
    scanf ("%c", &c);

    if ( (c >= 'a' && c <= 'z') || (c >= 'A' && c <= 'Z') )
        NSLog (@"It's an alphabetic character.");
    else if ( c >= '0' && c <= '9' )
        NSLog (@"It's a digit.");
    else
        NSLog (@"It's a special character.");

    [pool drain];
    return 0;
}
```

Program 6.7 Output

```
Enter a single character:
&
It's a special character.
```

Program 6.7 Output (Rerun)

```
Enter a single character:
8
It's a digit.
```

Program 6.7 Output (Rerun)

```
Enter a single character:
B
It's an alphabetic character.
```

The first test that is made after the character is read in determines whether the char variable c is an alphabetic character. This is done by testing whether the character is a lowercase letter or an uppercase letter. The former test is made by the following expression:

```
( c >= 'a' && c <= 'z' )
```

This expression is TRUE if c is within the range of characters 'a' through 'z'; that is, if c is a lowercase letter. The latter test is made by this expression:

```
( c >= 'A' && c <= 'Z' )
```

This expression is TRUE if c is within the range of characters 'A' through 'Z'; that is, if c is an uppercase letter. These tests work on computer systems that store characters inside the machine in a format known as ASCII.

If the variable c is an alphabetic character, the first if test succeeds and the message "It's an alphabetic character." is displayed. If the test fails, the else if clause is executed. This clause determines whether the character is a digit. Note that this test compares the character c against the *characters* '0' and '9' and *not* the *integers* 0 and 9. This is because a character was read in from the terminal, and the characters '0' to '9' are not the same as the numbers 0–9. In fact, in ASCII, the character '0' is actually represented internally as the number 48, the character '1' as the number 49, and so on.

If c is a digit character, the phrase "It's a digit." is displayed. Otherwise, if c is not alphabetic and is not a digit, the final else clause is executed and displays the phrase "It's a special character" at the terminal. Execution of the program is then complete.

Note that even though scanf is used here to read just a single character, you still must press the Enter key after the character is typed to send the input to the program. In general, whenever you're reading data from the terminal, the program doesn't see any of the data typed on the line until the Enter key is pressed.

Let's suppose for the next example that you want to write a program that allows the user to type in simple expressions of the following form:

number   operator   number

The program will evaluate the expression and display the results at the terminal. The operators you want to have recognized are the normal operators for addition, subtraction, multiplication, and division. Let's use the `Calculator` class from Program 4.6 in Chapter 4, "Data Types and Expressions," here. Each expression will be given to the calculator for computation.

The following program uses a large `if` statement with many `else if` clauses to determine which operation is to be performed.

> **Note**
>
> It's better to use routines in the standard library called `islower` and `isupper`, and avoid the internal representation issue entirely. To do that, include the line `#import <ctype.h>` in your program. However, we've put this here for illustrative purposes only.

Program 6.8

```
// Program to evaluate simple expressions of the form
//          number operator number

// Implement a Calculator class

#import <Foundation/Foundation.h>

@interface Calculator: NSObject
{
    double accumulator;
}

// accumulator methods
-(void)   setAccumulator: (double) value;
-(void)   clear;
-(double) accumulator;

// arithmetic methods
-(void)   add: (double) value;
-(void)   subtract: (double) value;
-(void)   multiply: (double) value;
-(void)   divide: (double) value;
@end

@implementation Calculator
-(void) setAccumulator: (double) value
{
    accumulator = value;
}
```

```
-(void) clear
{
    accumulator = 0;
}

-(double) accumulator
{
    return accumulator;
}

-(void) add: (double) value
{
    accumulator += value;
}

-(void) subtract: (double) value
{
    accumulator -= value;
}

-(void) multiply: (double) value
{
    accumulator *= value;
}

-(void) divide: (double) value
{
    accumulator /= value;
}
@end


int main (int argc, char *argv[])
{
    NSAutoreleasePool * pool = [[NSAutoreleasePool alloc] init];
    double      value1, value2;
    char        operator;
    Calculator  *deskCalc = [[Calculator alloc] init];

    NSLog (@"Type in your expression.");
    scanf ("%lf %c %lf", &value1, &operator, &value2);

    [deskCalc setAccumulator: value1];
    if ( operator == '+' )
        [deskCalc add: value2];
    else if ( operator == '-' )
```

```
        [deskCalc subtract: value2];
     else if ( operator == '*' )
        [deskCalc multiply: value2];
     else if ( operator == '/' )
        [deskCalc divide: value2];

     NSLog (@"%.2f", [deskCalc accumulator]);
     [deskCalc release];

     [pool drain];
     return 0;
}
```

Program 6.8 Output

```
Type in your expression.
```
123.5 + 59.3
```
182.80
```

Program 6.8 Output (Rerun)

```
Type in your expression.
```
198.7 / 26
```
7.64
```

Program 6.8 Output (Rerun)

```
Type in your expression.
```
89.3 * 2.5
```
223.25
```

The scanf call specifies that three values are to be read into the variables value1, operator, and value2. A double value can be read in with the %lf format characters. This is the format used to read in the value of the variable value1, which is the first operand of the expression.

Next, you read in the operator. Because the operator is a character ('+', '-', '*', or '/') and not a number, you read it into the character variable operator. The %c format characters tell the system to read in the next character from the terminal. The blank spaces inside the format string indicate that an arbitrary number of blank spaces are to be permitted on the input. This enables you to separate the operands from the operator with blank spaces when you type in these values.

After the two values and the operator have been read in, the program stores the first value in the calculator's accumulator. Next, you test the value of operator against the four permissible operators. When a correct match is made, the corresponding message is sent to the calculator to perform the operation. In the last NSLog, the value of the accumulator is retrieved for display. Execution of the program is then complete.

A few words about program thoroughness are in order at this point. Although the preceding program does accomplish the task that we set out to perform, the program is not really complete because it does not account for user mistakes. For example, what would happen if the user typed in a ? for the operator by mistake? The program would simply fall through the if statement and no messages would ever appear at the terminal to alert the user that he had incorrectly typed in his expression.

Another overlooked case is when the user types in a division operation with zero as the divisor. You know by now that you should never attempt to divide a number by zero in Objective-C. The program should check for this case.

Trying to predict the ways in which a program can fail or produce unwanted results and then taking preventive measures to account for such situations is a necessary part of producing good, reliable programs. Running a sufficient number of test cases against a program can often point a finger to portions of the program that do not account for certain cases. But it goes further than that. It must become a matter of self-discipline while coding a program to always ask, "What would happen if…?" and to insert the necessary program statements to handle the situation properly.

Program 6.8A, a modified version of Program 6.8, accounts for division by zero and the keying in of an unknown operator.

Program 6.8A

```
// Program to evaluate simple expressions of the form
//    value   operator   value

#import <Foundation/Foundation.h>

// Insert interface and implementation sections for
// Calculator class here

int main (int argc, char *argv[])
{
    NSAutoreleasePool * pool = [[NSAutoreleasePool alloc] init];
    double     value1, value2;
    char       operator;
    Calculator *deskCalc = [[Calculator alloc] init];

    NSLog (@"Type in your expression.");
    scanf ("%lf %c %lf", &value1, &operator, &value2);

    [deskCalc setAccumulator: value1];

    if ( operator == '+' )
       [deskCalc add: value2];
    else if ( operator == '-' )
```

```
        [deskCalc subtract: value2];
    else if ( operator == '*' )
        [deskCalc multiply: value2];
    else if ( operator == '/' )
        if ( value2 == 0 )
            NSLog (@"Division by zero.");
        else
            [deskCalc divide: value2];
    else
        NSLog (@"Unknown operator.");

    NSLog (@"%.2f", [deskCalc accumulator]);
    [deskCalc release];

    [pool drain];
    return 0;
}
```

Program 6.8A Output

```
Type in your expression.
123.5 + 59.3
182.80
```

Program 6.8A Output (Rerun)

```
Type in your expression.
198.7 / 0
Division by zero.
198.7
```

Program 6.8A Output (Rerun)

```
Type in your expression.
125 $ 28
Unknown operator.
125
```

When the operator that is typed in is the slash, for division, another test is made to determine whether value2 is 0. If it is, an appropriate message is displayed at the terminal; otherwise, the division operation is carried out and the results are displayed. Pay careful attention to the nesting of the if statements and the associated else clauses in this case.

The else clause at the end of the program catches any fall-throughs. Therefore, any value of operator that does not match any of the four characters tested causes this else clause to be executed, resulting in the display of "Unknown operator." at the terminal.

A better way to handle the division-by-zero problem is to perform the test inside the method that handles division. You can modify your `divide:` method as shown here:

```
-(void) divide: (double) value
{
   if (value != 0.0)
      accumulator /= value;
   else {
      NSLog (@"Division by zero.");
      accumulator = 99999999.;
   }
}
```

If `value` is nonzero, you perform the division; otherwise, you display the message and set the accumulator to `99999999`. This is arbitrary; you could have set it to zero or perhaps set a special variable to indicate an error condition. In general, it's better to have the method handle special cases than rely on the resourcefulness of the programmer using the method.

The `switch` Statement

The type of `if-else` statement chain you encountered in the last program example—with the value of a variable successively compared against different values—is so commonly used when developing programs that a special program statement exists in the Objective-C language for performing precisely this function. The name of the statement is the `switch` statement, and its general format is as follows:

```
switch ( expression )
{
    case value1:
        program statement
        program statement
          . . .
        break;
    case value2:
        program statement
        program statement
          . . .
        break;
      . . .
    case valuen:
        program statement
        program statement
          . . .
        break;
    default:
        program statement
        program statement
          . . .
```

```
        break;
}
```

The *expression* enclosed within parentheses is successively compared against the values *value1*, *value2*, . . ., *valuen*, which must be simple constants or constant expressions. If a case is found whose value is equal to the value of *expression*, the program statements that follow the case are executed. Note that when more than one such program statement is included, they do *not* have to be enclosed within braces.

The break statement signals the end of a particular case and causes execution of the switch statement to be terminated. Remember to include the break statement at the end of every case. Forgetting to do so for a particular case causes program execution to continue into the next case whenever that case is executed. Sometimes this is done intentionally; if you elect to do so, be sure to insert comments to alert others of your purpose.

The special optional case called default is executed if the value of *expression* does not match any of the case values. This is conceptually equivalent to the catchall else used in the previous example. In fact, the general form of the switch statement can be equivalently expressed as an if statement, as follows:

```
if ( expression == value1 )
{
    program statement
    program statement
        . . .
}
else if ( expression == value2 )
{
    program statement
    program statement
        . . .
}
    . . .
else if ( expression == valuen )
{
    program statement
    program statement
        . . .
}
else
{
    program statement
    program statement
        . . .
}
```

Bearing in mind the previous code, you can translate the big if statement from Program 6.8A into an equivalent switch statement. This is shown in Program 6.9.

Program 6.9

```
// Program to evaluate simple expressions of the form
//       value operator  value

#import <Foundation/Foundation.h>

// Insert interface and implementation sections for
// Calculator class here

int main (int argc, char *argv[])
{
    NSAutoreleasePool * pool = [[NSAutoreleasePool alloc] init];

    double  value1, value2;
    char    operator;
    Calculator *deskCalc = [[Calculator alloc] init];

     NSLog (@"Type in your expression.");
    scanf ("%lf %c %lf", &value1, &operator, &value2);

    [deskCalc setAccumulator: value1];

    switch ( operator ) {
       case '+':
          [deskCalc add: value2];
          break;
       case '-':
          [deskCalc subtract: value2];
          break;
       case '*':
          [deskCalc multiply: value2];
          break;
       case '/':
          [deskCalc divide: value2];
          break;
       default:
          NSLog (@"Unknown operator.");
          break;
    }

    NSLog (@"%.2f", [deskCalc accumulator]);
    [deskCalc release];

    [pool drain];
    return 0;
}
```

Program 6.9 Output

```
Type in your expression.
178.99 - 326.8
-147.81
```

After the expression has been read in, the value of `operator` is successively compared against the values specified by each case. When a match is found, the statements contained inside the case are executed. The `break` statement then sends execution out of the `switch` statement, where execution of the program is completed. If none of the cases matches the value of operator, the `default` case, which displays "Unknown operator.", is executed.

The `break` statement in the `default` case is actually unnecessary in the preceding program because no statements follow this case inside the `switch`. Nevertheless, it is a good programming habit to remember to include the `break` at the end of every case.

When writing a `switch` statement, bear in mind that no two case values can be the same. However, you can associate more than one case value with a particular set of program statements. This is done simply by listing the multiple case values (with the keyword `case` before the value and a colon after the value in each case) before the common statements that are to be executed. As an example, in the `switch` statement that follows, the `multiply:` method is executed if `operator` is equal to an asterisk or to the lowercase letter x:

```
switch ( operator )
{
    ...
    case '*':
    case 'x':
        [deskCalc multiply: value2];
        break;
    ...
}
```

Boolean Variables

Just about anyone learning to program soon faces the task of having to write a program to generate a table of prime numbers. To refresh your memory, a positive integer, p, is a prime number if it is not evenly divisible by any other integers other than 1 and itself. The first prime integer is defined to be 2. The next prime is 3 because it is not evenly divisible by any integers other than 1 and 3; and 4 is *not* prime because it *is* evenly divisible by 2.

You can take several approaches to generate a table of prime numbers. If you had the task of generating all prime numbers up to 50, for example, the most straightforward (and simplest) algorithm to generate such a table would simply test each integer, p, for divisibility by all integers from 2 through p-1. If any such integer evenly divided p, then p would not be prime; otherwise, it would be a prime number.

Program 6.10 generates a list of prime numbers from 2 to 50.

Program 6.10

```
// Program to generate a table of prime numbers

#import <Foundation/Foundation.h>

int main (int argc, char *argv[])
{
    NSAutoreleasePool * pool = [[NSAutoreleasePool alloc] init];

    int   p, d, isPrime;

    for ( p = 2; p <= 50; ++p ) {
        isPrime = 1;

        for ( d = 2; d < p; ++d )
            if ( p % d == 0 )
                isPrime = 0;

        if ( isPrime != 0 )
            NSLog (@"%i ", p);
    }

    [pool drain];
    return 0;
}
```

Program 6.10 Output

```
2
3
5
7
11
13
17
19
23
29
31
37
41
43
47
```

Several points are worth noting about Program 6.10. The outermost for statement sets up a loop to cycle through the integers 2–50. The loop variable p represents the value you are currently testing to see whether it is prime. The first statement in the loop assigns the value 1 to the variable isPrime. The use of this variable will become apparent shortly.

A second loop is set up to divide p by the integers 2 through p-1. Inside the loop, a test is performed to see whether the remainder of p divided by d is 0. If it is, you know that p cannot be prime because an integer other than 1 and itself evenly divides it. To signal that p is no longer a candidate as a prime number, the value of the variable isPrime is set equal to 0.

When the innermost loop finishes execution, the value of isPrime is tested. If its value is not equal to zero, no integer was found that evenly divided p; therefore, p must be a prime number, and its value is displayed.

You might have noticed that the variable isPrime takes on either 0 or 1, and no other values. Its value is 1 as long as p still qualifies as a prime number. But as soon as a single even divisor is found, its value is set to 0 to indicate that p no longer satisfies the criteria for being prime. Variables used in such a manner are generally referred to as *Boolean* variables. A flag typically assumes only one of two different values. Furthermore, the value of a flag usually is tested at least once in the program to see whether it is on (TRUE or YES) or off (FALSE or NO), and some particular action is taken based on the results of the test.

In Objective-C, the notion of a flag being TRUE or FALSE is most naturally translated into the values 1 and 0, respectively. So in Program 6.10, when you set the value of isPrime to 1 inside the loop, you are effectively setting it as TRUE to indicate that p "is prime." During the course of execution of the inner for loop, if an even divisor is found, the value of isPrime is set FALSE to indicate that p no longer "is prime."

It is no coincidence that the value 1 is typically used to represent the TRUE or on state and 0 is used to represent the FALSE or off state. This representation corresponds to the notion of a single bit inside a computer. When the bit is on, its value is 1; when it is off, its value is 0. But in Objective-C, there is an even more convincing argument in favor of these logic values. It has to do with the way the Objective-C language treats the concept of TRUE and FALSE.

When we began our discussions in this chapter, we noted that if the conditions specified inside the if statement are satisfied, the program statement that immediately followed is executed. But what exactly does *satisfied* mean? In the Objective-C language, *satisfied* means nonzero, and nothing more. Thus, the statement

```
if ( 100 )
    NSLog (@"This will always be printed.");
```

results in the execution of the NSLog statement because the condition in the if statement (in this case, simply the value 100) is nonzero and, therefore, is satisfied.

In each of the programs in this chapter, we used the notions of "nonzero means satisfied" and "zero means not satisfied." This is because, whenever a relational expression is evaluated in Objective-C, it is given the value 1 if the expression is satisfied and 0 if the expression is not satisfied. So, evaluation of the statement

```
if ( number < 0 )
    number = -number;
```

actually proceeds as follows: The relational expression `number < 0` is evaluated. If the condition is satisfied—that is, if `number` is less than `0`—the value of the expression is `1`; otherwise, its value is `0`.

The `if` statement tests the result of the expression evaluation. If the result is nonzero, the statement that immediately follows is executed; otherwise, the statement is skipped.

The preceding discussion also applies to the evaluation of conditions inside the `for`, `while`, and `do` statements. Evaluation of compound relational expressions such as in the following statement also proceeds as outlined previously:

```
while ( char != 'e' && count != 80 )
```

If both specified conditions are valid, the result is `1`, but if either condition is not valid, the result of the evaluation is `0`. The results of the evaluation are then checked. If the result is `0`, the `while` loop terminates; otherwise, it continues.

Returning to Program 6.10 and the notion of flags, it is perfectly valid in Objective-C to test whether the value of a flag is `TRUE` using an expression such as this one:

```
if ( isPrime )
```

This expression is equivalent to the following:

```
if ( isPrime != 0 )
```

To easily test whether the value of a flag is `FALSE`, you use the logical negation operator, `!`. In the expression that follows, the logical negation operator is used to test whether the value of `isPrime` is `FALSE` (read this statement as "if not `isPrime`"):

```
if ( ! isPrime )
```

In general, an expression such as this one negates the logical value of *expression*:

```
! expression
```

So if *expression* is `0`, the logical negation operator produces a `1`. And if the result of the evaluation of *expression* is nonzero, the negation operator yields a `0`.

The logical negation operator can be used to easily flip the value of a flag, as in the following expression:

```
my_move = ! my_move;
```

As you might expect, this operator has the same precedence as the unary minus operator, which means that it has higher precedence than all binary arithmetic operators and all relational operators. To test whether the value of a variable `x` is not less than the value of a variable `y`, such as in

```
! ( x < y )
```

the parentheses are required to ensure proper evaluation of the expression. Of course, you could have equivalently expressed the previous statement as follows:

```
x >= y
```

A couple of built-in features in Objective-C make working with Boolean variables a little easier. One is the special type BOOL, which can be used to declare variables that will contain either a true or a false value. The other is the built-in values YES and NO. Using these predefined values in your programs can make them easier to write and read. Take a look at Program 6.10, rewritten to take advantage of these features.

> **Note**
>
> The type BOOL is really added by a mechanism known as the preprocessor.

Program 6.10A

```
// Program to generate a table of prime numbers
// second version using BOOL type and predefined values

#import <Foundation/Foundation.h>

int main (int argc, char *argv[])
{
   NSAutoreleasePool * pool = [[NSAutoreleasePool alloc] init];

   int    p, d;
   BOOL   isPrime;

   for ( p = 2; p <= 50; ++p ) {
      isPrime = YES;

      for ( d = 2; d < p; ++d )
         if ( p % d == 0 )
            isPrime = NO;

      if ( isPrime == YES )
         NSLog (@"%i ", p);
   }

   [pool drain];
   return 0;
}
```

Program 6.10A Output

```
2
3
5
7
11
13
17
```

```
19
23
29
31
37
41
43
47
```

The Conditional Operator

Perhaps the most unusual operator in the Objective-C language is one called the conditional operator. Unlike all other operators in Objective-C—which are either unary or binary operators—the conditional operator is a *ternary* operator; that is, it takes three operands. The two symbols used to denote this operator are the question mark (?) and the colon (:). The first operand is placed before the ?, the second between the ? and the :, and the third after the :.

The general format of the conditional expression is shown here:

```
condition ? expression1 : expression2
```

In this syntax, *condition* is an expression, usually a relational expression, that the Objective-C system evaluates first whenever it encounters the conditional operator. If the result of the evaluation of *condition* is TRUE (that is, nonzero), *expression1* is evaluated and the result of the evaluation becomes the result of the operation. If *condition* evaluates FALSE (that is, zero), *expression2* is evaluated and its result becomes the result of the operation.

A conditional expression is most often used to assign one of two values to a variable, depending on some condition. For example, suppose you have an integer variable x and another integer variable s. If you wanted to assign -1 to s if x were less than 0, and the value of x^2 to s otherwise, you could write the following statement:

```
s = ( x < 0 ) ? -1 : x * x;
```

The condition x < 0 is first tested when the previous statement is executed. Parentheses are generally placed around the condition expression to aid in the statement's readability. This is usually not required, though, because the precedence of the conditional operator is very low—lower, in fact, than all other operators but the assignment operators and the comma operator.

If the value of x is less than zero, the expression immediately following the ? is evaluated. This expression is simply the constant integer value -1, which is assigned to the variable s if x is less than zero.

If the value of x is not less than zero, the expression immediately following the : is evaluated and assigned to s. So if x is greater than or equal to zero, the value of x * x, or x^2, is assigned to s.

As another example of the conditional operator, the following statement assigns to the variable max_value the maximum of a and b:

```
max_value = ( a > b ) ? a : b;
```

If the expression after the : (the "else" part) consists of another conditional operator, you can achieve the effects of an else if clause. For example, the sign function implemented in Program 6.6 can be written in one program line using two conditional operators, as follows:

```
sign = ( number < 0 ) ? -1 : (( number == 0 ) ? 0 : 1);
```

If number is less than zero, sign is assigned the value -1; if number is equal to zero, sign is assigned the value 0; otherwise, it is assigned the value 1. The parentheses around the "else" part of the previous expression are actually unnecessary. This is because the conditional operator associates from right to left, meaning that multiple uses of this operator in a single expression, such as in

```
e1 ? e2 : e3 ? e4 : e5
```

group from right to left and therefore are evaluated as follows:

```
e1 ? e2 : ( e3 ? e4 : e5 )
```

Conditional expressions don't have to be used on the right side of an assignment— they can be used in any situation in which expressions can be used. This means you can display the sign of the variable number without first assigning it to a variable using a NSLog statement, as shown here:

```
NSLog (@"Sign = %i", ( number < 0 ) ? -1
                          : ( number == 0 ) ? 0 : 1);
```

The conditional operator is very handy when writing preprocessor macros in Objective-C. You can see this in detail in Chapter 12, "The Preprocessor."

Exercises

1. Write a program that asks the user to type in two integer values. Test these two numbers to determine whether the first is evenly divisible by the second and then display an appropriate message at the terminal.

2. Program 6.8A displays the value in the accumulator even if an invalid operator is entered or division by zero is attempted. Fix that problem.

3. Modify the print method from the Fraction class so that whole numbers are displayed as such (so the fraction 5/1 should display as simply 5). Also modify the method to display fractions with a numerator of 0 as simply zero.

4. Write a program that acts as a simple printing calculator. The program should allow the user to type in expressions of the following form:

```
number   operator
```

The program should recognize the following operators:

```
+    -    *    /    S    E
```

The S operator tells the program to set the accumulator to the typed-in number, and the E operator tells the program that execution is to end. The arithmetic operations are performed on the contents of the accumulator, with the number that was keyed in acting as the second operand. The following is a sample run showing how the program should operate:

```
Begin Calculations
10 S                Set Accumulator to 10
= 10.000000         Contents of Accumulator
2 /                 Divide by 2
= 5.000000          Contents of Accumulator
55 -                Subtract 55
= -50.000000
100.25 S            Set Accumulator to 100.25
= 100.250000
4 *                 Multiply by 4
= 401.000000
0 E                 End of program
= 401.000000
End of Calculations.
```

Make sure that the program detects division by 0 and also checks for unknown operators. Use the `Calculator` class developed in Program 6.8 for performing your calculations.

5. We developed Program 5.9 to reverse the digits of an integer typed in from the terminal. However, this program does not function well if you type in a negative number. Find out what happens in such a case, and then modify the program so that negative numbers are correctly handled. By this, we mean that if the number - 8645 were typed in, for example, the output of the program should be 5468-.

6. Write a program that takes an integer keyed in from the terminal and extracts and displays each digit of the integer in English. So if the user types in 932, the program should display the following:

```
nine
three
two
```

(Remember to display **zero** if the user types in just 0.) Note: This exercise is a hard one!

7. Program 6.10 has several inefficiencies. One inefficiency results from checking even numbers. Because any even number greater than **2** obviously cannot be prime, the program could simply skip all even numbers as possible primes and as possible divisors. The inner **for** loop is also inefficient because the value of **p** is always divided by all values of **d** from **2** through **p–1**. You can avoid this inefficiency if you add a test for the value of **isPrime** in the conditions of the **for** loop. In this manner, you can set up the **for** loop to continue as long as no divisor is found and the value of **d** is less than **p**. Modify Program 6.10 to incorporate these two changes; then run the program to verify its operation.

More on Classes

In this chapter, you'll continue learning how to work with classes and write methods. You'll also apply some of the concepts you learned in the previous chapter, such as completing program looping, making decisions, and working with expressions. First we talk about splitting your program into multiple files to make working with larger programs easier.

Separate Interface and Implementation Files

It's time to get used to putting your class declarations and definitions in separate files.

If you're using Xcode, start a new project called `FractionTest`. Type the following program into the file `FractionTest.m`:

Program 7.1 Main Test Program: `FractionTest.m`

```
#import "Fraction.h"

int main (int argc, char *argv[])
{
    NSAutoreleasePool * pool = [[NSAutoreleasePool alloc] init];
    Fraction   *myFraction = [[Fraction alloc] init];

    // set fraction to 1/3

    [myFraction setNumerator: 1];
    [myFraction setDenominator: 3];

    // display the fraction

    NSLog (@"The value of myFraction is:");
    [myFraction print];
    [myFraction release];

    [pool drain];
    return 0;
}
```

Note that this file does not include the definition of the `Fraction` class. However, it does import a file called `Fraction.h`.

Typically, a class declaration (that is, the `@interface` section) is placed in its own file, called *class*`.h`. The definition (that is, the `@implementation` section) is normally placed in a file of the same name, using the extension `.m` instead. So let's put the declaration of the `Fraction` class in the file `Fraction.h` and the definition in `Fraction.m`.

To do this in Xcode, select New File from the File menu. In the left pane, select Cocoa. In the top-right pane, select Objective-C class. Your window should appear as shown in Figure 7.1.

Click Next. Type in Fraction.m for the file name. Leave the box that reads Also Create Fraction.h checked. The location for this file should be the same folder that contains the `FractionTest.m` file. Your window should look like Figure 7.2.

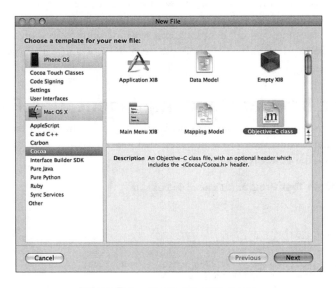

Figure 7.1   Xcode New File menu.

Now click Finish. Xcode has added two files to your project: `Fraction.h` and `Fraction.m`. Figure 7.3 shows this.

We're not working with Cocoa here, so change the line in the file `Fraction.h` that reads

```
#import <Cocoa/Cocoa.h>
```

to read

```
#import <Foundation/Foundation.h>
```

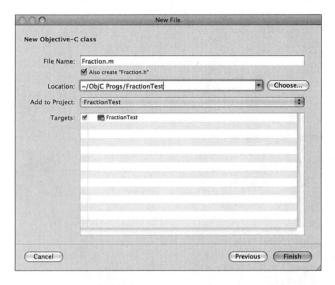

Figure 7.2   Adding a new class to your project.

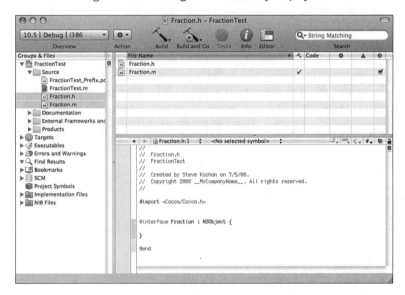

Figure 7.3   Xcode creates files for the new class.

In that same file (Fraction.h), you will now enter your interface section for the Fraction class, as shown in Program 7.1:

Program 7.1 Interface File `Fraction.h`

```
//
//  Fraction.h
//  FractionTest
//
//  Created by Steve Kochan on 7/5/08.
//  Copyright 2008 __MyCompanyName__. All rights reserved.
//

#import <Foundation/Foundation.h>

// The Fraction class

@interface Fraction : NSObject
{
  int   numerator;
  int   denominator;
}
-(void)    print;
-(void)    setNumerator: (int) n;
-(void)    setDenominator: (int) d;
-(int)     numerator;
-(int)     denominator;
-(double)  convertToNum;

@end
```

The interface file tells the compiler (and other programmers, as you'll learn later) what a `Fraction` looks like: It contains two instance variables called `numerator` and `denominator`, which are both integers. It also has six instance methods: `print`, `setNumerator:`, `setDenominator:`, `numerator`, `denominator`, and `convertToNum`. The first three methods don't return a value, the next two return an `int`, and the last one returns a `double`. The `setNumerator:` and `setDenominator:` methods each take an integer argument.

The details of the implementation for the `Fraction` class are in the file `Fraction.m`.

Program 7.1 Implementation File: `Fraction.m`

```
//
//  Fraction.m
//  FractionTest
//
//  Created by Steve Kochan on 7/5/08.
//  Copyright 2008 __MyCompanyName__. All rights reserved.
//

#import "Fraction.h"
```

```
@implementation Fraction
-(void) print
{
   NSLog (@"%i/%i", numerator, denominator);
}

-(void) setNumerator: (int) n
{
   numerator = n;
}

-(void) setDenominator: (int) d
{
   denominator = d;
}

-(int) numerator
{
   return numerator;
}

-(int) denominator
{
   return denominator;
}

-(double) convertToNum
{
   if (denominator != 0)
      return (double) numerator / denominator;
   else
      return 1.0;
}
@end
```

Note that the interface file is imported into the implementation file with the following statement:

```
#import "Fraction.h"
```

This is done so that the compiler knows about the class and methods you declared for your Fraction class and so that it can also ensure consistency between the two files. Recall also that you don't normally redeclare the class's instance variables inside the implementation section (although you can), so the compiler needs to get that information from the interface section contained in Fraction.h.

Another thing you should note is that the file that is imported is enclosed in a set of double quotes, not < and > characters, as was the case with <Foundation/Foundation.h>. The double quotes are used for *local* files (files that you create) instead of system files, and they tell the compiler where to look for the specified file. When you use double quotes, the compiler typically looks for the specified file first inside your current directory and then in a list of other places. If necessary, you can specify the actual places for the compiler to search.

Here is the test program for our example, which we have typed into the file FractionTest.m.

Program 7.1 Main Test Program: `FractionTest.m`

```
#import "Fraction.h"

int main (int argc, char *argv[])
{
    NSAutoreleasePool * pool = [[NSAutoreleasePool alloc] init];
     Fraction   *myFraction = [[Fraction alloc] init];

    // set fraction to 1/3

    [myFraction setNumerator: 1];
    [myFraction setDenominator: 3];

    // display the fraction

    NSLog (@"The value of myFraction is:");
    [myFraction print];
    [myFraction release];

    [pool drain];
    return 0;
}
```

Note again that the test program, FractionTest.m, includes the interface file Fraction.h, *not* the implementation file Fraction.m. Now you have your program split into three separate files. This might seem like a lot of work for a small program example, but the usefulness will become apparent when you start dealing with larger programs and sharing class declarations with other programmers.

You can now compile and run your program the same way you did before: Select Build and Go from the Build menu, or click the Build and Go icon in your main Xcode window.

If you're compiling your programs from the command line, give the Objective-C compiler both ".m" filenames. Using gcc, the command line looks like this:

```
gcc -framework Foundation Fraction.m FractionTest.m -o FractionTest
```

This builds an executable file called `FractionTest`. Here's the output after running the program:

Program 7.1 `FractionTest` **Output**

```
The value of myFraction is:
1/3
```

Synthesized Accessor Methods

As of Objective-C 2.0, you can have your setter and getter methods (collectively known as *accessor methods*) automatically generated for you. We haven't shown you how to do this up to this point because it was important for you to learn how to write these methods on your own. However, it's a nice convenience provided in the language, so it's time for you to learn how to take advantage of this feature.

The first step is to use the `@property` directive in your interface section to identify your properties. These properties are often your instance variables. In the case of our `Fraction` class, the two instance variables `numerator` and `denominator` fall into this category. Following is the new interface section with the new `@property` directive added.

```
@interface Fraction : NSObject
{
    int numerator;
    int denominator;
}

@property int numerator, denominator;

-(void)    print;
-(double)  convertToNum;
@end
```

Note that we no longer include the definitions for our getter and setter methods: `numerator`, `denominator`, `setNumerator:`, and `setDenominator:`. We're going to have the Objective-C compiler automatically generate or *synthesize* these for us. How is that done? Simply by using the `@synthesize` directive in the implementation section, as shown.

```
#import "Fraction.h"

@implementation Fraction

@synthesize numerator, denominator;

-(void) print
```

```
{
    NSLog (@"%i/%i", numerator, denominator);
}

-(double) convertToNum
{
    if (denominator != 0)
        return (double) numerator / denominator;
    else
        return 1.0;
}
@end
```

The following line tells the Objective-C compiler to generate a pair of getter and setter methods for each of the two listed instance variables, numerator and denominator:

```
@synthesize numerator, denominator;
```

In general, if you have an instance variable called *x*, including the following line in your implementation section causes the compiler to automatically synthesize a getter method called *x* and a setter method called setX:.

```
@synthesize x;
```

Even though this might not seem like a big deal here, having the compiler do this for you is worthwhile because the accessor methods that are generated will be efficient and will run safely with multiple threads, on multiple machines, with multiple cores.

Now go back to Program 7.1 and make the changes to the interface and implementation sections as indicated so that the accessor methods are synthesized for you. Verify that you still get the same output from the program without making any changes to FractionTest.m.

Accessing Properties Using the Dot Operator

The Objective-C language allows you to access properties using a more convenient syntax. To get the value of the numerator stored in myFraction, you could write this:

```
[myFraction numerator]
```

This sends the numerator message to the myFraction object, resulting in the return of the desired value. As of Objective-C 2.0, you can now also write the following equivalent expression using the dot operator:

```
myFraction.numerator
```

The general format here is:

```
instance.property
```

You can use a similar syntax to assign values as well:

```
instance.property = value
```

This is equivalent to writing the following expression:[*instance setProperty: value*]

In Program 7.1 you set the numerator and denominator of your fraction to 1/3 using the following two lines of code:

```
[myFraction setNumerator: 1];
[myFraction setDenominator: 3];
```

Here's an equivalent way to write the same two lines:

```
myFraction.numerator = 1;
myFraction.denominator = 3;
```

We use these new features for synthesizing methods and accessing properties throughout the remainder of this text.

Multiple Arguments to Methods

Let's continue to work with the Fraction class and make some additions. You have defined six methods. It would be nice to have a method to set both the numerator and the denominator with a single message. You define methods that take multiple arguments simply by listing each successive argument followed by a colon. This becomes part of the method name. For example, the method named addEntryWithName:andEmail: takes two arguments, presumably a name and an email address. The method addEntryWithName:andEmail:andPhone: takes three arguments: a name, an email address, and a phone number.

A method to set both the numerator and the denominator could be named setNumerator:andDenominator:, and you might use it like this:

```
[myFraction setNumerator: 1 andDenominator: 3];
```

That's not bad. And that was actually the first choice for the method name. But we can come up with a more readable method name. For example, how about setTo:over:? That might not look too appealing at first glance, but compare this message to set myFraction to 1/3 with the previous one:

```
[myFraction setTo: 1 over: 3];
```

I think that reads a little better, but the choice is up to you (some might actually prefer the first name because it explicitly references the instance variable names contained in the class). Again, choosing good method names is important for program readability. Writing out the actual message expression can help you pick a good one.

Let's put this new method to work. First, add the declaration of setTo:over: to the interface file, as shown in Program 7.2.

Program 7.2 Interface File: `Fraction.h`

```
#import <Foundation/Foundation.h>

// Define the Fraction class

@interface Fraction : NSObject
{
   int numerator;
   int denominator;
}

@property int numerator, denominator;

-(void)    print;
-(void)    setTo: (int) n over: (int) d;
-(double)  convertToNum;
@end
```

Next, add the definition for the new method to the implementation file.

Program 7.2 Implementation File: `Fraction.m`

```
#import "Fraction.h"

@implementation Fraction

@synthesize numerator, denominator;

-(void) print
{
   NSLog (@"%i/%i", numerator, denominator);
}

-(double) convertToNum
{
   if (denominator != 0)
     return (double) numerator / denominator;
   else
     return 1.0;
}

-(void) setTo: (int) n over: (int) d
{
   numerator = n;
   denominator = d;
}
@end
```

The new `setTo:over:` method simply assigns its two integer arguments, n and d, to the corresponding instance variables for the fraction, `numerator`, and `denominator`.

Here's a test program to try your new method.

Program 7.2 Test File: `FractionTest.m`

```
#import "Fraction.h"


int main (int argc, char *argv[])
{
    Fraction *aFraction = [[Fraction alloc] init];
    NSAutoreleasePool * pool = [[NSAutoreleasePool alloc] init];

    [aFraction setTo: 100 over: 200];
    [aFraction print];

    [aFraction setTo: 1 over: 3];
    [aFraction print];
    [aFraction release];

    [pool drain];
    return 0;
}
```

Program 7.2 Output

```
100/200
1/3
```

Methods Without Argument Names

When creating the name for a method, the argument names are actually optional. For example, you can declare a method like this:

```
-(int) set: (int) n: (int) d;
```

Note that, unlike in previous examples, no name is given for the second argument to the method here. This method is named `set::`, and the two colons mean the method takes two arguments, even though they're not all named.

To invoke the `set::` method, you use the colons as argument delimiters, as shown here:

```
[aFraction set: 1 : 3];
```

It's generally not good programming style to omit argument names when writing new methods because it makes the program harder to follow and makes the purpose of the method's actual parameters less intuitive.

Operations on Fractions

Let's continue to work with the `Fraction` class. First, you'll write a method that will enable you to add one fraction to another. You'll name the method `add:`, and you'll have it take a fraction as an argument. Here's the declaration for the new method:

```
-(void) add: (Fraction *) f;
```

Note the declaration for the argument `f`:

```
(Fraction *) f
```

This says that the argument to the `add:` method is of type class `Fraction`. The asterisk is necessary, so the following declaration is not correct:

```
(Fraction) f
```

You will be passing one fraction as an argument to your `add:` method, and you'll have the method add it to the receiver of the message; the following message expression adds the `Fraction` `bFraction` to the `Fraction` `aFraction`:

```
[aFraction add: bFraction];
```

Just as a quick math refresher, to add the fractions `a/b` and `c/d`, you perform the calculation as follows:

$$\frac{a}{b} + \frac{c}{d} = \frac{ad + bc}{bd}$$

You put this code for the new method into the `@implementation` section:

```
// add a Fraction to the receiver

- (void) add: (Fraction *) f
{
    // To add two fractions:
    // a/b + c/d = ((a*d) + (b*c)) / (b * d)

    numerator = numerator * f.denominator
                + denominator * f.numerator;
    denominator = denominator * f.denominator;
}
```

Don't forget that you can refer to the `Fraction` that is the receiver of the message by its fields: `numerator` and `denominator`. On the other hand, you can't directly refer to the instance variables of the argument `f` that way. Instead, you have to obtain them by applying the dot operator to `f` (or by sending an appropriate message to `f`).

Let's assume that you added the previous declarations and definitions for your new `add:` method to your interface and implementation files. Program 7.3 is a sample test program and output.

Program 7.3 Test File: `FractionTest.m`

```
#import "Fraction.h"

int main (int argc, char *argv[])
{
    NSAutoreleasePool * pool = [[NSAutoreleasePool alloc] init];

    Fraction *aFraction = [[Fraction alloc] init];
    Fraction *bFraction = [[Fraction alloc] init];

    // Set two fractions to 1/4 and 1/2 and add them together

    [aFraction setTo: 1 over: 4];
    [bFraction setTo: 1 over: 2];

    // Print the results

    [aFraction print];
    NSLog (@"+");
    [bFraction print];
    NSLog (@"=");

    [aFraction add: bFraction];
    [aFraction print];
    [aFraction release];
    [bFraction release];

    [pool drain];
    return 0;
}
```

Program 7.3 Output

```
1/4
+
1/2
=
6/8
```

The test program is straightforward enough. Two Fractions, called aFraction and bFraction, are allocated and initialized. Then they are set to the values 1/4 and 1/2, respectively. Next, the Fraction bFraction is added to the Fraction aFraction; the result of the addition is then displayed. Note again that the add: method adds the argument to the object of the message, so the object gets modified. This is verified when you print the value of aFraction at the end of main. You had to print the value of aFraction *before* invoking the add: method to get its value displayed before the method changed it. Later in this chapter, you'll redefine the add: method so that add: does not affect the value of its receiver.

Local Variables

You might have noticed that the result of adding 1/4 to 1/2 was displayed as 6/8, not as 3/4, which you might have preferred (or even expected!). That's because your addition routine just does the math and no more—it doesn't worry about reducing the result. So to continue our exercise of adding new methods to work with fractions, let's make a new reduce method to reduce a fraction to its simplest terms.

Reaching back to your high school math again, you can reduce a fraction by finding the largest number that evenly divides both the numerator and the denominator of your fraction and then dividing them by that number. Technically, you want to find the greatest common divisor (gcd) of the numerator and denominator. You already know how to do that from Program 5.7. You might want to refer to that program example just to refresh your memory.

With the algorithm in hand, you can now write your new reduce method:

```
- (void) reduce
{
    int  u = numerator;
    int  v = denominator;
    int  temp;

    while (v != 0) {
        temp = u % v;
        u = v;
        v = temp;
    }

    numerator /= u;
    denominator /= u;
}
```

Notice something new about this reduce method: It declares three integer variables called u, v, and temp. These variables are *local* variables, meaning that their values exist only during execution of the reduce method and that *they can be accessed only from within the method in which they are defined*. In that sense, they are similar to the variables you have been declaring inside your `main` routine; those variables were also local to `main` and could be accessed directly only from within the `main` routine. None of the methods you developed could directly access those variables defined in `main`.

Local variables have no default initial value, so you must set them to some value before using them. The three local variables in the `reduce` method are set to values before they are used, so that's not a problem here. And unlike your instance variables (which retain their values through method calls), these local variables have no memory. Therefore, after the method returns, the values of these variables disappear. Each time a method is called, each local variable defined in that method is initialized to the value specified (if any) with the variable's declaration.

Method Arguments

The names you use to refer to a method's arguments are also local variables. When the method is executed, whatever arguments are passed to the method are copied into these variables. Because the method is dealing with a copy of the arguments, *it cannot change the original values passed to the method.* This is an important concept. Suppose you had a method called `calculate:`, defined as follows:

```
-(void) calculate: (double) x
{
    x *= 2;
    ...
}
```

Also suppose that you used the following message expression to invoke it:

```
[myData calculate: ptVal];
```

Whatever value was contained in the variable `ptVal` would be copied into the local variable `x` when the `calculate` method was executed. So changing the value of `x` inside `calculate:` would have no effect on the value of `ptVal`—only on the copy of its value stored inside `x`.

Incidentally, in the case of arguments that are objects, you can change the instance variables stored in that object. You'll learn more about that in the next chapter.

The `static` Keyword

You can have a local variable retain its value through multiple invocations of a method by placing the keyword `static` in front of the variable's declaration. For example, the following declares the integer `hitCount` to be a static variable:

```
static int hitCount = 0;
```

Unlike other normal local variables, a static one does have an initial value of 0, so the initialization shown previously is redundant. Furthermore, they are initialized only once when program execution begins and retain their values through successive method calls.

The following code sequence might appear inside a `showPage` method that wanted to keep track of the number of times it was invoked (or, in this case, perhaps the number of pages that have been printed, for example):

```
-(void) showPage
{
    static int pageCount = 0;
      . . .
    ++pageCount;
      . . .
}
```

The local static variable would be set to 0 only once when the program started and would retain its value through successive invocations of the `showPage` method.

Note the difference between making `pageCount` a local static variable and making it an instance variable. In the former case, `pageCount` could count the number of pages printed by all objects that invoked the `showPage` method. In the latter case, the variable would count the number of pages printed by each individual object because each object would have its own copy of `pageCount`.

Remember that static or local variables can be accessed only from within the method in which they're defined. So even the static `pageCount` variable can be accessed only from within `showPage`. You can move the declaration of the variable *outside* any method declaration (typically near the beginning of your implementation file) to make it accessible to any methods, like so:

```
#import "Printer.h"
static int pageCount;

@implementation Printer
  . . .
@end
```

Now any instance or class method contained in the file can access the `pageCount` variable. Chapter 10, "More on Variables and Data Types," covers this topic of variable scope in greater detail.

Returning to fractions, you can incorporate the code for the `reduce` method into your `Fraction.m` implementation file. Don't forget to declare the `reduce` method in your `Fraction.h` interface file as well. With that done, you can test your new method in Program 7.4.

Program 7.4 Test File `FractionTest.m`

```
#import "Fraction.h"

int main (int argc, char *argv[])
{
```

```
    NSAutoreleasePool * pool = [[NSAutoreleasePool alloc] init];

    Fraction *aFraction = [[Fraction alloc] init];
    Fraction *bFraction = [[Fraction alloc] init];

    [aFraction setTo: 1 over: 4];    // set 1st fraction to 1/4
    [bFraction setTo: 1 over: 2];    // set 2nd fraction to 1/2

    [aFraction print];
    NSLog (@"+");
    [bFraction print];
    NSLog (@"=");

    [aFraction add: bFraction];

    // reduce the result of the addition and print the result

    [aFraction reduce];
    [aFraction print];

    [aFraction release];
    [bFraction release];

    [pool drain];
    return 0;
}
```

Program 7.4 Output

```
1/4
+
1/2
=
3/4
```

That's better!

The self Keyword

In Program 7.4, we decided to reduce the fraction outside of the add: method. We could have done it inside add: as well; the decision was completely arbitrary. However, how would we go about identifying the fraction to be reduced to our reduce method? We know how to identify instance variables inside a method directly by name, but we don't know how to directly identify the receiver of the message.

You can use the keyword `self` to refer to the object that is the receiver of the current method. If inside your `add:` method you wrote

```
[self reduce];
```

the `reduce` method would be applied to the `Fraction` that was the receiver of the `add:` method, which is what you want. You will see throughout this book how useful the `self` keyword can be. For now, use it in your `add:` method. Here's what the modified method looks like:

```
- (void) add: (Fraction *) f
{
    // To add two fractions:
    // a/b + c/d = ((a*d) + (b*c)) / (b * d)

    numerator = (numerator * [f denominator]) +
        (denominator * [f numerator]);
    denominator = denominator * [f denominator];

    [self reduce];
}
```

After the addition is performed, the fraction is reduced.

Allocating and Returning Objects from Methods

We noted that the `add:` method changes the value of the object that is receiving the message. Let's create a new version of `add:` that will instead make a new fraction to store the result of the addition. In this case, we need to return the new `Fraction` to the message sender. Here is the definition for the new `add:` method:

```
-(Fraction *) add: (Fraction *) f
{
    // To add two fractions:
    // a/b + c/d = ((a*d) + (b*c)) / (b * d)

    // result will store the result of the addition
    Fraction    *result = [[Fraction alloc] init];
    int         resultNum, resultDenom;

    resultNum = numerator * f.denominator +
        denominator * f.numerator;
    resultDenom = denominator * f.denominator;
```

```
    [result setTo: resultNum over: resultDenom];
    [result reduce];

    return result;
}
```

The first line of your method definition is this:

```
-(Fraction *) add: (Fraction *) f
```

It says that your `add:` method will return a `Fraction` object and that it will take one as its argument as well. The argument will be added to the receiver of the message, which is also a `Fraction`.

The method allocates and initializes a new `Fraction` object called `result` and then defines two local variables called `resultNum` and `resultDenom`. These will be used to store the resulting numerator and denominators from your addition.

After performing the addition as before and assigning the resulting numerators and denominators to your local variables, you can set `result` with the following message expression:

```
[result setTo: resultNum over: resultDenom];
```

After reducing the result, you return its value to the sender of the message with the `return` statement.

Note that the memory occupied by the `Fraction` `result` that is allocated inside the `add:` method is returned and does not get released. You can't release it from the `add:` method because the invoker of the method needs it. Therefore, it is imperative that the user of this method know that the object being returned is a new instance and must be subsequently released. This can be communicated through suitable documentation that is made available to users of the class.

Program 7.5 tests your new `add:` method.

Program 7.5 Test File `main.m`

```
#import "Fraction.h"

int main (int argc, char *argv[])
{
    NSAutoreleasePool * pool = [[NSAutoreleasePool alloc] init];

    Fraction *aFraction = [[Fraction alloc] init];
    Fraction *bFraction = [[Fraction alloc] init];

    Fraction *resultFraction;
```

```
[aFraction setTo: 1 over: 4];    // set 1st fraction to 1/4
[bFraction setTo: 1 over: 2];    // set 2nd fraction to 1/2

[aFraction print];
NSLog (@"+");
[bFraction print];
NSLog (@"=");

 resultFraction = [aFraction add: bFraction];
[resultFraction print];

// This time give the result directly to print
// memory leakage here!

[[aFraction add: bFraction] print];
[aFraction release];
[bFraction release];
[resultFraction release];

[pool drain];
return 0;
}
```

Program 7.5 Output

```
1/4
+
1/2
=
3/4
3/4
```

Some explanation is in order here. First, you define two Fractions—aFraction and bFraction—and set their values to 1/4 and 1/2, respectively. You also define a Fraction called resultFraction (why doesn't it have to be allocated and initialized?). This variable will store the result of your addition operations that follow.

The following lines of code first send the add: message to aFraction, passing along the Fraction bFraction as its argument:

```
resultFraction = [aFraction add: bFraction];
[resultFraction print];
```

The resulting Fraction that the method returns is stored in resultFraction and then displayed by passing it a print message. Note that you must be careful at the end of the program to release resultFraction, even though you didn't allocate it yourself in main. The `add:` method allocated it, but it's still your responsibility to clean it up. The following message expression might look nice, but it actually creates a problem:

```
[[aFraction add: bFraction] print];
```

Because you take the `Fraction` that `add:` returns and send it a message to `print`, you have no way of subsequently releasing the `Fraction` object that `add:` created. This is an example of *memory leakage*. If you do this type of nested messaging many times in your program, you'll end up accumulating storage for fractions whose memory will not be released. Each time, you would be adding, or *leaking*, just a little bit more memory that you could not directly recover.

One solution to the problem is to have the `print` method return its receiver, which you could then release. But that seems a little roundabout. A better solution is to divide the nested messages into two separate messages, as was done earlier in the program.

By the way, you could have avoided using the temporary variables `resultNum` and `resultDenom` completely in your `add:` method. Instead, this single message call would have done the trick:

```
[result setTo: numerator * f.denominator + denominator * f.numerator
        over: denominator * f.denominator];
```

We're not suggesting that you write such concise code. However, you might see it when you examine other programmers' code, so it is useful to learn how to read and understand these powerful expressions.

Let's take one last look at fractions in this chapter. For our example, let's consider calculation of the following series:

$$\sum_{i=1}^{n} 1/2^i$$

The sigma notation is shorthand for a summation. Its use here means to add the values of $1/2^i$, where i varies from 1 to n. That is, add `1/2 + 1/4 + 1/8` .... If you make the value of n large enough, the sum of this series should approach 1. Let's experiment with different values for n to see how close we get.

Program 7.6 prompts for the value of n to be entered and performs the indicated calculation.

Program 7.6 `FractionTest.m`

```
#import "Fraction.h"

int main (int argc, char *argv[])
{
    NSAutoreleasePool * pool = [[NSAutoreleasePool alloc] init];
```

```
    Fraction *aFraction = [[Fraction alloc] init];
    Fraction *sum = [[Fraction alloc] init], *sum2;
    int i, n, pow2;

    [sum setTo: 0 over: 1]; // set 1st fraction to 0

    NSLog (@"Enter your value for n:");
    scanf ("%i", &n);

    pow2 = 2;
    for (i = 1; i <= n; ++i) {
        [aFraction setTo: 1 over: pow2];
        sum2 = [sum add: aFraction];
        [sum release];  // release previous sum
        sum = sum2;
        pow2 *= 2;
    }

    NSLog (@"After %i iterations, the sum is %g", n, [sum convertToNum]);
    [aFraction release];
    [sum release];

    [pool drain];
    return 0;
}
```

Program 7.6 Output

```
Enter your value for n:
5
After 5 iterations, the sum is 0.96875
```

Program 7.6 Output (Rerun)

```
Enter your value for n:
10
After 10 iterations, the sum is 0.999023
```

Program 7.6 Output (Rerun)

```
Enter your value for n:
15
After 15 iterations, the sum is 0.999969
```

The Fraction sum is set to the value of 0 by setting its numerator to 0 and its denominator to 1 (what would happen if you set both its numerator and denominator to

0?). The program then prompts the user to enter a value for n and reads it using scanf. You then enter a for loop to calculate the sum of the series. First, you initialize the variable pow2 to 2. This variable is used to store the value of 2^i. Each time through the loop, its value is multiplied by 2.

The for loop starts at 1 and goes through n. Each time through the loop, you set aFraction to 1/pow2, or $1/2^i$. This value is then added to the cumulative sum by using the previously defined add: method. The result from add: is assigned to sum2 and not to sum, to avoid memory leakage problems. (What would happen if you assigned it directly to sum instead?) The old sum is then released, and the new sum, sum2, is assigned to sum for the next iteration through the loop. Study the way the fractions are released in the code so that you feel comfortable with the strategy used to avoid memory leakage. Also realize that if this were a for loop that was executed hundreds or thousands of times and you weren't judicious about releasing your fractions, you would quickly accumulate a lot of wasted memory space.

When the for loop is completed, you display the final result as a decimal value using the convertToNum method. You have just two objects left to release: aFraction and your final Fraction object stored in sum. Program execution is then complete.

The output shows what happens when we ran the program three separate times on a MacBook Air. The first time, the sum of the series was calculated and the resulting value of 0.96875 was displayed. The third time, we ran the program with a value of 15 for n, which gave us a result very close to 1.

Extending Class Definitions and the Interface File

You've now developed a small library of methods for working with fractions. In fact, here is the interface file, listed in its entirety, so you can see all you've accomplished with this class:

```
#import <Foundation/Foundation.h>


// Define the Fraction class

@interface Fraction : NSObject
{
  int  numerator;
  int  denominator;
}

@property int numerator, denominator;

-(void)        print;
-(void)        setTo: (int) n over: (int) d;
-(double)      convertToNum;
-(Fraction *)  add: (Fraction *) f;
-(void)        reduce;
@end
```

You might not need to work with fractions, but these examples have shown how you can continually refine and extend a class by adding new methods. You could hand this interface file to someone else working with fractions, and it would be sufficient for that person to be able to write programs to deal with fractions. If that person needed to add a new method, he could do so either directly, by extending the class definition, or indirectly, by defining his own subclass and adding his own new methods. You'll learn how to do that in the next chapter.

Exercises

1. Add the following methods to the `Fraction` class to round out the arithmetic operations on fractions. Reduce the result within the method in each case:
   ```
   // Subtract argument from receiver
   -(Fraction *) subtract: (Fraction *) f;
   // Multiply receiver by argument
   -(Fraction *) multiply: (Fraction *) f;
   // Divide receiver by argument
   -(Fraction *) divide: (Fraction *) f;
   ```

2. Modify the `print` method from your `Fraction` class so that it takes an additional `BOOL` argument that indicates whether the fraction should be reduced for display. If it is to be reduced, be sure you don't make any permanent changes to the fraction itself.

3. Modify Program 7.6 to also display the resulting sum as a fraction, not just as a real number.

4. Will your `Fraction` class work with negative fractions? For example, can you add `-1/4` and `-1/2` and get the correct result? When you think you have the answer, write a test program to try it.

5. Modify the `Fraction`'s `print` method to display fractions greater than 1 as mixed numbers. For example, the fraction `5/3` should be displayed as `1 2/3`.

6. Exercise 6 in Chapter 4, "Data Types and Expressions," defined a new class called `Complex` for working with complex imaginary numbers. Add a new method called `add:` that can be used to add two complex numbers. To add two complex numbers, you simply add the real parts and the imaginary parts, as shown here:
   `(5.3 + 7i) + (2.7 + 4i) = 8 + 11i`
   Have the `add:` method store and return the result as a new `Complex` number, based on the following method declaration:
   `-(Complex *) add: (Complex *) complexNum;`
   Make sure you address any potential memory leakage issues in your test program.

7. Given the `Complex` class developed in exercise 6 of Chapter 4 and the extension made in exercise 6 of this chapter, create separate `Complex.h` and `Complex.m` interface and implementation files. Create a separate test program file to test everything.

Inheritance

In this chapter, you'll learn about one of the key principles that makes object-oriented programming so powerful. Through the concept of *inheritance*, you will build on existing class definitions and customize them for your own applications.

It All Begins at the Root

You learned about the idea of a parent class in Chapter 3, "Classes, Objects, and Methods." A parent class can itself have a parent. The class that has no parent is at the top of the hierarchy and is known as a *root* class. In Objective-C, you have the capability to define your own root class, but it's something you normally won't want to do. Instead, you'll want to take advantage of existing classes. All the classes we've defined up to this point are descendants of the root class called NSObject, which you specified in your interface file like this:

```
@interface Fraction: NSObject
...
@end
```

The Fraction class is derived from the NSObject class. Because NSObject is at the top of the hierarchy (that is, there are no classes above it), it's called a *root* class, as shown in Figure 8.1. The Fraction class is known as a *child* or *subclass*.

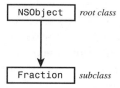

Figure 8.1   Root and subclass

From a terminology point of view, we can speak of classes, child classes, and parent classes. Analogously, we can talk about classes, subclasses, and superclasses. You should become familiar with both types of terminology.

Whenever a new class (other than a new root class) is defined, the class inherits certain properties. For example, all the instance variables and the methods from the parent implicitly become part of the new class definition. That means the subclass can access these methods and instance variables directly, as if they were defined directly within the class definition.

A simple example, albeit contrived, helps to illustrate this key concept of inheritance. Here's a declaration for an object called ClassA with one method called initVar:

```
@interface ClassA: NSObject
{
    int   x;
}

-(void) initVar;
@end
```

The initVar method simply sets the value of ClassA's instance variable to 100:

```
@implementation ClassA
-(void) initVar
{
    x = 100;
}
@end
```

Now let's also define a class called ClassB:

```
@interface ClassB: ClassA
-(void) printVar;
@end
```

The first line of the declaration

```
@interface ClassB: ClassA
```

says that instead of ClassB being a subclass of NSObject, ClassB is a subclass of ClassA. So although ClassA's parent (or superclass) is NSObject, ClassB's parent is ClassA. Figure 8.2 illustrates this.

As you can see from Figure 8.2, the root class has no superclass and ClassB, which is at the bottom of the hierarchy, has no subclass. Therefore, ClassA is a subclass of NSObject, and ClassB is a subclass of ClassA and also of NSObject (technically, it's a sub-subclass, or *grandchild*). Also, NSObject is a superclass of ClassA, which is a superclass of ClassB. NSObject is also a superclass of ClassB because it exists farther down its hierarchy.

Here's the full declaration for ClassB, which defines one method called printVar:

```
@interface ClassB: ClassA
```

```
-(void) printVar;
@end

@implementation ClassB
-(void) printVar
{
    NSLog (@"x = %i", x);
}
@end
```

The `printVar` method prints the value of the instance variable `x`, yet you haven't defined any instance variables in `ClassB`. That's because `ClassB` is a subclass of `ClassA`—therefore, it inherits all of `ClassA`'s instance variables (in this case, there's just one). Figure 8.3 depicts this.

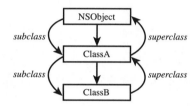

Figure 8.2   Subclasses and superclasses

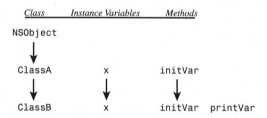

Figure 8.3   Inheriting instance variables and methods.

(Of course, Figure 8.3 doesn't show any of the methods or instance variables that are inherited from the `NSObject` class—there are several.)

Let's see how this works by putting it all together in a complete program example. For the sake of brevity, we'll put all the class declarations and definitions into a single file (see Program 8.1).

Program 8.1

```
// Simple example to illustrate inheritance

#import <Foundation/Foundation.h>

// ClassA declaration and definition

@interface ClassA: NSObject
{
    int  x;
}

-(void) initVar;
@end

@implementation ClassA
-(void) initVar
{
  x = 100;
}
@end

// Class B declaration and definition

@interface ClassB : ClassA
-(void) printVar;
@end

@implementation ClassB
-(void) printVar
{
  NSLog (@"x = %i", x);
}
@end

int main (int argc, char *argv[])
{
    NSAutoreleasePool * pool = [[NSAutoreleasePool alloc] init];

    ClassB  *b = [[ClassB alloc] init];

    [b initVar];      // will use inherited method
    [b printVar];     // reveal value of x;

    [b release];

    [pool drain];
    return 0;
}
```

Program 8.1 Output

```
x = 100
```

You begin by defining `b` to be a `ClassB` object. After allocating and initializing `b`, you send a message to apply the `initVar` method to it. But looking back at the definition of `ClassB`, you'll notice that you never defined such a method. `initVar` was defined in `ClassA`, and because `ClassA` is the parent of `ClassB`, `ClassB` gets to use all of `ClassA`'s methods. So with respect to `ClassB`, `initVar` is an *inherited* method.

> **Note**
>
> We briefly mentioned it up to this point, but `alloc` and `init` are methods you have used all along that are never defined in your classes. That's because you took advantage of the fact that they were inherited methods.

After sending the `initVar` message to `b`, you invoke the `printVar` method to display the value of the instance variable `x`. The output of `x = 100` confirms that `printVar` was capable of accessing this instance variable. That's because, as with the `initVar` method, it was inherited.

Remember that the concept of inheritance works all the way down the chain. So if you defined a new class called `ClassC`, whose parent class was `ClassB`, like so

```
@interface ClassC: ClassB;
    ...
@end
```

then `ClassC` would inherit all of `ClassB`'s methods and instance variables, which in turn inherited all of `ClassA`'s methods and instance variables, which in turn inherited all of `NSObject`'s methods and instance variables.

Be sure you understand that each instance of a class gets its own instance variables, even if they're inherited. A `ClassC` object and a `ClassB` object would therefore each have their own distinct instance variables.

Finding the Right Method

When you send a message to an object, you might wonder how the correct method is chosen to apply to that object. The rules are actually quite simple. First, the class to which the object belongs is checked to see whether a method is explicitly defined in that class with the specific name. If it is, that's the method that is used. If it's not defined there, the parent class is checked. If the method is defined there, that's what is used. If not, the search continues.

Parent classes are checked until one of two things happens: Either you find a class that contains the specified method or you don't find the method after going all the way back to the root class. If the first occurs, you're all set; if the second occurs, you have a problem, and a warning message is generated that looks like this:

```
warning: 'ClassB' may not respond to '-inity'
```

In this case, you inadvertently are trying to send a message called `inity` to a variable of type class `ClassB`. The compiler told you that variables of that type of class do not know how to respond to such a method. Again, this was determined after checking `ClassB`'s methods and its parents' methods back to the root class (which, in this case, is `NSObject`).

In some cases, a message is not generated if the method is not found. This involves using something known as *forwarding*, which is briefly discussed in Chapter 9, "Polymorphism, Dynamic Typing, and Dynamic Binding."

Extension Through Inheritance: Adding New Methods

Inheritance often is used to extend a class. As an example, let's assume that you've just been assigned the task of developing some classes to work with 2D graphical objects such as rectangles, circles, and triangles. For now, we'll worry about just rectangles. Let's go back to exercise 7 from Chapter 4, "Data Types and Expressions," and start with the `@interface` section from that example:

```
@interface Rectangle: NSObject
{
    int  width;
    int  height;
}

@property int width, height;
-(int)  area;
-(int)  perimeter;
@end
```

You'll have synthesized methods to set the rectangle's width and height and to return those values, and your own methods to calculate its area and perimeter. Let's add a method that will allow you to set both the width and the height of the rectangle with the same message call, which is as follows:

```
-(void) setWidth: (int) w andHeight: (int) h;
```

Assume that you typed this new class declaration into a file called `Rectangle.h`. Here's what the implementation file `Rectangle.m` might look like:

```
#import "Rectangle.h"

@implementation Rectangle

@synthesize width, height;

-(void) setWidth: (int) w andHeight: (int) h
{
    width = w;
    height = h;
}
```

```
-(int) area
{
    return width * height;
}

-(int) perimeter
{
    return (width + height) * 2;
}
@end
```

Each method definition is straightforward enough. Program 8.2 shows a `main` routine to test it.

Program 8.2

```
#import "Rectangle.h"

int main (int argc, char *argv[])
{
    NSAutoreleasePool * pool = [[NSAutoreleasePool alloc] init];

    Rectangle *myRect = [[Rectangle alloc] init];

    [myRect setWidth: 5 andHeight: 8];

    NSLog (@"Rectangle: w = %i, h = %i",
            myRect.width, myRect.height);
    NSLog (@"Area = %i, Perimeter = %i",
            [myRect area], [myRect perimeter]);
    [myRect release];

    [pool drain];
    return 0;
}
```

Program 8.2 Output

```
Rectangle: w = 5, h = 8
Area = 40, Perimeter = 26
```

`myRect` is allocated and initialized; then its width is set to 5 and its height to 8. The first line of output verifies this. Next, the area and the perimeter of the rectangle are calculated with the appropriate message calls, and the returned values are handed off to `NSLog` to be displayed.

Suppose that you now need to work with squares. You could define a new class called `Square` and define similar methods in it as in your `Rectangle` class. Alternately, you could recognize the fact that a square is just a special case of a rectangle whose width and height just happen to be the same.

Thus, an easy way to handle this is to make a new class called `Square` and have it be a subclass of `Rectangle`. That way, you get to use all of `Rectangle`'s methods and variables, in addition to defining your own. For now, the only methods you might want to add would be to set the side of the square to a particular value and retrieve that value. Program 8.3 shows the interface and implementation files for your new `Square` class.

Program 8.3 Square.h Interface File

```
#import "Rectangle.h"


@interface Square: Rectangle

-(void) setSide: (int) s;
-(int) side;
@end
```

Program 8.3 Square.m Implementation File

```
#import "Square.h"


@implementation Square: Rectangle

-(void) setSide: (int) s
{
    [self setWidth: s andHeight: s];
}

-(int) side
{
    return width;
}
@end
```

Notice what you did here. You defined your `Square` class to be a subclass of `Rectangle`, which is declared in the header file `Rectangle.h`. You didn't need to add any instance variables here, but you did add new methods called `setSide:` and `side`.

A square has only one side, but you're internally representing it as two numbers—that's okay. All that is hidden from the user of the `Square` class. You can always redefine your `Square` class later, if necessary; any users of the class don't have to be concerned with the internal details because of the notion of data encapsulation discussed earlier.

The `setSide:` method takes advantage of the fact that you already have a method inherited from your `Rectangle` class to set the values of the width and height of a rectangle.

So `setSide:` calls the `setWidth:andHeight:` method from the `Rectangle` class, passing the parameter `s` as the value for both the width and the height. You don't really have to do anything else. Someone working with a `Square` object can now set the dimensions of the square by using `setSide:` and can take advantage of the methods from the `Rectangle` class to calculate the square's area, perimeter, and so on. Program 8.3 shows the test program and output for your new `Square` class.

Program 8.3 Test Program

```
#import "Square.h"
#import <Foundation/Foundation.h>

int main (int argc, char *argv[])
{
    NSAutoreleasePool * pool = [[NSAutoreleasePool alloc] init];

    Square *mySquare = [[Square alloc] init];

    [mySquare setSide: 5];

    NSLog (@"Square s = %i", [mySquare side]);
    NSLog (@"Area = %i, Perimeter = %i",
        [mySquare area], [mySquare perimeter]);
    [mySquare release];

    [pool drain];
    return 0;
}
```

Program 8.3 Output

```
Square s = 5
Area = 25, Perimeter = 20
```

The way you defined the `Square` class is a fundamental technique of working with classes in Objective-C: extending what you or someone else has already done to suit your needs. In addition, a mechanism known as *categories* enables you to add new methods to an existing class definition in a modular fashion—that is, without having to constantly add new definitions to the same interface and implementation files. This is particularly handy when you want to do this to a class for which you don't have access to the source code. You'll learn about categories in Chapter 11, "Categories and Protocols."

A Point Class and Memory Allocation

The `Rectangle` class stores only the rectangle's dimensions. In a real-world graphical application, you might need to keep track of all sorts of additional information, such as the rectangle's fill color, line color, location (origin) inside a window, and so on. You can easily extend your class to do this. For now, let's deal with the idea of the rectangle's origin. Assume that the "origin" means the location of the rectangle's lower-left corner within some Cartesian coordinate system (x, y). If you were writing a drawing application, this point might represent the location of the rectangle inside a window, as depicted in Figure 8.4.

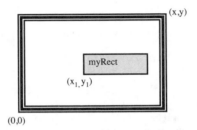

Figure 8.4   A rectangle drawn in a window

In Figure 8.4, the rectangle's origin is shown at (x_1, y_1).

You could extend your `Rectangle` class to store the x, y coordinate of the rectangle's origin as two separate values. Or you might realize that, in the development of your graphics application, you'll have to deal with a lot of coordinates and, therefore, decide to define a class called `XYPoint` (you might recall this problem from exercise 7 in Chapter 3):

```
#import <Foundation/Foundation.h>


@interface XYPoint: NSObject
{
    int   x;
    int   y;
}
@property int x, y;

-(void) setX: (int) xVal andY: (int) yVal;
@end
```

Now let's get back to your `Rectangle` class. You want to be able to store the rectangle's origin, so you'll add another instance variable, called `origin`, to the definition of your `Rectangle` class:

```
@interface Rectangle: NSObject
{
```

```
    int  width;
    int  height;
    XYPoint *origin;
}
        ...
```

It seems reasonable to add a method to set the rectangle's origin and to retrieve it. To illustrate an important point, we won't synthesize the accessor methods for the origin now. Instead, we'll write them ourselves.

The @class Directive

Now you can work with rectangles (and squares as well!) with the ability to set their widths, heights, and origins. First, let's take a complete look at your `Rectangle.h` interface file:

```
#import <Foundation/Foundation.h>


@class XYPoint;
@interface Rectangle: NSObject
{
    int  width;
    int  height;
    XYPoint *origin;
}

@property int width, height;

-(XYPoint *) origin;
-(void)  setOrigin: (XYPoint *) pt;
-(void)  setWidth: (int) w andHeight: (int) h;
-(int)   area;
-(int)   perimeter;
@end
```

You used a new directive in the `Rectangle.h` header file:

```
@class XYPoint;
```

You needed this because the compiler needs to know what an `XYPoint` is when it encounters it as one of the instance variables defined for a `Rectangle`. The class name is also used in the argument and return type declarations for your `setOrigin:` and `origin` methods, respectively. You do have another choice. You can import the header file instead, like so:

```
#import "XYPoint.h"
```

Using the @class directive is more efficient because the compiler doesn't need to process the entire XYPoint.h file (even though it is quite small); it just needs to know that XYPoint is the name of a class. If you need to reference one of the XYPoint classes methods, the @class directive does not suffice because the compiler would need more information; it would need to know how many arguments the method takes, what their types are, and what the method's return type is.

Let's fill in the blanks for your new XYPoint class and Rectangle methods so you can test everything in a program. First, Program 8.4 shows the implementation file for your XYPoint class.

First, Program 8.4 shows the new methods for the Rectangle class.

Program 8.4 Rectangle.m Added Methods

```
#import "XYPoint.h"


-(void) setOrigin: (XYPoint *) pt
{
    origin = pt;
}

-(XYPoint *) origin
{
    return origin;
}
@end
```

Following are the complete XYPoint and Rectangle class definitions, followed by a test program to try them out.

Program 8.4 XYPoint.h Interface File

```
#import <Foundation/Foundation.h>


@interface XYPoint: NSObject
{
    int  x;
    int  y;
}
@property int x, y;

-(void) setX: (int) xVal andY: (int) yVal;
@end
```

Program 8.4 `XYPoint.m` Implementation File

```
#import "XYPoint.h"


@implementation XYPoint

@synthesize x, y;
-(void) setX: (int) xVal andY: (int) yVal
{
    x = xVal;
    y = yVal;
}
@end
```

Program 8.4 `Rectangle.h` Interface File

```
#import <Foundation/Foundation.h>


@class XYPoint;
@interface Rectangle: NSObject
{
   int    width;
   int    height;
   XYPoint *origin;
}

@property int width, height;

-(XYPoint *) origin;
-(void)   setOrigin: (XYPoint *) pt;
-(void)   setWidth: (int) w andHeight: (int) h;
-(int)    area;
-(int)    perimeter;
@end
```

Program 8.4 `Rectangle.m` Implementation File

```
#import "Rectangle.h"


@implementation Rectangle

@synthesize width, height;

-(void) setWidth: (int) w andHeight: (int) h
```

```
{
    width = w;
    height = h;
}

-(void) setOrigin: (XYPoint *) pt
{
    origin = pt;
}

-(int) area
{
    return width * height;
}

-(int) perimeter
{
    return (width + height) * 2;
}

-(XYPoint *) origin
{
    return origin;
}
@end
```

Program 8.4 Test Program

```
#import "Rectangle.h"
#import "XYPoint.h"

int main (int argc, char *argv[])
{
    NSAutoreleasePool * pool = [[NSAutoreleasePool alloc] init];

    Rectangle *myRect = [[Rectangle alloc] init];
    XYPoint   *myPoint = [[XYPoint alloc] init];

    [myPoint setX: 100 andY: 200];

    [myRect setWidth: 5 andHeight: 8];
    myRect.origin = myPoint;

    NSLog (@"Rectangle w = %i, h = %i",
        myRect.width, myRect.height);
```

```
    NSLog (@"Origin at (%i, %i)",
        myRect.origin.x, myRect.origin.y);

    NSLog (@"Area = %i, Perimeter = %i",
        [myRect area], [myRect perimeter]);
    [myRect release];
    [myPoint release];

    [pool drain];
    return 0;
}
```

Program 8.4 Output

```
Rectangle w = 5, h = 8
Origin at (100, 200)
Area = 40, Perimeter = 26
```

Inside the `main` routine, you allocated and initialized a rectangle identified as `myRect` and a point called `myPoint`. Using the `setX:andY:` method, you set `myPoint` to `(100, 200)`. After setting the width and the height of the rectangle to `5` and `8`, respectively, you invoked the `setOrigin` method to set the rectangle's origin to the point indicated by `myPoint`. The three `NSLog` calls then retrieve and print the values. The expression

```
myRect.origin.x
```

takes the `XYPoint` object returned by the accessor method `origin` method and applies the dot operator to get the x-coordinate of the rectangle's origin. In a similar manner, the following expression retrieves the y-coordinate of the rectangle's origin:

```
myRect.origin.y
```

Classes Owning Their Objects

Can you explain the output from Program 8.5?

Program 8.5

```
#import "Rectangle.h"
#import "XYPoint.h"

int main (int argc, char *argv[])
{
    NSAutoreleasePool * pool = [[NSAutoreleasePool alloc] init];

    Rectangle *myRect = [[Rectangle alloc] init];
    XYPoint   *myPoint = [[XYPoint alloc] init];
```

```
    [myPoint setX: 100 andY: 200];

    [myRect setWidth: 5 andHeight: 8];
    myRect.origin = myPoint;

    NSLog (@"Origin at (%i, %i)",
        myRect.origin.x, myRect.origin.y);
    [myPoint setX: 50 andY: 50];
    NSLog (@"Origin at (%i, %i)",
        myRect.origin.x, myRect.origin.y);
    [myRect release];
    [myPoint release];

    [pool drain];
    return 0;
}
```

Program 8.5 Output

```
Origin at (100, 200)
Origin at (50, 50)
```

You changed the XYPoint myPoint from (100, 200) in the program to (50, 50), and apparently it also changed the rectangle's origin! But why did that happen? You didn't explicitly reset the rectangle's origin, so why did the rectangle's origin change? If you go back to the definition of your setOrigin: method, perhaps you'll see why:

```
-(void) setOrigin: (XYPoint *) pt
{
    origin = pt;
}
```

When the setOrigin: method is invoked with the expression

```
myRect.origin = myPoint;
```

the value of myPoint is passed as the argument to the method. This value points to where this XYPoint object is stored in memory, as depicted in Figure 8.5.

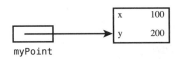

Figure 8.5   The **XYPoint myPoint** in memory

That value stored inside `myPoint`, which is a pointer into memory, is copied into the local variable `pt` as defined inside the method. Now both `pt` and `myPoint` reference the same data stored in memory. Figure 8.6 illustrates this.

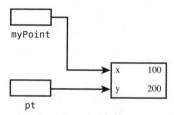

Figure 8.6   Passing the rectangle's origin to the method

When the origin variable is set to `pt` inside the method, the pointer stored inside `pt` is copied into the instance variable `origin`, as depicted in Figure 8.7.

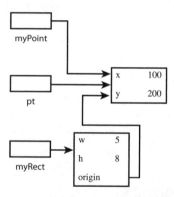

Figure 8.7   Setting the rectangle's origin

Because `myPoint` and the origin variable stored in `myRect` reference the same area in memory (as does the local variable `pt`), when you subsequently change the value of `myPoint` to `(50, 50)`, the rectangle's origin is changed as well.

You can avoid this problem by modifying the `setOrigin:` method so that it allocates its own point and sets the `origin` to that point. This is shown here:

```
-(void) setOrigin: (XYPoint *) pt
{
    origin = [[XYPoint alloc] init];

    [origin setX: pt.x andY: pt.y];
}
```

The method first allocates and initializes a new `XYPoint`. The message expression

```
[origin setX: pt.x andY: pt.y];
```

sets the newly allocated `XYPoint` to the x, y coordinate of the argument to the method. Study this message expression until you fully understand how it works.

The change to the `setOrigin:` method means that each `Rectangle` instance now owns its `origin XYPoint` instance. Even though it is now responsible for allocating the memory for that `XYPoint`, it should also now become responsible for releasing that memory. In general, when a class contains other objects, at times you will want to have it own some or all of those objects. In the case of a rectangle, it makes sense for the `Rectangle` class to own its origin because that is a basic attribute of a rectangle.

But how do you release the memory used by your `origin`? Releasing the rectangle's memory does not also release the memory you allocated for the origin. One way to release the memory is to insert a line such as the following into `main`:

```
[[myRect origin] release];
```

This releases the `XYPoint` object that the `origin` method returns. You must do this before you release the memory for the `Rectangle` object itself because none of the variables contained in an object is valid after an object's memory is released. So the correct code sequence would be as follows:

```
[[myRect origin] release];    // Release the origin's memory
[myRect release];             // Release the rectangle's memory
```

It's a bit of a burden to have to remember to release the origin's memory yourself. After all, you weren't the one who allocated it; the `Rectangle` class did. In the next section, "Overriding Methods," you learn how to have the `Rectangle` release the memory.

With your modified method, recompiling and rerunning Program 8.5 produces the error messages shown as Figure 8.8.

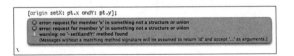

Figure 8.8   Compiler error messages

Oops! The problem here is that you've used some methods from the `XYPoint` class in your modified method, so now the compiler needs more information about it than the `@class` directive provides. In this case, you must go back and replace that directive with an `import` instead, like so:

```
#import "XYPoint.h"
```

Program 8.5B Output

```
Origin at (100, 200)
Origin at (100, 200)
```

That's better. This time, changing the value of `myPoint` to (50, 50) inside `main` had no effect on the rectangle's origin because a copy of the point was created inside the `Rectangle`'s `setOrigin:` method.

Incidentally, we didn't synthesize the `origin` methods here because the synthesized setter `setOrigin:` method would have behaved just like the one you originally wrote. That is, by default, the action of a synthesized setter is to simply copy the object pointer, not the object itself.

You can synthesize a different type of setter method that instead does make a copy of the object. However, to do that, you need to learn how to write a special copying method. We revisit this topic in Chapter 17, "Memory Management."

Overriding Methods

We noted earlier in this chapter that you can't remove or subtract methods through inheritance. However, you can change the definition of an inherited method by *overriding* it.

Returning to your two classes, `ClassA` and `ClassB`, assume that you want to write your own `initVar` method for `ClassB`. You already know that `ClassB` will inherit the `initVar` method defined in `ClassA`, but can you make a new method with the same name to replace the inherited method? The answer is yes, and you do so simply by defining a new method with the same name. A method defined with the same name as that of a parent class replaces, or overrides, the inherited definition. Your new method must have the same return type and take the same number and type of arguments as the method you are overriding.

Program 8.6 shows a simple example to illustrate this concept.

Program 8.6

```
// Overriding Methods

#import <Foundation/Foundation.h>

// ClassA declaration and definition

@interface ClassA: NSObject
{
    int x;
}

-(void) initVar;
@end

@implementation ClassA
-(void) initVar
{
    x = 100;
}
```

```
@end

// ClassB declaration and definition

@interface ClassB: ClassA
-(void) initVar;
-(void) printVar;
@end

@implementation ClassB
-(void) initVar     // added method
{
    x = 200;
}

-(void) printVar
{
    NSLog (@"x = %i", x);
}
@end

int main (int argc, char *argv[])
{
    NSAutoreleasePool * pool = [[NSAutoreleasePool alloc] init];

    ClassB  *b = [[ClassB alloc] init];

    [b initVar];   // uses overriding method in B

    [b printVar];   // reveal value of x;
    [b release];

    [pool drain];
    return 0;
}
```

Program 8.6 Output
```
x = 200
```

Clearly, the message

```
[b initVar];
```

causes the initVar method defined in ClassB to be used, and not the one defined in ClassA, as was the case with the previous example. Figure 8.9 illustrates this.

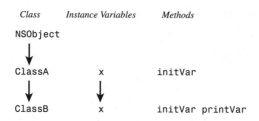

Class	Instance Variables	Methods
NSObject		
ClassA	x	initVar
ClassB	x	initVar printVar

Figure 8.9   Overriding the **initVar** method

Which Method Is Selected?

We covered how the system searches up the hierarchy for a method to apply to an object. If you have methods in different classes with the same name, the correct method is chosen based on the class of the receiver of the message. Program 8.7 uses the same class definition for ClassA and ClassB as before.

Program 8.7

```
#import <Foundation/Foundation.h>


// insert definitions for ClassA and ClassB here

int main (int argc, char *argv[])
{
   NSAutoreleasePool * pool = [[NSAutoreleasePool alloc] init];

   ClassA   *a = [[ClassA alloc] init];
   ClassB   *b = [[ClassB alloc] init];

   [a initVar];    // uses ClassA method
   [a printVar];   // reveal value of x;

   [b initVar];    // use overriding ClassB method
   [b printVar];   // reveal value of x;
   [a release];
   [b release];

   [pool drain];
   return 0;
}
```

You'll get this warning message when you build this program:

```
warning: 'ClassA' may not respond to '-printVar'
```

What happened here? We talked about this in an earlier section. Take a look at the declaration for ClassA:

```
// ClassA declaration and definition
```

```
@interface ClassA: NSObject
{
    int  x;
}

-(void) initVar;
@end
```

Notice that no `printVar` method is declared. That method is declared and defined in `ClassB`. Therefore, even though `ClassB` objects and their descendants can use this method through inheritance, `ClassA` objects cannot because the method is defined farther down in the hierarchy.

> **Note**
>
> You can coerce the use of this method in some ways, but we don't go into that here—besides, it's not good programming practice.

Returning to our example, let's add a `printVar` method to `ClassA` so you can display the value of its instance variables:

```
// ClassA declaration and definition

@interface ClassA: NSObject
{
    int  x;
}

-(void) initVar;
-(void) printVar;
@end

@implementation ClassA
-(void) initVar
{
    x = 100;
}

-(void) printVar
{
    NSLog (@"x = %i", x);
}

@end
```

`ClassB`'s declaration and definition remain unchanged. Let's try compiling and running this program again.

Program 8.7 Output

```
x = 100
x = 200
```

Now we can talk about the actual example. First, a and b are defined to be ClassA and ClassB objects, respectively. After allocation and initialization, a message is sent to a asking it to apply the initVar method. This method is defined in the definition of ClassA, so this method is selected. The method simply sets the value of the instance variable x to 100 and returns. The printVar method, which you just added to ClassA, is invoked next to display the value of x.

As with the ClassA object, the ClassB object b is allocated and initialized, its instance variable x is set to 200, and finally its value displayed.

Be sure that you understand how the proper method is chosen for a and b based on which class they belong to. This is a fundamental concept of object-oriented programming in Objective-C.

As an exercise, consider removing the printVar method from ClassB. Would this work? Why or why not?

Overriding the dealloc Method and the Keyword super

Now that you know how to override methods, let's return to Program 8.5B to learn a better approach to releasing the memory occupied by the origin. The setOrigin: method now allocates its own XYPoint origin object, and you are responsible for releasing its memory. The approach used in Program 8.6 was to have main release that memory with a statement such as follows:

```
[[myRect origin] release];
```

You don't have to worry about releasing all the individual members of a class; you can override the inherited dealloc method (it's inherited from NSObject) and release the origin's memory there.

> **Note**
>
> You don't override the release method—you override dealloc instead. As you'll learn in a later chapter, release sometimes gives up the memory an object used, and sometimes it doesn't. It gives up the memory taken by an object only if no one else is referencing that object. And it does this by invoking the object's dealloc method, the method that actually releases the memory.

If you decide to override dealloc, you also have to be sure to release the memory taken up not only by your own instance variables, but by any inherited ones as well.

To do this, you need to take advantage of the special keyword super, which refers to the parent class of the message receiver. You can send a message to super to execute an overridden method. This is the most common use for this keyword. So the message expression

```
[super release];
```

when used inside a method invokes the `release` method that is defined in (or inherited by) the parent class. The method is invoked on the receiver of the message—in other words, on `self`.

Therefore, the strategy for overriding the `dealloc` method for your `Rectangle` class is to first release the memory taken up by your `origin` and then invoke the `dealloc` method from the parent class to complete the job. This releases the memory taken up by the `Rectangle` object itself. Here is the new method:

```
-(void) dealloc
{
    if (origin)
        [origin release];
    [super dealloc];
}
```

The `dealloc` method is defined to not return a value. Inside the `dealloc` method, a test is made to see if `origin` is nonzero before releasing it. The origin of the rectangle possibly was never set; in this case, it has its default value of zero. Then we invoke the `dealloc` method from the parent class, which is the same method the `Rectangle` class would have inherited if it had not been overridden.

You can also write the `dealloc` method more simply as

```
-(void) dealloc
{
    [origin release];
    [super dealloc];
}
```

because it's okay to send a message to a nil object. Also, you're careful to `release` origin and not `dealloc` it here. If no one else is using the origin, the `release` will end up invoking the `dealloc` method on the origin anyway to free up its space.

With your new method, you now have to release just the rectangles that you allocate, without having to worry about the `XYPoint` objects they contain. The two `release` messages shown in Program 8.5 will now suffice to release all the objects you allocated in the program, including the `XYPoint` object that `setOrigin:` creates:

```
[myRect release];
[myPoint release];
```

One issue remains: If you set the origin of a single `Rectangle` object to different values during the execution of your program, you must release the memory taken up by the old origin before you allocate and assign the new one. For example, consider the following code sequence:

```
myRect.origin = startPoint;
```

```
myRect.origin = endPoint;
   ...
[startPoint release];
[endPoint release];
[myRect release];
```

The copy of the XYPoint startPoint stored in the origin member of myRect will not be released because it is overwritten by the second origin (endPoint) that is stored there. That origin is released properly when the rectangle itself is released, based on your new release method.

You would have to ensure that, before you set a new origin in your rectangle, the old one was released. You could handle this in the setOrigin: method, as follows:

```
-(void) setOrigin: (XYPoint *) pt
{
    if (origin)
      [origin release];

    origin = [[XYPoint alloc] init];

    [origin setX: pt.x andY: pt.y];
}
```

Luckily, when you synthesize your accessor methods, you can also have the compiler automatically handle this issue for you.

Extension Through Inheritance: Adding New Instance Variables

Not only can you add new methods to effectively extend the definition of a class, but you can also add new instance variables. In both cases, the effect is cumulative. You can never subtract methods or instance variables through inheritance; you can only add—or, in the case of methods, add or override.

Let's return to your simple ClassA and ClassB classes and make some changes. Add a new instance variable, y, to ClassB, like so:

```
@interface ClassB: ClassA
{
    int  y;
}

-(void) printVar;
@end
```

Even though ClassB might appear to have only one instance variable, called y, based on the previous declaration, it actually has two: It inherits the variable x from ClassA and adds its own instance variable y.

> **Note**
>
> Of course, it also has instance variables that it inherits from the NSObject class, but we choose to ignore this detail for now.

Let's put this together in a simple example to illustrate this concept (see Program 8.8).

Program 8.8

```
// Extension of instance variables


#import <Foundation/Foundation.h>

// Class A declaration and definition

@interface ClassA: NSObject
{
   int  x;
}

-(void) initVar;
@end

@implementation ClassA
-(void) initVar
{
   x = 100;
}
@end


// ClassB declaration and definition

@interface ClassB: ClassA
{
   int  y;
}
-(void)  initVar;
-(void)  printVar;
@end

@implementation ClassB
-(void) initVar
{
   x = 200;
   y = 300;
}

-(void) printVar
{
```

```
    NSLog (@"x = %i", x);
    NSLog (@"y = %i", y);
}
@end

int main (int argc, char *argv[])
{
    NSAutoreleasePool * pool = [[NSAutoreleasePool alloc] init];

    ClassB *b = [[ClassB alloc] init];

    [b initVar];  // uses overriding method in ClassB
    [b printVar];  // reveal values of x and y;

    [b release];
    [pool drain];
    return 0;
}
```

Program 8.8 Output

```
x = 200
y = 300
```

The ClassB object b is initialized by invoking the initVar method defined within ClassB. Recall that this method overrides the initVar method from ClassA. This method also sets the value of x (which was inherited from ClassA) to 200 and y (which was defined in ClassB) to 300. Next, the printVar method is used to display the value of these two instance variables.

Many more subtleties surround the idea of choosing the right method in response to a message, particularly when the receiver can be one of several classes. This is a powerful concept known as *dynamic binding*, and it is the topic of the next chapter.

Abstract Classes

What better way to conclude this chapter than with a bit of terminology? We introduce it here because it's directly related to the notion of inheritance.

Sometimes classes are created just to make it easier for someone to create a subclass. For that reason, these classes are called *abstract* classes or, equivalently, *abstract superclasses*. Methods and instance variables are defined in the class, but no one is expected to actually create an instance from that class. For example, consider the root object NSObject. Can you think of any use for defining an object from that class?

The Foundation framework, covered in Part II, "The Foundation Framework," has several of these so-called abstract classes. As an example, the Foundation's NSNumber class is an abstract class that was created for working with numbers as objects. Integers and floating-point numbers typically have different storage requirements. Separate subclasses of NSNumber exist for each numeric type. Because these subclasses, unlike their abstract superclasses, actually exist, they are known as *concrete* subclasses. Each concrete subclass falls under the NSNumber class umbrella and is collectively referred to as a *cluster*. When you send a message to the NSNumber class to create a new integer object, the appropriate subclass is used to allocate the necessary storage for an integer object and to set its value appropriately. These subclasses are actually private. You don't access them directly yourself; they are accessed indirectly through the abstract superclass. The abstract superclass gives a common interface for working with all types of number objects and relieves you of the burden of having to know which type of number you have stored in your number object and how to set and retrieve its value.

Admittedly, this discussion might seem a little "abstract" (sorry!); don't worry—just a basic grasp of the concept is sufficient here.

Exercises

1. Add a new class called ClassC, which is a subclass of ClassB, to Program 8.1. Make an initVar method that sets the value of its instance variable x to 300. Write a test routine that declares ClassA, ClassB, and ClassC objects and invokes their corresponding initVar methods.

2. When dealing with higher-resolution devices, you might need to use a coordinate system that enables you to specify points as floating-point values instead of as simple integers. Modify the XYPoint and Rectangle classes from this chapter to deal with floating-point numbers. The rectangle's width, height, area, and perimeter should all work with floating-point numbers as well.

3. Modify Program 8.1 to add a new class called ClassB2 that, like ClassB, is a subclass of ClassA.
   What can you say about the relationship between ClassB and ClassB2?
   Identify the hierarchical relationship between the NSObject class, ClassA, ClassB, and ClassB2.
   What is the superclass of ClassB?
   What is the superclass of ClassB2?
   How many subclasses can a class have, and how many superclasses can it have?

4. Write a Rectangle method called translate: that takes a vector called XYPoint (x_v, y_v) as its argument. Have it translate the rectangle's origin by the specified vector.

5. Define a new class called GraphicObject, and make it a subclass of NSObject. Define instance variables in your new class as follows:
   ```
   int    fillColor;   // 32-bit color
   BOOL   filled;      // Is the object filled?
   int    lineColor;   // 32-bit line color
   ```

Write methods to set and retrieve the variables defined previously.
Make the Rectangle class a subclass of GraphicObject.
Define new classes, Circle and Triangle, which are also subclasses of
GraphicObject. Write methods to set and retrieve the various parameters for these
objects and also to calculate the circle's circumference and area, and the triangle's
perimeter and area.

6. Write a Rectangle method called intersect: that takes a rectangle as an argument and returns a rectangle representing the overlapping area between the two rectangles. For example, given the two rectangles shown in Figure 8.10, the method should return a rectangle whose origin is at (400, 420), whose width is 50, and whose height is 60.

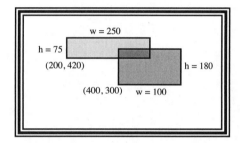

Figure 8.10   Intersecting rectangles

If the rectangles do not intersect, return one whose width and height are zero and whose origin is at (0,0).

7. Write a method for the Rectangle class called draw that draws a rectangle using dashes and vertical bar characters. The following code sequence

```
Rectangle *myRect = [[Rectangle alloc] init];
[myRect setWidth: 10 andHeight: 3];
[myRect draw];
[myRect release];
```
would produce the following output:

```
 ------
|      |
|      |
|      |
 ------
```

Note

You should use printf to draw your characters, since NSLog will display a new line each time it's called.

9

Polymorphism, Dynamic Typing, and Dynamic Binding

In this chapter, you'll learn about the features of the Objective-C language that make it such a powerful programming language and that distinguish it from some other object-oriented programming languages such as C++. This chapter describes three key concepts: polymorphism, dynamic typing, and dynamic binding. *Polymorphism* enables programs to be developed so that objects from different classes can define methods that share the same name. *Dynamic typing* defers the determination of the class that an object belongs to until the program is executing. *Dynamic binding* defers the determination of the actual method to invoke on an object until program execution time.

Polymorphism: Same Name, Different Class

Program 9.1 shows the interface file for a class called `Complex`, which is used to represent complex numbers in a program.

Program 9.1 Interface File `Complex.h`

```
// Interface file for Complex class

#import <Foundation/Foundation.h>

@interface Complex: NSObject
{
   double real;
   double imaginary;
}

@property double real, imaginary;
-(void)    print;
-(void)    setReal: (double) a andImaginary: (double) b;
-(Complex *) add: (Complex *) f;
@end
```

You should have completed the implementation section for this class in Exercises 6 and 7 from Chapter 7, "More on Classes." We added an additional `setReal:andImaginary:` method to enable you to set both the real and imaginary parts of your number with a single message and also synthesized accessor methods. This is shown in the following.

Program 9.1 Implementation File `Complex.m`

```
// Implementation file for Complex class

#import "Complex.h"

@implementation Complex

@synthesize real, imaginary;

-(void) print
{
    NSLog (@" %g + %gi ", real, imaginary);
}

-(void) setReal: (double) a andImaginary: (double) b
{
    real = a;
    imaginary = b;
}

-(Complex *) add: (Complex *) f
{
    Complex *result = [[Complex alloc] init];

    [result setReal: real + [f real]
          andImaginary: imaginary + [f imaginary]];

    return result;
}
@end
```

Program 9.1 Test Program `main.m`

```
// Shared Method Names: Polymorphism

#import "Fraction.h"
#import "Complex.h"

int main (int argc, char *argv[])
{
```

```objc
    NSAutoreleasePool * pool = [[NSAutoreleasePool alloc] init];

    Fraction *f1 = [[Fraction alloc] init];
    Fraction *f2 = [[Fraction alloc] init];
    Fraction *fracResult;
    Complex *c1 = [[Complex alloc] init];
    Complex *c2 = [[Complex alloc] init];
    Complex *compResult;

    [f1 setTo: 1 over: 10];
    [f2 setTo: 2 over: 15];


    [c1 setReal: 18.0 andImaginary: 2.5];
    [c2 setReal: -5.0 andImaginary: 3.2];

    // add and print 2 complex numbers

    [c1 print]; NSLog (@"        +"); [c2 print];
    NSLog (@"---------");
    compResult = [c1 add: c2];
    [compResult print];
    NSLog (@"\n");

    [c1 release];
    [c2 release];
    [compResult release];

    // add and print 2 fractions
    [f1 print]; NSLog (@"   +"); [f2 print];
    NSLog (@"----");
    fracResult = [f1 add: f2];
    [fracResult print];

    [f1 release];
    [f2 release];
    [fracResult release];

    [pool drain];
    return 0;
}
```

Program 9.1 Output

```
18 + 2.5i
        +
-5 + 3.2i
---------
13 + 5.7i

1/10
   +
2/15
----
7/30
```

Note that both the `Fraction` and `Complex` classes contain `add:` and `print` methods. So when executing the message expressions

```
compResult = [c1 add: c2];
[compResult print];
```

how does the system know which methods to execute? It's simple: The Objective-C run-time knows that `c1`, the receiver of the first message, is a `Complex` object. Therefore, it selects the `add:` method defined for the `Complex` class.

The Objective-C runtime system also determines that `compResult` is a `Complex` object, so it selects the `print` method defined in the `Complex` class to display the result of the addition. The same discussion applies to the following message expressions:

```
fracResult = [f1 add: f2];
[fracResult print];
```

Note

As described more completely in Chapter 13, "Underlying Language Features," the system always carries information about the class to which an object belongs. This enables it to make these key decisions at runtime instead of at compile time.

The corresponding methods from the `Fraction` class are chosen to evaluate the message expression based on the class of `f1` and `fracResult`.

As mentioned, the capability to share the same method name across different classes is known as polymorphism. Polymorphism enables you to develop a set of classes that each can respond to the same method name. Each class definition encapsulates the code needed to respond to that particular method, and this makes it independent of the other class definitions. This also enables you to later add new classes that can respond to methods with the same name.

> **Note**
>
> Before leaving this section, note that both the Fraction and Complex classes should be re-
> sponsible for releasing the results that are produced by their add:methods, and not the
> test program. In fact, these objects should be autoreleased. We'll talk about that more in
> Chapter 17, "Memory Management."

Dynamic Binding and the `id` Type

Chapter 4 briefly touched on the id data type and noted that it is a generic object type.
That is, id can be used for storing objects that belong to any class. The real power of this
data type is exploited when it's used this way to store different types of objects in a variable during the execution of a program. Study Program 9.2 and its associated output.

Program 9.2

```
// Illustrate Dynamic Typing and Binding


#import "Fraction.h"
#import "Complex.h"

int main (int argc, char *argv[])
{
    NSAutoreleasePool * pool = [[NSAutoreleasePool alloc] init];

    id      dataValue;
    Fraction *f1 = [[Fraction alloc] init];
    Complex   *c1 = [[Complex alloc] init];

    [f1 setTo: 2 over: 5];
    [c1 setReal: 10.0 andImaginary: 2.5];

    // first dataValue gets a fraction

    dataValue = f1;
    [dataValue print];

    // now dataValue gets a complex number

    dataValue = c1;
    [dataValue print];

    [c1 release];
    [f1 release];

    [pool drain];
    return 0;
}
```

Program 9.2 Output

```
2/5
10 + 2.5i
```

The variable `dataValue` is declared as an `id` object type. Therefore, `dataValue` can be used to hold any type of object in the program. Note that no asterisk is used in the declaration line:

```
id dataValue;
```

The `Fraction` `f1` is set to `2/5`, and the `Complex` number `c1` is set to `(10 + 2.5i)`. The assignment

```
dataValue = f1;
```

stores the `Fraction` `f1` in `dataValue`. Now, what can you do with `dataValue`? Well, you can invoke any of the methods that you can use on a `Fraction` object with `dataValue`, even though the type of `dataValue` is an `id` and not a `Fraction`. But if `dataValue` can store any type of object, how does the system know which method to invoke? That is, when it encounters the message expression

```
[dataValue print];
```

how does it know which `print` method to invoke? You have `print` methods defined for both the `Fraction` and `Complex` classes.

As noted previously, the answer lies in the fact that the Objective-C system always keeps track of the class to which an object belongs. It also lies in the concepts of dynamic typing and dynamic binding—that is, the system makes the decision about the class of the object, and, therefore, which method to invoke dynamically, at runtime instead of at compile time.

So during execution of the program, before the system sends the `print` message to `dataValue`, it first checks the class of the object stored inside `dataValue`. In the first case of Program 9.2, this variable contains a `Fraction`, so the `print` method defined in the `Fraction` class is used. This is verified by the output from the program.

In the second case, the same thing happens. First, the `Complex` number `c1` is assigned to `dataValue`. Next, the following message expression is executed:

```
[dataValue print];
```

This time, because `dataValue` contains an object belonging to the `Complex` class, the corresponding `print` method from that class is selected for execution.

This is a simple example, but you can extrapolate this concept to more sophisticated applications. When combined with polymorphism, dynamic binding and dynamic typing enable you to easily write code that can send the same message to objects from different classes.

For example, consider a `draw` method that can be used to paint graphical objects on the screen. You might have different `draw` methods defined for each of your graphical objects, such as text, circles, rectangles, windows, and so on. If the particular object to be drawn is stored inside an `id` variable called `currentObject`, for example, you could paint it on the screen simply by sending it the `draw` message:

```
[currentObject draw];
```

You could even test it first to ensure that the object stored in `currentObject` actually responds to a `draw` method. You'll see how to do that later in this chapter, in the section called "Asking Questions About Classes."

Compile Time Versus Runtime Checking

Because the type of object stored inside an `id` variable can be indeterminate at compile time, some tests are deferred until runtime—that is, while the program is executing.

Consider the following sequence of code:

```
Fraction *f1 = [[Fraction alloc] init];
[f1 setReal: 10.0 andImaginary: 2.5];
```

Recalling that the `setReal:andImaginary:` method applies to complex numbers and not fractions, the following message is issued when you compile the program containing these lines:

```
prog3.m: In function 'main':
prog3.m:13: warning: 'Fraction' does not respond to 'setReal:andImaginary:'
```

The Objective-C compiler knows that `f1` is a `Fraction` object because it has been declared that way. It also knows that when it sees the message expression

```
[f1 setReal: 10.0 andImaginary: 2.5];
```

the `Fraction` class does not have a `setReal:andImaginary:` method (and did not inherit one, either). Therefore, it issues the warning message shown previously.

Now consider the following code sequence:

```
id dataValue = [[Fraction alloc] init];
  ...
[dataValue setReal: 10.0 andImaginary: 2.5];
```

These lines do not produce a warning message from the compiler because the compiler doesn't know what type of object is stored inside `dataValue` when processing your source file.

No error message is reported until you run the program containing these lines. The error looks something like this:

```
objc: Fraction: does not recognize selector -setReal:andImaginary:
dynamic3: received signal: Abort trap
When attempting to execute the expression
[dataValue setReal: 10.0 andImaginary: 2.5];
```

The runtime system first checks the type of object stored inside `dataValue`. Because `dataValue` has a `Fraction` stored in it, the runtime system checks to ensure that the method `setReal:andImaginary:` is one of the methods defined for the class `Fraction`. Because it's not, the error message shown previously is issued and the program is terminated.

The `id` Data Type and Static Typing

If an `id` data type can be used to store any object, why don't you just declare all your objects as type `id`? For several reasons, you don't want to get into the habit of overusing this generic class data type.

First, when you define a variable to be an object from a particular class, you are using what's known as *static* typing. The word *static* refers to the fact that the variable is always used to store objects from the particular class. So the class of the object stored in that type is predeterminate, or *static*. When you use static typing, the compiler ensures, to the best of its ability, that the variable is used consistently throughout the program. The compiler can check to ensure that a method applied to an object is defined or inherited by that class; if not, it issues a warning message. Thus, when you declare a `Rectangle` variable called `myRect` in your program, the compiler checks that any methods you invoke on `myRect` are defined in the `Rectangle` class or are inherited from its superclass.

> **Note**
>
> Certain techniques make it possible to invoke methods that are specified by a variable, in which case the compiler can't check that for you.

However, if the check is performed for you at runtime anyway, why do you care about static typing? You care because it's better to get your errors out during the compilation phase of your program than during the execution phase. If you leave it until runtime, you might not even be the one running the program when the error occurs. If your program is put into production, some poor unsuspecting user might discover when running the program that a particular object does not recognize a method.

Another reason for using static typing is that it makes your programs more readable. Consider the following declaration:

```
id    f1;
```

versus

```
Fraction *f1;
```

Which do you think is more understandable—that is, which makes the intended use of the variable `f1` clearer? The combination of static typing and meaningful variable names (which we intentionally did not choose in the previous example) can go a long way toward making your program more self-documenting.

Argument and Return Types with Dynamic Typing

If you use dynamic typing to invoke a method, note the following rule: If a method with the same name is implemented in more than one of your classes, each method must agree on the type of each argument and the type of value it returns so that the compiler can generate the correct code for your message expressions.

The compiler performs a consistency check among each class declaration it has seen. If one or more methods conflict in either argument or return type, the compiler issues a warning message. For example, both the `Fraction` and `Complex` classes contain `add:` methods. However, the Fraction class takes as its argument and returns a Fraction object, whereas the `Complex` class takes and returns a `Complex` object. If `frac1` and `myFract` are `Fraction` objects, and `comp1` and `myComplex` are `Complex` objects, statements such as

```
result = [myFract add: frac1];
```

and

```
result = [myComplex add: comp1];
```

do not cause any problems This is because, in both cases, the receiver of the message is statically typed and the compiler can check for consistent use of the method as it is defined in the receiver's class.

If `dataValue1` and `dataValue2` are `id` variables, the statement

```
result = [dataValue1 add: dataValue2];
```

causes the compiler to generate code to pass the argument to an `add:` method and handle its returned value by making assumptions.

At runtime, the Objective-C runtime system will check the actual class of the object stored inside `dataValue1` and select the appropriate method from the correct class to execute. However, in a more general case, the compiler might generate the incorrect code to pass arguments to a method or handle its return value. This would happen if one method took an object as its argument and the other took a floating-point value, for example. Or if one method returned an object and the other returned an integer, for example. If the inconsistency between two methods is just a different type of object (for example, the `Fraction`'s `add:` method takes a `Fraction` object as its argument and returns one, and the `Complex`'s `add:` method takes and returns a `Complex` object), the compiler will still generate the correct code because memory addresses (that is, pointers) are passed as references to objects anyway.

Asking Questions About Classes

As you start working with variables that can contain objects from different classes, you might need to ask questions such as the following:

- Is this object a rectangle?
- Does this object support a `print` method?
- Is this object a member of the `Graphics` class or one of its descendants?

You can then use the answers to these questions to execute different sequences of code, avoid an error, or check the integrity of your program while it's executing.

Table 9.1 summarizes some of the basic methods that the NSObject class supports for asking these types of questions. In this table, *class-object* is a class object (typically generated with the class method), and *selector* is a value of type SEL (typically created with the @selector directive).

Table 9.1   **Methods for Working with Dynamic Types**

Method	Question or Action
-(BOOL) isKindOfClass: *class-object*	Is the object a member of *class-object* or a descendant?
-(BOOL) isMemberOfClass: *class-object*	Is the object a member of *class-object?*
-(BOOL) respondsToSelector: *selector*	Can the object respond to the method specified by *selector*?
+(BOOL) instancesRespondToSelector: *selector*	Can instances of the specified class respond to *selector*?
+(BOOL)isSubclassOfClass: *class-object*	Is the object a subclass of the specified class?
-(id) performSelector: *selector*	Apply the method specified by *selector*.
-(id) performSelector: *selector* withObject: *object*	Apply the method specified by *selector*, passing the argument *object*.
-(id) performSelector: *selector* withObject: *object1* withObject: *object2*	Apply the method specified by *selector* with the arguments *object1* and *object2*.

Other methods are not covered here. One enables you to ask whether an object conforms to a protocol (see Chapter 11, "Tying Up Some Loose Ends"). Others enable you to ask about dynamically resolving methods (not covered in this text).

To generate a class object from a class name or another object, you send it the class message. So to get a class object from a class named Square, you write the following:

```
[Square class]
```

If mySquare is an instance of Square object, you get its class by writing this:

```
[mySquare class]
```

To see whether the objects stored in the variables obj1 and obj2 are instances from the same class, you write this:

```
if ([obj1 class] == [obj2 class])
    ...
```

To see if the variable `myFract` is a `Fraction` class object, you test the result from the expression, like this:

```
[myFract isMemberOfClass: [Fraction class]]
```

To generate one of the so-called selectors listed in Table 9.1, you apply the `@selector` directive to a method name. For example, the following produces a value of type `SEL` for the method named `alloc`, which you know is a method inherited from the `NSObject` class:

```
@selector (alloc)
```

The following expression produces a selector for the `setTo:over:` method that you implemented in your `Fraction` class (remember those colon characters in the method names):

```
@selector (setTo:over:)
```

To see whether an instance of the `Fraction` class responds to the `setTo:over:` method, you can test the return value from the expression, like this:

```
[Fraction instancesRespondToSelector: @selector (setTo:over:)]
```

Remember, the test covers inherited methods, not just one that is directly defined in the class definition.

The `performSelector:` method and its variants (not shown in Table 9.1) enable you to send a message to an object, where the message can be a selector stored inside a variable. For example, consider this code sequence:

```
SEL     action;
id      graphicObject;
...
action = @selector (draw);
...
[graphicObject performSelector: action];
```

In this example, the method indicated by the `SEL` variable `action` is sent to whatever graphical object is stored in `graphicObject`. Presumably, the action might vary during program execution—perhaps based on the user's input—even though we've shown the action as `draw`. To first ensure that the object can respond to the action, you might want to use something like this:

```
if ([graphicObject respondsToSelector: action] == YES)
    [graphicObject performSelector: action]
else
    // error handling code here
```

> **Note**
>
> You can also catch an error by overriding the doesNotRecognize: method. This method is invoked whenever an unrecognized message is sent to a class and is passed the unrecognized selector as its argument.

You can employ other strategies as well: You can forward the message to someone else to handle using the forward:: method, or you can try to send the method anyway and catch an exception if it occurs. We cover this latter technique shortly.

Program 9.3 asks some questions about the Square and Rectangle classes defined in Chapter 8, "Inheritance." Try to predict the results from this program before looking at the actual output (no peeking!).

Program 9.3

```
#import "Square.h"

int main (int argc, char *argv[])
{
    NSAutoreleasePool * pool = [[NSAutoreleasePool alloc] init];

    Square *mySquare = [[Square alloc] init];


    // isMemberOf:

    if ( [mySquare isMemberOfClass: [Square class]] == YES )
        NSLog (@"mySquare is a member of Square class");

    if ( [mySquare isMemberOfClass: [Rectangle class]] == YES )
        NSLog (@"mySquare is a member of Rectangle class");

    if ( [mySquare isMemberOfClass: [NSObject class]] == YES )
        NSLog (@"mySquare is a member of NSObject class");

    // isKindOf:

    if ( [mySquare isKindOfClass: [Square class]] == YES )
        NSLog (@"mySquare is a kind of Square");

    if ( [mySquare isKindOfClass: [Rectangle class]] == YES )
        NSLog (@"mySquare is a kind of Rectangle");

    if ( [mySquare isKindOfClass: [NSObject class]] == YES )
```

```
        NSLog (@"mySquare is a kind of NSObject");

    // respondsTo:

    if ( [mySquare respondsToSelector: @selector (setSide:)] == YES )
        NSLog (@"mySquare responds to setSide: method");

    if ( [mySquare respondsToSelector: @selector (setWidth:andHeight:)] == YES )
        NSLog (@"mySquare responds to setWidth:andHeight: method");

    if ( [Square respondsToSelector: @selector (alloc)] == YES )
        NSLog (@"Square class responds to alloc method");

    // instancesRespondTo:

    if ([Rectangle instancesRespondToSelector: @selector (setSide:)] == YES)
        NSLog (@"Instances of Rectangle respond to setSide: method");

    if ([Square instancesRespondToSelector: @selector (setSide:)] == YES)
        NSLog (@"Instances of Square respond to setSide: method");

    if ([Square isSubclassOfClass: [Rectangle class]] == YES)
        NSLog (@"Square is a subclass of a rectangle");

    [mySquare release];

    [pool drain];
    return 0;
}
```

Make sure you build this program with the implementation files for the Square, Rectangle, and XYPoint classes, which were all presented in Chapter 8, "Inheritance."

Program 9.3 Output
```
mySquare is a member of Square class
mySquare is a kind of Square
mySquare is a kind of Rectangle
mySquare is a kind of NSObject
mySquare responds to setSide: method
mySquare responds to setWidth:andHeight: method
Square class responds to alloc method
Instances of Square respond to setSide: method
Square is a subclass of a rectangle
```

The output from Program 9.3 should be clear. Remember that isMemberOfClass: tests for direct membership in a class, whereas isKindOfClass: checks for membership in the inheritance hierarchy. Thus, mySquare is a member of the Square class—but it's also "kind of" a Square, Rectangle, and NSObject because it exists in that class hierarchy (obviously, all objects should return YES for the isKindOf: test on the NSObject class, unless you've defined a new root object).

The test

```
if ( [Square respondsTo: @selector (alloc)] == YES )
```

tests whether the class Square responds to the class method alloc, which it does because it's inherited from the root object NSObject. Realize that you can always use the class name directly as the receiver in a message expression, and you don't have to write this in the previous expression (although you could if you wanted):

```
[Square class]
```

That's the only place you can get away with that. In other places, you need to apply the class method to obtain the class object.

Exception Handling Using @try

Good programming practice dictates that you try to anticipate problems that can occur in your program. You can do this by testing for conditions that could cause a program to terminate abnormally and handling these situations, perhaps by logging a message and gracefully terminating the program or taking some other corrective action. For example, you saw earlier in this chapter how you can test to see if an object responds to a particular message. In the case of error avoidance, performing this test while the program is executing can enable you to avoid sending an unrecognized message to an object. When an attempt is made to send such an unrecognized message, your program will typically terminate immediately by throwing what's known as an *exception*.

Take a look at Program 9.4. We have no method called noSuchMethod defined in the Fraction class. When you compile the program, you will get warning messages to that effect.

Program 9.4

```
#import "Fraction.h"


int main (int argc, char *argv [])

{
    NSAutoreleasePool * pool = [[NSAutoreleasePool alloc] init];
    Fraction *f = [[Fraction alloc] init];
    [f noSuchMethod];
    NSLog (@"Execution continues!");
    [f release];
    [pool drain];
    return 0;
}
```

You can go ahead and run the program despite the warning messages you receive. If you do, you can expect to see your program terminate abnormally with errors similar to these:

Program 9.4 Output

```
-[Fraction noSuchMethod]: unrecognized selector sent to instance 0x103280
*** Terminating app due to uncaught exception 'NSInvalidArgumentException',
    reason: '*** -[Fraction noSuchMethod]: unrecognized selector sent
            to instance 0x103280'
Stack: (
   2482717003,
   2498756859,
   2482746186,
   2482739532,
   2482739730
)
Trace/BPT trap
```

To avoid abnormal program termination in a case such as this, you can put one or more statements inside a special statement block, which takes the following format:

```
@try {
    statement
    statement
    ...
}
@catch (NSException *exception) {
    statement
    statement
    ...
}
```

Execution proceeds as normal with each *statement* in the @try block. However, if one of the statements in the block throws an exception, execution is not terminated but instead goes immediately to the @catch block, where it continues. Inside that block, you can handle the exception. One plausible sequence of actions here would be to log an error message, clean up, and terminate execution.

Program 9.5 illustrates exception handling. It is followed by the program's output.

Program 9.5 Exception Handling

```
#import "Fraction.h"

int main (int argc, char *argv [])

{
```

```
    NSAutoreleasePool * pool = [[NSAutoreleasePool alloc] init];
    Fraction *f = [[Fraction alloc] init];

    @try {
        [f noSuchMethod];
    }
    @catch (NSException *exception) {
        NSLog(@"Caught %@%@", [exception name], [exception reason]);
    }
    NSLog (@"Execution continues!");
    [f release];
    [pool drain];
    return 0;
}
```

Program 9.5 Output

```
*** -[Fraction noSuchMethod]:  unrecognized selector sent to instance 0x103280
Caught NSInvalidArgumentException: *** -[Fraction noSuchMethod]:
unrecognized selector sent to instance 0x103280
Execution continues!
```

When the exception occurs, the @catch block gets executed. An NSException object that contains information about the exception gets passed as the argument into this block. As you can see, the name method retrieves the name of the exception, and the reason method gives the reason (which the runtime system also previously printed automatically).

After the last statement in the @catch block is executed (we have only one here), the program continues execution with the statement immediately following the block. In this case, we execute an NSLog call to verify that execution has continued and has not been terminated.

This is a very simple example to illustrate how to catch exceptions in a program. An @finally block can be used to include code to execute whether or not a statement in a @try block throws an exception.

An @throw directive enables you to throw your own exception. You can use it to throw a specific exception, or inside a @catch block to throw the same exception that took you into the block like this:

```
@throw;
```

You might want to do this after handling an exception yourself (perhaps after performing cleanup work, for example). You can then let the system handle the rest of the work for you. Finally, you can have multiple @catch blocks that are sequenced to catch and handle different type of exceptions.

Exercises

1. What will happen if you insert the message expression
   ```
   [compResult reduce];
   ```
   into Program 9.1 after the addition is performed (but before `compResult` is released)? Try it and see.

2. Can the id variable `dataValue`, as defined in Program 9.2, be assigned a `Rectangle` object as you defined it in Chapter 8? That is, is the statement
   ```
   dataValue = [[Rectangle alloc] init];
   ```
   valid? Why or why not?

3. Add a `print` method to your `XYPoint` class defined in Chapter 8. Have it display the point in the format (x, y). Then modify Program 9.2 to incorporate an `XYPoint` object. Have the modified program create an `XYPoint` object, set its value, assign it to the id variable `dataValue`, and then display its value.

4. Based on the discussions about argument and return types in this chapter, modify both `add:` methods in the `Fraction` and `Complex` classes to take and return id objects. Then write a program that incorporates the following code sequence:
   ```
   result = [dataValue1 add: dataValue2];
   [result print];
   ```
   Here, `result`, `dataValue1`, and `dataValue2` are id objects. Make sure you set `dataValue1` and `dataValue2` appropriately in your program and release all objects before your program terminates.

Note

You'll have to change the name of the methods to something other than `add:`. That's because the system's `NSObjectController` class also has an `add:` method. As noted on the top of page 195, if multiple methods of the same name exist in different classes and the type of the receiver isn't known at compile time, the compiler will perform a consistency check to make sure the arguments and return types are consistent among the similarly named methods.

5. Given the `Fraction` and `Complex` class definitions you have been using in this text and the following definitions
   ```
   Fraction *fraction = [[Fraction alloc] init];
   Complex  *complex  = [[Complex alloc] init];
   id        number   = [[Complex alloc] init];
   ```
   determine the return value from the following message expressions. Then type them into a program to verify the results.

```
[fraction isMemberOfClass: [Complex class]];
[complex isMemberOfClass: [NSObject class]];
[complex isKindOfClass: [NSObject class]];
[fraction isKindOfClass: [Fraction class]];
[fraction respondsToSelector: @selector (print)];
[complex respondsToSelector: @selector (print)];
[Fraction instancesRespondToSelector: @selector (print)];
[number respondsToSelector: @selector (print)];
[number isKindOfClass: [Complex class]];
[number respondsToSelector: @selector (release)];
[[number class] respondsToSelector: @selector (alloc)];
```

More on Variables
and Data Types

In this chapter, we go into more detail about variable scope, initialization methods for objects, and data types.

The initialization of an object deserves some special attention, which we give it here.

We talked briefly about the scope of instance variables as well as static and local variables in Chapter 7, "More on Classes." We talk more about static variables here and introduce the concept of global and external ones. In addition, you can give certain directives to the Objective-C compiler, to more precisely control the scope of your instance variables. We cover these directives in this chapter as well.

An *enumerated* data type enables you to define the name for a data type to be used only to store a specified list of values. The Objective-C language's `typedef` statement lets you assign your own name to a built-in or derived data type. Finally, in this chapter, we describe in more detail the precise steps the Objective-C compiler follows when converting data types in the evaluation of expressions.

Initializing Classes

You've seen the pattern before: You allocate a new instance of an object and then initialize it, using a familiar sequence like this:

```
Fraction *myFract = [[Fraction alloc] init];
```

After these two methods are invoked, you typically assign some values to the new object, like this:

```
[myFract setTo: 1 over: 3];
```

The process of initializing an object followed by setting it to some initial values is often combined into a single method. For example, you can define an `initWith::` method that initializes a fraction and sets its numerator and denominator to the two (unnamed) supplied arguments.

A class that contains many methods and instance variables in it commonly has several initialization methods as well. For example, the Foundation framework's NSArray class contains the following six initialization methods:

```
initWithArray:
initWithArray:copyItems:
initWithContentsOfFile:
initWithContentsOfURL:
initWithObjects:
initWithObjects:count:
```

An array might be allocated and then initialized with a sequence like this:

```
myArray = [[NSArray alloc] initWithArray: myOtherArray];
```

It's common practice for all the initializers in a class to begin with init....As you can see, the NSArray's initializers follow that convention. You should adhere to the following two strategies when writing initializers.

If your class contains more than one initializer, one of them should be your *designated* initializer and all the other initialization methods should use it. Typically, that is your most complex initialization method (usually, the one that takes the most arguments). Creating a designated initializer centralizes your main initialization code in a single method. Anyone subclassing your class can then override your designated initializer, to ensure that new instances are properly initialized.

Ensure that any inherited instance variables get properly initialized. The easiest way to do that is to first invoke the parent's designated initialization method, which is most often init. After that, you can initialize your own instance variables.

Based on that discussion, your initialization method initWith:: for your Fraction class might look like this:

```
-(Fraction *) initWith: (int) n: (int) d
{
   self = [super init];

   if (self)
      [self setTo: n over: d];

   return self;
}
```

This method invokes the parent initializer first, which is NSObject's init method (recall that this is Fraction's parent). You must assign the result back to self because an initializer has the right to change or move the object in memory.

Following the initialization of super (and its success, as indicated by the return of a nonzero value) you use the setTo:over: method to set the numerator and denominator of your Fraction. As with other initialization methods, you are expected to return the initialized object, which you do here.

Program 10.1 tests your new `initWith::` initialization method.

Program 10.1

```
#import "Fraction.h"

int main (int argc, char *argv[])
{
   NSAutoreleasePool * pool = [[NSAutoreleasePool alloc] init];

   Fraction *a, *b;

   a = [[Fraction alloc] initWith: 1: 3];
   b = [[Fraction alloc] initWith: 3: 7];

   [a print];
   [b print];

   [a release];
   [b release];

   [pool drain];
   return 0;
}
```

Program 10.1 Output

```
1/3
3/7
```

When your program begins execution, it sends the `initialize` call method to all your classes. If you have a class and associated subclasses, the parent class gets the message first. This message is sent only once to each class, and it is guaranteed to be sent before any other messages are sent to the class. The purpose is for you to perform any class initialization at that point. For example, you might want to initialize some static variables associated with that class at that time.

Scope Revisited

You can influence the scope of the variables in your program in several ways. You can do this with instance variables as well as with normal variables defined either outside or inside functions. In the following discussion, we use the term *module* to refer to any number of method or function definitions contained within a single source file.

Directives for Controlling Instance Variable Scope

You know by now that instance variables have scope that is limited to the instance methods defined for the class. So any instance method can access its instance variables directly by name, without having to do anything special.

You also know that instance variables are inherited by a subclass. Inherited instance variables can also be accessed directly by name from within any method defined in that subclass. Again, this is without having to do anything special.

You can put four directives in front of your instance variables when they are declared in the interface section, to more precisely control their scope:

- **@protected**—Methods defined in the class and any subclasses can directly access the instance variables that follow. This is the default case.

- **@private**—Methods defined in the class can directly access the instance variables that follow, but subclasses cannot.

- **@public**—Methods defined in the class and any other classes or modules can directly access the instance variables that follow.

- **@package**—For 64-bit images, the instance variable can be accessed anywhere within the image that implements the class.

If you wanted to define a class called `Printer` that kept two instance variables, called `pageCount` and `tonerLevel` private, and was accessible only by methods in the `Printer` class, you might use an interface section that looks like this:

```
@interface Printer: NSObject
{
@private
    int   pageCount;
    int   tonerLevel;
@protected
    // other instance variables
}
  ...
@end
```

Anyone subclassing `Printer` would be incapable of accessing these two instance variables because they were made private.

These special directives act like "switches"; all variables that appear after one of these directives (until the right curly brace that marks the end of the variable declarations) have the specified scope unless another directive is used. In the previous example, the `@protected` directive ensures that instance variables that follow, up to the `}`, will be accessible by subclasses and by the `Printer` class methods.

The `@public` directive makes instance variables accessible by other methods or functions through the use of the pointer operator (`->`), which is covered in Chapter 13, "Underlying C Language Features." Making an instance variable public is not considered good programming practice because it defeats the concept of data encapsulation (that is, a class hiding its instance variables).

External Variables

If you write the statement

```
int gMoveNumber = 0;
```

at the beginning of your program—outside any method, class definition, or function—its value can be referenced from anywhere in that module. In such a case, we say that gMoveNumber is defined as a *global* variable. By convention, a lowercase *g* is commonly used as the first letter of a global variable, to indicate its scope to the program's reader.

Actually, this same definition of the variable gMoveNumber also makes its value accessible from other files. Specifically, the preceding statement defines the variable gMoveNumber not just as a global variable, but as an *external* global variable.

An *external* variable is one whose value can be accessed and changed by any other methods or functions. Inside the module that wants to access the external variable, the variable is declared in the normal fashion and the keyword extern is placed before the declaration. This signals to the system that a globally defined variable from another file is to be accessed. The following is an example of how to declare the variable gMoveNumber as an external variable:

```
extern int gMoveNumber;
```

The module in which the preceding declaration appeared can now access and modify the value of gMoveNumber. Other modules can also access the value of gMoveNumber by using a similar extern declaration in the file.

Consider this important rule to follow when working with external variables: The variable must be defined someplace among your source files. This is done by declaring the variable outside any method or function and is *not* preceded by the keyword extern, like this:

```
int gMoveNumber;
```

Here, an initial value can be optionally assigned to the variable, as shown previously.

The second way to define an external variable is to declare the variable outside any function, placing the keyword extern in front of the declaration and explicitly assigning an initial value to it, like this:

```
extern int gMoveNumber = 0;
```

However, this is not the preferred way to do this, and the compiler warns you that you've declared the variable extern and assigned it a value at the same time. That's because using the word extern makes it a declaration for the variable, not a definition. Remember, a declaration doesn't cause storage for a variable to be allocated, but a definition does. The previous example violates this rule by forcing a declaration to be treated as a definition (by assigning it an initial value).

When dealing with external variables, you can declare a variable as `extern` in many places, but you can define it only once.

Consider a small program example to illustrate the use of external variables. Suppose we have defined a class called `Foo`, and we type the following code into a file called `main.m`:

```
#import "Foo.h"

int gGlobalVar = 5;

int main (int argc, char *argc[])
{
    NSAutoreleasePool * pool = [[NSAutoreleasePool alloc] init];
    Foo *myFoo = [[Foo alloc] init];
    NSLog (@"%i ", gGlobalVar);

    [myFoo setgGlobalVar: 100];
    NSLog (@"%i", gGlobalVar);
    [myFoo release];
    [pool drain];
    return 0;
}
```

The definition of the global variable `gGlobalVar` in the previous program makes its value accessible by any method (or function) that uses an appropriate `extern` declaration. Suppose your `Foo` method `setgGlobalVar:` looks like this:

```
-(void) setgGlobalVar: (int) val
{
   extern int gGlobalVar;
   gGlobalVar = val;
}
```

This program would produce the following output:

```
5
100
```

This would verify that the method `setgGlobalVar:` is capable of accessing and changing the value of the external variable `gGlobalVar`.

If many methods needed to access the value of `gGlobalVar`, making the `extern` declaration just once at the front of the file would be easier. However, if only one method or a small number of methods needed to access this variable, there would be something to be said for making separate `extern` declarations in each such method; it would make the program more organized and would isolate the use of the particular variable to those functions that actually used it. Note that if the variable is defined inside the file containing the code that accesses the variable, the individual `extern` declarations are not re-quired.

Static Variables

The example just shown goes against the notion of data encapsulation and good object-oriented programming techniques. However, you might need to work with variables whose values are shared across different method invocations. Even though it might not make sense to make `gGlobalVar` an instance variable in the `Foo` class, a better approach might be to "hide" it within the `Foo` class by restricting its access to setter and getter methods defined for that class.

You now know that any variable defined outside a method is not only a global vari-able, but an external one as well. Many situations arise in which you want to define a variable to be global but not external. In other words, you want to define a global variable to be local to a particular module (file). It would make sense to want to define a variable this way if no methods other than those contained inside a particular class definition needed access to the particular variable. You can accomplish this by defining the variable to be *static* inside the file that contains the implementation for the particular class.

If made outside any method (or function), the following statement makes the value of `gGlobalVar` accessible from any subsequent point in the file in which the definition ap-pears, but not from methods or functions contained in other files:

```
static int gGlobalVar = 0;
```

Recall that class methods do not have access to instance variables (you might want to think about why that's the case again). However, you might want a class method to be ca-pable of setting and accessing variables. A simple example is a class allocator method that you want to keep track of the number of objects it has allocated. You would accomplish this task by setting up a static variable inside the implementation file for the class. The al-location method could then access this variable directly because it would not be an in-stance variable. The users of the class would not need to know about this variable. Because it's defined as a static variable in the implementation file, its scope would be re-stricted to that file. Users thus wouldn't have direct access to it, and the concept of data encapsulation would not be violated. You could write a method to retrieve the value of this variable if access was needed from outside the class.

Program 10.2 extends the `Fraction` class definition with the addition of two new methods. The `allocF` class method allocates a new `Fraction` and keeps track of how many `Fractions` it has allocated, whereas the `count` method returns that count. Note that this latter method is also a class method. It could have been implemented as an instance method as well, but it makes more sense to ask the class how many instances it has allo-cated instead of sending the message to a particular instance of the class.

These are the declarations for the two new class methods to be added to the `Fraction.h` header file:

```
+(Fraction *) allocF;
```

```
+(int) count;
```

Notice that the inherited `alloc` method wasn't overridden here; instead, you defined your own allocator method. Your method will take advantage of the inherited `alloc` method. Place this code in your `Fraction.m` implementation file:

```
static int gCounter;

@implementation Fraction

+(Fraction *) allocF
{
    extern int gCounter;
    ++gCounter;

    return [Fraction alloc];
}

+(int) count
{
    extern int gCounter;

    return gCounter;
}
// other methods from Fraction class go here
    ...
@end
```

Note

It's not considered good programming practice to override `alloc`, as this method deals with the physical allocation of the memory. You shouldn't have to get involved at that level.

The static declaration of gCounter makes it accessible to any method defined in the implementation section, yet it does not make it accessible from outside the file. The `allocF` method simply increments the `gCounter` variable and then uses the `alloc` method to create a new `Fraction`, returning the result. The `count` method simply returns the value of the counter, thus isolating its direct access from the user.

Recall that the `extern` declarations are not required in the two methods because the gCounter variable is defined within the file. It simply helps the reader of the method understand that a variable defined outside the method is being accessed. The *g* prefix for the variable name also serves the same purpose for the reader; for that reason, most programmers typically do not include the `extern` declarations.

Program 10.2 tests the new methods.

Program 10.2

```
#import "Fraction.h"


int main (int argc, char *argv[])
{
    NSAutoreleasePool * pool = [[NSAutoreleasePool alloc] init];
    Fraction *a, *b, *c;

    NSLog (@"Fractions allocated: %i", [Fraction count]);

    a = [[Fraction allocF] init];
    b = [[Fraction allocF] init];
    c = [[Fraction allocF] init];

    NSLog (@"Fractions allocated: %i", [Fraction count]);
    [a release];
    [b release];
    [c release];

    [pool drain];
    return 0;
}
```

Program 10.2 Output

```
Fractions allocated: 0
Fractions allocated: 3
```

When the program begins execution, the value of gCounter is automatically set to 0 (recall that you can override the inherited class `initialize` method if you want to perform any special initialization of the class as a whole, such as set the value of other static variables to some nonzero values). After allocating (and then initializing) three `Fractions` using the `allocF` method, the `count` method retrieves the `counter` variable, which is correctly set to 3. You could also add a setter method to the class if you wanted to reset the counter or set it to a particular value. You don't need that for this application, though.

Storage Class Specifiers

You've already encountered storage class specifiers that you can place in front of variable names, such as `extern` and `static`. Here we'll discuss more specifiers that give the compiler information about the intended use of a variable in your program.

auto

This keyword is used to declare an automatic local variable, as opposed to a `static` one. It is the default for a variable declared inside a function or method—but you'll never see anyone using it. Here's an example:

```
auto int index;
```

This declares `index` to be an automatic local variable, meaning that it automatically is allocated when the block (which can be a curly-braced sequence of statements, a method, or a function) is entered and is automatically deallocated when the block is exited. Because this is the default inside a block, the statement

```
int index;
```

is equivalent to this:

```
auto int index;
```

Unlike static variables, which have default initial values of 0, automatic variables are undefined unless you explicitly assign them values.

const

The compiler enables you to associate the `const` attribute to variables whose values the program will not change. That is, this tells the compiler that the specified variables have a *const*ant value throughout the program's execution. If you try to assign a value to a `const` variable after initializing it or try to increment or decrement it, the compiler issues a warning message. As an example of the `const` attribute, the following line declares the `const` variable `pi`:

```
const double pi = 3.141592654;
```

This tells the compiler that the program will not modify this variable. Of course, because the value of a `const` variable cannot be subsequently modified, you must initialize it when it is defined.

Defining a variable as a `const` variable aids in the self-documentation process and tells the reader of the program that the program will not change the variable's value.

volatile

This is sort of the inverse to `const`. It tells the compiler explicitly that the specified variable *will* change its value. It's included in the language to prevent the compiler from optimizing away seemingly redundant assignments to a variable or repeated examination of a variable without its value seemingly changing. A good example to consider is an I/O port, which involves an understanding of pointers (see Chapter 13).

Let's say that you have the address of an output port stored in a variable in your program called `outPort`. If you wanted to write two characters to the port—let's say an *O* followed by an *N*—you might write the following code:

```
*outPort = 'O';
*outPort = 'N';
```

This first line says to store the character O at the memory address specified by `outPort`. The second says to then store the character N at the same location. A smart compiler might notice two successive assignments to the same location and, because `outPort` isn't being modified in between, simply remove the first assignment from the program. To prevent this from happening, you declare outPort to be a volatile variable, like this:

```
volatile char *outPort;
```

Enumerated Data Types

The Objective-C language enables you to specify a range of values that can be assigned to a variable. An enumerated data type definition is initiated by the keyword enum. Immediately following this keyword is the name of the enumerated data type, followed by a list of identifiers (enclosed in a set of curly braces) that define the permissible values that can be assigned to the type. For example, the following statement defines a data type flag:

```
enum flag { false, true };
```

In theory, this data type can be assigned the values true and false inside the program, and no other values. Unfortunately, the Objective-C compiler does not generate warning messages if this rule is violated.

To declare a variable to be of type enum flag, you again use the keyword enum, followed by the enumerated type name, followed by the variable list. So the following statement defines the two variables endOfData and matchFound to be of type flag:

```
enum flag endOfData, matchFound;
```

The only values (in theory, that is) that can be assigned to these variables are the names true and false. Thus, statements such as

```
endOfData = true;
```

and

```
if ( matchFound == false )
    ...
```

are valid.

If you want to have a specific integer value associated with an enumeration identifier, the integer can be assigned to the identifier when the data type is defined. Enumeration identifiers that subsequently appear in the list are assigned sequential integer values beginning with the specified integer value plus one.

In the following definition, an enumerated data type, direction, is defined with the values up, down, left, and right:

```
enum direction { up, down, left = 10, right };
```

The compiler assigns the value 0 to up because it appears first in the list, assigns 1 to down because it appears next, assigns 10 to left because it is explicitly assigned this value, and assigns 11 to right because it is the incremented value of the preceding enum in the list.

Enumeration identifiers can share the same value. For example, in

```
enum boolean { no = 0, false = 0, yes = 1, true = 1 };
```

assigning either the value no or `false` to an `enum boolean` variable assigns it the value 0; assigning either `yes` or `true` assigns it the value 1.

As another example of an enumerated data type definition, the following defines the type `enum month`, with permissible values that can be assigned to a variable of this type being the names of the months of the year:

```
enum month { january = 1, february, march, april, may, june, july,
        august, september, october, november, december };
```

The Objective-C compiler actually treats enumeration identifiers as integer constants. If your program contains these two lines, the value 2 would be assigned to `thisMonth` (and not the name `february`):

```
enum month thisMonth;

    ...
thisMonth = february;
```

Program 10.3 shows a simple program using enumerated data types. The program reads a month number and then enters a `switch` statement to see which month was entered. Recall that the compiler treats enumeration values as integer constants, so they're valid case values. The variable `days` is assigned the number of days in the specified month, and its value is displayed after the `switch` is exited. A special test is included to see whether the month is February.

Program 10.3

```
#import <Foundation/Foundation.h>
// print the number of days in a month
int main (int argc, char *argv[])
{
    NSAutoreleasePool * pool = [[NSAutoreleasePool alloc] init];

    enum month { january = 1, february, march, april, may, june,
                july, august, september, october, november,
                december };
    enum month amonth;
    int     days;

    NSLog (@"Enter month number: ");
    scanf ("%i", &amonth);
```

```
    switch (amonth) {
       case january:
       case march:
       case may:
       case july:
       case august:
       case october:
       case december:
                days = 31;
                break;
       case april:
       case june:
       case september:
       case november:
                days = 30;
                break;
       case february:
                days = 28;
                break;
       default:
                NSLog (@"bad month number");
                days = 0;
                break;
    }

    if ( days != 0 )
       NSLog (@"Number of days is %i", days);

    if ( amonth == february )
       NSLog (@"...or 29 if it's a leap year");

    [pool drain];
    return 0;
}
```

Program 10.3 Output

```
Enter month number:
5
Number of days is 31
```

Program 10.3 Output (Rerun)

```
Enter month number:
2
Number of days is 28
...or 29 if it's a leap year
```

You can explicitly assign an integer value to an enumerated data type variable; you should do this using the type cast operator. Therefore, if `monthValue` were an integer variable that had the value 6, for example, this expression would be permissible:

```
lastMonth = (enum month) (monthValue - 1);
```

If you don't use the type cast operator, the compiler (unfortunately) won't complain about it.

When using programs with enumerated data types, try not to rely on the fact that the enumerated values are treated as integers. Instead, treat them as distinct data types. The enumerated data type gives you a way to associate a symbolic name with an integer number. If you subsequently need to change the value of that number, you must change it only in the place where the enumeration is defined. If you make assumptions based on the actual value of the enumerated data type, you defeat this benefit of using an enumeration.

Some variations are permitted when defining an enumerated data type: The name of the data type can be omitted, and variables can be declared to be of the particular enumerated data type when the type is defined. As an example showing both of these options, the statement

```
enum { east, west, south, north } direction;
```

defines an (unnamed) enumerated data type with values `east`, `west`, `south`, or `north` and declares a variable (`direction`) to be of that type.

Defining an enumerated data type within a block limits the scope of that definition to the block. On the other hand, defining an enumerated data type at the beginning of the program, outside any block, makes the definition global to the file.

When defining an enumerated data type, you must make certain that the enumeration identifiers are unique with respect to other variable names and enumeration identifiers defined within the same scope.

The `typedef` Statement

Objective-C provides a capability that enables the programmer to assign an alternative name to a data type. This is done with a statement known as `typedef`. The following statement defines the name `Counter` to be equivalent to the Objective-C data type `int`:

```
typedef int Counter;
```

You can subsequently declare variables to be of type `Counter`, as in the following statement:

```
Counter  j, n;
```

The Objective-C compiler treats the declaration of the variables `j` and `n`, shown previously, as normal integer variables. The main advantage of the use of the `typedef` in this case is in the added readability it lends to the definition of the variables. The definition of `j` and `n` makes clear the intended purpose of these variables in the program. Declaring them to be of type int in the traditional fashion would not have made the intended use of these variables clear.

The following typedef defines a type named NumberObject to be a Number object:

```
typedef Number *NumberObject;
```

Variables subsequently declared to be of type NumberObject, as in

```
NumberObject myValue1, myValue2, myResult;
```

are treated as if they were declared in the normal way in your program:

```
Number *myValue1, *myValue2, *myResult;
```

To define a new type name with typedef, follow this procedure:

1. Write the statement as if a variable of the desired type were being declared.

2. Where the name of the declared variable would normally appear, substitute the new type name.

3. In front of everything, place the keyword typedef.

As an example of this procedure, to define a type called Direction to be an enumerated data type that consists of the directions east, west, north, and south, write out the enumerated type definition and substitute the name Direction where the variable name would normally appear. Before everything, place the keyword typedef:

```
typedef enum { east, west, south, north } Direction;
```

With this typedef in place, you can subsequently declare variables to be of type Direction, as in the following:

```
Direction step1, step2;
```

The Foundation framework has the following typedef definition for NSComparisonResult in one of its header files:

```
enum _NSComparisonResult {
   NSOrderedAscending = -1, NSOrderedSame, NSOrderedDescending
};

typedef NSInteger NSComparisonResult;
```

Some of the methods in the Foundation framework that perform comparisons return a value of this type. For example, Foundation's string-comparison method, called compare:, returns a value of type NSComparisonResult after comparing two strings that are NSString objects. The method is declared like this:

```
-(NSComparisonResult) compare: (NSString *) string;
```

To test whether two `NSString` objects called `userName` and `savedName` are equal, you might include a line like this in your program:

```
if ( [userName compare: savedName] == NSOrderedSame) {
    // The names match
    ...
}
```

This actually tests whether the result from the `compare:` method is zero.

Data Type Conversions

Chapter 4, "Data Types and Expressions," briefly addressed the fact that sometimes the system implicitly makes conversions when expressions are evaluated. You examined a case with the data types `float` and `int`. You saw how an operation that involves a `float` and an `int` was carried out as a floating-point operation, with the integer data item automatically converted to a floating point.

You also saw how the type cast operator can be used to explicitly dictate a conversion. So given that `total` and `n` are both integer variables

```
average = (float) total / n;
```

the value of the variable `total` is converted to type `float` before the operation is performed, thereby guaranteeing that the division will be carried out as a floating-point operation.

Conversion Rules

The Objective-C compiler adheres to very strict rules when it comes to evaluating expressions that consist of different data types.

The following summarizes the order in which conversions take place in the evaluation of two operands in an expression:

1. If either operand is of type `long double`, the other is converted to `long double`, and that is the type of the result.

2. If either operand is of type `double`, the other is converted to `double`, and that is the type of the result.

3. If either operand is of type `float`, the other is converted to `float`, and that is the type of the result.

4. If either operand is of type `_Bool`, `char`, `short int`, or `bit field`,[1] or of an enumerated data type, it is converted to `int`.

---

[1] Chapter 13 briefly discusses bit fields.

5. If either operand is of type `long long int`, the other is converted to `long long int`, and that is the type of the result.

6. If either operand is of type `long int`, the other is converted to `long int`, and that is the type of the result.

7. If this step is reached, both operands are of type `int`, and that is the type of the result.

This is actually a simplified version of the steps involved in converting operands in an expression. The rules get more complicated when `unsigned` operands are involved. For the complete set of rules, see Appendix B, "Objective-C Language Summary."

Realize from this series of steps that whenever you reach a step that says "that is the type of the result," you're done with the conversion process.

As an example of how to follow these steps, let's see how the following expression would be evaluated, where f is defined to be a `float`, i an `int`, l a `long int`, and s a `short int` variable:

```
f * i + l / s
```

Consider first the multiplication of f by i, which is the multiplication of a `float` by an `int`. From step 3, you know that, because f is of type `float`, the other operand (i) will also be converted to type `float`, and that will be the type of the result of the multiplication.

Next, l is divided by s, which is the division of a `long int` by a `short int`. Step 4 tells you that the `short int` will be promoted to an `int`. Continuing, step 6 shows that because one of the operands (l) is a `long int`, the other operand will be converted to a `long int`, which will also be the type of the result. This division will therefore produce a value of type `long int`, with any fractional part resulting from the division truncated.

Finally, step 3 indicates that, if one of the operands in an expression is of type `float` (as is the result of multiplying f * i), the other operand will be converted to type `float`, which will be the type of the result. Therefore, *after* the division of l by s, the result of the operation will be converted to type `float` and then added into the product of f and i. The final result of the preceding expression will therefore be a value of type `float`.

Remember, the type cast operator can always be used to explicitly force conversions and thereby control the way in which a particular expression is evaluated.

Thus, if you didn't want the result of dividing l by s to be truncated in the preceding expression evaluation, you could have type-cast one of the operands to type `float`, thereby forcing the evaluation to be performed as a floating-point division:

```
f * i + (float) l / s
```

In this expression, l would be converted to `float` before the division operation was performed because the type cast operator has higher precedence than the division operator. Because one of the operands of the division would then be of type `float`, the other (s) would be automatically converted to type `float`, and that would be the type of the result.

Sign Extension

Whenever a signed int or signed short int is converted into an integer of a larger size, the sign is extended to the left when the conversion is performed. This ensures that a short int that has a value of -5, for example, will also have the value -5 when converted to a long int. Whenever an unsigned integer is converted to an integer of a larger size, no sign extension occurs, as you would expect.

On some machines (such as on the Intel processors used in the current Macintosh line of computers as well as on the ARM processors currently used in the iPhone and iTouch), characters are treated as signed quantities. This means that when a character is converted to an integer, sign extension occurs. As long as characters are used from the standard ASCII character set, this never poses a problem. However, if a character value is used that is not part of the standard character set, its sign can be extended when converted to an integer. For example, on a Mac, the character constant '\377' is converted to the value -1 because its value is negative when treated as a signed 8-bit quantity.

Recall that the Objective-C language permits character variables to be declared unsigned, thus avoiding this potential problem. That is, an unsigned char variable never has its sign extended when converted to an integer; its value always is greater than or equal to zero. For the typical 8-bit character, a signed character variable therefore has the range of values from −128 to +127, inclusive. An unsigned character variable can range in value from 0 to 255, inclusive.

If you want to force sign extension on your character variables, you can declare such variables to be of type signed char. This ensures that sign extension occurs when the character value is converted to an integer, even on machines that don't do so by default.

In Chapter 15, "Numbers, Strings, and Collections," you'll learn about dealing with multibyte Unicode characters. This is the preferred way to deal with strings that can contain characters from character sets containing millions of characters.

Exercises

1. Using the Rectangle class from Chapter 8, "Inheritance," add an initializer method according to the following declaration:
    ```
    -(Rectangle *) initWithWidth: (int) w andHeight: (int) h;
    ```

2. Given that you label the method developed in exercise 1 the designated initializer for the Rectangle class, and based on the Square and Rectangle class definitions from Chapter 8, add an initializer method to the Square class according to the following declaration:
    ```
    -(Square *) initWithSide: (int) side;
    ```

3. Add a counter to the `Fraction` class's `add:` method to count the number of times it is invoked. How can you retrieve the value of the counter?

4. Using `typedef` and enumerated data types, define a type called `Day` with the possible values `Sunday`, `Monday`, `Tuesday`, `Wednesday`, `Thursday`, `Friday`, and `Saturday`.

5. Using `typedef`, define a type called `FractionObj` that enables you to write statements such as the following:
```
FractionObj f1 = [[Fraction alloc] init],
           f2 = [[Fraction alloc] init];
```

6. Based on the following definitions
```
float     f = 1.00;
short int i = 100;
long int  l = 500L;
double    d = 15.00;
```
and the seven steps outlined in this chapter for the conversion of operands in expressions, determine the type and value of the following expressions:
```
f + i
l / d
i / l + f
l * i
f / 2
i / (d + f)
l / (i * 2.0)
l + i / (double) l
```

7. Write a program to ascertain whether sign extension is performed on signed `char` variables on your machine.

11

Categories and Protocols

In this chapter, you'll learn about how to add methods to a class in a modular fashion through the use of categories and how to create a standardized list of methods for others to implement.

Categories

Sometimes you might be working with a class definition and want to add some new methods to it. For example, you might decide for your `Fraction` class that, in addition to the `add:` method for adding two fractions, you want to have methods to subtract, multiply, and divide two fractions.

As another example, say you are working on a large programming project and, as part of that project, your group is defining a new class that contains many different methods. You have been assigned the task of writing methods for the class that work with the file system. Other project members have been assigned methods responsible for creating and initializing instances of the class, performing operations on objects in the class, and drawing representations of objects from the class on the screen.

As a final example, suppose you've learned how to use a class from the library (for example, the Foundation framework's array class called `NSArray`) and realize that you wish the class had implemented one or more methods. Of course, you could write a new subclass of the `NSArray` class and implement the new methods, but perhaps an easier way exists.

A practical solution for all these situations is *categories*. A category provides an easy way for you to modularize the definition of a class into groups or categories of related methods. It also gives you an easy way to extend an existing class definition without even having access to the original source code for the class and without having to create a subclass. This is a powerful yet easy concept for you to learn.

Let's get back to the first case and show how to add a new category to the `Fraction` class to handle the four basic math operations. We first show you the original `Fraction` interface section:

```
#import <Foundation/Foundation.h>
```

```
// Define the Fraction class

@interface Fraction : NSObject
{
    int numerator;
    int denominator;
}

@property int numerator, denominator;
-(void)  setTo: (int) n over: (int) d;
-(Fraction *) add: (Fraction *) f;
-(void)   reduce;
-(double) convertToNum;
-(void)   print;
@end
```

Next, let's remove the `add:` method from this interface section and add it to a new category, along with the other three math operations you want to implement. Here's what the interface section would look like for your new `MathOps` category:

```
#import "Fraction.h"
@interface Fraction (MathOps)
-(Fraction *) add: (Fraction *) f;
-(Fraction *) mul: (Fraction *) f;
-(Fraction *) sub: (Fraction *) f;
-(Fraction *) div: (Fraction *) f;
@end
```

Realize that even though this is an interface section definition, it is an extension to an existing one. Therefore, you must include the original interface section so that the compiler knows about the `Fraction` class (unless you incorporate the new category directly into the original `Fraction.h` header file, which is an option).

After the `#import`, you see the following line:

```
@interface Fraction (MathOps)
```

This tells the compiler that you are defining a new category for the `Fraction` class and that its name is `MathOps`. The category name is enclosed in a pair of parentheses after the class name. Notice that you don't list the `Fraction`'s parent class here; the compiler already knows it from `Fraction.h`. Also, you don't tell it about the instance variables, as you've done in all the previous interface sections you've defined. In fact, if you try to list the parent class or the instance variables, you'll get a syntax error from the compiler.

This interface section tells the compiler you are adding an extension to the class called `Fraction` under the category named `MathOps`. The `MathOps` category contains four instance methods: `add:`, `mul:`, `sub:`, and `div:`. Each method takes a fraction as its argument and returns one as well.

You can put the definitions for all your methods into a single implementation section. That is, you could define all the methods from the interface section in `Fraction.h` plus all the methods from the `MathOps` category in one implementations section. Alternatively, you could define your category's methods in a separate implementation section. In such a case, the implementation section for these methods must also identify the category to which the methods belong. As with the interface section, you do this by enclosing the category name inside parentheses after the class name, like this:

```
@implementation Fraction (MathOps)
    // code for category methods
    ...
@end
```

In Program 11.1, the interface and implementation sections for the new `MathOps` category are grouped together, along with a test routine, into a single file.

Program 11.1 MathOps Category and Test Program

```
#import "Fraction.h"

@interface Fraction (MathOps)
-(Fraction *) add: (Fraction *) f;
-(Fraction *) mul: (Fraction *) f;
-(Fraction *) sub: (Fraction *) f;
-(Fraction *) div: (Fraction *) f;
@end

@implementation Fraction (MathOps)
-(Fraction *) add: (Fraction *) f
{
    // To add two fractions:
    // a/b + c/d = ((a*d) + (b*c)) / (b * d)

    Fraction *result = [[Fraction alloc] init];
    int      resultNum, resultDenom;

    resultNum = (numerator * f.denominator) +
        (denominator * f.numerator);
    resultDenom = denominator * f.denominator;

    [result setTo: resultNum over: resultDenom];
    [result reduce];

    return result;
}

-(Fraction *) sub: (Fraction *) f
{
```

```
    // To sub two fractions:
    // a/b - c/d = ((a*d) - (b*c)) / (b * d)

    Fraction *result = [[Fraction alloc] init];
    int      resultNum, resultDenom;

    resultNum = (numerator * f.denominator) -
          (denominator * f.numerator);
    resultDenom = denominator * f.denominator;

    [result setTo: resultNum over: resultDenom];
    [result reduce];

    return result;
}

-(Fraction *) mul: (Fraction *) f
{
    Fraction  *result = [[Fraction alloc] init];

    [result setTo: numerator * f.numerator
              over: denominator * f.denominator];
    [result reduce];

    return result;
}

-(Fraction *) div: (Fraction *) f
{
    Fraction  *result = [[Fraction alloc] init];

    [result setTo: numerator * f.denominator
              over: denominator * f.numerator];
    [result reduce];

    return result;
}
@end

int main (int argc, char *argv[])
{
    NSAutoreleasePool * pool = [[NSAutoreleasePool alloc] init];

    Fraction *a = [[Fraction alloc] init];
    Fraction *b = [[Fraction alloc] init];
    Fraction *result;

    [a setTo: 1 over: 3];
    [b setTo: 2 over: 5];

    [a print]; NSLog (@"  +"); [b print]; NSLog (@"-----");
    result = [a add: b];
```

```
    [result print];
    NSLog (@"\n");
    [result release];

    [a print]; NSLog (@"  -"); [b print]; NSLog (@"-----");
    result = [a sub: b];
    [result print];
    NSLog (@"\n");
    [result release];

    [a print]; NSLog (@"  *"); [b print]; NSLog (@"-----");
    result = [a mul: b];
    [result print];
    NSLog (@"\n");
    [result release];

    [a print]; NSLog (@"  /"); [b print]; NSLog (@"-----");
    result = [a div: b];
    [result print];
    NSLog (@"\n");
    [result release];
    [a release];
    [b release];

    [pool drain];
    return 0;
}
```

Program 11.1 Output

```
1/3
  +
2/5
-----
11/15

1/3
  -
2/5
-----
-1/15

1/3
  *
2/5
-----
2/15

1/3
  /
2/5
-----
5/6
```

Realize once again that it is certainly legal in Objective-C to write a statement such as this:

```
[[a div: b] print];
```

This line directly prints the result of dividing `Fraction` a by b and thereby avoids the intermediate assignment to the variable `result`, as was done in Program 11.1. However, you need to perform this intermediate assignment so you can capture the resulting `Fraction` and subsequently release its memory. Otherwise, your program will leak memory every time you perform an arithmetic operation on a fraction.

Program 11.1 puts the interface and implementation sections for the new category into the same file with the test program. As mentioned previously, the interface section for this category could go either in the original `Fraction.h` header file so that all methods would be declared in one place or in its own header file.

If you put your category into a master class definition file, all users of the class have access to the methods in the category. If you don't have the capability to modify the original header file directly (consider adding a category to an existing class from a library, as shown in Part II, "The Foundation Framework"), you have no choice but to keep it separate.

Some Notes About Categories

Some points about categories are worth mentioning. First, although a category has access to the instance variables of the original class, it can't add any of its own. If you need to do that, consider subclassing.

Also, a category can override another method in the class, but this is typically considered poor programming practice. For one thing, after you override a method, you can no longer access the original method. Therefore, you must be careful to duplicate all the functionality of the overridden method in your replacement. If you do need to override a method, subclassing might be the right choice. If you override a method in a subclass, you can still reference the parent's method by sending a message to `super`. So you don't have to understand all the intricacies of the method you are overriding; you can simply invoke the parent's method and add your own functionality to the subclass's method.

You can have as many categories as you like, following the rules we've outlined here. If a method is defined in more than one category, the language does not specify which one will be used.

Unlike a normal interface section, you don't need to implement all the methods in a category. That's useful for incremental program development because you can declare all the methods in the category and implement them over time.

Remember that extending a class by adding new methods with a category affects not just that class, but all its subclasses as well. This can be potentially dangerous if you add new methods to the root object `NSObject`, for example, because everyone will inherit those new methods, whether or not that was your intention.

The new methods you add to an existing class through a category can serve your purposes just fine, but they might be inconsistent with the original design or intentions of the class. Turning a `Square` into a `Circle` (admittedly, an exaggeration), for example, by adding a new category and some methods muddies the definition of the class and is not good programming practice.

Also, object/category named pairs must be unique. Only one `NSString (Private)` category can exist in a given Objective-C namespace. This can be tricky because the Objective-C namespace is shared between the program code and all the libraries, frameworks, and plug-ins. This is especially important for Objective-C programmers writing screensavers, preference panes, and other plug-ins because their code will be injected into application or framework code that they do not control.

Protocols

A *protocol* is a list of methods that is shared among classes. The methods listed in the protocol do not have corresponding implementations; they're meant to be implemented by someone else (like you!). A protocol provides a way to define a set of methods that are somehow related with a specified name. The methods are typically documented so that you know how they are to perform and so that you can implement them in your own class definitions, if desired.

If you decide to implement all of the required methods for a particular protocol, you are said to *conform to* or *adopt* that protocol.

Defining a protocol is easy: You simply use the `@protocol` directive followed by the name of the protocol, which is up to you. After that, you declare methods just as you did with your interface section. All the method declarations, up to the `@end` directive, become part of the protocol.

If you choose to work with the Foundation framework, you'll find that several protocols are defined. One of them, called `NSCopying`, declares a method that you need to implement if your class is to support copying of objects through the `copy` (or `copyWithZone:`) method. (Chapter 18, "Copying Objects," covers the topic of copying objects in detail.)

Here's how the `NSCopying` protocol is defined in the standard Foundation header file `NSObject.h`:

```
@protocol NSCopying
- (id)copyWithZone: (NSZone *)zone;
@end
```

If you adopt the NSCopying protocol in your class, you must implement a method called copyWithZone:. You tell the compiler that you are adopting a protocol by listing the protocol name inside a pair of angular brackets (<...>) on the @interface line. The protocol name comes after the name of the class and its parent class, as in the following:

```
@interface AddressBook: NSObject <NSCopying>
```

This says that AddressBook is an object whose parent is NSObject and states that it conforms to the NSCopying protocol. Because the system already knows about the method(s) previously defined for the protocol (in this example, it knows from the header file NSObject.h), you don't declare the methods in the interface section. However, you need to define them in your implementation section.

In this example, in the implementation section for AddressBook, the compiler expects to see the copyWithZone: method defined.

If your class adopts more than one protocol, just list them inside the angular brackets, separated by commas:

```
@interface AddressBook: NSObject <NSCopying, NSCoding>
```

This tells the compiler that the AddressBook class adopts the NSCopying and NSCoding protocols. Again, the compiler expects to see all the required methods listed for those protocols implemented in the AddressBook implementation section.

If you define your own protocol, you don't have to actually implement it yourself. However, you're alerting other programmers that if they want to adopt the protocol, they do have to implement the methods. Those methods can be inherited from a superclass. Thus, if one class conforms to the NSCopying protocol, its subclasses do as well (although that doesn't mean the methods are correctly implemented for that subclass).

You can use a protocol to define methods that you want other people who subclass your class to implement. Perhaps you could define a Drawing protocol for your GraphicObject class; in it, you could define paint, erase, and outline methods:

```
@protocol Drawing
-(void) paint;
-(void) erase;
@optional
-(void) outline;
@end
```

As the creator of the GraphicObject class, you don't necessarily want to implement these painting methods. However, you want to specify the methods that someone who subclasses the GraphicObject class needs to implement to conform to a standard for drawing objects he's trying to create.

> **Note**
>
> Note the use of the @optional directive here. Any methods that are listed following that directive are optional. That is, an adopter of the Drawing protocol does not have to implement the outline method to conform to the protocol. (And you can subsequently switch back to listing required methods by using the @required directive inside the protocol definition.)

So if you create a subclass of GraphicObject called Rectangle and advertise (that is, *document*) that your Rectangle class conforms to the Drawing protocol, users of the class will know that they can send paint, erase, and (possibly) outline messages to instances from that class.

> **Note**
>
> Well that's the theory, anyway. The compiler lets you say that you conform to a protocol and issues warning messages only if you don't implement the methods.

Notice that the protocol doesn't reference any classes; it's *classless*. Any class can conform to the Drawing protocol, not just subclasses of GraphicObject.

You can check to see whether an object conforms to a protocol by using the conformsToProtocol: method. For example, if you had an object called currentObject and wanted to see whether it conformed to the Drawing protocol so you could send it drawing messages, you could write this:

```
id currentObject;
 ...
if ([currentObject conformsToProtocol: @protocol (Drawing)] == YES)
{
  // Send currentObject paint, erase and/or outline msgs
  ...
}
```

The special @protocol directive as used here takes a protocol name and produces a Protocol object, which is what the conformsToProtocol: method expects as its argument.

You can enlist the aid of the compiler to check for conformance with your variables by including the protocol name inside angular brackets after the type name, like this:

```
id <Drawing> currentObject;
```

This tells the compiler that currentObject will contain objects that conform to the Drawing protocol. If you assign a statically typed object to currentObject that does not conform to the Drawing protocol (say that you have a Square class that does not conform), the compiler issues a warning message that looks like this:

```
warning: class 'Square' does not implement the 'Drawing' protocol
```

This is a compiler check here, so assigning an `id` variable to `currentObject` would not generate this message because the compiler has no way of knowing whether the object stored inside an `id` variable conforms to the `Drawing` protocol.

You can list more than one protocol if the variable will hold an object conforming to more than one protocol, as in this line:

```
id <NSCopying, NSCoding> myDocument;
```

When you define a protocol, you can extend the definition of an existing one. This protocol declaration says that the `Drawing3D` protocol also adopts the `Drawing` protocol:

```
@protocol Drawing3D <Drawing>
```

Thus, whichever class adopts the `Drawing3D` protocol must implement the methods listed for that protocol, as well as the methods from the `Drawing` protocol.

Finally, a category also can adopt a protocol, like this:

```
@interface Fraction (Stuff) <NSCopying, NSCoding>
```

Here `Fraction` has a category, `Stuff` (okay, not the best choice of names!), that adopts the `NSCopying` and `NSCoding` protocols.

As with class names, protocol names must be unique.

Informal Protocols

You might come across the notion of an *informal* protocol in your readings. This is really a category that lists a group of methods but does not implement them. Everyone (or just about everyone) inherits from the same root object, so informal categories are often defined for the root class. Sometimes informal protocols are also referred to as *abstract* protocols.

If you look at the header file `<NSScriptWhoseTests.h>`, you might find some method declarations that look like this:

```
@interface NSObject (NSComparisonMethods)
- (BOOL)isEqualTo:(id)object;
- (BOOL)isLessThanOrEqualTo:(id)object;
- (BOOL)isLessThan:(id)object;
- (BOOL)isGreaterThanOrEqualTo:(id)object;
- (BOOL)isGreaterThan:(id)object;
- (BOOL)isNotEqualTo:(id)object;
- (BOOL)doesContain:(id)object;
- (BOOL)isLike:(NSString *)object;
- (BOOL)isCaseInsensitiveLike:(NSString *)object;
@end
```

This defines a category called `NSComparisonMethods` for the `NSObject` class. This informal protocol lists a group of methods (here, nine are listed) that can be implemented as part of this protocol. An informal protocol is really no more than a grouping of methods under a name. This can help somewhat from the point of documentation and modularization of methods.

The class that declares the informal protocol doesn't implement the methods in the class itself, and a subclass that chooses to implement the methods needs to redeclare them in its interface section, as well as implement one or more of them. Unlike formal protocols, the compiler gives no help with informal protocols; there's no concept of conformance or testing by the compiler.

If an object adopts a formal protocol, the object must conform to all the required messages in the protocol. This can be enforced at runtime as well as compile time. If an object adopts an informal protocol, the object might not need to adopt all methods in the protocol, depending on the protocol. Conformance to an informal protocol can be enforced at runtime (via `respondsToSelector:`) but not at compile time.

> **Note**
>
> The previously-described @optional directive that was added to the Objective-C 2.0 language is meant to replace the use of informal protocols. You can see this used for several of the UIKit classes (UIKit is part of the Cocoa Touch frameworks).

Composite Objects

You've learned several ways to extend the definition of a class through techniques such as subclassing and using categories. Another technique involves defining a class that consists of one or more objects from other classes. An object from this new class is known as a *composite* object because it is composed of other objects.

As an example, consider the `Square` class you defined in Chapter 8, "Inheritance." You defined this as a subclass of a `Rectangle` because you recognized that a square was just a rectangle with equal sides. When you define a subclass, it inherits all the instance variables and methods of the parent class. In some cases, this is undesirable—for example, some of the methods defined in the parent class might not be appropriate for use by the subclass. The `Rectangle`'s `setWidth:andHeight:` method is inherited by the `Square` class but really does not apply to a square (even though it will work properly). Furthermore, when you create a subclass, you must ensure that all the inherited methods work properly because users of the class will have access to them.

As an alternative to subclassing, you can define a new class that contains as one of its instance variables an object from the class you want to extend. Then you have to define only those methods in the new class that are appropriate for that class. Getting back to the `Square` example, here's an alternative way to define a `Square`:

```
@interface Square: NSObject
{
    Rectangle *rect;
}
-(int) setSide: (int) s;
-(int) side;
-(int) area;
```

```
-(int) perimeter;
@end
```

The `Square` class is defined here with four methods. Unlike the subclass version, which gives you direct access to the `Rectangle`'s methods (`setWidth:`, `setHeight:`, `setWidth:andHeight:`, `width`, and `height`), those methods are not in this definition for a `Square`. That makes sense here because those methods really don't fit in when you deal with squares.

If you define your `Square` this way, it becomes responsible for allocating the memory for the rectangle it contains. For example, without overriding methods, the statement

```
Square *mySquare = [[Square alloc] init];
```

allocates a new `Square` object but does not allocate a `Rectangle` object stored in its instance variable, `rect`.

A solution is to override `init` or add a new method such as `initWithSide:` to do the allocation. That method can allocate the `Rectangle rect` and set its side appropriately. You also need to override the `dealloc` method (which you saw how to do with the `Rectangle` class in Chapter 8) to release the memory used by the `Rectangle rect` when the `Square` itself is freed.

When defining your methods in your `Square` class, you can still take advantage of the `Rectangle`'s methods. For example, here's how you could implement the `area` method:

```
-(int) area
{
  return [rect area];
}
```

Implementing the remaining methods is left as an exercise for you (see Exercise 5, which follows).

Exercises

1. Extend the `MathOps` category from Program 11.1 to also include an `invert` method, which returns a `Fraction` that is an inversion of the receiver.

2. Add a category to the `Fraction` class called `Comparison`. In this category, add two methods according to these declarations:
   ```
   -(BOOL) isEqualTo: (Fraction *) f;
   -(int) compare: (Fraction *) f;
   ```
   The first method should return `YES` if the two fractions are identical and should return `NO` otherwise. Be careful about comparing fractions (for example, comparing `3/4` to `6/8` should return `YES`).
   The second method should return −1 if the receiver compares less than the fraction represented by the argument, return 0 if the two are equal, and return 1 if the receiver is greater than the argument.

3. Extend the `Fraction` class by adding methods that conform to the informal proto-col `NSComparisonMethods`, as listed earlier in this chapter. Implement the first six methods from that protocol (`isEqualTo:`, `isLessThanOrEqualTo:`, `is-LessThan:`, `isGreaterThanOrEqualTo:`, `isGreaterThan:`, `isNotEqualTo:`) and test them.

4. The functions `sin ()`, `cos ()`, and `tan ()` are part of the Standard Library (as `scanf ()` is). These functions are declared in the header file `<math.h>`, which you should import into your program with the following line:

   ```
   #import <math.h>
   ```

   You can use these functions to calculate the sine, cosine, or tangent, respectively, of their `double` argument, which is expressed in radians. The result is also returned as a double precision floating-point value. So you can use this line to calculate the sine of `d`, with the angle `d` expressed in radians:

   ```
   result = sin (d);
   ```

   Add a category called `Trig` to the `Calculator` class defined in Chapter 6, "Making Decisions." Add methods to this category to calculate the sine, cosine, and tangent based on these declarations:

   ```
   -(double) sin;
   -(double) cos;
   -(double) tan;
   ```

5. Given the discussion on composite objects from this chapter and the following in-terface section:

   ```
   @interface Square: NSObject
   {
       Rectangle *rect;
   }
   -(Square*) initWithSide: (int) s;
   -(void) setSide: (int) s;
   -(int) side;
   -(int) area;
   -(int) perimeter;
   -(void)  dealloc;  // Override to release the Rectangle object's
   memory
   @end
   ```

   write the implementation section for a `Square` and a test program to check its methods.

12

The Preprocessor

The preprocessor provides the tools that enable you to develop programs that are easier to develop, read, modify, and port to different systems. You can also use the preprocessor to literally customize the Objective-C language to suit a particular programming application or your own programming style.

The preprocessor is a part of the Objective-C compilation process that recognizes special statements that can be interspersed throughout a program. As its name implies, the preprocessor actually processes these statements before analysis of the Objective-C program itself takes place. Preprocessor statements are identified by the presence of a pound sign (#), which must be the first nonspace character on the line. As you will see, preprocessor statements have a syntax that is slightly different from that of normal Objective-C statements. We begin by examining the `#define` statement.

The `#define` Statement

One of the primary uses of the `#define` statement is to assign symbolic names to program constants. The preprocessor statement

```
#define  TRUE  1
```

defines the name TRUE and makes it equivalent to the value 1. The name TRUE can subsequently be used anywhere in the program where the constant 1 could be used. Whenever this name appears, the preprocessor automatically substitutes its defined value of 1 into the program. For example, you might have the following Objective-C statement that uses the defined name TRUE:

```
gameOver = TRUE;
```

This statement assigns the value of TRUE to gameOver. You don't need to concern yourself with the actual value you defined for TRUE, but because you do know that you defined it to be 1, the preceding statement would have the effect of assigning 1 to gameOver. The preprocessor statement

```
#define  FALSE  0
```

defines the name FALSE and makes its subsequent use in the program equivalent to specifying the value 0. Therefore, the statement

```
gameOver = FALSE;
```

assigns the value of FALSE to gameOver, and the statement

```
if ( gameOver == FALSE )
    ...
```

compares the value of gameOver against the defined value of FALSE.

A defined name is *not* a variable. Therefore, you cannot assign a value to it unless the
result of substituting the defined value is a variable. Whenever a defined name is used in a
program, the preprocessor automatically substitutes into the program whatever appears to
the right of the defined name in the #define statement. It's analogous to doing a search
and replace with a text editor; in this case, the preprocessor replaces all occurrences of the
defined name with its associated text.

Notice that the #define statement has a special syntax: No equals sign is used to assign
the value 1 to TRUE. Furthermore, a semicolon does *not* appear at the end of the statement. Soon you will understand why this special syntax exists.

#define statements are often placed toward the beginning of the program, after
#import or #include statements. This is not required; they can appear anywhere in the
program. However, a name must be defined before it is referenced by the program. Defined names do not behave like variables: There is no such thing as a local define. After a
name has been defined, it can subsequently be used *anywhere* in the program. Most programmers place their defines inside header files so they can be used by more than one
source file.

As another example of the use of a defined name, suppose you wanted to write two
methods to find the area and circumference of a Circle object. Because both of these
methods need to use the constant π, which is not a particularly easy constant to remember, it might make sense to define the value of this constant once at the start of the program and then use this value where necessary in each method.

So you could include the following in your program:

```
#define PI    3.141592654
```

Then you could use it in your two Circle methods (this assumes that the Circle class
has an instance variable called radius) like this:

```
-(double) area
{
    return PI * radius * radius;
}


-(double) circumference
{
    return 2.0 * PI * radius;
}
```

Assigning a constant to a symbolic name frees you from having to remember the particular constant value every time you want to use it in a program. Furthermore, if you ever need to change the value of the constant (if perhaps you found out that you were using the wrong value, for example), you would have to change the value in only one place in the program: in the #define statement. Without this approach, you would have to search throughout the program and explicitly change the value of the constant whenever it was used.

You might have realized that all the defines shown so far (TRUE, FALSE, and PI) have been written in capital letters. This is done to visually distinguish a defined value from a variable. Some programmers adopt the convention that all defined names be capitalized, so that determining when a name represents a variable or an object, a class name, or a defined name is easy. Another common convention is to prefix the define with the letter *k*. In that case, the following characters of the name are not capitalized. kMaximumValues and kSignificantDigits are examples of two defined names that adhere to this convention.

Using a defined name for a constant value helps make programs more readily extendable. For example, when you learn how to work with arrays, instead of hard-coding in the size of the array you want to allocate, you can define a value as follows:

```
#define MAXIMUM_DATA_VALUES  1000
```

Then you can base all references on the array's size (such as allocation of the array in memory) and valid indexes into this array on this defined value.

Also, if the program were written to use MAXIMUM_DATA_VALUES in all cases where the size of the array was used, the preceding definition could be the only statement in the program that would have to be changed if you later needed to change the array size.

More Advanced Types of Definitions

A definition for a name can include more than a simple constant value. It can include an expression and, as you will see shortly, just about anything else!

The following defines the name TWO_PI as the product of 2.0 and 3.141592654:

```
#define TWO_PI  2.0 * 3.141592654
```

You can subsequently use this defined name anywhere in a program where the expression 2.0 * 3.141592654 would be valid. So you could replace the return statement of the circumference method from the previous example with the following statement:

```
return TWO_PI * radius;
```

Whenever a defined name is encountered in an Objective-C program, everything that appears to the right of the defined name in the #define statement is literally substituted for the name at that point in the program. Thus, when the preprocessor encounters the name TWO_PI in the return statement shown previously, it substitutes for this name whatever appeared in the #define statement for this name. Therefore, the preprocessors literally substitutes `2.0 * 3.141592654` whenever the defined name `TWO_PI` occurs in the program.

The fact that the preprocessor performs a literal text substitution whenever the defined name occurs explains why you don't usually want to end your `#define` statement with a semicolon. If you did, the semicolon would also be substituted into the program wherever the defined name appeared. If you had defined `PI` as

```
#define PI    3.141592654;
```

and then written

```
return 2.0 * PI * r;
```

the preprocessor would replace the occurrence of the defined name `PI` by `3.141592654;`. The compiler would therefore see this statement as

```
return 2.0 * 3.141592654; * r;
```

after the preprocessor had made its substitution, which would result in a syntax error. Remember not to put a semicolon at the end of your define statements unless you're really sure you want one there.

A preprocessor definition does not have to be a valid Objective-C expression in its own right, as long as the resulting expression is valid wherever it is used. For instance, you could set up these definitions:

```
#define AND    &&
#define OR     ||
```

Then you could write expressions such as

```
if ( x > 0 AND x < 10 )
   ...
```

and

```
if ( y == 0 OR y == value )
   ...
```

You could even include a `#define` for the equality test:

```
#define EQUALS  ==
```

Then, you could write the following statement:

```
if ( y EQUALS 0 OR y EQUALS value )
   ...
```

This removes the very real possibility of mistakenly using a single equals sign for the equality test.

Although these examples illustrate the power of the `#define`, you should note that it is commonly considered bad programming practice to redefine the syntax of the underlying language in such a manner. Plus, it makes it harder for someone else to understand your code.

To make things even more interesting, a defined value can itself reference another defined value. So these two #define lines are perfectly valid:

```
#define PI     3.141592654
#define TWO_PI  2.0 * PI
```

The name TWO_PI is defined in terms of the previously defined name PI, thus obviating the need to spell out the value 3.141592654 again.

Reversing the order of the defines, as in this example, is also valid:

```
#define TWO_PI  2.0 * PI
#define PI     3.141592654
```

The rule is that you can reference other defined values in your definitions as long as everything is defined at the time the defined name is used in the program.

Good use of #defines often reduces the need for comments within the program. Consider the following statement:

```
if ( year % 4 == 0 && year % 100 != 0 || year % 400 == 0 )
    ...
```

This expression tests whether the variable year is a leap year. Now consider the following #define statement and the subsequent if statement:

```
#define IS_LEAP_YEAR  year % 4 == 0 && year % 100 != 0 \
                 || year % 400 == 0

    ...
if ( IS_LEAP_YEAR )
    ...
```

Normally, the preprocessor assumes that a definition is contained on a single line of the program. If a second line is needed, the last character on the line must be a backslash character. This character signals a continuation to the preprocessor and is otherwise ignored. The same holds true for more than one continuation line; each line to be continued must end with a backslash character.

The preceding if statement is far easier to understand than the one shown directly before it. No comment is needed because the statement is self-explanatory. Of course, the definition restricts you to testing the variable year to see whether it's a leap year. If would be nice if you could write a definition to see whether any year were a leap year, not just the variable year. Actually, you can write a definition to take one or more arguments, which leads us to our next point of discussion.

IS_LEAP_YEAR can be defined to take an argument called y, as follows:

```
#define IS_LEAP_YEAR(y)  y % 4 == 0 && y % 100 != 0 \
                 || y % 400 == 0
```

Unlike in a method definition, you do not define the type of the argument y here because you are merely performing a literal text substitution—you are not calling a function. Note that when defining a name with arguments, no spaces are permitted between the defined name and the left parenthesis of the argument list.

With the previous definition, you can write a statement such as the following:

```
if ( IS_LEAP_YEAR (year) )
    ...
```

This tests whether the value of `year` is a leap year. Or you could write this to test whether the value of `nextYear` is a leap year:

```
if ( IS_LEAP_YEAR (nextYear) )
    ...
```

In the preceding statement, the definition for `IS_LEAP_YEAR` is directly substituted inside the `if` statement, with the argument `nextYear` replacing `y` wherever it appears in the definition. So the compiler would actually see the `if` statement as follows:

```
if ( nextYear % 4 == 0 && nextYear % 100 != 0 || nextYear % 400 == 0 )
    ...
```

Definitions are frequently called *macros*. This terminology is more often applied to definitions that take one or more arguments.

This macro, called `SQUARE`, simply squares its argument:

```
#define SQUARE(x) x * x
```

Although the macro definition for `SQUARE` is straightforward, you must avoid an interesting pitfall when defining macros. As we have described, the statement

```
y = SQUARE (v);
```

assigns the value of v^2 to `y`. Think about what would happen in the case of the following statement:

```
y = SQUARE (v + 1);
```

This statement does *not* assign the value of $(v + 1)^2$ to `y`, as you would expect. Because the preprocessor performs a literal text substitution of the argument into the macro definition, the preceding expression is actually evaluated as follows:

```
y = v + 1 * v + 1;
```

This obviously does not produce the expected results. To handle this situation properly, parentheses are needed in the definition of the `SQUARE` macro:

```
#define SQUARE(x)  ( (x) * (x) )
```

Even though the previous definition might look strange, remember that the entire expression as given to the `SQUARE` macro is literally substituted wherever `x` appears in the definition. With your new macro definition for `SQUARE`, the statement

```
y = SQUARE (v + 1);
```

is then correctly evaluated as

```
y = ( (v + 1) * (v + 1) );
```

The following macro lets you easily create new fractions from your `Fraction` class on the fly:

```
#define MakeFract(x,y) ([[Fraction alloc] initWith: x over: y])
```

Then you can write expressions such as

```
myFract = MakeFract (1, 3);  // Make the fraction 1/3
```

The conditional expression operator can be particularly handy when defining macros. The following defines a macro called `MAX` that gives the maximum of two values:

```
#define MAX(a,b)  ( ((a) > (b)) ? (a) : (b) )
```

This macro enables you to subsequently write statements such as this:

```
limit = MAX (x + y, minValue);
```

This assigns to `limit` the maximum of `x + y` and `minValue`. Parentheses are placed around the entire `MAX` definition to ensure that an expression such as this is evaluated properly:

```
MAX (x, y) * 100
```

Parentheses are individually placed around each argument to ensure that expressions such as the following are correctly evaluated:

```
MAX (x & y, z)
```

The `&` operator is the bitwise AND operator, and it has lower precedence than the `>` operator used in the macro. Without the parentheses in the macro definition, the `>` operator would be evaluated before the bitwise AND, producing the incorrect result.

The following macro tests whether a character is a lowercase letter:

```
#define IS_LOWER_CASE(x) ( ((x) >= 'a') && ((x) <= 'z') )
```

It thereby permits you to write expressions such as this:

```
if ( IS_LOWER_CASE (c) )
    ...
```

You can even use this macro in another macro definition to convert a character from lower case to upper case, leaving any nonlowercase character unchanged:

```
#define TO_UPPER(x) ( IS_LOWER_CASE (x) ? (x) - 'a' + 'A' : (x) )
```

Again, you are dealing with a standard ASCII character set here. When you learn about Foundation string objects in Part II, you'll see how to perform case conversion that will work for international (Unicode) character sets as well.

The # Operator

If you place a # in front of a parameter in a macro definition, the preprocessor creates a constant C-style string out of the macro argument when the macro is invoked. For example, the definition

```
#define str(x)  # x
```

causes the subsequent invocation

```
str (testing)
```

to be expanded into

```
"testing"
```

by the preprocessor. The `printf` call

```
printf (str (Programming in Objective-C is fun.\n));
```

is therefore equivalent to

```
printf ("Programming in Objective-C is fun.\n");
```

The preprocessor inserts double quotation marks around the actual macro argument. The preprocessor preserves any double quotation marks or backslashes in the argument. So

```
str ("hello")
```

produces

```
"\"hello\""
```

A more practical example of the # operator might be in the following macro definition:

```
#define printint(var)  printf (# var " = %i\n", var)
```

This macro is used to display the value of an integer variable. If `count` is an integer variable with a value of `100`, the statement

```
printint (count);
```

is expanded into this:

```
printf ("count" " = %i\n", count);
```

The compiler concatenates two adjacent literal strings to make a single string. Therefore, after concatenation is performed on the two adjacent strings, the statement becomes the following:

```
printf ("count = %i\n", count);
```

The ## Operator

The ## operator is used in macro definitions to join two tokens. It is preceded (or followed) by the name of a parameter to the macro. The preprocessor takes the actual argument to the macro that is supplied when the macro is invoked and creates a single token out of that argument and whatever token follows (or precedes) the ##.

Suppose, for example, that you have a list of variables x1 through x100. You can write a macro called printx that simply takes as its argument an integer value 1–100 and displays the corresponding x variable, as shown here:

```
#define printx(n)  printf ("%i\n", x ## n)
```

The portion of the define that reads

```
x ## n
```

says to use the tokens that occur before and after the ## (the letter x and the argument n, respectively) and make a single token out of them. So the call

```
printx (20);
```

is expanded into the following:

```
printf ("%i\n", x20);
```

The printx macro can even use the previously defined printint macro to get the variable name as well as its value displayed:

```
#define printx(n)  printint(x ## n)
```

The invocation

```
printx (10);
```

first expands into

```
printint (x10);
```

and then into

```
printf ("x10" " = %i\n", x10);
```

and finally into the following:

```
printf ("x10 = %i\n", x10);
```

The #import Statement

When you have programmed in Objective-C for a while, you will find yourself developing your own set of macros, which you will want to use in each of your programs. But instead of having to type these macros into each new program you write, the preprocessor enables you to collect all your definitions into a separate file and then include them in your program, using the #import statement. These files—similar to the ones you've previously encountered but haven't written yourself—normally end with the characters .h and are referred to as *header* or *include* files.

Suppose you were writing a series of programs for performing various metric conversions. You might want to set up some #define statements for the various constants you would need for performing your conversions:

```
#define INCHES_PER_CENTIMETER  0.394
#define CENTIMETERS_PER_INCH  (1 / INCHES_PER_CENTIMETER)

#define QUARTS_PER_LITER      1.057
#define LITERS_PER_QUART      (1 / QUARTS_PER_LITER)

#define OUNCES_PER_GRAM       0.035
#define GRAMS_PER_OUNCE       (1 / OUNCES_PER_GRAM)
   ...
```

Suppose you entered the previous definitions into a separate file on the system called metric.h. Any program that subsequently needed to use any of the definitions contained in the metric.h file could do so by simply issuing this preprocessor directive:

```
#import "metric.h"
```

This statement must appear before any of the #define statements contained in metric.h are referenced and is typically placed at the beginning of the source file. The preprocessor looks for the specified file on the system and effectively copies the contents of the file into the program at the precise point at which the #import statement appears. So any statements inside the file are treated just as if they had been directly typed into the program at that point.

The double quotation marks around the header filename instruct the preprocessor to look for the specified file in one or more file directories (typically, first in the directory that contains the source file, but the actual places the preprocessor searches can be specified in Xcode by modifying the appropriate Project Settings).

Enclosing the filename within the characters < and > instead, as in

```
#import <Foundation/Foundation.h>
```

causes the preprocessor to look for the include file only in the special "system" header file directory or directories the current directory will not be searched. Again, with Xcode, you can alter these directories by selecting Project, Edit Project Settings from the menu.

> **Note**
>
> When compiling programs for this section of the book, the Foundation.h header file was imported from this directory on my system:
> /Developers/SDKs/MacOSX10.5.sdk/System/Library/Frameworks/Foundation.fr amework/Versions/C/Headers.

To see how include files are used in an actual program example, type the six #define statements given previously into a file called metric.h. Then type and run Program 12.1 in the normal manner.

Program 12.1

```
/* Illustrate the use of the #import statement
   Note: This program assumes that definitions are
   set up in a file called metric.h        */

#import <Foundation/Foundation.h>
#import "metric.h"

int main (int argc, char *argv[])
{
    NSAutoreleasePool * pool = [[NSAutoreleasePool alloc] init];
    float liters, gallons;

    NSLog (@"*** Liters to Gallons ***");
    NSLog (@"Enter the number of liters:");
    scanf ("%f", &liters);

    gallons = liters * QUARTS_PER_LITER / 4.0;
    NSLog (@"%g liters = %g gallons", liters, gallons);

    [pool drain];
    return 0;
}
```

Program 12.1 Output

```
*** Liters to Gallons ***
Enter the number of liters:
55.75
55.75 liters = 14.7319 gallons.
```

Program 12.1 is rather simple because it shows only a single defined value (QUARTS_PER_LITER) being referenced from the include file metric.h. Nevertheless, the point is well made: After the definitions have been entered into metric.h, they can be used in any program that uses an appropriate #import statement.

One of the nicest things about the import file capability is that it enables you to centralize your definitions, thus ensuring that all programs reference the same value. Furthermore, errors discovered in one of the values contained in the include file need be corrected in only that one spot, thus eliminating the need to correct every program that uses the value. Any program that referenced the incorrect value would simply have to be recompiled and would not have to be edited.

Other system include files contain declarations for various functions stored inside the underlying C system library. For example, the file `limits.h` contains system-dependent values that specify the sizes of various characters and integer data types. For instance, the maximum size of an `int` is defined by the name `INT_MAX` inside this file. The maximum size of an `unsigned long int` is defined by `ULONG_MAX`, and so on.

The `float.h` header file gives information about floating-point data types. For example, `FLT_MAX` specifies the maximum floating-point number, and `FLT_DIG` specifies the number of decimal digits of precision for a `float` type.

The file `string.h` contains declarations for the library routines that perform character string operations such as copying, comparing, and concatenating. If you're working with the `Foundation` string classes exclusively (discussed in Chapter 15, "Numbers, Strings, and Collections"), you probably won't need to use any of these routines in your programs.

Conditional Compilation

The Objective-C preprocessor offers a feature known as *conditional compilation.* Conditional compilation is often used to create one program that can be compiled to run on different computer systems. It is also often used to switch on or off various statements in the program, such as debugging statements that print the values of variables or trace the flow of program execution.

The #ifdef, #endif, #else, and #ifndef Statements

Unfortunately, a program sometimes must rely on system-dependent parameters that need to be specified differently on different processors (for example, Power PC versus Intel) or on a particular version of the operating system (for example, Tiger versus Leopard).

If you had a large program that had many such dependencies on the particular hardware and/or software of the computer system (you should minimize this as much as possible), you might end up with many defines whose values would have to be changed when the program was moved to another computer system.

You can help reduce the problem of having to change these defines when the program is moved and can incorporate into the program the values of these defines for each different machine by using the conditional compilation capabilities of the preprocessor. As a simple example, the following statements have the effect of defining `DATADIR` to "/uxn1/data" if the symbol `MAC_OS_X` has been previously defined, and to "\usr\data" otherwise:

```
#ifdef MAC_OS_X
#   define DATADIR  "/uxn1/data"
#else
#   define DATADIR  "\usr\data"
#endif
```

As you can see here, you are allowed to put one or more spaces after the # that begins a preprocessor statement.

The #ifdef, #else, and #endif statements behave as you would expect. If the symbol specified on the #ifdef line has been already defined—through a #define statement or through the command line when the program is compiled—the compiler processes lines that follow up to a #else, #elif, or #endif; otherwise, they are ignored.

To define the symbol POWER_PC to the preprocessor, the statement

```
#define POWER_PC   1
```

or even just

```
#define POWER_PC
```

will suffice. As you can see, no text at all has to appear after the defined name to satisfy the #ifdef test. The compiler also permits you to define a name to the preprocessor when the program is compiled by using a special option to the compiler command. The command line

```
gcc —framework Foundation -D POWER_PC program.m —
```

defines the name POWER_PC to the preprocessor, causing all #ifdef POWER_PC statements inside program.m to evaluate as TRUE (note that you must type the -D POWER_PC before the program name on the command line). This technique enables you to define names without having to edit the source program.

In Xcode, you add new defined names and specify their values by selecting Add User-Defined Setting under Project Settings.

The #ifndef statement follows along the same lines as the #ifdef. This statement is used in a similar way, except that it causes the subsequent lines to be processed if the indicated symbol is *not* defined.

As already mentioned, conditional compilation is useful when debugging programs. You might have many NSLog calls embedded in your program that are used to display intermediate results and trace the flow of execution. You can turn on these statements by conditionally compiling them into the program if a particular name, such as DEBUG, is defined. For example, you could use a sequence of statements such as the following to display the value of some variables only if the program had been compiled with the name DEBUG defined:

```
#ifdef DEBUG
  NSLog (@"User name = %s, id = %i", userName, userId);
#endif
```

You might have many such debugging statements throughout the program. Whenever the program is being debugged, it can be compiled with the DEBUG defined to have all the debugging statements compiled. When the program is working correctly, it can be recompiled without DEBUG defined. This has the added benefit of reducing the size of the program because all your debugging statements are not compiled in.

The #if and #elif Preprocessor Statements

The #if preprocessor statement offers a more general way of controlling conditional compilation. The #if statement can be used to test whether a constant expression evaluates to nonzero. If the result of the expression is nonzero, subsequent lines up to a #else, #elif, or #endif are processed; otherwise, they are skipped.

As an example of how this can be used, the following lines appear in the Foundation header file NSString.h:

```
#if MAC_OS_X_VERSION_MIN_REQUIRED < MAC_OS_X_VERSION_10_5
#define NSMaximumStringLength    (INT_MAX-1)
#endif
```

This tests the value of the defined variable MAC_OS_X_VERSION_MIN_REQUIRED against the defined variable MAC_OS_X_VERSION_10_5. If the former is less than the latter, the #define that follows is processed; otherwise, it is skipped. Presumably, this sets the maximum length of a string to the maximum size of an integer minus 1 if the program is being compiled on MAC OS X 10.5 or later versions.

The special operator

```
defined (name)
```

can also be used in #if statements. This set of preprocessor statements does the same thing:

```
#if defined (DEBUG)
   ...
#endif
```

and

```
#ifdef DEBUG
   ...
#endif
```

The following statements appear in the NSObjcRuntime.h header file for the purpose of defining NS_INLINE (if it's not previously defined) based on the particular compiler that is being used:

```
#if !defined(NS_INLINE)
    #if defined(__GNUC__)
        #define NS_INLINE static __inline__attribute__((always_inline))
    #elif defined(__MWERKS__) || defined(__cplusplus)
        #define NS_INLINE static inline
    #elif defined(_MSC_VER)
        #define NS_INLINE static __inline
    #elif defined(__WIN32__)
        #define NS_INLINE static __inline__
    #endif
#endif
```

Another common use of `#if` is in code sequences that look like this:

```
#if defined (DEBUG) && DEBUG
...
#endif
```

This causes the statements after the `#if` and up to the `#endif` to be processed only if `DEBUG` is defined and has a nonzero value.

The `#undef` Statement

Sometimes you need to cause a defined name to become undefined. You do this with the `#undef` statement. To remove the definition of a particular name, you write the following:

```
#undef name
```

Thus, this statement removes the definition of `POWER_PC`:

```
#undef POWER_PC
```

Subsequent `#ifdef POWER_PC` or `#if defined (POWER_PC)` statements evaluate to `FALSE`.

This concludes our discussion on the preprocessor. Appendix B, "Objective-C Language Summary," describes some other preprocessor statements that we didn't cover here.

Exercises

1. Locate the system header files `limits.h` and `float.h` on your machine. Examine the files to see what's in them. If these files include other header files, be sure to track them down as well, to examine their contents.

2. Define a macro called `MIN` that gives the minimum of two values. Then write a program to test the macro definition.

3. Define a macro called `MAX3` that gives the maximum of three values. Write a program to test the definition.

4. Write a macro called `IS_UPPER_CASE` that gives a nonzero value if a character is an uppercase letter.

5. Write a macro called `IS_ALPHABETIC` that gives a nonzero value if a character is an alphabetic character. Have the macro use the `IS_LOWER_CASE` macro defined in the chapter text and the `IS_UPPER_CASE` macro defined in Exercise 4.

6. Write a macro called `IS_DIGIT` that gives a nonzero value if a character is a digit 0 through 9. Use this macro in the definition of another macro called `IS_SPECIAL`, which gives a nonzero result if a character is a special character (that is, not alphabetic and not a digit). Be sure to use the `IS_ALPHABETIC` macro developed in Exercise 5.

7. Write a macro called ABSOLUTE_VALUE that computes the absolute value of its argument. Make sure that the macro properly evaluates an expression such as this:

   ABSOLUTE_VALUE (x + delta)

8. Consider the definition of the printint macro from this chapter:

   ```
   #define printx(n)   printf ("%i\n", x ## n)
   ```

   Could the following be used to display the values of the 100 variables x1–x100? Why or why not?

   ```
   for ( i = 1; i <= 100; ++i )
     printx (i);
   ```

13

Underlying C Language Features

This chapter describes features of the Objective-C language that you don't necessarily need to know to write Objective-C programs. In fact, most of these come from the underlying C programming language. Features such as functions, structures, pointers, unions, and arrays are best learned on a need-to-know basis. Because C is a procedural language, some of these features go against the grain of object-oriented programming. They can also interfere with some of the strategies implemented by the Foundation framework, such as the memory allocation methodology or work with character strings containing multibyte characters.

> **Note**
>
> There are ways to work with multibyte characters at the C level, but Foundation provides a much more elegant solution with its `NSString` class.

On the other hand, some applications can require you to use a lower-level approach, perhaps for the sake of optimization. If you're working with large arrays of data, for example, you might want to use the built-in data structures of C instead of the array objects of Foundation (which are described in Chapter 15, "Numbers, Strings, and Collections"). Functions also come in handy if used properly to group repetitive operations and modularize a program.

Skim this chapter to get an overview of the material, and come back after you've finished reading Part II, "The Foundation Framework." Or you can skip it altogether and go on to Part II, which covers the Foundation framework. If you end up supporting someone else's code or start digging through some of the Foundation framework header files, you will encounter some of the constructs covered in this chapter. Several of the Foundation data types, such as `NSRange`, `NSPoint`, and `NSRect`, require a rudimentary understanding of structures, which are described here. In such cases, you can return to this chapter and read the appropriate section to gain an understanding of the concepts.

Arrays

The Objective-C language enables the user to define a set of ordered data items known as an *array*. This section describes how to define and manipulate arrays. Later sections illustrate how arrays work together with functions, structures, character strings, and pointers.

Suppose you wanted to read a set of grades into the computer and then perform some operations on these grades, such as rank them in ascending order, compute their average, or find their median. In the process of ranking a set of grades, you cannot perform such an operation until you enter every grade.

In Objective-C, you can define a variable called `grades` that represents not a single value of a grade, but an entire set of grades. You can then reference each element of the set using a number called an *index* number, or *subscript*. Whereas in mathematics a subscripted variable, x_i, refers to the *i*th element x in a set, in Objective-C the equivalent notation is this:

```
x[i]
```

So the expression

```
grades[5]
```

(read as "grades sub 5") refers to element number 5 in the array called `grades`. In Objective-C, array elements begin with the number 0, so

```
grades[0]
```

actually refers to the first element of the array.

You can use an individual array element anywhere that you can use a normal variable. For example, you can assign an array value to another variable with a statement such as this:

```
g = grades[50];
```

This statement assigns the value contained in `grades[50]` to `g`. More generally, if `i` is declared to be an integer variable, the statement

```
g = grades[i];
```

assigns the value contained in element number `i` of the `grades` array to `g`.

A value can be stored in an element of an array simply by specifying the array element on the left side of an equals sign. In the statement

```
grades[100] = 95;
```

the value 95 is stored in element number 100 of the `grades` array.

You can easily sequence through the elements in the array by varying the value of a variable that is used as a subscript into the array. Therefore, the `for` loop

```
for ( i = 0; i < 100; ++i )
    sum += grades[i];
```

sequences through the first 100 elements of the array grades (elements 0–99) and adds the value of each grade into sum. When the for loop is finished, the variable sum contains the total of the first 100 values of the grades array (assuming that sum was set to 0 before the loop was entered).

As with other types of variables, you must declare arrays before you can use them. Declaring an array involves declaring the type of element that will be contained in the array, such as int, float, or an object, as well as the maximum number of elements that will be stored inside the array.

The definition

```
Fraction *fracts [100];
```

defines fracts to be an array containing 100 fractions. You can make valid references to this array by using subscripts 0–99.

The expression

```
fracts[2] = [fracts[0] add: fracts[1]];
```

invokes the Fraction's add: method to add the first two fractions from the fracts array and stores the result in the third location of the array.

Program 13.1 generates a table of the first 15 Fibonacci numbers. Try to predict its output. What relationship exists between each number in the table?

Program 13.1

```
// Program to generate the first 15 Fibonacci numbers
#import <Foundation/Foundation.h>

int main (int argc, char *argv[])
{
    NSAutoreleasePool * pool = [[NSAutoreleasePool alloc] init];
    int Fibonacci[15], i;

    Fibonacci[0] = 0;  /* by definition */
    Fibonacci[1] = 1;  /*   ditto    */

    for ( i = 2; i < 15; ++i )
        Fibonacci[i] = Fibonacci[i-2] + Fibonacci[i-1];

    for ( i = 0; i < 15; ++i )
        NSLog (@"%i", Fibonacci[i]);

    [pool drain];
    return 0;
}
```

Program 13.1 Output

```
0
1
1
2
3
5
8
13
21
34
55
89
144
233
377
```

The first two Fibonacci numbers, which we call F_0 and F_1, are defined to be 0 and 1, respectively. Thereafter, each successive Fibonacci number F_i is defined to be the sum of the two preceding Fibonacci numbers F_{i-2} and F_{i-1}. So F_2 is calculated by adding the values of F_0 and F_1. In the preceding program, this corresponds directly to calculating Fibonacci[2] by adding the values Fibonacci[0] and Fibonacci[1]. This calculation is performed inside the for loop, which calculates the values of F_2–F_{14} (or, equivalently, Fibonacci[2] through Fibonacci[14]).

Initializing Array Elements

Just as you can assign initial values to variables when they are declared, you can assign initial values to the elements of an array. This is done by simply listing the initial values of the array, starting from the first element. Values in the list are separated by commas, and the entire list is enclosed in a pair of braces.

The statement

```
int integers[5] = { 0, 1, 2, 3, 4 };
```

sets the value of integers[0] to 0, integers[1] to 1, integers[2] to 2, and so on.

Arrays of characters are initialized in a similar manner; thus, the statement

```
char letters[5] = { 'a', 'b', 'c', 'd', 'e' };
```

defines the character array letters and initializes the five elements to the characters 'a', 'b', 'c', 'd', and 'e', respectively.

You don't have to completely initialize an entire array. If fewer initial values are specified, only an equal number of elements are initialized; the remaining values in the array are set to zero. Thus, the declaration

```
float sample_data[500] = { 100.0, 300.0, 500.5 };
```

initializes the first three values of `sample_data` to 100.0, 300.0, and 500.5 and sets the remaining 497 elements to 0.

By enclosing an element number in a pair of brackets, you can initialize specific array elements in any order. For example,

```
int x = 1233;
int a[] = { [9] = x + 1, [2] = 3, [1] = 2, [0] = 1 };
```

defines a 10-element array called a (based on the highest index in the array) and initializes the last element to the value of x + 1 (1234). In addition, it initializes the first three elements to 1, 2, and 3, respectively.

Character Arrays

Program 13.2 illustrates how you can use a character array. However, one point is worthy of discussion. Can you spot it?

Program 13.2

```
#import <Foundation/Foundation.h>

int main (int argc, char *argv[])
{
    NSAutoreleasePool * pool = [[NSAutoreleasePool alloc] init];
    char word[] = { 'H', 'e', 'l', 'l', 'o', '!' };
    int  i;

    for ( i = 0; i < 6; ++i )
        NSLog (@"%c", word[i]);

    [pool drain];
    return 0;
}
```

Program 13.2 Output

```
H
e
l
l
o
!
```

The most notable point in the preceding program is the declaration of the character array word. The array makes no mention of the number of elements. The Objective-C language enables you to define an array without specifying the number of elements. In this case, the size of the array is determined automatically based on the number of initialization elements. Because Program 13.2 has six initial values listed for the array word, the Objective-C language implicitly dimensions the array to six elements.

This approach works fine as long as you initialize every element in the array at the point that the array is defined. If this is not to be the case, you must explicitly dimension the array.

If you put a terminating null character ('\0') at the end of a character array, you create what is often called a *character string*. If you substituted the initialization of word in Program 13.2 with this line

```
char word[] = { 'H', 'e', 'l', 'l', 'o', '!', '\0' };
```

you could have subsequently displayed the string with a single NSLog call, like this:

```
NSLog (@"%s", word);
```

This works because the %s format characters tell NSLog to keep displaying characters until a terminating null character is reached. That's the character you put at the end of your word array.

Multidimensional Arrays

The types of arrays you've seen thus far are all linear arrays—that is, they all deal with a single dimension. The language enables you to define arrays of any dimension. This section takes a look at two-dimensional arrays.

One of the most natural applications for a two-dimensional array arises in the case of a matrix. Consider the 4×5 matrix shown here:

10	5	–3	17	82
9	0	0	8	–7
32	20	1	0	14
0	0	8	7	6

In mathematics, an element of a matrix commonly is referred to by using a double subscript. If the preceding matrix were called M, the notation $M_{i,j}$ would refer to the element in the ith row, jth column, where i ranges from 1 through 4 and j ranges from 1 through 5. The notation $M_{3,2}$ would refer to the value 20, which is found in the third row, second column of the matrix. In a similar fashion, $M_{4,5}$ would refer to the element contained in the fourth row, fifth column (the value 6).

In Objective-C, an analogous notation is used when referring to elements of a two-dimensional array. However, because Objective-C likes to start numbering things at 0, the first row of the matrix is actually row 0 and the first column of the matrix is column 0. The preceding matrix would then have row and column designations as shown in the following diagram:

Row (i)	Column (j)				
	0	**1**	**2**	**3**	**4**
0	10	5	−3	17	82
1	9	0	0	8	−7
2	32	20	1	0	14
3	0	0	8	7	6

Whereas in mathematics the notation $M_{i,j}$ is used, in Objective-C the equivalent notation is as follows:

```
M[i][j]
```

Remember, the first index number refers to the row number, whereas the second index number references the column. Therefore, the statement

```
sum = M[0][2] + M[2][4];
```

adds the value contained in row 0, column 2 (which is -3) to the value contained in row 2, column 4 (which is 14) and assigns the result of 11 to the variable sum.

Two-dimensional arrays are declared the same way that one-dimensional arrays are; thus,

```
int M[4][5];
```

declares the array M to be a two-dimensional array consisting of 4 rows and 5 columns, for a total of 20 elements. Each position in the array is defined to contain an integer value.

Two-dimensional arrays can be initialized in a manner analogous to their one-dimensional counterparts. When listing elements for initialization, the values are listed by row. Brace pairs are used to separate the list of initializers for one row from the next. Thus, to define and initialize the array M to the elements listed in the preceding table, you can use a statement such as the following:

```
int M[4][5] = {
              { 10, 5, -3, 17, 82 },
              { 9, 0, 0, 8, -7 },
              { 32, 20, 1, 0, 14 },
              { 0, 0, 8, 7, 6 }
      };
```

Pay particular attention to the syntax of the previous statement. Note that commas are required after each brace that closes off a row, except in the case of the last row. The use of the inner pairs of braces is actually optional. If these aren't supplied, initialization proceeds by row. Therefore, the previous statement could also have been written as follows:

```
int M[4][5] = { 10, 5, -3, 17, 82, 9, 0, 0, 8, -7, 32,
              20, 1, 0, 14, 0, 0, 8, 7, 6 };
```

As with one-dimensional arrays, the entire array need not be initialized. A statement such as the following initializes only the first three elements of each row of the matrix to the indicated values:

```
int M[4][5] = {
        { 10, 5, -3 },
        { 9, 0, 0 },
        { 32, 20, 1 },
        { 0, 0, 8 }
    };
```

The remaining values are set to 0. Note that, in this case, the inner pairs of braces are required to force the correct initialization. Without them, the first two rows and the first two elements of the third row would have been initialized instead. (Verify for yourself that this would be the case.)

Functions

The NSLog routine is an example of a function that you have used in every program so far. Indeed, every program also has used a function called main. Let's go back to the first program you wrote (Program 2.1), which displayed the phrase "Programming is fun." at the terminal:

```
#import <Foundation/Foundation.h>

int main (int argc, char *argv[])
{
    NSAutoreleasePool * pool = [[NSAutoreleasePool alloc] init];

    NSLog (@"Programming is fun.");
    [pool drain];
    return 0;
}
```

This function, called printMessage, produces the same output:

```
void printMessage (void)
{
    NSLog (@"Programming is fun.");
}
```

The only difference between printMessage and the function main from Program 2.1 is the first line. The first line of a function definition tells the compiler four things about the function:

- Who can call it
- The type of value it returns
- Its name
- The number and type of arguments it takes

The first line of the `printMessage` function definition tells the compiler that `printMessage` is the name of the function and that it returns no value (the first use of the keyword `void`). Unlike methods, you don't put the function's return type inside a set of parentheses. In fact, you get a compiler error message if you do.

After telling the compiler that `printMessage` doesn't return a value, the second use of the keyword `void` says that it takes no arguments.

Recall that `main` is a specially recognized name in the Objective-C system that always indicates where the program is to begin execution. There always must be a `main`. So you can add a `main` function to the preceding code to end up with a complete program, as shown in Program 13.3.

Program 13.3

```
#import <Foundation/Foundation.h>


void printMessage (void)
{
   NSLog (@"Programming is fun.");
}

int main (int argc, char *argv[])
{
   NSAutoreleasePool * pool = [[NSAutoreleasePool alloc] init];

   printMessage ();
   [pool drain];
   return 0;
}
```

Program 13.3 Output

```
Programming is fun.
```

Program 13.3 consists of two functions: `printMessage` and `main`. As mentioned earlier, the idea of calling a function is not new. Because `printMessage` takes no arguments, you call it simply by listing its name followed by a pair of open and close parentheses.

Arguments and Local Variables

In Chapter 5, "Program Looping," you developed programs for calculating triangular numbers. Here you define a function to generate a triangular number and call it, appropriately enough, `calculateTriangularNumber`. As an argument to the function, you specify which triangular number to calculate. The function then calculates the desired number and displays the results. Program 13.4 shows the function to accomplish the task and a `main` routine to try it.

Program 13.4

```
#import <Foundation/Foundation.h>


// Function to calculate the nth triangular number

void calculateTriangularNumber (int n)
{
   int i, triangularNumber = 0;

   for ( i = 1; i <= n; ++i )
       triangularNumber += i;

   NSLog (@"Triangular number %i is %i", n, triangularNumber);
}

int main (int argc, char *argv[])
{
    NSAutoreleasePool * pool = [[NSAutoreleasePool alloc] init];

    calculateTriangularNumber (10);
    calculateTriangularNumber (20);
    calculateTriangularNumber (50);

    [pool drain];
    return 0;
}
```

Program 13.4 Output
```
Triangular number 10 is 55
Triangular number 20 is 210
Triangular number 50 is 1275
```

The first line of the `calculateTriangularNumber` function is this:

```
void calculateTriangularNumber (int n)
```

It tells the compiler that `calculateTriangularNumber` is a function that returns no value (the keyword `void`) and that it takes a single argument, called n, which is an `int`. Note again that you can't put the argument type inside parentheses, as you are accustomed to doing when you write methods.

The opening curly brace indicates the beginning of the function's definition. Because you want to calculate the *n*th triangular number, you must set up a variable to store the value of the triangular number as it is being calculated. You also need a variable to act as your loop index. The variables `TriangularNumber` and `i` are defined for these purposes and are declared to be of type `int`. You define and initialize these variables in the same manner that you defined and initialized your variables inside the `main` routine in previous programs.

Local variables in functions behave the same way they do in methods: If an initial value is given to a variable inside a function, that initial value is assigned to the variable each time the function is called.

Variables defined inside a function (as in methods) are known as *automatic local* variables because they are automatically "created" each time the function is called and their values are local to the function.

Static local variables are declared with the keyword `static`, retain their values through function calls, and have default initial values of 0.

The value of a local variable can be accessed only by the function in which the variable is defined. Its value cannot be directly accessed from outside the function.

Returning to our program example, after the local variables have been defined, the function calculates the triangular number and displays the results at the terminal. The closed brace then defines the end of the function.

Inside the `main` routine, the value 10 is passed as the argument in the first call to `calculateTriangularNumber`. Execution then transfers directly to the function where the value 10 becomes the value of the formal parameter n inside the function. The function then calculates the value of the 10th triangular number and displays the result.

The next time `calculateTriangularNumber` is called, the argument 20 is passed. In a similar process, as described earlier, this value becomes the value of n inside the function. The function then calculates the value of the 20th triangular number and displays the answer.

Returning Function Results

As with methods, a function can return a value. The type of value returned with the `return` statement must be consistent with the return type declared for the function. A function declaration that starts like this

```
float kmh_to_mph (float km_speed)
```

begins the definition of a function `kmh_to_mph`, which takes one `float` argument called `km_speed` and returns a floating-point value. Similarly,

```
int gcd (int u, int v)
```

defines a function called `gcd` with integer arguments u and v and returns an integer value.

Let's rewrite the greatest common divisor algorithm used in Program 5.7 in function form. The two arguments to the function are the two numbers whose greatest common divisor (`gcd`) you want to calculate (see Program 13.5).

Program 13.5

```
#import <Foundation/Foundation.h>

// This function finds the greatest common divisor of two
//  nonnegative integer values and returns the result
```

```
int gcd (int u, int v)
{
    int temp;

    while ( v != 0 )
    {
        temp = u % v;
        u = v;
        v = temp;
    }

    return u;
}

main ()
{
    NSAutoreleasePool * pool = [[NSAutoreleasePool alloc] init];
    int result;

    result = gcd (150, 35);
    NSLog (@"The gcd of 150 and 35 is %i", result);

    result = gcd (1026, 405);
    NSLog (@"The gcd of 1026 and 405 is %i", result);

    NSLog (@"The gcd of 83 and 240 is %i", gcd (83, 240));
    [pool drain];
    return 0;
}
```

Program 13.5 Output
```
The gcd of 150 and 35 is 5
The gcd of 1026 and 405 is 27
The gcd of 83 and 240 is 1
```

The function gcd is defined to take two integer arguments. The function refers to these arguments through their formal parameter names: u and v. After declaring the variable temp to be of type int, the program displays the values of the arguments u and v, together with an appropriate message at the terminal. The function then calculates and returns the greatest common divisor of the two integers.

The statement

```
result = gcd (150, 35);
```

says to call the function gcd with the arguments 150 and 35, and to store the value that this function returns in the variable result.

If the return type declaration for a function is omitted, the compiler assumes that the function will return an integer—if it returns a value at all. Many programmers take advantage of this fact and omit the return type declaration for functions that return integers. However, this is a bad programming habit that you should avoid. The compiler will warn you that the return type defaults to `int`, which is an indication that you're doing something wrong!

The default return type for functions differs from that for methods. Recall that, if no return type is specified for a method, the compiler assumes that it returns a value of type `id`. Again, you should always declare the return type for a method instead of relying on this fact.

Declaring Return Types and Argument Types

We mentioned earlier that the Objective-C compiler assumes that a function returns a value of type `int` as the default case. More specifically, whenever a call is made to a function, the compiler assumes that the function returns a value of type `int` unless either of the following has occurred:

- The function has been defined in the program before the function call is encountered.
- The value returned by the function has been declared before the function call is encountered. Declaring the return and argument types for a function is known as a *prototype* declaration.

The function declaration not only is used to declare the function's return type, but it also is used to tell the compiler how many arguments the function takes and what their types are. This is analogous to declaring methods inside the `@interface` section when defining a new class.

To declare `absoluteValue` as a function that returns a value of type `float` and that takes a single argument, also of type `float`, you could use the following prototype declaration:

```
float absoluteValue (float);
```

As you can see, you have to specify just the argument type inside the parentheses, not its name. You can optionally specify a "dummy" name after the type, if you like:

```
float absoluteValue (float x);
```

This name doesn't have to be the same as the one used in the function definition—the compiler ignores it anyway.

A foolproof way to write a prototype declaration is to simply make a copy of the first line from the actual definition of the function. Remember to place a semicolon at the end.

If the function takes a variable number of arguments (such as is the case with `NSLog` and `scanf`), the compiler must be informed. The declaration

```
void NSLog (NSString *format, ...);
```

tells the compiler that `NSLog` takes an `NSString` object as its first argument and is followed by any number of additional arguments (the use of the `...`). `NSLog` is declared in the special file `Foundation/Foundation.h`[1], which is why you have been placing the following line at the start of each of your programs:

```
#import <Foundation/Foundation.h>
```

Without this line, the compiler can assume that `NSLog` takes a fixed number of arguments, which can result in incorrect code being generated.

The compiler automatically converts your numeric arguments to the appropriate types when a function is called only if you have placed the function's definition or have declared the function and its argument types before the call.

Consider some reminders and suggestions about functions:

- By default, the compiler assumes that a function returns an `int`.
- When defining a function that returns an `int`, define it as such.
- When defining a function that doesn't return a value, define it as `void`.
- The compiler converts your arguments to agree with the ones the function expects only if you have previously defined or declared the function.

To be safe, declare all functions in your program, even if they are defined before they are called. (You might decide later to move them someplace else in your file or even to another file.) A good strategy is to put your function declarations inside a header file and then just import that file into your modules.

Functions are *external* by default. That is, the default scope for a function is that it can be called by any functions or methods contained in any files that are linked with the function. You can limit the scope of a function by making it static. You do this by placing the keyword `static` in front of the function declaration, as shown here:

```
static int gcd (int u, int v)
{
    ...
}
```

A static function can be called only by other functions or methods that appear in the same file that contains the function's definition.

Functions, Methods, and Arrays

To pass a single array element to a function or method, you specify the array element as an argument in the normal fashion. So if you had a `squareRoot` function to calculate square roots and wanted to take the square root of `averages[i]` and assign the result to a variable called `sq_root_result`, a statement such as this one would work:

```
sq_root_result = squareRoot (averages[i]);
```

---

[1] Technically speaking, its defined in the file `NSObjCRuntime.h`, which is imported from inside the file `Foundation.h`

Passing an entire array to a function or method is an entirely new ballgame. To pass an array, you need to list only the name of the array, without any subscripts, inside the call to the function or method invocation. As an example, if you assume that `grade_scores` has been declared as an array containing 100 elements, the expression

```
minimum (grade_scores)
```

passes the entire 100 elements contained in the array `grade_scores` to the function called `minimum`. Naturally, the `minimum` function must be expecting an entire array to be passed as an argument and must make the appropriate formal parameter declaration.

This function finds the minimum integer value in an array containing a specified number of elements:

```
// Function to find the minimum in an array

int minimum (int values[], int numElements)
{
    int minValue, i;

    minValue = values[0];

    for ( i = 1; i < numElements; ++i )
        if ( values[i] < minValue )
            minValue = values[i];

    return (minValue);
}
```

The function `minimum` is defined to take two arguments: first, the array whose minimum you want to find and, second, the number of elements in the array. The open and close brackets that immediately follow `values` in the function header inform the Objective-C compiler that `values` is an array of integers. The compiler doesn't care how large it is.

The formal parameter `numElements` serves as the upper limit inside the `for` statement. Thus, the `for` statement sequences through the array from `values[1]` through the last element of the array, which is `values[numElements - 1]`.

If a function or method changes the value of an array element, that change is made to the original array that was passed to the function or method. This change remains in effect even after the function or method has completed execution.

The reason an array behaves differently from a simple variable or an array element—whose value a function or method cannot change—is worthy of a bit of explanation. We stated that when a function or method is called, the values passed as arguments are copied into the corresponding formal parameters. This statement is still valid. However, when dealing with arrays, the entire contents of the array are not copied into the formal parameter array. Instead, a pointer is passed indicating where in the computer's memory the array is located. So any changes made to the formal parameter array are actually made to the original array, not to a copy of the array. Therefore, when the function or method returns, these changes remain in effect.

Multidimensional Arrays

You can pass a multidimensional array element to a function or method just as any ordinary variable or single-dimensional array element can. The statement

```
result = squareRoot (matrix[i][j]);
```

calls the `squareRoot` function, passing the value contained in `matrix[i][j]` as the argument.

You can pass an entire multidimensional array as an argument the same way you do with a single-dimensional array: You simply list the name of the array. For example, if the matrix `measuredValues` is declared to be a two-dimensional array of integers, you can use the Objective-C statement

```
scalarMultiply (measuredValues, constant);
```

to invoke a function that multiplies each element in the matrix by the value of `constant`. This implies, of course, that the function itself can change the values contained inside the `measuredValues` array. The discussion pertaining to this topic for single-dimensional arrays also applies here: An assignment made to any element of the formal parameter array inside the function makes a permanent change to the array that was passed to the function.

We mentioned that, when declaring a single-dimensional array as a formal parameter, you don't need the actual dimension of the array. You simply use a pair of empty brackets to inform the Objective-C compiler that the parameter is an array. This does not totally apply in the case of multidimensional arrays. For a two-dimensional array, you can omit the number of rows in the array, but the declaration must contain the number of columns in the array. The declarations

```
int arrayValues[100][50]
```

and

```
int arrayValues[][50]
```

are both valid declarations for a formal parameter array called `arrayValues` that contains 100 rows by 50 columns. However, the declarations

```
int arrayValues[100][]
```

and

```
int arrayValues[][]
```

are not valid because you must specify the number of columns in the array.

Structures

The Objective-C language provides another tool besides arrays for grouping elements. You also can use *structures*, which form the basis for the discussions in this section.

Suppose you wanted to store a date—say, 7/18/09—inside a program, perhaps to be used for the heading of some program output or even for computational purposes. A natural method for storing the date is to simply assign the month to an integer variable called month, the day to an integer variable day, and the year to an integer variable year. So the statements

```
int month = 7, day = 18, year = 2009;
```

would work just fine. This is a totally acceptable approach. But what if your program also needed to store several dates? It would be much better to somehow group these sets of three variables.

You can define a structure called date in the Objective-C language that consists of three components that represent the month, day, and year. The syntax for such a definition is rather straightforward:

```
struct date
{
    int month;
    int day;
    int year;
};
```

The date structure just defined contains three integer members, called month, day, and year. Essentially, the definition of date defines a new type in the language, in that variables can subsequently be declared to be of type struct date, as in the following definition:

```
struct date today;
```

You can also define a variable called purchaseDate to be of the same type with a separate definition:

```
struct date purchaseDate;
```

Or you can simply include the two definitions on the same line:

```
struct date today, purchaseDate;
```

Unlike variables of type int, float, or char, a special syntax is needed when dealing with structure variables. A member of a structure is accessed by specifying the variable name, followed by a period (called the *dot operator*) and then the member name. For example, to set the value of day in the variable today to 21, you would write this:

```
today.day = 21;
```

Note that no spaces are permitted between the variable name, the period, and the member name.

Now, wait a second! Wasn't this the same operator we used to invoke an property on an object? Recall that we could write the statement

```
myRect.width = 12;
```

to invoke the `Rectangle` object's setter method (called `setWidth`), passing it the argument value of 12. No confusion arises here: The compiler determines whether it's a structure or an object to the left of the dot operator and handles the situation properly.

Returning to the `struct date` example, to set `year` in `today` to 2010, you can use this expression:

```
today.year = 2010;
```

Finally, to test the value of `month` to see whether it is equal to 12, you can use a statement such as this:

```
if ( today.month == 12 )
    next_month = 1;
```

Program 13.6 incorporates the preceding discussions into an actual program.

Program 13.6

```
#import <Foundation/Foundation.h>

int main (int argc, char *argv[])
{
    NSAutoreleasePool * pool = [[NSAutoreleasePool alloc] init];

    struct date
    {
        int month;
        int day;
        int year;
    };

    struct date today;

    today.month = 9;
    today.day = 25;
    today.year = 2009;

    NSLog (@"Today's date is %i/%i/%.2i.", today.month,
            today.day, today.year % 100);

    [pool drain];
    return 0;
}
```

Program 13.6 Output

```
Today's date is 9/25/09.
```

The first statement inside `main` defines the structure called `date` to consist of three integer members, called `month`, `day`, and `year`. In the second statement, the variable `today` is declared to be of type `struct date`. So the first statement simply defines what a `date` structure looks like to the Objective-C compiler and causes no storage to be reserved inside the computer. The second statement declares a variable to be of type `struct date` and, therefore, does reserve memory for storing the three integer members of the structure variable `today`.

After the assignments, an appropriate `NSLog` call displays the values contained inside the structure. The remainder of `today.year` divided by 100 is calculated before being passed to the `NSLog` function so that just `09` displays for the year. The `%.2i` format characters in the `NSLog` call specify a minimum of two characters to be displayed, thus forcing the display of the leading zero for the year.

When it comes to the evaluation of expressions, structure members follow the same rules as ordinary variables in the Objective-C language. Division of an integer structure member by another integer is performed as an integer division, as shown here:

```
century = today.year / 100 + 1;
```

Suppose you wanted to write a simple program that accepted today's date as input and displayed tomorrow's date to the user. At first glance, this seems a perfectly simple task to perform. You can ask the user to enter today's date and then calculate tomorrow's date by a series of statements, like so:

```
tomorrow.month = today.month;
tomorrow.day  = today.day + 1;
tomorrow.year = today.year;
```

Of course, the previous statements would work fine for most dates, but the following two cases would not be properly handled:

- If today's date fell at the end of a month
- If today's date fell at the end of a year (that is, if today's date were December 31)

One way to easily determine whether today's date falls at the end of a month is to set up an array of integers that corresponds to the number of days in each month. A lookup inside the array for a particular month then gives the number of days in that month (see Program 13.7).

Program 13.7

```
// Program to determine tomorrow's date

#import <Foundation/Foundation.h>

struct date
{
```

```
      int month;
      int day;
      int year;
};

// Function to calculate tomorrow's date

struct date dateUpdate (struct date today)
{
    struct date tomorrow;
    int numberOfDays (struct date d);

    if ( today.day != numberOfDays (today) )
    {
        tomorrow.day = today.day + 1;
        tomorrow.month = today.month;
        tomorrow.year = today.year;
    }
    else if ( today.month == 12 )    // end of year
    {
        tomorrow.day = 1;
        tomorrow.month = 1;
        tomorrow.year = today.year + 1;
    }
    else
    {                       // end of month
        tomorrow.day = 1;
        tomorrow.month = today.month + 1;
        tomorrow.year = today.year;
    }

    return (tomorrow);
}

// Function to find the number of days in a month

int numberOfDays (struct date d)
{
    int answer;
    BOOL isLeapYear (struct date d);
    int daysPerMonth[12] =
        { 31, 28, 31, 30, 31, 30, 31, 31, 30, 31, 30, 31 };

    if ( isLeapYear (d) == YES && d.month == 2 )
        answer = 29;
    else
        answer = daysPerMonth[d.month - 1];
```

```
    return (answer);
}

// Function to determine if it's a leap year

BOOL isLeapYear (struct date d)
{
 if ( (d.year % 4 == 0 && d.year % 100 != 0) ||
        d.year % 400 == 0 )
    return YES;
 else
    return NO;
}

int main (int argc, char *argv[])
{
    NSAutoreleasePool * pool = [[NSAutoreleasePool alloc] init];
    struct date dateUpdate (struct date today);
    struct date thisDay, nextDay;

    NSLog (@"Enter today's date (mm dd yyyy): ");
    scanf ("%i%i%i", &thisDay.month, &thisDay.day,
            &thisDay.year);

    nextDay = dateUpdate (thisDay);

    NSLog (@"Tomorrow's date is %i/%i/%.2i.",nextDay.month,
            nextDay.day, nextDay.year % 100);

    [pool drain];
    return 0;
}
```

Program 13.7 Output

```
Enter today's date (mm dd yyyy):
2 28 2012
Tomorrow's date is 2/29/12.
```

Program 13.7 Output (Rerun)

```
Enter today's date (mm dd yyyy):
10 2 2009
Tomorrow's date is 10/3/09.
```

Program 13.7 Output (Rerun)

```
Enter today's date (mm dd yyyy):
12 31 2010
Tomorrow's date is 1/1/10.
```

Even though you're not working with any classes in this program, the file Foundation.h was imported because you wanted to use the BOOL type and the defines YES and NO. They're defined in that file.

Notice that the definition of the date structure appears first and outside of any function. This is because structure definitions behave much like variables: If a structure is defined within a particular function, only that function knows of its existence. This is a *local* structure definition. If you define the structure outside any function, that definition is *global*. A global structure definition enables any variables that are subsequently defined in the program (either inside or outside a function) to be declared as that structure type. Structure definitions that more than one file share are typically centralized in a header file and then imported into the files that want to use the structure.

Inside the main routine, the declaration

```
struct date dateUpdate (struct date today);
```

tells the compiler that the dateUpdate function takes a date structure as its argument and returns one as well. You don't need the declaration here because the compiler has already seen the actual function definition earlier in the file. However, it's still good programming practice. For example, if you subsequently separated the function definition and main into separate source files, the declaration would be necessary.

As with ordinary variables—and unlike arrays—any changes that the function makes to the values contained in a structure argument have no effect on the original structure. They affect only the copy of the structure that is created when the function is called.

After a date has been entered and stored inside the date structure variable thisDay, the dateUpdate function is called like this:

```
nextDay = dateUpdate (thisDay);
```

This statement calls dateUpdate, passing it the value of the date structure thisDay.

Inside the dateUpdate function, the prototype declaration

```
int numberOfDays (struct date d);
```

informs the Objective-C compiler that the numberOfDays function returns an integer value and takes a single argument of type struct date.

The statement

```
if ( today.day != numberOfDays (today) )
```

specifies that the structure `today` is to be passed as an argument to the `numberOfDays` function. Inside that function, the appropriate declaration must be made to inform the system that a structure is expected as an argument, like so:

```
int numberOfDays (struct date d)
```

The `numberOfDays` function begins by determining whether it is a leap year and whether the month is February. The former determination is made by calling another function called `isLeapYear`.

The `isLeapYear` function is straightforward enough; it simply tests the year contained in the `date` structure given as its argument and returns `YES` if it is a leap year and `NO` if it is not.

Make sure that you understand the hierarchy of function calls in Program 13.7: The `main` function calls `dateUpdate`, which calls `numberOfDays`, which itself calls the function `isLeapYear`.

Initializing Structures

Initializing structures is similar to initializing arrays—the elements are simply listed inside a pair of braces, with a comma separating each element.

To initialize the `date` structure variable `today` to July 2, 2011, you can use this statement:

```
struct date today = { 7, 2, 2011 };
```

As with the initialization of an array, fewer values can be listed than the structure contains. So the statement

```
struct date today = { 7 };
```

sets `today.month` to 7 but gives no initial value to `today.day` or `today.year`. In such a case, their default initial values are undefined.

Specific members can be designated for initialization in any order with the notation

```
.member = value
```

in the initialization list, as in

```
struct date today = { .month = 7, .day = 2, .year = 2011 };
```

and

```
struct date today = { .year = 2011 };
```

The last statement just sets the year in the structure to 2011. As you know, the other two members are undefined.

Arrays of Structures

Working with arrays of structures is pretty straightforward. The definition

```
struct date birthdays[15];
```

defines the array `birthdays` to contain 15 elements of type `struct date`. Referencing a particular structure element inside the array is quite natural. To set the second birthday inside the `birthdays` array to February 22, 1996, this sequence of statements works:

```
birthdays[1].month = 2;
birthdays[1].day   = 22;
birthdays[1].year = 1996;
```

The statement

```
n = numberOfDays (birthdays[0]);
```

sends the first date in the array to the `numberOfDays` function to find out how many days are contained in the month that date specifies.

Structures Within Structures

Objective-C provides an enormous amount of flexibility in defining structures. For instance, you can define a structure that itself contains other structures as one or more of its members, or you can define structures that contain arrays.

You have seen how to logically group the month, day, and year into a structure called `date`. Suppose you had an analogous structure called `time` that you used to group the hour, minutes, and seconds representing a time. In some applications, you might need to logically group both a date and a time. For example, you might need to set up a list of events that are to occur at a particular date and time.

The previous discussion implies that you want to have a convenient means of associating both the date and the time. You can do this in Objective-C by defining a new structure (perhaps called `date_and_time`) that contains as its members two elements: the date and the time:

```
struct date_and_time
{
    struct date  sdate;
    struct time  stime;
};
```

The first member of this structure is of type `struct date` and is called `sdate`, and the second member of the `date_and_time` structure is of type `struct time` and is called `stime`. This definition of a `date_and_time` structure requires that a `date` structure and a `time` structure be previously defined to the compiler.

Variables can now be defined as type `struct date_and_time`:

```
struct date_and_time event;
```

To reference the `date` structure of the variable `event`, the syntax is the same:

```
event.sdate
```

Therefore, you could call your dateUpdate function with this date as the argument and assign the result back to the same place by a statement, like so:

```
event.sdate = dateUpdate (event.sdate);
```

You can do the same with the time structure contained within your date_and_time structure:

```
event.stime = timeUpdate (event.stime);
```

To reference a particular member inside one of these structures, add a period followed by the member name to the end:

```
event.sdate.month = 10;
```

This statement sets the month of the date structure contained within event to October, and the statement

```
++event.stime.seconds;
```

adds 1 to the seconds contained within the time structure.

You can initialize the event variable in the expected manner:

```
struct date_and_time event =
    { { 12, 17, 1989 }, { 3, 30, 0 } };
```

This sets the date in the variable event to December 17, 1989, and sets the time to 3:30:00.

Naturally, you can set up an array of date_and_time structures, as is done with the following declaration:

```
struct date_and_time events[100];
```

The array events is declared to contain 100 elements of type struct date_and_time. The 4th date_and_time contained within the array is referenced in the usual way as events[3], and the 25th date in the array can be sent to your dateUpdate function as follows:

```
events[24].sdate = dateUpdate (events[24].sdate);
```

To set the first time in the array to noon, you can use the following series of statements:

```
events[0].stime.hour    = 12;
events[0].stime.minutes = 0;
events[0].stime.seconds = 0;
```

Additional Details About Structures

We should mention that you have some flexibility in defining a structure. First, you can declare a variable to be of a particular structure type at the same time that the structure is defined. You do this simply by including the variable name(s) before the terminating semicolon of the structure definition. For example, the following statement defines the structure date and also declares the variables todaysDate and purchaseDate to be of this type:

```
struct date
{
    int month;
    int day;
    int year;
} todaysDate, purchaseDate;
```

You can also assign initial values to the variables in the normal fashion. Thus, the following defines the structure date and the variable todaysDate with initial values as indicated:

```
struct date
{
    int month;
    int day;
    int year;
} todaysDate = { 9, 25, 2010 };
```

If all the variables of a particular structure type are defined when the structure is defined, you can omit the structure name. So the following statement defines an array called dates to consist of 100 elements:

```
struct
{
    int month;
    int day;
    int year;
} dates[100];
```

Each element is a structure containing three integer members: month, day, and year. Because you did not supply a name to the structure, the only way to subsequently declare variables of the same type is to explicitly define the structure again.

Bit Fields

Two methods in Objective-C can pack information together. One way is to simply represent the data inside an integer and then access the desired bits of the integer using the bit operators described in Chapter 4, "Data Types and Expressions."

Another way is to define a structure of packed information using an Objective-C construct known as a *bit field*. This method uses a special syntax in the structure definition that enables you to define a field of bits and assign a name to that field.

To define bit field assignments, you can define a structure called packedStruct, for example, as follows:

```
struct packedStruct
{
    unsigned int f1:1;
    unsigned int f2:1;
    unsigned int f3:1;
    unsigned int type:4;
    unsigned int index:9;
};
```

The structure packedStruct is defined to contain five members. The first member, called f1, is an unsigned int. The :1 that immediately follows the member name specifies that this member is to be stored in 1 bit. The flags f2 and f3 are similarly defined as being a single bit in length. The member type is defined to occupy 4 bits, whereas the member index is defined as being 9 bits long.

The compiler automatically packs the preceding bit field definitions together. The nice thing about this approach is that the fields of a variable defined to be of type packedStruct can now be referenced in the same convenient way that normal structure members are referenced. So if you declared a variable called packedData as follows

```
struct packedStruct packedData;
```

you could easily set the type field of packedData to 7 with this simple statement:

```
packedData.type = 7;
```

You could also set this field to the value of n with this similar statement:

```
packedData.type = n;
```

In this last case, you needn't worry about whether the value of n is too large to fit into the type field; only the low-order 4 bits of n are assigned to packedData.type.

Extraction of the value from a bit field is also automatically handled, so the statement

```
n = packedData.type;
```

extracts the type field from packedData (automatically shifting it into the low-order bits as required) and assigns it to n.

You can use bit fields in normal expressions and automatically convert them to integers. Therefore, the statement

```
i = packedData.index / 5 + 1;
```

is perfectly valid, as is the following:

```
if ( packedData.f2 )
  . . .
```

This tests whether flag f2 is on or off. One point worth noting about bit fields is that no guarantee states whether the fields are internally assigned from left to right or from right to left. So if bit fields are assigned from right to left, f1 would be in the low-order bit position, f2 in the bit position immediately to the left of f1, and so on. This should not present a problem unless you are dealing with data that a different program or a different machine created.

You can also include normal data types within a structure that contains bit fields. So if you wanted to define a structure that contains an int, a char, and two 1-bit flags, the following definition would be valid:

```
struct table_entry
{
    int     count;
    char    c;
    unsigned int f1:1;
    unsigned int f2:1;
};
```

Bit fields are packed into *units* as they appear in the structure definition, where the size of a *unit* is defined by the implementation and is most likely a word. The Objective-C compiler does not rearrange the bit field definitions to try to optimize storage space.

A bit field that has no name can be specified to cause bits inside a word to be skipped. The following definition defines a structure, x_entry, that contains a 4-bit field called type and a 9-bit field called count:

```
struct x_entry
{
    unsigned int type:4;
    unsigned int :3;
    unsigned int count:9;
};
```

The unnamed field specifies that 3 bits separate type from the count field.

A final point on the specification of fields concerns the special case of an unnamed field of length 0. You can be use this to force alignment of the next field in the structure at the start of a unit boundary.

Don't Forget About Object-Oriented Programming!

Now you know how to define a structure to store a date, and you've written various routines to manipulate that date structure. But what about object-oriented programming? Shouldn't you have made a class called Date instead and then developed methods to work with a Date object? Wouldn't that be a better approach? Well, yes. Hopefully, that entered your mind when we discussed storing dates in your program.

Certainly, if you have to work with a lot of dates in your programs, defining a class and methods to work with dates is a better approach. In fact, the Foundation framework has a couple of classes, called NSDate and NSCalendarDate, defined for such purposes. We leave it as an exercise for you to implement a Date class to deal with dates as objects instead of as structures.

Pointers

Pointers enable you to effectively represent complex data structures, change values passed as arguments to functions and methods, and more concisely and efficiently deal with arrays. At the end of this chapter, we also clue you in about how important they are to the implementation of objects in the Objective-C language.

We introduced the concept of a pointer in Chapter 8, "Inheritance," when we talked about the `Point` and `Rectangle` classes and stated that you can have multiple references to the same object.

To understand the way pointers operate, you first must understand the concept of *indirection*. We witness this concept in our everyday life. For example, suppose that I needed to buy a new toner cartridge for my printer. In the company that I work for, the purchasing department handles all purchases. So I would call Jim in purchasing and ask him to order the new cartridge for me. Jim then would call the local supply store to order the cartridge. To obtain my new cartridge, I would take an indirect approach because I would not be ordering the cartridge directly from the supply store.

This same notion of indirection applies to the way pointers work in Objective-C. A pointer provides an indirect means of accessing the value of a particular data item. And just as there are reasons it makes sense to go through the purchasing department to order new cartridges (I don't have to know which particular store the cartridges are being ordered from, for example), good reasons exist for why sometimes it makes sense to use pointers in Objective-C.

But enough talk; it's time to see how pointers actually work. Suppose you've defined a variable called `count` as follows:

```
int count = 10;
```

You can define another variable, called `intPtr`, that enables you to indirectly access the value of `count` with the following declaration:

```
int *intPtr;
```

The asterisk defines to the Objective-C system that the variable `intPtr` is of type pointer to `int`. This means that the program will use `intPtr` to indirectly access the value of one or more integer variables.

You have seen how we used the `&` operator in the `scanf` calls of previous programs. This unary operator, known as the *address* operator, makes a pointer to a variable in Objective-C. So if x is a variable of a particular type, the expression `&x` is a pointer to that variable. If you want, you can assign the expression `&x` to any pointer variable that has been declared to be a pointer of the same type as x.

Therefore, with the definitions of `count` and `intPtr` as given, you can write a statement such as

```
intPtr = &count;
```

to set up the indirect reference between intPtr and count. The address operator assigns to the variable intPtr not the value of count, but a pointer to the variable count. Figure 13.1 illustrates the link made between intPtr and count. The directed line illustrates the idea that intPtr does not directly contain the value of count, but contains a pointer to the variable count.

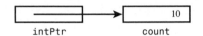

intPtr   count

Figure 13.1   Pointer to an integer

To reference the contents of count through the pointer variable intPtr, you use the indirection operator, which is the asterisk (*). If x were defined to be of type int, the statement

```
x = *intPtr;
```

would assign the value that is indirectly referenced through intPtr to the variable x. Because intPtr was previously set pointing to count, this statement would have the effect of assigning the value contained in the variable count—which is 10—to the variable x.

Program 13.8 incorporates the previous statements and illustrates the two fundamental pointer operators: the address operator (&) and the indirection operator (*).

Program 13.8

```
// Program to illustrate pointers

#import <Foundation/Foundation.h>

int main (int argc, char *argv[])
{
  NSAutoreleasePool * pool = [[NSAutoreleasePool alloc] init];
  int   count = 10, x;
  int   *intPtr;

  intPtr = &count;
  x = *intPtr;

  NSLog (@"count = %i, x = %i", count, x);

  [pool drain];
  return 0;
}
```

Program 13.8 Output

```
count = 10, x = 10
```

The variables count and x are declared to be integer variables in the normal fashion. On the next line, the variable intPtr is declared to be of type "pointer to int." Note that the two lines of declarations could have been combined into a single line:

```
int count = 10, x, *intPtr;
```

Next, the address operator is applied to the variable count, which has the effect of creating a pointer to this variable, which the program then assigns to the variable intPtr.

Execution of the next statement in the program

```
x = *intPtr;
```

proceeds as follows: The indirection operator tells the Objective-C system to treat the variable intPtr as containing a pointer to another data item. This pointer is then used to access the desired data item, whose type is specified by the declaration of the pointer variable. Because you told the compiler when you declared the variable that intPtr points to integers, the compiler knows that the value referenced by the expression *intPtr is an integer. Also, because you set intPtr to point to the integer variable count in the previous program statement, this expression indirectly accesses the value of count.

Program 13.9 illustrates some interesting properties of pointer variables. This program uses a pointer to a character.

Program 13.9

```
#import <Foundation/Foundation.h>

int main (int argc, char *argv[])
{
    NSAutoreleasePool * pool = [[NSAutoreleasePool alloc] init];
    char c = 'Q';
    char *charPtr = &c;

    NSLog (@"%c %c", c, *charPtr);

    c = '/';
    NSLog (@"%c %c", c, *charPtr);

    *charPtr = '(';
    NSLog (@"%c %c", c, *charPtr);

    [pool drain];
    return 0;
}
```

Program 13.9 Output

```
Q Q
/ /
( (
```

The character variable c is defined and initialized to the character 'Q'. In the next line of the program, the variable charPtr is defined to be of type "pointer to char," meaning that whatever value is stored inside this variable should be treated as an indirect reference (pointer) to a character. Notice that you can assign an initial value to this variable in the normal fashion. The value you assign to charPtr in the program is a pointer to the variable c, which is obtained by applying the address operator to the variable c. (Note that this initialization would have generated a compiler error had c been defined after this statement because a variable must always be declared before its value can be referenced in an expression.)

The declaration of the variable charPtr and the assignment of its initial value could have been equivalently expressed in two separate statements, as follows

```
char *charPtr;
charPtr = &c;
```

(and not by the statements

```
char *charPtr;
*charPtr = &c;
```

as might be implied from the single line declaration).

Remember that the value of a pointer in Objective-C is meaningless until it is set to point to something.

The first NSLog call simply displays the contents of the variable c and the contents of the variable referenced by charPtr. Because you set charPtr to point to the variable c, the value displayed is the contents of c, as verified by the first line of the program's output.

In the next line of the program, the character '/' is assigned to the character variable c. Because charPtr still points to the variable c, displaying the value of *charPtr in the subsequent NSLog call correctly displays this new value of c at the terminal. This is an important concept. Unless the value of charPtr changes, the expression *charPtr always accesses the value of c. Thus, as the value of c changes, so does the value of *charPtr.

The previous discussion can help you understand how the program statement that appears next in the program works. We mentioned that unless charPtr were changed, the expression *charPtr would always reference the value of c. Therefore, in the expression

```
*charPtr = '(';
```

the left parenthesis character is being assigned to c. More formally, the character '(' is assigned to the variable that charPtr points to. You know that this variable is c because you placed a pointer to c in charPtr at the beginning of the program.

The previous concepts are the key to your understanding of pointer operation. Review them at this point if they still seem a bit unclear.

Pointers and Structures

You have seen how to define a pointer to point to a basic data type such as an `int` or a `char`. But you can also define a pointer to point to a structure. Earlier in this chapter, you defined your `date` structure as follows:

```
struct date
{
    int month;
    int day;
    int year;
};
```

Just as you defined variables to be of type `struct date`, as in

```
struct date  todaysDate;
```

you can define a variable to be a pointer to a `struct date` variable:

```
struct date *datePtr;
```

You can then use the variable `datePtr`, as just defined, in the expected fashion. For example, you can set it to point to `todaysDate` with the following assignment statement:

```
datePtr = &todaysDate;
```

After such an assignment, you can indirectly access any of the members of the `date` structure that `datePtr` points to in the following way:

```
(*datePtr).day = 21;
```

This statement sets the day of the `date` structure pointed to by `datePtr` to 21. The parentheses are required because the structure member operator . has higher precedence than the indirection operator `*`.

To test the value of `month` stored in the `date` structure that `datePtr` points to, you can use a statement such as this:

```
if ( (*datePtr).month == 12 )
    . . .
```

Pointers to structures are so often used that the language has a special operator. The structure pointer operator `->`, which is the dash followed by the greater-than sign, permits expressions that would otherwise be written as

```
(*x).y
```

to be more clearly expressed as

```
x->y
```

So you can conveniently write the previous `if` statement as follows:

```
if ( datePtr->month == 12 )
    . . .
```

We rewrote Program 13.6, the first program to illustrate structures, using the concept of structure pointers. Program 13.10 presents this program.

Program 13.10

```
// Program to illustrate structure pointers
#import <Foundation/Foundation.h>

int main (int argc, char *argv[])
{
   NSAutoreleasePool * pool = [[NSAutoreleasePool alloc] init];

   struct date
   {
      int month;
      int day;
      int year;
   };

   struct date today, *datePtr;

   datePtr = &today;
   datePtr->month = 9;
   datePtr->day = 25;
   datePtr->year = 2009;

   NSLog (@"Today's date is %i/%i/%.2i.",
         datePtr->month, datePtr->day, datePtr->year % 100);
   [pool drain];
   return 0;
}
```

Program 13.10 Output

```
Today's date is 9/25/09.
```

Pointers, Methods, and Functions

You can pass a pointer as an argument to a method or function in the normal fashion, and you can have a function or method return a pointer as its result. When you think about it, that's what your `alloc` and `init` methods have been doing all along—returning pointers. We cover that in more detail at the end of this chapter.

Now consider Program 13.11.

Program 13.11

```
// Pointers as arguments to functions
#import <Foundation/Foundation.h>

void exchange (int *pint1, int *pint2)
```

```
{
    int temp;

    temp = *pint1;
    *pint1 = *pint2;
    *pint2 = temp;
}

int main (int argc, char *argv[])
{
    NSAutoreleasePool * pool = [[NSAutoreleasePool alloc] init];
    void exchange (int *pint1, int *pint2);
    int  i1 = -5, i2 = 66, *p1 = &i1, *p2 = &i2;

    NSLog (@"i1 = %i, i2 = %i", i1, i2);

    exchange (p1, p2);
    NSLog (@"i1 = %i, i2 = %i", i1, i2);

    exchange (&i1, &i2);
    NSLog (@"i1 = %i, i2 = %i", i1, i2);

    [pool drain];
    return 0;
}
```

Program 13.11 Output

```
i1 = -5, i2 = 66
i1 = 66, i2 = -5
i1 = -5, i2 = 66
```

The purpose of the exchange function is to interchange the two integer values that its two arguments point to. The local integer variable temp is used to hold one of the integer values while the exchange is made. Its value is set equal to the integer that pint1 points to. The integer that pint2 points to is then copied into the integer that pint1 points to, and the value of temp is then stored in the integer that pint2 points to, thus making the exchange complete.

The main routine defines integers i1 and i2 with values of -5 and 66, respectively. Two integer pointers, p1 and p2, are then defined and set to point to i1 and i2, respectively. The program next displays the values of i1 and i2 and calls the exchange function, passing the two pointers (p1 and p2) as arguments. The exchange function exchanges the value contained in the integer that p1 points to with the value contained in the integer that p2 points to. Because p1 points to i1, and p2 to i2, the function exchanges the values of i1 and i2. The output from the second NSLog call verifies that the exchange worked properly.

The second call to `exchange` is a bit more interesting. This time, the arguments passed to the function are pointers to `i1` and `i2` that are manufactured on the spot by applying the address operator to these two variables. Because the expression `&i1` produces a pointer to the integer variable `i1`, this is in line with the type of argument your function expects for the first argument (a pointer to an integer). The same applies for the second argument. As you can see from the program's output, the exchange function did its job and switched the values of `i1` and `i2` to their original values.

Study Program 13.11 in detail. It illustrates with a small example the key concepts when dealing with pointers in Objective-C.

Pointers and Arrays

If you have an array of 100 integers called `values`, you can define a pointer called `valuesPtr`, which you can use to access the integers contained in this array with the following statement:

```
int *valuesPtr;
```

When you define a pointer that will be used to point to the elements of an array, you don't designate the pointer as type "pointer to array"; instead, you designate the pointer as pointing to the type of element contained in the array.

If you had an array of `Fraction` objects called `fracts`, you could similarly define a pointer to be used to point to elements in `fracts` with the following statement:

```
Fraction **fractsPtr;
```

Note that this is the same declaration used to define a `Fraction` object.

To set `valuesPtr` to point to the first element in the `values` array, you simply write this:

```
valuesPtr = values;
```

The address operator is not used in this case because the Objective-C compiler treats the occurrence of an array name without a subscript as a pointer to the first element of the array. Therefore, simply specifying `values` without a subscript produces a pointer to the first element of values.

An equivalent way of producing a pointer to the start of `values` is to apply the address operator to the first element of the array. Thus, the statement

```
valuesPtr = &values[0];
```

serves the same purpose of placing a pointer to the first element of `values` in the pointer variable `valuesPtr`.

To display the `Fraction` object in the array `fracts` that `fractsPtr` points to, you would write this statement:

```
[*fractsPtr print];
```

The real power of using pointers to arrays comes into play when you want to sequence through the elements of an array. If `valuesPtr` is defined as mentioned previously and is set pointing to the first element of `values`, you can use the expression

```
*valuesPtr
```

to access the first integer of the `values` array—that is, `values[0]`. To reference `values[3]` through the `valuesPtr` variable, you can add 3 to `valuesPtr` and then apply the indirection operator:

```
*(valuesPtr + 3)
```

In general, you can use the expression

```
*(valuesPtr + i)
```

to access the value contained in `values[i]`.

So to set `values[10]` to 27, you would write the following expression:

```
values[10] = 27;
```

Or, using `valuesPtr`, you would write this:

```
*(valuesPtr + 10) = 27;
```

To set `valuesPtr` to point to the second element of the `values` array, you apply the address operator to `values[1]` and assign the result to `valuesPtr`:

```
valuesPtr = &values[1];
```

If `valuesPtr` points to `values[0]`, you can set it to point to `values[1]` by simply adding 1 to the value of `valuesPtr`:

```
valuesPtr += 1;
```

This is a perfectly valid expression in Objective-C and can be used for pointers to any data type.

In general, if `a` is an array of elements of type `x`, `px` is of type "pointer to `x`," and `i` and `n` are integer constants of variables, the statement

```
px = a;
```

sets `px` to point to the first element of `a`, and the expression

```
*(px + i)
```

subsequently references the value contained in `a[i]`. Furthermore, the statement

```
px += n;
```

sets `px` to point to n elements further in the array, no matter what type of element the array contains.

Suppose that `fractsPtr` points to a fraction stored inside an array of fractions. Further suppose that you want to add it to the fraction contained in the next element of the array and assign the result to the `Fraction` object `result`. You could do this by writing the following:

```
result = [*fractsPtr add: *(fractsPtr + 1)];
```

The increment and decrement operators (++ and --) are particularly handy when dealing with pointers. Applying the increment operator to a pointer has the same effect as adding 1 to the pointer, whereas applying the decrement operator has the same effect as subtracting 1 from the pointer. So if `textPtr` were defined as a `char` pointer and were set to point to the beginning of an array of `chars` called `text`, the statement

```
++textPtr;
```

would set `textPtr` to point to the next character in `text`, which is `text[1]`. In a similar fashion, the statement

```
--textPtr;
```

would set `textPtr` to point to the previous character in `text` (assuming, of course, that `textPtr` was not pointing to the beginning of `text` before this statement executed).

Comparing two pointer variables in Objective-C is perfectly valid. This is particularly useful when comparing two pointers in the same array. For example, you could test the pointer `valuesPtr` to see whether it points past the end of an array containing 100 elements by comparing it to a pointer to the last element in the array. So the expression

```
valuesPtr > &values[99]
```

would be TRUE (nonzero) if `valuesPtr` was pointing past the last element in the `values` array, and it would be FALSE (zero) otherwise. From our earlier discussions, you can replace the previous expression with its equivalent:

```
valuesPtr > values + 99
```

This is possible because `values` used without a subscript is a pointer to the beginning of the `values` array. (Remember that it's the same as writing `&values[0]`.)

Program 13.12 illustrates pointers to arrays. The `arraySum` function calculates the sum of the elements contained in an array of integers.

Program 13.12

```
// Function to sum the elements of an integer array

#import <Foundation/Foundation.h>

int arraySum (int array[], int n)
{
    int sum = 0, *ptr;
    int *arrayEnd = array + n;

    for ( ptr = array; ptr < arrayEnd; ++ptr )
        sum += *ptr;
```

```
   return (sum);
}

int main (int argc, char *argv[])
{
   NSAutoreleasePool * pool = [[NSAutoreleasePool alloc] init];
   int arraySum (int array[], int n);
   int values[10] = { 3, 7, -9, 3, 6, -1, 7, 9, 1, -5 };

   NSLog (@"The sum is %i", arraySum (values, 10));
   [pool drain];
   return 0;
}
```

Program 13.12 Output

```
The sum is 21
```

Inside the arraySum function, the integer pointer arrayEnd is defined and set pointing immediately after the last element of array. A for loop is then set up to sequence through the elements of array; then the value of ptr is set to point to the beginning of array when the loop is entered. Each time through the loop, the element of array that ptr points to is added into sum. The for loop then increments the value of ptr to set it to point to the next element in array. When ptr points past the end of array, the for loop is exited and the value of sum is returned to the caller.

Is It an Array, or Is It a Pointer?

To pass an array to a function, you simply specify the name of the array, as you did previously with the call to the arraySum function. But we also mentioned in this section that to produce a pointer to an array, you need only specify the name of the array. This implies that in the call to the arraySum function, a pointer to the array values was passed to the function. This is precisely the case and explains why you can change the elements of an array from within a function.

But if a pointer to the array is passed to the function, why isn't the formal parameter inside the function declared to be a pointer? In other words, in the declaration of array in the arraySum function, why isn't this declaration used?

```
int *array;
```

Shouldn't all references to an array from within a function be made using pointer variables?

To answer these questions, we must first reiterate what we have already said about pointers and arrays. We mentioned that if valuesPtr points to the same type of element as contained in an array called values, the expression *(valuesPtr + i) is in equivalent to the expression values[i], assuming that valuesPtr has been set to point to the be-

ginning of `values`. What follows from this is that you can also use the expression
`*(values + i)` to reference the ith element of the array `values`—and, in general, if x is
an array of any type, the expression `x[i]` can always be equivalently expressed in Objective-C as `*(x + i)`.

As you can see, pointers and arrays are intimately related in Objective-C, which is why
you can declare `array` to be of type "array of `int`s" inside the `arraySum` function or to be
of type "pointer to `int`." Either declaration works fine in the preceding program—try it
and see.

If you will be using index numbers to reference the elements of an array, declare the
corresponding formal parameter to be an array. This more correctly reflects the function's
use of the array. Similarly, if you will be using the argument as a pointer to the array, declare it to be of type pointer.

Pointers to Character Strings

One of the most common applications of using a pointer to an array is as a pointer to a
character string. The reasons are ones of notational convenience and efficiency. To show
how easily you can use pointers to character strings, let's write a function called
`copyString` to copy one string into another. If you were writing this function using
your normal array-indexing methods, you might code the function as follows:

```
void copyString (char to[], char from[])
{
    int i;

    for ( i = 0; from[i] != '\0'; ++i )
        to[i] = from[i];

    to[i] = '\0';
}
```

The `for` loop is exited before the null character is copied into the `to` array, thus explaining the need for the last statement in the function.

If you write `copyString` using pointers, you no longer need the index variable `i`.
Program 13.13 shows a pointer version.

Programming 13.13

```
#import <Foundation/Foundation.h>

void copyString (char *to, char *from)
{
    for ( ; *from != '\0'; ++from, ++to )
        *to = *from;

    *to = '\0';
}
```

```
int main (int argc, char *argv[])
{
    NSAutoreleasePool * pool = [[NSAutoreleasePool alloc] init];
    void copyString (char *to, char *from);
    char string1[] = "A string to be copied."²;
    char string2[50];

    copyString (string2, string1);
    NSLog (@"%s", string2);

    copyString (string2, "So is this.");
    NSLog (@"%s", string2);

    [pool drain];
    return 0;
}
```

Program 13.13 Output

```
A string to be copied.
So is this.
```

The copyString function defines the two formal parameters, to and from, as character pointers and not as character arrays, as was done in the previous version of copyString. This reflects how the function will use these two variables.

A for loop is then entered (with no initial conditions) to copy the string that from points to into the string that to points to. Each time through the loop, the from and to pointers are each incremented by 1. This sets the from pointer pointing to the next character that is to be copied from the source string and sets the to pointer pointing to the location in the destination string where the next character is to be stored.

When the from pointer points to the null character, the for loop is exited. The function then places the null character at the end of the destination string.

In the main routine, the copyString function is called twice—the first time to copy the contents of string1 into string2, and the second time to copy the contents of the constant character string "So is this." into string2.

---

² Note the use of the strings "A string to be copied." and "So is this" in the program. These are not string objects, but C-style character strings, as distinguished by the fact that an @ character does not precede the string. The two types are not interchangeable. If a function expects an array of char as an argument, you may pass it either an array of type char or a literal C-style character string, but not a character string object.

Constant Character Strings and Pointers

The fact that the call

```
copyString (string2, "So is this.");
```

works in the previous program implies that when a constant character string is passed as an argument to a function, that character string is actually passed to a pointer. Not only is this true in this case, but it can also be generalized by saying that whenever a constant character string is used in Objective-C, a pointer to that character string is produced.

This point might sound a bit confusing now, but, as we briefly noted in Chapter 4, constant character strings that we mention here are called C-style strings. These are not objects. As you know, a constant character string object is created by putting an @ sign in front of the string, as in @"This is okay.". You can't substitute one for the other.

So if textPtr is declared to be a character pointer, as in

```
char *textPtr;
```

then the statement

```
textPtr = "A character string.";
```

assigns to textPtr a pointer to the constant character string "A character string." Be careful to make the distinction here between character pointers and character arrays because the type of assignment shown previously is not valid with a character array. For example, if text were defined instead to be an array of chars, with a statement such as

```
char text[80];
```

you could not write a statement such as this:

```
text = "This is not valid.";
```

The only time Objective-C lets you get away with performing this type of assignment to a character array is when initializing it:

```
char text[80] = "This is okay.";
```

Initializing the text array in this manner does not have the effect of storing a pointer to the character string "This is okay." inside text. Instead, the actual characters themselves are followed by a terminating null character, inside corresponding elements of the text array.

If text were a character pointer, initializing text with the statement

```
char *text = "This is okay.";
```

would assign to it a pointer to the character string "This is okay."

The Increment and Decrement Operators Revisited

Up to this point, whenever you used the increment or decrement operator, that was the only operator that appeared in the expression. When you write the expression ++x, you know that this adds 1 to the value of the variable x. And as you have just seen, if x is a pointer to an array, this sets x to point to the next element of the array.

You can use the increment and decrement operators in expressions where other operators also appear. In such cases, it becomes important to know more precisely how these operators work.

Whenever you used the increment and decrement operators, you always placed them before the variables that were being incremented or decremented. So to increment a variable i, you simply wrote the following:

```
++i;
```

You can also place the increment operator after the variable, like so:

```
i++;
```

Both expressions are valid, and both achieve the same result—incrementing the value of i. In the first case, where the ++ is placed before its operand, the increment operation is more precisely identified as a *pre-increment*. In the second case, where the ++ is placed after its operand, the operation is identified as a *post-increment*.

The same discussion applies to the decrement operator. So the statement

```
--i;
```

technically performs a pre-decrement of i, whereas the statement

```
i--;
```

performs a post-decrement of i. Both have the same net result of subtracting 1 from the value of i.

When the increment and decrement operators are used in more complex expressions, the distinction between the pre- and post- nature of these operators is realized.

Suppose that you have two integers, called i and j. If you set the value of i to 0 and then write the statement

```
j = ++i;
```

the value assigned to j is 1—not 0, as you might expect. In the case of the pre-increment operator, the variable is incremented before its value is used in an expression. Therefore, in the previous expression, the value of i is first incremented from 0 to 1 and then its value is assigned to j, as if the following two statements had been written instead:

```
++i;
j = i;
```

If you use the post-increment operator in the statement

```
j = i++;
```

i is incremented after its value has been assigned to j. So if i were 0 before the previous statement were executed, 0 would be assigned to j and then i would be incremented by 1, as if these statements were used instead:

```
j = i;
++i;
```

As another example, if i is equal to 1, the statement

```
x = a[--i];
```

has the effect of assigning the value of a[0] to x because the variable i is decremented before its value is used to index into a. The statement

```
x = a[i--];
```

used instead assigns the value of a[1] to x because i would be decremented after its value was used to index into a.

As a third example of the distinction between the pre- and post- increment and decrement operators, the function call

```
NSLog (@"%i", ++i);
```

increments i and then sends its value to the NSLog function, whereas the call

```
NSLog (@"%i", i++);
```

increments i after its value has been sent to the function. So if i were equal to 100, the first NSLog call would display 101 at the terminal, whereas the second NSLog call would display 100. In either case, the value of i would be equal to 101 after the statement had been executed.

As a final example on this topic before we present a program, if textPtr is a character pointer, the expression

```
*(++textPtr)
```

first increments textPtr and then fetches the character it points to, whereas the expression

```
*(textPtr++)
```

fetches the character that textPtr points to before its value is incremented. In either case, the parentheses are not required because the * and ++ operators have equal precedence but associate from right to left.

Let's go back to the copyString function from Program 13.13 and rewrite it to incorporate the increment operations directly into the assignment statement.

Because the to and from pointers are incremented each time after the assignment statement inside the for loop is executed, they should be incorporated into the assignment statement as post-increment operations. The revised for loop of Program 13.13 then becomes this:

```
for ( ; *from != '\0'; )
    *to++ = *from++;
```

Execution of the assignment statement inside the loop would proceed as follows. The character that `from` points to would be retrieved, and then `from` would be incremented to point to the next character in the source string. The referenced character would be stored inside the location that `to` points to; then `to` would be incremented to point to the next location in the destination string.

The previous `for` statement hardly seems worthwhile because it has no initial expression and no looping expression. In fact, the logic would be better served when expressed in the form of a `while` loop. This has been done in Program 13.14, which presents the new version of the `copyString` function. The `while` loop uses the fact that the null character is equal to the value `0`, as experienced Objective-C programmers commonly do.

Program 13.14

```
// Function to copy one string to another
//          pointer version 2

#import <Foundation/Foundation.h>
void copyString (char *to, char *from)
{
    while ( *from )
        *to++ = *from++;
    *to = '\0';
}

int main (int argc, char *argv[])
{
    NSAutoreleasePool * pool = [[NSAutoreleasePool alloc] init];
    void copyString (char *to, char *from);
    char string1[] = "A string to be copied.";
    char string2[50];

    copyString (string2, string1);
    NSLog (@"%s", string2);

    copyString (string2, "So is this.");
    NSLog (@"%s", string2);
    [pool drain];
    return 0;
}
```

Program 13.14 Output

```
A string to be copied.
So is this.
```

Operations on Pointers

As you have seen in this chapter, you can add or subtract integer values from pointers. Furthermore, you can compare two pointers to see whether they are equal or whether one pointer is less than or greater than another pointer. The only other operation permitted on pointers is the subtraction of two pointers of the same type. The result of subtracting two pointers in Objective-C is the number of elements contained between the two pointers. Thus, if a points to an array of elements of any type and b points to another element somewhere further along in the same array, the expression b - a represents the number of elements between these two pointers. For example, if p points to some element in an array x, the statement

```
n = p - x;
```

assigns to the variable n (assumed here to be an integer variable) the index number of the element inside x that p points to. Therefore, if p had been set pointing to the 100th element in x by a statement such as

```
p = &x[99];
```

the value of n after the previous subtraction was performed would be 99.

Pointers to Functions

Of a slightly more advanced nature, but presented here for the sake of completeness, is the notion of a pointer to a function. When working with pointers to functions, the Objective-C compiler needs to know not only that the pointer variable points to a function, but also the type of value returned by that function, as well as the number and types of its arguments. To declare a variable, fnPtr, to be of type "pointer to function that returns an int and that takes no arguments," you would write this declaration:

```
int (*fnPtr) (void);
```

The parentheses around *fnPtr are required; otherwise, the Objective-C compiler treats the preceding statement as the declaration of a function called fnPtr that returns a pointer to an int (because the function call operator () has higher precedence than the pointer indirection operator *).

To set your function pointer to point to a specific function, you simply assign the name of the function to it. Therefore, if lookup were a function that returned an int and that took no arguments, the statement

```
fnPtr = lookup;
```

would store a pointer to this function inside the function pointer variable fnPtr. Writing a function name without a subsequent set of parentheses is treated in an analogous way to writing an array name without a subscript. The Objective-C compiler automatically produces a pointer to the specified function. An ampersand is permitted in front of the function name, but it's not required.

If the `lookup` function has not been previously defined in the program, you must declare the function before the previous assignment can be made. A statement such as

```
int lookup (void);
```

would be needed before a pointer to this function could be assigned to the variable `fnPtr`.

You can call the function indirectly referenced through a pointer variable by applying the function call operator to the pointer, listing any arguments to the function inside the parentheses. For example

```
entry = fnPtr ();
```

calls the function that `fnPtr` points to, storing the returned value inside the variable `entry`.

One common application for pointers to functions is passing them as arguments to other functions. The Standard Library uses this in the function `qsort`, which performs a *quick sort* on an array of data elements. This function takes as one of its arguments a pointer to a function that is called whenever `qsort` needs to compare two elements in the array being sorted. In this manner, `qsort` can be used to sort arrays of any type because the actual comparison of any two elements in the array is made by a user-supplied function, not by the `qsort` function itself.

In the Foundation framework, some methods take a function pointer as an argument. For example, the method `sortUsingFunction:context:` is defined in the `NSMutableArray` class and calls the specified function whenever two elements in an array to be sorted need to be compared.

Another common application for function pointers is to create *dispatch* tables. You can't store functions themselves inside the elements of an array. However, you can store function pointers inside an array. Given this, you can create tables that contain pointers to functions to be called. For example, you might create a table for processing different commands that a user will enter. Each entry in the table could contain both the command name and a pointer to a function to call to process that particular command. Now, whenever the user entered a command, you could look up the command inside the table and invoke the corresponding function to handle it.

Pointers and Memory Addresses

Before we end this discussion of pointers in Objective-C, we should point out the details of how they are actually implemented. A computer's memory can be conceptualized as a sequential collection of storage cells. Each cell of the computer's memory has a number, called an *address*, associated with it. Typically, the first address of a computer's memory is numbered 0. On most computer systems, a *cell* is 1 byte.

The computer uses memory to store the instructions of your computer program and to store the values of the variables associated with a program. So if you declare a variable called `count` to be of type `int`, the system would assign location(s) in memory to hold the value of count while the program is executing. For example, this location might be at address $1000FF_{16}$ inside the computer's memory.

Luckily, you don't need to concern yourself with the particular memory addresses assigned to variables—the system automatically handles them. However, the knowledge that each variable is associated with a unique memory address will help you understand the way pointers operate.

Whenever you apply the address operator to a variable in Objective-C, the value generated is the actual address of that variable inside the computer's memory. (Obviously, this is where the address operator gets its name.) So the statement

```
intPtr = &count;
```

assigns to intPtr the address in the computer's memory that has been assigned to the variable count. Thus, if count were located at address $1000FF_{16}$, this statement would assign the value 0x1000FF to intPtr.

Applying the indirection operator to a pointer variable, as in the expression

```
*intPtr
```

has the effect of treating the value contained in the pointer variable as a memory address. The value stored at that memory address is then fetched and interpreted in accordance with the type declared for the pointer variable. So if intPtr were of type pointer to int, the system would interpret the value stored in the memory address given by *intPtr as an integer.

Unions

One of the more unusual constructs in the Objective-C programming language is the *union*. This construct is used mainly in more advanced programming applications when you need to store different types of data in the same storage area. For example, if you wanted to define a single variable called x that could be used to store a single character, a floating-point number, or an integer, you would first define a union, called (perhaps) mixed, as follows:

```
union mixed
{
    char  c;
    float f;
    int   i;
};
```

The declaration of a union is identical to that of a structure, except that the keyword union is used where the keyword struct is otherwise specified. The real difference between structures and unions has to do with the way memory is allocated. Declaring a variable to be of type union mixed, as in

```
union mixed x;
```

does not define x to contain three distinct members called c, f, and i; instead, it defines x
to contain a single member that is called either c, f, or i. In this way, you can use the
variable x to store either a char, a float, or an int, but not all three (and not even two
of the three). You can store a character in the variable x with the following statement:

```
x.c = 'K';
```

To store a floating-point value in x, use the notation x.f:

```
x.f = 786.3869;
```

Finally, to store the result of dividing an integer count by 2 into x, use this statement:

```
x.i = count / 2;
```

Because the float, char, and int members of x coexist in the same place in memory,
only one value can be stored in x at a time. Furthermore, you must ensure that the value
retrieved from a union is consistent with the way it was last stored in the union.

When defining a union, the name of the union is not required and variables can be
declared at the same time that the union is defined. You can also declare pointers to
unions, and their syntax and rules for performing operations are the same as for structures. Finally, you can initialize a union variable like so:

```
union mixed x = { '#' };
```

This sets the first member of x, which is c, to the character #. A particular member can
also be initialized by name, like this:

```
union mixed x = {.f=123.4;};
```

You can initialize an automatic union variable to another union variable of the same
type.

A union enables you to define arrays that you can use to store elements of different
data types. For example, the following statement sets up an array called table, consisting
of kTableEntries elements:

```
struct
{
    char *name;
    int  type;
    union
    {
        int   i;
        float f;
        char  c;
    } data;
} table [kTableEntries];
```

Each element of the array contains a structure consisting of a character pointer called
name, an integer member called type, and a union member called data. Each data member of the array can contain an int, a float, or a char. You might use the integer mem-

ber `type` to keep track of the type of value stored in the member `data`. For example, you could assign it the value `INTEGER` (defined appropriately, we assume) if it contained an `int`, `FLOATING` if it contained a `float`, and `CHARACTER` if it contained a `char`. This information would enable you to know how to reference the particular `data` member of a particular array element.

To store the character '#' in `table[5]` and subsequently set the `type` field to indicate that a character is stored in that location, you would use the following two statements:

```
table[5].data.c = '#';
table[5].type = CHARACTER;
```

When sequencing through the elements of `table`, you could determine the type of data value stored in each element by setting up an appropriate series of test statements. For example, the following loop would display each name and its associated value from `table` at the terminal:

```
enum symbolType { INTEGER, FLOATING, CHARACTER };
  ...

for ( j = 0; j < kTableEntries; ++j )
{
   NSLog (@"%s ", table[j].name);

   switch ( table[j].type )
   {
      case INTEGER:
           NSLog (@"%i", table[j].data.i);
           break;
      case FLOATING:
           NSLog (@"%g", table[j].data.f);
           break;
      case CHARACTER:
           NSLog (@"%c", table[j].data.c);
           break;
      default:
           NSLog (@"Unknown type (%i), element %i",
                    table[j].type, j );
           break;
   }
}
```

The type of application illustrated previously might be practical in storing a symbol table, which might contain the name of each symbol, its type, and its value (and perhaps other information about the symbol as well).

They're Not Objects!

Now you know how to define arrays, structures, character strings, and unions, and how to manipulate them in your program. Remember one fundamental thing: *They're not objects.* Thus, you can't send messages to them. You also can't use them to take maximum advantage of nice things such as the memory-allocation strategy that the Foundation framework provides. That's one of the reasons I encouraged you to skip this chapter and return to it later. In general, you're better served learning how to use the Foundation's classes that define arrays and strings as objects than using the ones built into the language. Resort to using the types defined in this chapter only if you really need to—and hopefully you won't!

Miscellaneous Language Features

Some language features didn't fit well into any of the other chapters, so we've included them here.

Compound Literals

A *compound literal* is a type name enclosed in parentheses followed by an initialization list. It creates an unnamed value of the specified type, which has scope limited to the block in which it is created or global scope if defined outside any block. In the latter case, the initializers must all be constant expressions.

Consider an example:

```
(struct date) {.month = 7, .day = 2, .year = 2004}
```

This expression produces a structure of type `struct date` with the specified initial values. You can assign this to another `struct date` structure, like so:

```
theDate = (struct date) {.month = 7, .day = 2, .year = 2004};
```

Or you can pass it to a function or method that expects an argument of `struct date`, like so:

```
setStartDate ((struct date) {.month = 7, .day = 2, .year = 2004});
```

In addition, you can define types other than structures. For example, if `intPtr` is of type `int *`, the statement

```
intPtr = (int [100]) {[0] = 1, [50] = 50, [99] = 99 };
```

(which can appear anywhere in the program) sets `intptr` pointing to an array of 100 integers, whose 3 elements are initialized as specified.

If the size of the array is not specified, the initializer list determines it.

The goto Statement

Executing a goto statement causes a direct branch to be made to a specified point in the program. To identify where in the program the branch is to be made, a label is needed. A *label* is a name formed with the same rules as variable names; it must be immediately followed by a colon. The label is placed directly before the statement to which the branch is to be made and must appear in the same function or method as the goto.

For example, the statement

```
goto out_of_data;
```

causes the program to branch immediately to the statement that is preceded by the label out_of_data;. This label can be located anywhere in the function or method, before or after the goto, and might be used as shown here:

```
out_of_data: NSLog (@"Unexpected end of data.");
    . . .
```

Lazy programmers frequently abuse the goto statement to branch to other portions of their code. The goto statement interrupts the normal sequential flow of a program. As a result, programs are harder to follow. Using many gotos in a program can make it impossible to decipher. For this reason, goto statements are not considered part of good programming style.

The null Statement

Objective-C permits you to place a solitary semicolon wherever a normal program statement can appear. The effect of such a statement, known as the *null* statement, is that nothing is done. This might seem quite useless, but programmers often do this in while, for, and do statements. For example, the purpose of the following statement is to store all the characters read in from *standard input* (your terminal, by default) in the character array that text points to until a newline character is encountered. This statement uses the library routine getchar, which reads and returns a single character at a time from standard input:

```
while ( (*text++ = getchar ()) != '' )
    ;
```

All the operations are performed inside the looping conditions part of the while statement. The null statement is needed because the compiler takes the statement that follows the looping expression as the body of the loop. Without the null statement, the compiler would treat whatever statement follows in the program as the body of the program loop.

The Comma Operator

At the bottom of the precedence totem pole, so to speak, is the comma operator. In Chapter 5, "Program Looping," we pointed out that inside a for statement, you can include more than one expression in any of the fields by separating each expression with a comma. For example, the for statement that begins

```
for ( i = 0, j = 100; i != 10; ++i, j -= 10 )
    ...
```

initializes the value of i to 0 and j to 100 before the loop begins, and it increments the value of i and subtracts 10 from the value of j after the body of the loop is executed.

Because all operators in Objective-C produce a value, the value of the comma operator is that of the rightmost expression.

The `sizeof` Operator

Although you should never make assumptions about the size of a data type in your program, sometimes you need to know this information. This might be when performing dynamic memory allocation using library routines such as `malloc`, or when writing or archiving data to a file. Objective-C provides an operator called `sizeof` that you can use to determine the size of a data type or object. The `sizeof` operator returns the size of the specified item in bytes. The argument to the `sizeof` operator can be a variable, an array name, the name of a basic data type, an object, the name of a derived data type, or an expression. For example, writing

```
sizeof (int)
```

gives the number of bytes needed to store an integer. On my MacBook Air, this produces a result of 4 (or 32 bits). If x is declared as an array of 100 `ints`, the expression

```
sizeof (x)
```

would give the amount of storage required to store the 100 integers of x.

Given that `myFract` is a `Fraction` object that contains two int instance variables (`numerator` and `denominator`), the expression

```
sizeof (myFract)
```

produces the value 4 on any system that represents pointers using 4 bytes. In fact, this is the value that `sizeof` yields for any object because here you are asking for the size of the pointer to the object's data. To get the size of the actual data structure to store an instance of a `Fraction` object, you would instead write the following:

```
sizeof (*myFract)
```

On my MacBook Air, this gives me a value of 12. That's 4 bytes each for the `numerator` and `denominator`, plus another 4 bytes for the inherited `isa` member mentioned in the section "How Things Work," at the end of this chapter.

The expression

```
sizeof (struct data_entry)
```

has as its value the amount of storage required to store one `data_entry` structure. If `data` is defined as an array of `struct data_entry` elements, the expression

```
sizeof (data) / sizeof (struct data_entry)
```

gives the number of elements contained in data (data must be a previously defined array, not a formal parameter or externally referenced array). The expression

```
sizeof (data) / sizeof (data[0])
```

produces the same result.

Use the sizeof operator wherever possible, to avoid having to calculate and hard-code sizes into your programs.

Command-Line Arguments

Often a program is developed that requires the user to enter a small amount of information at the terminal. This information might consist of a number indicating the triangular number you want to have calculated or a word you want to have looked up in a dictionary.

Instead of having the program request this type of information from the user, you can supply the information to the program at the time the program is executed. *Command-line arguments* provide this capability.

We have pointed out that the only distinguishing quality of the function main is that its name is special; it specifies where program execution is to begin. In fact, the runtime system actually calls upon the function main at the start of program execution, just as you would call a function from within your own program. When main completes execution, control returns to the runtime system, which then knows that your program has completed.

When the runtime system calls main, two arguments are passed to the function. The first argument, called argc by convention (for *argument c*ount), is an integer value that specifies the number of arguments typed on the command line. The second argument to main is an array of character pointers, called argv by convention (for *arg*ument *v*ector). In addition, argc + 1 character pointers are contained in this array. The first entry in this array is either a pointer to the name of the program that is executing or a pointer to a null string if the program name is not available on your system. Subsequent entries in the array point to the values specified in the same line as the command that initiated execution of the program. The last pointer in the argv array, argv[argc], is defined to be null.

To access the command-line arguments, the main function must be appropriately declared as taking two arguments. The conventional declaration we have used in all the programs in this book suffices:

```
int main (int argc, char *argv[])
{
    ...
}
```

Remember, the declaration of argv defines an array that contains elements of type "pointer to char." As a practical use of command-line arguments, suppose that you had developed a program that looks up a word inside a dictionary and prints its meaning. You can use command-line arguments so that the word whose meaning you want to find can be specified at the same time that the program is executed, as in the following command:

```
lookup aerie
```

This eliminates the need for the program to prompt the user to enter a word because it is typed on the command line.

If the previous command were executed, the system would automatically pass to the `main` function a pointer to the character string "aerie" in `argv[1]`. Recall that `argv[0]` would contain a pointer to the name of the program, which, in this case, would be "lookup".

The `main` routine might appear as shown:

```
#include <Foundation/Foundation.h>

int main (int argc, char *argv[])
{
    struct entry dictionary[100] =
        { { "aardvark", "a burrowing African mammal"    },
          { "abyss",    "a bottomless pit"              },
          { "acumen",   "mentally sharp; keen"          },
          { "addle",    "to become confused"            },
          { "aerie",    "a high nest"                   },
          { "affix",    "to append; attach"             },
          { "agar",     "a jelly made from seaweed"     },
          { "ahoy",     "a nautical call of greeting"   },
          { "aigrette", "an ornamental cluster of feathers" },
          { "ajar",     "partially opened"              } };

    int  entries = 10;
    int  entryNumber;
    int  lookup (struct entry dictionary [], char search[],
                 int entries);

    if ( argc != 2 )
    {
        NSLog (@"No word typed on the command line.");
        return (1);
    }

    entryNumber = lookup (dictionary, argv[1], entries);

    if ( entryNumber != -1 )
        NSLog (@"%s", dictionary[entryNumber].definition);
    else
        NSLog (@"Sorry, %s is not in my dictionary.", argv[1]);
```

```
    return (0);
}
```

The `main` routine tests to ensure that a word was typed after the program name when the program was executed. If it wasn't, or if more than one word was typed, the value of `argc` is not equal to 2. In that case, the program writes an error message to standard error and terminates, returning an exit status of 1.

If `argc` is equal to 2, the `lookup` function is called to find the word that `argv[1]` points to in the dictionary. If the word is found, its definition is displayed.

Remember that command-line arguments are always stored as character strings. So execution of the program `power` with the command-line arguments 2 and 16, as in

`power 2 16`

stores a pointer to the character string "2" inside `argv[1]` and a pointer to the string "16" inside `argv[2]`. If the program is to interpret arguments as numbers (as we suspect is the case in the `power` program), the program itself must convert them. Several routines are available in the program library for doing such conversions: `sscanf`, `atof`, `atoi`, `strtod`, and `strtol`. In Part II, you'll learn how to use a class called `NSProcessInfo` to access the command-line arguments as string objects instead of as C strings.

How Things Work

We would be remiss if we finished this chapter without first tying a couple things together. Because the Objective-C language has the C language underneath, it's worth mentioning some of the connections between the two. You can ignore these implementation details or use them to better understand how things work, in the same way that learning about pointers as memory addresses can help you better understand pointers. We don't get too detailed here; we just state four facts about the relationship between Objective-C and C.

Fact #1: Instance Variables are Stored in Structures

When you define a new class and its instance variables, those instance variables are actually stored inside a structure. That's how you can manipulate objects; they're really structures whose members are your instance variables. So the inherited instance variables plus the ones you added in your class comprise a single structure. When you allocate a new object using `alloc`, enough space is reserved to hold one of these structures.

One of the inherited members (it comes from the root object) of the structure is a protected member called `isa` that identifies the class to which the object belongs. Because it's part of the structure (and, therefore, part of the object), it is carried around with the object. In that way, the runtime system can always identify the class of an object (even if you assign it to a generic `id` object variable) by just looking at its `isa` member.

You can gain direct access to the members of an object's structure by making them `@public` (see the discussion in Chapter 10, "More on Variables and Data Types"). If you did that with the `numerator` and `denominator` members of your `Fraction` class, for example, you could write expressions such as

```
myFract->numerator
```

in your program to directly access the `numerator` member of the `Fraction` object `myFract`. But we strongly advise against doing that. As we mentioned in Chapter 10, it goes against the grain of data encapsulation.

Fact #2: An Object Variable is Really a Pointer

When you define an object variable such as a `Fraction`, as in

```
Fraction *myFract;
```

you're really defining a pointer variable called `myFract`. This variable is defined to point to something of type `Fraction`, which is the name of your class. When you allocate a new instance of a `Fraction`, with

```
myFract = [Fraction alloc];
```

you're allocating space to store a new `Fraction` object in memory (that is, space for a structure) and then storing the pointer to that structure that is returned inside the pointer variable `myFract`.

When you assign one object variable to another, as in

```
myFract2 = myFract1;
```

you're simply copying pointers. Both variables end up pointing to the same structure stored somewhere in memory. Making a change to one of the members referenced (that is, pointed to) by `myFract2` therefore changes the same instance variable (that is, structure member) that `myFract1` references.

Fact #3: Methods are Functions, and Message Expressions are Function Calls

Methods are really functions. When you invoke a method, you call a function associated with the class of the receiver. The arguments passed to the function are the receiver (`self`) and the method's arguments. So all the rules about passing arguments to functions, return values, and automatic and static variables are the same whether you're talking about a function or a method. The Objective-C compiler creates a unique name for each function using a combination of the class name and the method name.

Fact #4: The `id` Type is a Generic Pointer Type

Because objects are referenced through pointers, which are just memory addresses, you can freely assign them between `id` variables. A method that returns an `id` type consequently just returns a pointer to some object in memory. You can then assign that value to any object variable. Because the object carries its `isa` member wherever it goes, its class can always be identified, even if you store it in a generic object variable of type `id`.

Exercises

1. Write a function that calculates the average of an array of 10 floating-point values and returns the result.

2. The `reduce` method from your `Fraction` class finds the greatest common divisor of the numerator and denominator to reduce the fraction. Modify that method so that it uses the `gcd` function from Program 13.5 instead. Where do you think you should place the function definition? Are there any benefits to making the function static? Which approach do you think is better, using a `gcd` function or incorporating the code directly into the method as you did previously? Why?

3. An algorithm known as the *Sieve of Erastosthenes* can generate prime numbers. The algorithm for this procedure is presented here. Write a program that implements this algorithm. Have the program find all prime numbers up to $n = 150$. What can you say about this algorithm as compared to the ones used in the text for calculating prime numbers?

   Step 1: Define an array of integers P. Set all elements P_i to 0, 2 `<=` i `<=` n.

   Step 2: Set i to 2.

   Step 3: If $i > n$, the algorithm terminates.

   Step 4: If P_i is 0, i is prime.

   Step 5: For all positive integer values of j, such that i×j`<=n`, n, set $P_{i \times j}$ to 1.

   Step 6: Add 1 to i and go to step 3.

4. Write a function to add all the `Fractions` passed to it in an array and to return the result as a `Fraction`.

5. Write a `typedef` definition for a `struct date` called `Date` that enables you to make declarations such as

   `Date todaysDate;`

   in your program.

6. As noted in the text, defining a `Date` class instead of a `date` structure is more consistent with the notion of object-oriented programming. Define such a class with appropriate setter and getter methods. Also add a method called `dateUpdate` to return the day after its argument.

   Do you see any advantages of defining a `Date` as a class instead of as a structure? Do you see any disadvantages?

7. Given the following definitions

```
char *message = "Programming in Objective-C is fun";
char message2[] = "You said it";
int  x = 100;
```

determine whether each NSLog call from the following sets is valid and produces the same output as other calls from the set.

```
/*** set 1 ***/
NSLog (@"Programming in Objective-C is fun");
NSLog (@"%s", "Programming in Objective-C is fun");
NSLog (@"%s", message);

/*** set 2 ***/
NSLog (@"You said it");
NSLog (@"%s", message2);
NSLog (@"%s", &message2[0]);

/*** set 3 ***/
NSLog (@"said it");
NSLog (@"%s", message2 + 4);
NSLog (@"%s", &message2[4]);
```

8. Write a program that prints all its command-line arguments, one per line at the terminal. Notice the effect of enclosing arguments that contain space characters inside quotation marks.

9. Which of the following statements produce the output This is a test? Explain.

```
NSLog (@"This is a test");
NSLog ("This is a test");

NSLog (@"%s", "This is a test");
NSLog (@"%s", @"This is a test");

NSLog ("%s", "This is a test");
NSLog ("%s", @"This is a test");

NSLog (@"%@", @"This is a test");
NSLog (@"%@", "This is a test");
```

Part II

The Foundation
Framework

14

Introduction to the Foundation Framework

A framework is a collection of classes, methods, functions, and documentation logically grouped together to make developing programs easier. On Mac OS X, more than 80 frameworks are available for developing applications so that you can easily work with the Mac's Address Book structure, burn CDs, play back DVDs, play movies with QuickTime, play songs, and so on.

The framework that provides the base or foundation for all your program development is called the Foundation framework. This framework, the subject of the second part of this book, enables you to work with basic objects, such as numbers and strings, and with collections of objects, such as arrays, dictionaries, and sets. Other capabilities provide for working with dates and times, using automated memory management, working with the underlying file system, storing (or *archiving*) objects, and working with geometric data structures such as points and rectangles.

The Application Kit framework contains an extensive collection of classes and methods to develop interactive graphical applications. These provide the capability to easily work with text, menus, toolbars, tables, documents, the pasteboard, and windows. In Mac OS X, the term *Cocoa* collectively refers to the Foundation framework and the Application Kit framework. The term *Cocoa Touch* collectively refers to the Foundation framework and the UIKit framework. Part III, "Cocoa and the iPhone SDK," provides some more detail on this subject. Many resources are also listed in Appendix D, "Resources."

Foundation Documentation

For reference purposes, you should know where the Foundation header files are stored on your system. They are kept in the following directory:

```
/System/Library/Frameworks/Foundation.framework/Headers
```

> **Note**
>
> The header files are actually *linked* to another directory where they are stored, but that really makes no difference to you.

Navigate to this directory on your system and familiarize yourself with its contents. You should also take advantage of the Foundation framework documentation that is stored on your system (buried deep in the `/Developer/Documentation` directory) and that is also available online at Apple's website. Most documentation exists in the form of HTML files for viewing by a browser or as Acrobat `pdf` files. Contained in this documentation is a description of all the Foundation classes and all the implemented methods and functions.

If you're using Xcode to develop your programs, you have easy access to documentation through the Documentation window that is available from Xcode's Help menu. This window enables you to easily search and access documentation that is stored locally on your computer or is available online. Figure 14.1 shows the results of searching for the string "foundation framework" in the Xcode documentation window. From the pane that shows the header "Foundation Framework Reference," you can easily access the documentation for all Foundation classes.

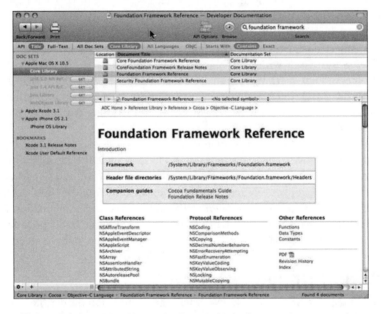

Figure 14.1   Using Xcode for Foundation reference documentation

If you're editing a file in Xcode and you want to get immediate access to the documentation for a particular header file, method, or class, you can simply highlight the text in your editor window and right-click it. From the menu that appears, you can either select Find Selected Text in Documentation or select Find Selected Text in API Reference, as appropriate. Xcode will search the documentation library and display the results that match your query.

Let's see how this works. The `NSString` class is a Foundation class that you use to work with strings. (It is explained in great detail in the next chapter.) Suppose you are editing a program that uses this class, and you want more information about it and its methods. You can highlight the word `NSString` wherever it appears in your edit window and right-click on it. If you then select Find Selected Text in API Reference from the menu that appears, you' get a document window displayed that looks similar to that shown in Figure 14.2.

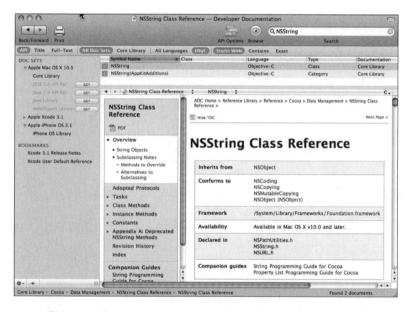

Figure 14.2   Obtaining documentation for the NSString class.

If you scroll down in the pane labeled NSString Class Reference, you'll find (among other things) a list of all the methods this class supports. This is an easy way to find information about the methods a class implements, including how they work and their expected arguments.

You can also access the documentation online at developer.apple.com/referencelibrary and navigate your way to the Foundation reference documentation (by following the Cocoa, Frameworks, Foundation Framework Reference links). At this website, you'll also find a wide assortment of documents covering specific programming issues, such as memory management, strings, and file management.

Unless you *subscribe* to a particular document set with Xcode, the online documentation might be more current than that stored on your disk.

This concludes our brief introduction to the Foundation framework. Now it's time to learn about some if its classes and how you can put them to work in your applications.

15

Numbers, Strings, and Collections

This chapter describes how to work with some of the basic objects provided in the Foundation framework. These include numbers, strings, and collections, which refers to the capability to work with groups of objects in the form of arrays, dictionaries, and sets.

The Foundation framework contains a plethora of classes, methods, and functions for you to use. Approximately 125 header files are available under Mac OS X. As a convenience, you can simply use the following import:

```
#import <Foundation/Foundation.h>
```

Because the `Foundation.h` file imports virtually all the other Foundation header files, you don't have to worry about whether you are importing the correct header file. Xcode automatically insert this header file into your program, as you've seen in each example throughout this book.

Using this statement can add significant time to your compiles. However, you can avoid this extra time by using *precompiled* headers. These are files that the compiler has preprocessed. By default, all Xcode projects benefit from precompiled headers.

In this chapter, you use the specific header files for each object you use. This will be a useful exercise to help you become familiar with what each header file contains.

> **Note**
>
> If you like, you can continue to just import `Foundation.h`, but if you do import the individual files shown in each example, you should delete the file *project_name*_Prefix.pch that XCode automatically includes for you when you create a new Foundation Tool project. When you delete that file from your project, be sure to select "Delete References" when prompted by Xcode.

Number Objects

All the numeric data types we've dealt with up to now, such as integers, floats, and longs, are basic data types in the Objective-C language—that is, they are not objects. For example, you can't send messages to them. Sometimes, though, you need to work with these values as objects. For example, the Foundation object NSArray enables you to set up an array in which you can store values. These values have to be objects, so you can't directly store any of your basic data types in these arrays. Instead, to store any of the basic numeric data types (including the char data type), you can use the NSNumber class to create objects from these data types. (See Program 15.1.)

Program 15.1

```
// Working with Numbers


#import <Foundation/NSObject.h>
#import <Foundation/NSAutoreleasePool.h>
#import <Foundation/NSValue.h>

#import <Foundation/NSString.h>

int main (int argc, char *argv[])
{
    NSAutoreleasePool * pool = [[NSAutoreleasePool alloc] init];
    NSNumber          *myNumber, *floatNumber, *intNumber;
    NSInteger          myInt;

    // integer value

    intNumber = [NSNumber numberWithInteger: 100];
    myInt = [intNumber integerValue];
    NSLog (@"%li", (long) myInt);

    // long value

    myNumber = [NSNumber numberWithLong: 0xabcdef];
    NSLog (@"%lx", [myNumber longValue]);

    // char value

    myNumber = [NSNumber numberWithChar: 'X'];
    NSLog (@"%c", [myNumber charValue]);


    // float value

    floatNumber = [NSNumber numberWithFloat: 100.00];
    NSLog (@"%g", [floatNumber floatValue]);
```

```
    // double

    myNumber = [NSNumber numberWithDouble: 12345e+15];
    NSLog (@"%lg", [myNumber doubleValue]);

    // Wrong access here

    NSLog (@"%i", [myNumber integerValue]);

    // Test two Numbers for equality

    if ([intNumber isEqualToNumber: floatNumber] == YES)
        NSLog (@"Numbers are equal");
    else
        NSLog (@"Numbers are not equal");

    // Test if one Number is <, ==, or > second Number

    if ([intNumber compare: myNumber] == NSOrderedAscending)
        NSLog (@"First number is less than second");

    [pool drain];
    return 0;
}
```

Program 15.1 Output

```
100
abcdef
X
100
1.2345e+19
0
Numbers are equal
First number is less than second
```

The file `<Foundation/NSValue.h>` is needed to work with objects from the `NSNumber` class.

A Quick Look at the Autorelease Pool

The first line in Program 15.1 has appeared in every program in this book. The following line reserves space in memory for an autorelease pool that you assign to `pool`:

```
NSAutoreleasePool * pool = [[NSAutoreleasePool alloc] init];
```

The autorelease pool provides for the automatic release of memory used by objects that are added to this pool. An object is added to the pool when it is sent an `autorelease` message. When the pool is released, so are all the objects that were added to it. Therefore, all such objects are destroyed unless they have been specified to exist beyond the scope of the autorelease pool (as indicated by their *reference counts*).

In general, you don't need to worry about releasing an object that a Foundation method returns. Sometimes the object is owned by the method that returns it. Other times, the object is newly created and added to the autorelease pool by the method. As described in detail in Part I, "The Objective-C 2.0 Language," you still need to release any objects (including Foundation objects) that you explicitly create using the `alloc` method when you're done using them.

> **Note**
>
> You also need to release objects created by a copy method, as you'll learn in Chapter 17.

Chapter 17, "Memory Management," fully describes reference counts, the autorelease pool, and the concept of automatic *garbage collection*.

Let's return to Program 15.1. The `NSNumber` class contains many methods that allow you to create `NSNumber` objects with initial values. For example, the line

```
intNumber = [NSNumber numberWithInteger: 100];
```

creates an object from an integer whose value is `100`.

The value retrieved from an `NSNumber` object must be consistent with the type of value that was stored in it. So in the statement that follows in the program, the message expression

```
[intNumber integerValue]
```

retrieves the integer value stored inside `intNumber` and stores it inside the `NSInteger` variable `myInt`. Note that `NSInteger` is not an object, but a typedef for basic date type. It is `typedef`'ed either to a `long` for 64-bit builds or to an `int` for 32-bit builds. A similar `typedef` for `NSUInteger` exists for working with unsigned integers in your program.

In the `NSLog` call, we cast the `NSInteger` `myInt` to a `long` and use the format characters `%li` to ensure that the value will be passed and displayed correctly even if the program is compiled for a 32-bit architecture.

For each basic value, a class method allocates an `NSNumber` object and sets it to a specified value. These methods begin with `numberWith` followed by the type, as in `numberWithLong:`, `numberWithFloat:`, and so on. In addition, instance methods can be used to set a previously allocated `NSNumber` object to a specified value. These all begin with `initWith`, as in `initWithLong:` and `initWithFloat:`.

Table 15.1 lists the class and instance methods for setting values for `NSNumber` objects and the corresponding instance methods for retrieving their values.

Table 15.1 **NSNumber Creation and Retrieval Methods**

Creation and Initialization Class Method	Initialization Instance Method	Retrieval Instance Method
numberWithChar:	initWithChar:	charValue
numberWithUnsignedChar:	initWithUnsignedChar:	unsignedCharValue
numberWithShort:	initWithShort:	shortValue
numberWithUnsignedShort:	initWithUnsignedShort:	unsignedShortValue
numberWithInteger:	initWithInteger:	integerValue
numberWithUnsignedInteger:	initWithUnsignedInteger:	unsignedIntegerValue
numberWithInt:	initWithInt:	intValue
numberWithUnsignedInt:	initWithUnsignedInt:	unsignedIntValue
numberWithLong:	initWithLong:	longValue
numberWithUnsignedLong:	initWithUnsignedLong:	unsignedLongValue
numberWithLongLong:	initWithLongLong:	longlongValue
numberWithUnsignedLongLong:	initWithUnsignedLongLong:	unsignedLongLongValue
numberWithFloat:	initWithFloat:	floatValue
numberWithDouble:	initWithDouble:	doubleValue
numberWithBool:	initWithBool:	boolValue

Returning to Program 15.1, the program next uses the class methods to create long, char, float, and double NSNumber objects. Notice what happens after you create a double object with the line

```
myNumber = [NSNumber numberWithDouble: 12345e+15];
```

and then try to (incorrectly) retrieve and display its value with the following line:

```
NSLog (@"%i", [myNumber integerValue]);
```

You get this output:

0

Also, you get no error message from the system. In general, it's up to you to ensure that if you store a value in an NSNumber object, you retrieve it in a consistent manner.

Inside the if statement, the message expression

```
[intNumber isEqualToNumber: floatNumber]
```

uses the isEqualToNumber: method to numerically compare two NSNumber objects. The program tests the Boolean value returned to see whether the two values are equal.

You can use the compare: method to test whether one numeric value is numerically less than, equal to, or greater than another. The message expression

```
[intNumber compare: myNumber]
```

returns the value NSOrderedAscending if the numeric value stored in intNumber is less than the numeric value contained in myNumber, returns the value NSOrderedSame if the two numbers are equal, and returns the value NSOrderedDescending if the first number is greater than the second. The values returned are defined in the header file NSObject.h for you.

Note that you can't reinitialize the value of a previously created NSNumber object. For example, you can't set the value of an integer stored in the NSNumber object myNumber with a statement such as follows:

```
[myNumber initWithInt: 1000];
```

This statement generates an error when the program is executed. All number objects must be newly created, meaning that you must invoke either one of the methods listed in the first column of Table 15.1 on the NSNumber class or one of the methods listed in column 2 with the result from the alloc method:

```
myNumber = [[NSNumber alloc] initWithInt: 1000];
```

Of course, based on previous discussions, if you create myNumber this way, you are responsible for subsequently releasing it when you're done using it with a statement such as follows:

```
[myNumber release];
```

You'll encounter NSNumber objects again in programs throughout the remainder of this chapter.

String Objects

You've encountered string objects in your programs before. Whenever you enclosed a sequence of character strings inside a pair of double quotes, as in

```
@"Programming is fun"
```

you created a character string object in Objective-C. The Foundation framework supports a class called NSString for working with character string objects. Whereas C-style strings consist of char characters, NSString objects consist of unichar characters. A unichar character is a multibyte character according to the Unicode standard. This enables you to work with character sets that can contain literally millions of characters. Luckily, you don't have to worry about the internal representation of the characters in your strings because the NSString class automatically handles this for you.[1] By using the methods from this class, you can more easily develop applications that can be *localized*—that is, made to work in different languages all over the world.

---

[1] Currently, unichar characters occupy 16 bits, but the Unicode standard provides for characters larger than that size. So in the future, unichar characters might be larger than 16 bits. The bottom line is to never make an assumption about the size of a Unicode character.

As you know, you create a constant character string object in Objective-C by putting the @ character in front of the string of double-quoted characters. So the expression

```
@"Programming is fun"
```

creates a constant character string object. In particular, it is a constant character string that belongs to the class NSConstantString. NSConstantString is a subclass of the string object class NSString. To use string objects in your program, include the following line:

```
#import <Foundation/NSString.h>
```

More on the NSLog Function

Program 15.2, which follows, shows how to define an NSString object and assign an initial value to it. It also shows how to use the format characters %@ to display an NSString object.

Program 15.2

```
#import <Foundation/NSObject.h>
#import <Foundation/NSString.h>
#import <Foundation/NSAutoreleasePool.h>

int main (int argc, char *argv[])
{
    NSAutoreleasePool * pool = [[NSAutoreleasePool alloc] init];
    NSString *str = @"Programming is fun";

    NSLog (@"%@", str);

    [pool drain];
    return 0;
}
```

Program 15.2 Output

```
Programming is fun
```

In the line

```
  NSString *str = @"Programming is fun";
```

the constant string object Programming is fun is assigned to the NSString variable str. Its value is then displayed using NSLog.

The NSLog format characters %@ can be used to display not just NSString objects, but any object. For example, given the following

```
NSNumber *intNumber = [NSNumber numberWithInteger: 100];
```

the NSLog call

```
NSLog (@"%@", intNumber);
```

produces the following output:

```
100
```

You can even use the `%@` format characters to display the entire contents of arrays, dictionaries, and sets. In fact, they can display your own class objects as well, as long as you override the `description` method inherited by your class. If you don't override the method, `NSLog` simply displays the name of the class and the address of your object in memory (that's the default implementation for the `description` method that is inherited from the `NSObject` class).

Mutable Versus Immutable Objects

When you create a string object by writing an expression such as

```
@"Programming is fun"
```

you create an object whose contents cannot be changed. This is referred to as an *immutable* object. The `NSString` class deals with immutable strings. Frequently, you'll want to deal with strings and change characters within the string. For example, you might want to delete some characters from a string or perform a search-and-replace operation on a string. These types of strings are handled through the `NSMutableString` class.

Program 15.3 shows basic ways to work with immutable character strings in your programs.

Program 15.3

```
// Basic String Operations

#import <Foundation/NSObject.h>
#import <Foundation/NSString.h>
#import <Foundation/NSAutoreleasePool.h>

int main (int argc, char *argv[])
{
    NSAutoreleasePool  *pool = [[NSAutoreleasePool alloc] init];
    NSString *str1 = @"This is string A";
    NSString *str2 = @"This is string B";
    NSString *res;
    NSComparisonResult  compareResult;

    // Count the number of characters

    NSLog (@"Length of str1: %lu", [str1 length]);

    // Copy one string to another

    res = [NSString stringWithString: str1];
    NSLog (@"copy: %@", res);
```

```
    // Copy one string to the end of another

    str2 = [str1 stringByAppendingString: str2];
    NSLog (@"Concatentation: %@", str2);

    // Test if 2 strings are equal

    if ([str1 isEqualToString: res] == YES)
       NSLog (@"str1 == res");
    else
       NSLog (@"str1 != res");

    // Test if one string is <, == or > than another

    compareResult = [str1 compare: str2];

    if  (compareResult == NSOrderedAscending)
       NSLog (@"str1 < str2");
    else if (compareResult == NSOrderedSame)
       NSLog (@"str1 == str2");
    else  // NSOrderedDescending
       NSLog (@"str1 > str2");

    // Convert a string to uppercase

    res = [str1 uppercaseString];
    NSLog (@"Uppercase conversion: %s", [res UTF8String]);

    // Convert a string to lowercase

    res = [str1 lowercaseString];
    NSLog (@"Lowercase conversion: %@", res);

    NSLog (@"Original string: %@", str1);

    [pool drain];
    return 0;
}
```

Program 15.3 Output

```
Length of str1: 16
Copy: This is string A
Concatentation: This is string AThis is string B
str1 == res
str1 < str2
Uppercase conversion: THIS IS STRING A
Lowercase conversion: this is string a
Original string: This is string A
```

Program 15.3 first declares three immutable NSString objects: str1, str2, and res. The first two are initialized to constant character string objects. The declaration

```
NSComparisonResult compareResult;
```

declares compareResult to hold the result of the string comparison that will be performed later in the program.

You can use the length method to count the number of characters in a string. It returns an unsigned integer value of type NSUInteger. The output verifies that the string

```
@"This is string A"
```

contains 16 characters. The statement

```
res = [NSString stringWithString: str1];
```

shows how to create a new character string with the contents of another. The resulting NSString object is assigned to res and is then displayed to verify the results. An actual copy of the string contents is made here, not just another reference to the same string in memory. That means that str1 and res refer to two different string objects, which is different than simply performing a simple assignment, as follows:

```
res = str1;
```

This simply creates another reference to the same object in memory.

The stringByAppendingString: method can join two character strings. So the expression

```
[str1 stringByAppendingString: str2]
```

creates a new string object that consists of the characters str1 followed by str2, returning the result. The original string objects, str1 and str2, are not affected by this operation (they can't be because they're both immutable string objects).

The isEqualToString: method is used next to test to see whether two character strings are equal—that is, whether they contain the same characters. You can use the compare: method instead if you need to determine the ordering of two character strings—for example, if you wanted to sort an array of them. Similar to the compare: method you used earlier for comparing two NSNumber objects, the result of the comparison is NSOrderedAscending if the first string is lexically less than the second string, NSOrderedSame if the two strings are equal, and NSOrderedDescending if the first string is lexically greater than the second. If you don't want to perform a case-sensitive comparison, use the caseInsensitiveCompare: method instead of compare: to compare two strings. In such a case, the two string objects @"Gregory" and @"gregory" would compare as equal with caseInsensitiveCompare:.

The uppercaseString and lowercaseString are the last two NSString methods used in Program 15.3 to convert strings to upper case and lower case, respectively. Again, the conversion does not affect the original strings, as the last line of output verifies.

Program 15.4 illustrates additional methods for dealing with strings. These methods enable you to extract substrings from a string, as well as search one string for the occurrence of another.

Some methods require that you identify a substring by specifying a range. A *range* consists of a starting index number plus a character count. Index numbers begin with zero, so the first three characters in a string would be specified by the pair of numbers {0, 3}. Some methods of the NSString class (and other Foundation classes as well) use the special data type NSRange to create a range specification. It is defined in <Foundation/NSRange.h> (which is included for you from inside <Foundation/NSString.h>) and is actually a typedef definition for a structure that has two members, location and length, each of which is defined as type NSUInteger. Program 15.4 uses this data type.

> **Note**
>
> You can read about structures in Chapter 13, "Underlying C Language Features." However, you can probably gain enough information to work with them from the discussion that follows in this chapter.

Program 15.4

```
// Basic String Operations - Continued


#import <Foundation/NSObject.h>
#import <Foundation/NSString.h>
#import <Foundation/NSAutoreleasePool.h>

int main (int argc, char *argv[])
{
   NSAutoreleasePool  *pool = [[NSAutoreleasePool alloc] init];
   NSString   *str1 = @"This is string A";
   NSString   *str2 = @"This is string B";
   NSString   *res;
   NSRange    subRange;

   // Extract first 3 chars from string

   res = [str1 substringToIndex: 3];
   NSLog (@"First 3 chars of str1: %@", res);

   // Extract chars to end of string starting at index 5

   res = [str1 substringFromIndex: 5];
   NSLog (@"Chars from index 5 of str1: %@", res);

   // Extract chars from index 8 through 13 (6 chars)

   res = [[str1 substringFromIndex: 8] substringToIndex: 6];
   NSLog (@"Chars from index 8 through 13: %@", res);

   // An easier way to do the same thing

   res = [str1 substringWithRange: NSMakeRange (8, 6)];
```

```
NSLog (@"Chars from index 8 through 13: %@", res);

// Locate one string inside another

subRange = [str1 rangeOfString: @"string A"];
NSLog (@"String is at index %lu, length is %lu",
    subRange.location, subRange.length);


subRange = [str1 rangeOfString: @"string B"];

if (subRange.location == NSNotFound)
   NSLog (@"String not found");
else
   NSLog (@"String is at index %lu, length is %lu",
       subRange.location, subRange.length);

[pool drain];
return 0;
}
```

Program 15.4 Output

```
First 3 chars of str1: Thi
Chars from index 5 of str1: is string A
Chars from index 8 through 13: string
Chars from index 8 through 13: string
String is at index 8, length is 8
String not found
```

The substringToIndex: method creates a substring from the leading characters in a string up to but not including the specified index number. Because indexing begins at 0, the argument of 3 extracts characters 0, 1, and 2 from the string and returns the resulting string object. For any of the string methods that take an index number as one of their arguments, you get a "Range or index out of bounds" error message if you provide an invalid index number in the string.

The substringFromIndex: method returns a substring from the receiver beginning with the character at the specified index and up through the end of the string.

The expression

```
res = [[str1 substringFromIndex: 8] substringToIndex: 6];
```

shows how the two methods can be combined to extract a substring of characters from inside a string. The substringFromIndex: method is first used to extract characters from index number 8 through the end of the string; then substringToIndex: is applied to the result to get the first six characters. The net result is a substring representing the range of characters {8, 6} from the original string.

The `substringWithRange:` method does in one step what we just did in two: It takes a range and returns a character in the specified range. The special function

```
NSMakeRange (8, 6)
```

creates a range from its argument and returns the result. This is given as the argument to the `substringWithRange:` method.

To locate one string inside another, you can use the `rangeOfString:` method. If the specified string is found inside the receiver, the returned range specifies precisely where in the string it was found. However, if the string is not found, the range that is returned has its `location` member set to `NSNotFound`.

So the statement

```
subRange = [str1 rangeOfString: @"string A"];
```

assigns the `NSRange` structure returned by the method to the `NSRange` variable `subRange`. Be sure to note that `subRange` is not an object variable, but a *structure* variable (the declaration for `subRange` in the program also does not contain an asterisk). Its members can be retrieved by using the structure member operator dot (.). So the expression `subRange.location` gives the value of the `location` member of the structure, and `subRange.length` gives the `length` member. These values are passed to the `NSLog` function to be displayed.

Mutable Strings

The `NSMutableString` class can be used to create string objects whose characters can be changed. Because this class is a subclass of `NSString`, all `NSString`'s methods can be used as well.

When we speak of mutable versus immutable string objects, we talk about changing the actual characters within the string. Either a mutable or an immutable string object can always be set to a completely different string object during execution of the program. For example, consider the following:

```
str1 = @"This is a string";
   ...
str1 = [str1 substringFromIndex: 5];
```

In this case, `str1` is first set to a constant character string object. Later in the program, it is set to a substring. In such a case, `str1` can be declared as either a mutable or an immutable string object. Be sure you understand this point.

Program 15.5 shows some ways to work with mutable strings in your programs.

Program 15.5

```objc
// Basic String Operations - Mutable Strings


#import <Foundation/NSObject.h>
#import <Foundation/NSString.h>
#import <Foundation/NSAutoreleasePool.h>

int main (int argc, char *argv[])
{
   NSAutoreleasePool  * pool = [[NSAutoreleasePool alloc] init];
   NSString  *str1 = @"This is string A";
   NSString  *search, *replace;
   NSMutableString  *mstr;
   NSRange   substr;

   // Create mutable string from nonmutable

   mstr = [NSMutableString  stringWithString: str1];
   NSLog (@"%@", mstr);

   // Insert characters

   [mstr insertString: @" mutable" atIndex: 7];
   NSLog (@"%@", mstr);

   // Effective concatentation if insert at end

   [mstr insertString: @" and string B" atIndex: [mstr length]];
   NSLog (@"%@", mstr);

   //  Or can use appendString directly

   [mstr appendString: @" and string C"];
   NSLog (@"%@", mstr);

   // Delete substring based on range

   [mstr deleteCharactersInRange: NSMakeRange (16, 13)];
   NSLog (@"%@", mstr);

   // Find range first and then use it for deletion

   substr = [mstr  rangeOfString: @"string B and "];
```

```
    if (substr.location != NSNotFound) {
       [mstr deleteCharactersInRange: substr];
       NSLog (@"%@", mstr);
    }

    // Set the mutable string directly

    [mstr setString: @"This is string A"];
    NSLog (@"%@", mstr);

    // Now let's replace a range of chars with another

    [mstr replaceCharactersInRange: NSMakeRange(8, 8)
                        withString: @"a mutable string"];
    NSLog (@"%@", mstr);

    // Search and replace

    search = @"This is";
    replace = @"An example of";

    substr = [mstr  rangeOfString: search];

    if (substr.location != NSNotFound) {
       [mstr replaceCharactersInRange: substr
                          withString: replace];
       NSLog (@"%@", mstr);
    }

    // Search and replace all occurrences

    search = @"a";
    replace = @"X";

    substr = [mstr rangeOfString: search];

    while (substr.location != NSNotFound) {
       [mstr replaceCharactersInRange: substr
                          withString: replace];
          substr = [mstr rangeOfString: search];
    }

    NSLog (@"%@", mstr);

    [pool drain];
    return 0;
}
```

Program 15.5 Output

```
This is string A
This is mutable string A
This is mutable string A and string B
This is mutable string A and string B and string C
This is mutable string B and string C
This is mutable string C
This is string A
This is a mutable string
An example of a mutable string
An exXmple of X mutXble string
```

The declaration

```
NSMutableString *mstr;
```

declares `mstr` to be a variable that holds a character string object whose contents might change during execution of the program. The line

```
    mstr = [NSMutableString stringWithString: str1];
```

sets `mstr` to the string object whose contents are a copy of the characters in `str1`, or "This is string A". When the `stringWithString:` method is sent to the `NSMutableString` class, a mutable string object is returned. When it's sent to the `NSString` class, as in Program 15.5, you get an immutable string object instead.

The `insertString:atIndex:` method inserts the specified character string into the receiver beginning at the specified index number. In this case, you insert the string @" mutable" into the string beginning at index number 7, or in front of the eighth character in the string. Unlike the immutable string object methods, no value is returned here because the receiver is modified—you can do that because it's a mutable string object.

The second `insertString:atIndex:` invocation uses the `length` method to insert one character string at the end of another. The `appendString:` method makes this task a little simpler.

By using the `deleteCharactersInRange:` method, you can remove a specified number of characters from a string. The range `{16, 13}`, when applied to the string

```
This is mutable string A and string B and string C
```

deletes the 13 characters "string A and" beginning with index number 16 (or the 17th character in the string). This is depicted in Figure 15.1.

```
This is mutable string A and string B and string C
```

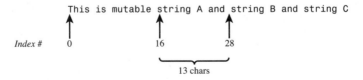

Figure 15.1   Indexing into a string

The `rangeOfString:` method is used in the lines that follow in Program 15.5 to show how a string can first be located and then deleted. After first verifying that the string `@"string B and"` does exist in `mstr`, the `deleteCharactersInRange:` method is used to delete the characters, using the range returned from the `rangeOfString:` method as its argument.

You can use the `setString:` method to directly set the contents of a mutable string object. After using this method to set `mstr` to the string `@"This is string A"`, the `replaceCharactersInRange:` method replaces some of the characters in the string with another string. The sizes of the strings do not have to be the same; you can replace one string with another of equal or unequal sizes. So in the statement

```
[mstr replaceCharactersInRange: NSMakeRange(8, 8)
               withString: @"a mutable string"];
```

the 8 characters "string A" are replaced with the 16 characters "a mutable string".

The remaining lines in the program example show how to perform search and replace operations. In the first case, you locate the string `@"This is"` inside the string `mstr`, which has been set to `@"This is a mutable string"`. This string is found inside the search string and gets replaced by the string `@"An example of"`. The net result is that `mstr` gets changed to the string `@"An example of a mutable string"`.

The program next sets up a loop to illustrate how to implement a search-and-replace-all operation. The search string is set to `@"a"` and the replacement string is set to `@"X"`.

If the replacement string also contains the search string (for example, consider replacing the string `"a"` with the string `"aX"`), you end up with an infinite loop.

Second, if the replacement string is empty (that is, if it contains no characters), you effectively delete all occurrences of the search string. An empty constant character string object is specified by an adjacent pair of quotation marks, with no intervening spaces:

```
replace = @"";
```

Of course, if you just wanted to delete an occurrence of a string, you could use the `deleteCharactersInRange:` method instead, as you've already seen.

Finally, the `NSMutableString` class also contains a method called `replaceOccurrencesOfString:withString:options:range:` that you can use to do a search-and-replace-all on a string. In fact, you could have replaced the `while` loop from Program 15.5 with this single statement:

```
[mstr replaceOccurrencesOfString: search
               withString: replace
                  options: nil
                    range: NSMakeRange (0, [mstr length])];
```

This achieves the same result and averts the potential of an infinite loop because the method prevents such a thing from happening.

Where Are All Those Objects Going?

Programs 15.4 and 15.5 deal with many string objects that various NSString and NSMutableString methods create and return. As discussed at the beginning of this chapter, you are not responsible for releasing the memory these objects use; the objects' creators are. Presumably, the creators have added all these objects to the autorelease pool, and the objects will be freed when the pool is released. However, be aware that if you are developing a program that creates a lot of temporary objects, the memory these objects use can accumulate. In such cases, you might need to adopt different strategies that allow for memory to be released during your program's execution, not just at the end. Chapter 17 describes this concept. For now, just realize that these objects take up memory that can expand as your program executes.

The NSString class contains more than 100 methods that can work with immutable string objects. Table 15.2 summarizes some of the more commonly used ones, and Table 15.3 lists some of the additional methods that the NSMutableString class provides. Some other NSString methods (such as working with pathnames and reading the contents of a file into a string) are introduced to you throughout the remainder of this book.

In Tables 15.2 and 15.3, *url* is an NSURL object, *path* is an NSString object specifying the path to a file, *nsstring* is an NSString object, *i* is an NSUInteger value representing a valid character number in a string, *enc* is an NSStringEncoding object that specifies the character encoding, *err* is an NSError object that describes an error if one occurs, *size* and *opts* are NSUIntegers, and *range* is an NSRange object indicating a valid range of characters within a string.

Table 15.2 **Common NSString Methods**

Method	Description
+(id) stringWithContentsOfFile: *path* encoding: *enc* error: *err*	Creates a new string and sets it to the *path* contents of a file specified by *path* using character encoding *enc*, returning error in *err* if non-nil
+(id) stringWithContentsOfURL: *url* encoding: *enc* error: *err*	Creates a new string and sets it to the contents of *url* using character encoding *enc*, returning error in *err* if non-nil
+(id) string	Creates a new empty string
+(id) stringWithString: *nsstring*	Creates a new string, setting it to *nsstring*
-(id) initWithString: *nsstring*	Sets a newly allocated string to *nsstring*
-(id) initWithContentsOfFile: *path* encoding: *enc* error: *err*	Sets a string to the contents of a file specified by *path*

Table 15.2   **Common NSString Methods**

Method	Description
`-(id) initWithContentsOfURL:` `url` `encoding` `enc` `error:` `err`	Sets a string to the contents of `url` (`NSURL *`) `url` using character encoding `enc`, returning error in `err` if non-nil
`-(NSUInteger) length`	Returns the number of characters in the string
`-(unichar) characterAtIndex:` `i`	Returns the Unicode character at index `i`
`-(NSString *)` `substringFromIndex:` `i`	Returns a substring from the character at `i` to the end
`-(NSString *)` `substringWithRange:` `range`	Returns a substring based on a specified range
`-(NSString *) substringToIndex:` `i`	Returns a substring from the start of the string up to the character at index `i`
`-(NSComparator *)` `caseInsensitiveCompare:` `nsstring`	Compares two strings, ignoring case
`-(NSComparator *) compare:` `nsstring`	Compares two strings
`-(BOOL) hasPrefix:` `nsstring`	Tests whether a string begins with `nsstring`
`-(BOOL) hasSuffix:` `nsstring`	Tests whether a string ends with `nsstring`
`-(BOOL) isEqualToString:` `nsstring`	Tests whether two strings are equal
`-(NSString *) capitalizedString`	Returns a string with the first letter of every word capitalized (and the remaining letters in each word converted to lower case)
`-(NSString *) lowercaseString`	Returns a string converted to lower case
`-(NSString *) uppercaseString`	Returns a string converted to upper case
`-(const char *) UTF8String`	Returns a string converted to a UTF-8 C-style character string
`-(double) doubleValue`	Returns a string converted to a double
`-(float) floatValue`	Returns a string converted to a floating value
`-(NSInteger) integerValue`	Returns a string converted to an `NSInteger` integer
`-(int) intValue`	Returns a string converted to an integer

The methods in Table 15.3 either create or modify NSMutableString objects.

Table 15.3   **Common NSMutableString Methods**

Method	Description
+(id) stringWithCapacity: *size*	Creates a string initially containing *size* characters.
-(id) initWithCapacity: *size*	Initializes a string with an initial capacity of *size* characters.
-(void) setString: *nsstring*	Sets a string to *nsstring.*
-(void) appendString: *nsstring*	Appends *nsstring* to the end of the receiver.
-(void) deleteCharactersInRange: *range*	Deletes characters in a specified *range*.
-(void) insertString: *nstring* atIndex: *i*	Inserts *nsstring* into the receiver starting at index *i*.
-(void) replaceCharactersInRange: *range* withString: *nsstring*	Replaces characters in a specified *range* with *nsstring*.
-(void) replaceOccurrencesOf String: *nsstring* withString: *nsstring2* options: *opts* range: *range*	Replaces all occurrences of *nsstring* with *nsstring2* within a specified *range* and according to options *opts*. Options can include a bitwise-ORed combination of NSBackwardsSearch (the search starts from the end of range), NSAnchoredSearch (*nsstring* must match from the beginning of the range only), NSLiteralSearch (performs a byte-by-byte comparison), and NSCaseInsensitiveSearch.

NSString objects are used extensively throughout the remainder of this text. If you need to parse strings into tokens, you can take a look at Foundation's NSScanner class.

Array Objects

A Foundation array is an ordered collection of objects. Most often, elements in an array are of one particular type, but that's not required. Just as there are mutable and immutable strings, are there mutable and immutable arrays. *Immutable* arrays are handled by the NSArray class, whereas *mutable* ones are handled by NSMutableArray. The latter is a subclass of the former, which means it inherits its methods. To work with array objects in your programs, include the following line:

```
#import <Foundation/NSArray.h>
```

Program 15.6 sets up an array to store the names of the months of the year and then prints them.

Program 15.6

```
#import <Foundation/NSObject.h>
#import <Foundation/NSArray.h>
#import <Foundation/NSString.h>
#import <Foundation/NSAutoreleasePool.h>

int main (int argc, char *argv[])
{
   int      i;
   NSAutoreleasePool   * pool = [[NSAutoreleasePool alloc] init];

   // Create an array to contain the month names

   NSArray  *monthNames = [NSArray  arrayWithObjects:
      @"January", @"February", @"March", @"April",
      @"May", @"June", @"July", @"August", @"September",
      @"October", @"November", @"December", nil ];

   // Now list all the elements in the array

   NSLog (@"Month    Name");
   NSLog (@"=====    ====");

   for (i = 0; i < 12; ++i)
      NSLog (@" %2i      %@", i + 1, [monthNames objectAtIndex: i]);

   [pool drain];
   return 0;
}
```

Program 15.6 Output

```
Month   Name
=====   ====
  1     January
  2     February
  3     March
  4     April
  5     May
  6     June
  7     July
  8     August
  9     September
 10     October
 11     November
 12     December
```

You can use the class method `arrayWithObjects:` to create an array with a list of objects as its elements. In such a case, the objects are listed in order and are separated by commas. This is a special syntax used by methods that can take a variable number of arguments. To mark the end of the list, `nil` must be specified as the last value in the list—it isn't actually stored inside the array.

In Program 15.7 `monthNames` is set to the 12 string values specified by the arguments to `arrayWithObjects:`.

Elements are identified in an array by their index numbers. Similar to `NSString` objects, indexing begins with zero. So an array containing 12 elements has valid index numbers 0–11. To retrieve an element of an array using its index number, you use the `objectAtIndex:` method.

The program simply executes a `for` loop to extract each element from the array using the `objectAtIndex:` method. Each retrieved element is displayed with `NSLog`.

Program 15.7 generates a table of prime numbers. Because you will be adding prime numbers to your array as they are generated, a mutable array is required. The `NSMutableArray primes` is allocated using the `arrayWithCapacity:` method. The argument of 20 that you give specifies the initial capacity of the array; a mutable array's capacity automatically increases as necessary while the program is running.

Even though prime numbers are integers, you can't directly store `int` values inside your array. Your array can hold only objects. Thus, you need to store `NSNumber` integer objects inside your `primes` array.

Program 15.7

```
#import <Foundation/NSObject.h>
#import <Foundation/NSArray.h>
#import <Foundation/NSString.h>
#import <Foundation/NSAutoreleasePool.h>
#import <Foundation/NSValue.h>

#define MAXPRIME    50
```

```
int main (int argc, char *argv[])
{
    int      i, p, prevPrime;
    BOOL     isPrime;
    NSAutoreleasePool   * pool = [[NSAutoreleasePool alloc] init];

    // Create an array to store the prime numbers

    NSMutableArray  *primes =
        [NSMutableArray arrayWithCapacity: 20];

    // Store the first two primes (2 and 3) into the array

    [primes  addObject: [NSNumber numberWithInteger: 2]];
    [primes  addObject: [NSNumber numberWithInteger: 3]];

    // Calculate the remaining primes

    for (p = 5; p <= MAXPRIME; p += 2) {
        // we're testing to see if p is prime

        isPrime = YES;

        i = 1;

        do {
            prevPrime = [[primes objectAtIndex: i] integerValue];

            if (p % prevPrime == 0)
                isPrime = NO;

            ++i;
        } while ( isPrime == YES && p / prevPrime >= prevPrime);

        if (isPrime)
            [primes addObject: [NSNumber numberWithInteger: p]];
    }


    // Display the results

    for (i = 0; i < [primes count]; ++i)
        NSLog (@"%li", (long) [[primes objectAtIndex: i] integerValue]);

    [pool drain];
    return 0;
}
```

Program 15.7 Output

```
2
3
5
7
11
13
17
19
23
29
31
37
41
43
47
```

You define `kMaxPrime` to the maximum prime number you want the program to calculate, which, in this case, is `50`.

After allocating your `primes` array, you set the first two elements of the array using these statements:

```
[primes addObject: [NSNumber numberWithInteger: 2]];
[primes addObject: [NSNumber numberWithInteger: 3]];
```

The `addObject:` method adds an object to the end of an array. Here you add the `NSNumber` objects created from the integer values `2` and `3`, respectively.

The program then enters a `for` loop to find prime numbers starting with `5`, going up to `kMaxPrime` and skipping the even numbers in between (`p += 2`).

For each possible prime candidate `p`, you want to see whether it is evenly divisible by the previously discovered primes. If it is, it's not prime. As an added optimization, you test the candidate for even division only by earlier primes up to its square root. That's because if a number is not prime, it must be divisible by a prime number that is less than or equal to its square root (ahh, back to high school math again!). So the expression

```
p / prevPrime >= prevPrime
```

remains true only as long as `prevPrime` is less than the square root of `p`.

If the `do-while` loop exits with the flag `isPrime` still equal to `YES`, you have found another prime number. In that case, the candidate `p` is added to the `primes` array and execution continues.

Just a comment about program efficiency here: The Foundation classes for working with arrays provide many conveniences. However, in the case of manipulating large arrays of numbers with complex algorithms, learning how to perform such a task using the lower-level array constructs provided by the language might be more efficient, in terms of both memory usage and execution speed. Refer to the section titled "Arrays" in Chapter 13 for more information.

Making an Address Book

Let's take a look at an example that starts to combine a lot of what you've learned to this point by creating an address book.[2] Your address book will contain address cards. For the sake of simplicity, your address cards will contain only a person's name and email address. Extend this concept to other information, such as address and phone number, is straight-forward, but we leave that as an exercise for you at the end of this chapter.

Creating an Address Card

We start by defining a new class called `AddressCard`. You'll want the capability to create a new address card, set its name and email fields, retrieve those fields, and print the card. In a graphics environment, you could use some nice routines such as those provided by the Application Kit framework to draw your card onscreen. But here you stick to a simple Console interface to display your address cards.

Program 15.8 shows the interface file for your new `AddressCard` class. We're not going to synthesize the accessor methods yet; writing them yourself offers valuable lessons.

Program 15.8 Interface File AddressCard.h

```
#import <Foundation/NSObject.h>
#import <Foundation/NSString.h>

@interface AddressCard: NSObject
{
  NSString   *name;
  NSString   *email;
}


-(void) setName: (NSString *) theName;
-(void) setEmail: (NSString *) theEmail;

-(NSString *) name;
-(NSString *) email;

-(void) print;

@end
```

---

[2] Mac OS X provides an entire Address Book framework, which offers extremely powerful capabilities for working with address books.

This is straightforward, as is the implementation file in Program 15.8.

Program 15.8 Implementation File AddressCard.m

```
#import "AddressCard.h"


@implementation AddressCard

-(void) setName: (NSString *) theName
{
   name = [[NSString alloc] initWithString: theName];
}

-(void) setEmail: (NSString *) theEmail
{
    email = [[NSString alloc] initWithString: theEmail];
}

-(NSString *) name
{
  return name;
}


-(NSString *) email
{
  return email;
}

-(void) print
{
    NSLog (@"====================================");
    NSLog (@"|                                  |");
    NSLog (@"|   %-31s |", [name UTF8String]);
    NSLog (@"|   %-31s |", [email UTF8String]);
    NSLog (@"|                                  |");
    NSLog (@"|                                  |");
    NSLog (@"|                                  |");
    NSLog (@"|        O                O        |");
    NSLog (@"====================================");

}
@end
```

You could have the setName: and setEmail: methods store the objects directly in their respective instance variables with method definitions like these:

```
-(void) setName: (NSString *) theName
{
   name = theName;
}
```

```
-(void) setEmail: (NSString *) theEmail
{
    email = theEmail;
}
```

But the `AddressCard` object would not own its member objects. We talked about the motivation for an object to take ownership with respect to the `Rectangle` class owning its `origin` object in Chapter 8, "Inheritance."

Defining the two methods in the following way would also be an incorrect approach because the `AddressCard` methods would still not own their name and email objects—`NSString` would own them:

```
-(void) setName: (NSString *) theName
{
    name = [NSString stringWithString: theName];
}

-(void) setEmail: (NSString *) theEmail
{
    email = [NSString stringWithString: theEmail];
}
```

Returning to Program 15.8, the `print` method tries to present the user with a nice display of an address card in a format resembling a Rolodex card (remember those?). The `%-31s` characters to `NSLog` indicate to display a UTF8 C-string within a field width of 31 characters, left-justified. This ensures that the right edges of your address card line up in the output. It's used in this example strictly for cosmetic reasons.

With your AddressCard class in hand, you can write a test program to create an address card, set its values, and display it (see Program 15.8).

Program 15.8 Test Program

```
#import "AddressCard.h"
#import <Foundation/NSAutoreleasePool.h>

int main (int argc, char *argv[])
{
    NSAutoreleasePool * pool = [[NSAutoreleasePool alloc] init];
    NSString    *aName = @"Julia Kochan";
    NSString    *aEmail = @"jewls337@axlc.com";
    AddressCard *card1 = [[AddressCard alloc] init];
```

```
    [card1 setName: aName];
    [card1 setEmail: aEmail];

    [card1 print];

    [card1 release];
    [pool drain];
    return 0;
}
```

Program 15.8 Output

```
=======================================
|                                     |
| Julia Kochan                        |
| jewls337@axlc.com                   |
|                                     |
|                                     |
|                                     |
|          O              O           |
=======================================
```

In this program, the line

```
[card1 release];
```

is used to release the memory your address card uses. You should realize from previous discussions that releasing an `AddressCard` object this way does not also release the memory you allocated for its `name` and `email` members. To make the `AddressCard` leak free, you need to override the `dealloc` method to release these members whenever the memory for an `AddressCard` object is released.

This is the `dealloc` method for your `AddressCard` class:

```
-(void) dealloc
{
    [name release];
    [email release];
    [super dealloc];
}
```

The `dealloc` method must release its own instance variables before using `super` to destroy the object itself. That's because an object is no longer valid after it has been deallocated.

To make your `AddressCard` leak free, you must also modify your `setName:` and `setEmail:` methods to release the memory used by the objects stored in their respective instance variables. If someone changes the name on a card, you need to release the memory that the old name takes up before you replace it with the new one. Similarly, for the email address, you must release the memory it uses before you replace it with the new one.

These are the new `setName:` and `setEmail:` methods that ensure that we have a class that handles memory management properly:

```
-(void) setName: (NSString *) theName
{
   [name release];
   name = [[NSString alloc] initWithString: theName];
}

-(void) setEmail: (NSString *) theEmail
{
   [email release];
   email = [[NSString alloc] initWithString: theEmail];
}
```

You can send a message to a nil object; therefore, the message expressions

```
[name release];
```

and

```
[email release];
```

are okay even if `name` or `email` have not been previously set.

Synthesized `AddressCard` Methods

Now that we've discussed the correct way to write the accessor methods `setName:` and `setEmail:`, and you understand the important principles, we can go back and let the system generate the accessor methods for you. Consider the second version of the `AddressCard` interface file:

```
#import <Foundation/NSObject.h>
#import <Foundation/NSString.h>

@interface AddressCard: NSObject
{
   NSString     *name;
   NSString     *email;
}

@property (copy, nonatomic) NSString *name, *email;
-(void) print;
@end
```

The line

```
@property (copy, nonatomic) NSString *name, *email;
```

lists the *attributes* copy and nonatomic for the properties. The copy attribute says to make a copy of the instance variable in its setter method, as you did in the version you wrote. The default action is not to make a copy, but to instead perform a simple assignment (that's the default attribute assign), an incorrect approach that we recently discussed.

The nonatomic attribute specifies that the getter method should not *retain* or *autorelease* the instance variable before returning its value. Chapter 18 discusses this topic in greater detail.

Program 15.9 is the new AddressCard implementation file that specifies that the accessor methods be synthesized.

Program 15.9 Implementation File AddressCard.m with Synthesized Methods

```
#import "AddressCard.h"


@implementation AddressCard

@synthesize name, email;
-(void) print
{
    NSLog (@"===================================");
    NSLog (@"|                                 |");
    NSLog (@"|   %-31s |", [name UTF8String]);
    NSLog (@"|   %-31s |", [email UTF8String]);
    NSLog (@"|                                 |");
    NSLog (@"|                                 |");
    NSLog (@"|                                 |");
    NSLog (@"|         O             O         |");
    NSLog (@"===================================");

}
@end
```

We leave it as an exercise to you to verify that the new AddressCard definition with its synthesized accessor methods works with the test program shown in Program 15.9.

Now let's add another method to your AddressCard class. You might want to set both the name and email fields of your card with one call. To do so, add a new method, setName:andEmail:.[3] The new method looks like this:

```
-(void) setName: (NSString *) theName andEmail: (NSString *) theEmail
{
    self.name = theName;
    self.email = theEmail;
}
```

---

[3] *You also might want an* `initWithName:andEmail:` *initialization method, but we don't show that here.*

By relying on the synthesized setter methods to set the appropriate instance variables (instead of setting them directly inside the method yourself), you add a level of abstraction and, therefore, make the program slightly more independent of its internal data structures. You also take advantage of the synthesized method's properties, which in this case, copy instead of assign the value to the instance variable.

Program 15.9 tests your new method.

Program 15.9 Test Program

```
#import <Foundation/NSAutoreleasePool.h>
#import "AddressCard.h"

int main (int argc, char *argv[])
{
    NSAutoreleasePool * pool = [[NSAutoreleasePool alloc] init];

    NSString   *aName = @"Julia Kochan";
    NSString   *aEmail = @"jewls337@axlc.com";
    NSString   *bName = @"Tony Iannino";
    NSString   *bEmail = @"tony.iannino@techfitness.com";

    AddressCard    *card1 = [[AddressCard alloc] init];
    AddressCard    *card2 = [[AddressCard alloc] init];

    [card1 setName: aName andEmail: aEmail];
    [card2 setName: bName andEmail: bEmail];

    [card1 print];
    [card2 print];
    [card1 release];
    [card2 release];
    [pool drain];
    return 0;
}
```

Program 15.9 Output

```
======================================
|                                    |
|  Julia Kochan                      |
|  jewls337@axlc.com                 |
|                                    |
|                                    |
|                                    |
|        O           O               |
======================================
```

```
=====================================
|                                   |
|  Tony Iannino                     |
|  tony.iannino@techfitness.com     |
|                                   |
|                                   |
|                                   |
|          O           O            |
=====================================
```

Your `AddressCard` class seems to be working okay. What if you wanted to work with a lot of `AddressCards`? It would make sense to collect them together, which is exactly what you'll do by defining a new class called `AddressBook`. The `AddressBook` class will store the name of an address book and a collection of `AddressCards`, which you'll store in an array object. To start, you'll want the ability to create a new address book, add new address cards to it, find out how many entries are in it, and list its contents. Later, you'll want to be able to search the address book, remove entries, possibly edit existing entries, sort it, or even make a copy of its contents.

Let's get started with a simple `interface` file (see Program 15.10).

Program 15.10 AddressBook.h Interface File

```
#import <Foundation/NSArray.h>
#import "AddressCard.h"

@interface AddressBook: NSObject
{
    NSString        *bookName;
    NSMutableArray  *book;
}

-(id) initWithName: (NSString *) name;
-(void) addCard: (AddressCard *) theCard;
-(int)  entries;
-(void) list;
-(void) dealloc;

@end
```

The `initWithName:` method sets up the initial array to hold the address cards and store the name of the book, whereas the `addCard:` method adds an `AddressCard` to the book. The `entries` method reports the number of address cards in your book, and the `list` method gives a concise listing of its entire contents. Program 15.10 shows the implementation file for your `AddressBook` class.

Program 15.10 AddressBook.m Implementation File

```objc
#import "AddressBook.h"


@implementation AddressBook;

// set up the AddressBook's name and an empty book

-(id) initWithName: (NSString *) name
{
    self = [super init];

    if (self) {
        bookName = [[NSString alloc] initWithString: name];
        book = [[NSMutableArray alloc] init];
    }

    return self;
}

-(void) addCard: (AddressCard *) theCard
{
    [book addObject: theCard];
}

-(int) entries
{
    return [book count];
}


-(void) list
{
    NSLog (@"======== Contents of: %@ =========", bookName);

    for ( AddressCard *theCard in book )
        NSLog (@"%-20s    %-32s", [theCard.name UTF8String],
                    [theCard.email UTF8String]);

    NSLog (@"=================================================");
}

-(void) dealloc
{
    [bookName release];
    [book release];
    [super dealloc];
}
@end
```

The `initWithName:` method first calls the `init` method for the superclass to perform its initialization. Next, it creates a string object (using `alloc` so it owns it) and sets it to the name of the address book passed in as `name`. This is followed by the allocation and initialization of an empty mutable array that is stored in the instance variable `book`.

You defined `initWithName:` to return an `id` object, instead of an `AddressBook` one. If `AddressBook` is subclassed, the receiver to the `initWithName:` message (and therefore the return value) isn't an `AddressBook` object; its type is that of the subclass. For that reason, you define the return type as a generic object type.

Notice also that in `initWithName:`, you take ownership of the `bookName` and `book` instance variables by using `alloc`. For example, if you created the array for `book` using the `NSMutableArray` array method, as in

```
book = [NSMutableArray array];
```

you would still not be the owner of the `book` array; `NSMutableArray` would own it. Thus, you wouldn't be able to release its memory when you freed up the memory for an `AddressBook` object.

The `addCard:` method takes the `AddessCard` object given as its argument and adds it to the address book.

The `count` method gives the number of elements in an array. The `entries` method uses this to return the number of address cards stored in the address book.

Fast Enumeration

The `list` method's `for` loop shows a construct you haven't seen before:

```
for ( AddressCard *theCard in book )
     NSLog (@"%-20s    %-32s", [theCard.name UTF8String],
                 [theCard.email UTF8String]);
```

This uses a technique known as *fast enumeration* to sequence through each element of the `book` array. The syntax is simple enough: You define a variable that will hold each element in the array in turn (`AddressCard *theCard`). You follow that with the keyword `in`, and then you list the name of the array. When the `for` loop executes, it assigns the first element in the array to the specified variable and then executes the body of the loop. Then it assigns the second element in the array to the variable and executes the body of the loop. This continues in sequence until all elements of the array have been assigned to the variable and the body of the loop has executed each time.

Note that if `theCard` had been previously defined as an `AddressCard` object, the `for` loop would more simply become this:

```
for ( theCard in book )
    ...
```

Program 15.10 is a test program for your new AddressBook class.

Program 15.10 Test Program

```
#import "AddressBook.h"
#import <Foundation/NSAutoreleasePool.h>

int main (int argc, char *argv[])
{
    NSAutoreleasePool * pool = [[NSAutoreleasePool alloc] init];

    NSString  *aName = @"Julia Kochan";
    NSString  *aEmail = @"jewls337@axlc.com";
    NSString  *bName = @"Tony Iannino";
    NSString  *bEmail = @"tony.iannino@techfitness.com";
    NSString  *cName = @"Stephen Kochan";
    NSString  *cEmail = @"steve@kochan-wood.com";
    NSString  *dName = @"Jamie Baker";
    NSString  *dEmail = @"jbaker@kochan-wood.com";

    AddressCard *card1 = [[AddressCard alloc] init];
    AddressCard *card2 = [[AddressCard alloc] init];
    AddressCard *card3 = [[AddressCard alloc] init];
    AddressCard *card4 = [[AddressCard alloc] init];

    AddressBook  *myBook = [AddressBook alloc];

    // First set up four address cards

    [card1 setName: aName andEmail: aEmail];
    [card2 setName: bName andEmail: bEmail];
    [card3 setName: cName andEmail: cEmail];
    [card4 setName: dName andEmail: dEmail];

    // Now initialize the address book

    myBook = [myBook initWithName: @"Linda's Address Book"];

    NSLog (@"Entries in address book after creation: %i",
            [myBook entries]);

    // Add some cards to the address book

    [myBook addCard: card1];
    [myBook addCard: card2];
    [myBook addCard: card3];
    [myBook addCard: card4];
```

```
    NSLog (@"Entries in address book after adding cards: %i",
            [myBook entries]);

    // List all the entries in the book now

    [myBook list];

    [card1 release];
    [card2 release];
    [card3 release];
    [card4 release];
    [myBook release];
    [pool drain];
    return 0;
}
```

Program 15.10 Output

```
Entries in address book after creation: 0
Entries in address book after adding cards: 4


======== Contents of: Linda's Address Book =========
Julia Kochan         jewls337@axlc.com
Tony Iannino         tony.iannino@techfitness.com
Stephen Kochan       steve@kochan-wood.com
Jamie Baker          jbaker@kochan-wood.com
===================================================
```

The program sets up four address cards and then creates a new address book called Linda's Address Book. The four cards are then added to the address book using the addCard: method, and the list method is used to list and verify the contents of the address book.

Looking Up Someone in the Address Book

When you have a large address book, you don't want to list its complete contents each time you want to look up someone. Therefore, adding a method to do that for you makes sense. Let's call the method lookup: and have it take as its argument the name to locate. The method will search the address book for a match (ignoring case) and return the matching entry, if found. If the name does not appear in the phone book, you'll have it return nil.

Here's the new lookup: method:

```
// lookup address card by name — assumes an exact match


-(AddressCard *) lookup: (NSString *) theName
{
```

```
        for ( AddressCard *nextCard in book )
            if ( [[nextCard name] caseInsensitiveCompare: theName] == NSOrderedSame )
                return nextCard;

        return nil;
}
```

If you put the declaration for this method in your interface file and the definition in the implementation file, you can write a test program to try your new method. Program 15.11 shows such a program, followed immediately by its output.

Program 15.11 Test Program

```
#import "AddressBook.h"
#import <Foundation/NSAutoreleasePool.h>

int main (int argc, char *argv[])
{
    NSAutoreleasePool * pool = [[NSAutoreleasePool alloc] init];

    NSString    *aName = @"Julia Kochan";
    NSString    *aEmail = @"jewls337@axlc.com";
    NSString    *bName = @"Tony Iannino";
    NSString    *bEmail = @"tony.iannino@techfitness.com";
    NSString    *cName = @"Stephen Kochan";
    NSString    *cEmail = @"steve@kochan-wood.com";
    NSString    *dName = @"Jamie Baker";
    NSString    *dEmail = @"jbaker@kochan-wood.com";
    AddressCard    *card1 = [[AddressCard alloc] init];
    AddressCard    *card2 = [[AddressCard alloc] init];
    AddressCard    *card3 = [[AddressCard alloc] init];
    AddressCard    *card4 = [[AddressCard alloc] init];

    AddressBook    *myBook = [AddressBook alloc];
    AddressCard    *myCard;

    // First set up four address cards

    [card1 setName: aName andEmail: aEmail];
    [card2 setName: bName andEmail: bEmail];
    [card3 setName: cName andEmail: cEmail];
    [card4 setName: dName andEmail: dEmail];

    myBook = [myBook initWithName: @"Linda's Address Book"];

    // Add some cards to the address book

    [myBook addCard: card1];
    [myBook addCard: card2];
```

```
    [myBook addCard: card3];
    [myBook addCard: card4];

    // Look up a person by name

    NSLog (@"Lookup: Stephen Kochan");
    myCard = [myBook lookup: @"stephen kochan"];

    if (myCard != nil)
       [myCard print];
    else
       NSLog (@"Not found!");

    // Try another lookup

    NSLog (@"Lookup: Haibo Zhang");
    myCard = [myBook lookup: @"Haibo Zhang"];

    if (myCard != nil)
       [myCard print];
    else
       NSLog (@"Not found!");

    [card1 release];
    [card2 release];
    [card3 release];
    [card4 release];
    [myBook release];

    [pool drain];
    return 0;
}
```

Program 15.11 Output

```
Lookup: Stephen Kochan
====================================
|                                  |
|  Stephen Kochan                  |
|  steve@kochan-wood.com           |
|                                  |
|                                  |
|                                  |
|        O             O           |
====================================

Lookup: Haibo Zhang
Not found!
```

When the `lookup:` method located Stephen Kochan in the address book (taking advantage of the fact that a non-case-sensitive match was made), the method gave the resulting address card to the **AddressCard**'s `print` method for display. In the case of the second lookup, the name Haibo Zhang was not found.

This lookup message is very primitive because it needs to find an exact match of the entire name. A better method would perform partial matches and be able to handle multiple matches. For example, the message expression

```
[myBook lookup: @"steve"]
```

could match entries for "Steve Kochan", "Fred Stevens", and "steven levy". Because multiple matches would exist, a good approach might be to create an array containing all the matches and return the array to the method caller (see exercise 2 at the end of this chapter), like so:

```
matches = [myBook lookup: @"steve"];
```

Removing Someone from the Address Book

No address book manager that enables you to add an entry would be complete without the capability to also remove an entry. You can make a `removeCard:` method to remove a particular **AddressCard** from the address book. Another possibility would be to create a `remove:` method that removes someone based on name (see exercise 6 at the end of this chapter).

Because you've made a couple changes to your interface file, Program 15.12 shows it again with the new `removeCard:` method. It's followed by your new `removeCard:` method.

Program 15.12 Addressbook.h Interface File

```
#import <Foundation/NSArray.h>
#import "AddressCard.h"

@interface AddressBook: NSObject
{
   NSString       *bookName;
   NSMutableArray *book;
}

-(id) initWithName: (NSString *) name;

-(void) addCard: (AddressCard *) theCard;
-(void) removeCard: (AddressCard *) theCard;

-(AddressCard *) lookup: (NSString *) theName;
-(int) entries;
-(void) list;

@end
```

Here's the new `removeCard` method:

```
-(void) removeCard: (AddressCard *) theCard
{
    [book removeObjectIdenticalTo: theCard];
}
```

For purposes of what's considered an *identical* object, we are using the idea of the same location in memory. So the `removeObjectIdenticalTo:` method does *not* consider two address cards that contain the same information but are located in different places in memory (which might happen if you made a copy of an `AddressCard`, for example) to be identical.

Incidentally, the `removeObjectIdenticalTo:` method removes all objects identical to its argument. However, that's an issue only if you have multiple occurrences of the same object in your arrays.

You can get more sophisticated with your approach to equal objects by using the `removeObject:` method and then writing your own `isEqual:` method for testing whether two objects are equal. If you use `removeObject:`, the system automatically invokes the `isEqual:` method for each element in the array, giving it the two elements to compare. In this case, because your address book contains `AddressCard` objects as its elements, you would have to add an `isEqual:` method to that class (you would be overriding the method that the class inherits from `NSObject`). The method could then decide for itself how to determine equality. It would make sense to compare the two corresponding names and emails. If both were equal, you could return `YES` from the method; otherwise, you could return `NO`. Your method might look like this:

```
-(BOOL) isEqual: (AddressCard *) theCard
{
    if ([name isEqualToString: theCard.name] == YES &&
            [email isEqualToString: theCard.email] == YES)
        return YES;
    else
        return NO;
}
```

Note that other `NSArray` methods, such as `containsObject:` and `indexOfObject:`, also rely on this `isEqual:` strategy for determining whether two objects are considered equal.

Program 15.12 tests the new `removeCard:` method.

Program 15.12 Test Program

```objc
#import "AddressBook.h"
#import <Foundation/NSAutoreleasePool.h>

int main (int argc, char *argv[])
{
    NSAutoreleasePool * pool = [[NSAutoreleasePool alloc] init];

    NSString   *aName = @"Julia Kochan";
    NSString   *aEmail = @"jewls337@axlc.com";
    NSString   *bName = @"Tony Iannino";
    NSString   *bEmail = @"tony.iannino@techfitness.com";
    NSString   *cName = @"Stephen Kochan";
    NSString   *cEmail = @"steve@kochan-wood.com";
    NSString   *dName = @"Jamie Baker";
    NSString   *dEmail = @"jbaker@kochan-wood.com";

    AddressCard *card1 = [[AddressCard alloc] init];
    AddressCard *card2 = [[AddressCard alloc] init];
    AddressCard *card3 = [[AddressCard alloc] init];
    AddressCard *card4 = [[AddressCard alloc] init];

    AddressBook  *myBook = [AddressBook alloc];
    AddressCard  *myCard;

    // First set up four address cards

    [card1 setName: aName andEmail: aEmail];
    [card2 setName: bName andEmail: bEmail];
    [card3 setName: cName andEmail: cEmail];
    [card4 setName: dName andEmail: dEmail];

    myBook = [myBook initWithName: @"Linda's Address Book"];

    // Add some cards to the address book

    [myBook addCard: card1];
    [myBook addCard: card2];
    [myBook addCard: card3];
    [myBook addCard: card4];

    // Look up a person by name

    NSLog (@"Lookup: Stephen Kochan");
    myCard = [myBook lookup: @"Stephen Kochan"];

    if (myCard != nil)
       [myCard print];
    else
       NSLog (@"Not found!");
```

```
    // Now remove the entry from the phone book

    [myBook removeCard: myCard];
    [myBook list];    // verify it's gone

    [card1 release];
    [card2 release];
    [card3 release];
    [card4 release];
    [myBook release];
    [pool drain];

  return 0;
}
```

Program 15.12 Output

```
Lookup: Stephen Kochan
=====================================
|                                   |
| Stephen Kochan                    |
| steve@kochan-wood.com             |
|                                   |
|                                   |
|                                   |
|       O           O               |
=====================================

======== Contents of: Linda's Address Book =========
Julia Kochan       jewls337@axlc.com
Tony Iannino       tony.iannino@techfitness.com
Jamie Baker        jbaker@kochan-wood.com
====================================================
```

After looking up Stephen Kochan in the address book and verifying that he's there, you pass the resulting AddressCard to your new removeCard: method to be removed. The resulting listing of the address book verifies the removal.

Sorting Arrays

If your address book contains a lot of entries, alphabetizing it might be convenient. You can easily do this by adding a sort method to your AddressBook class and by taking advantage of an NSMutableArray method called sortUsingSelector:. This method takes as its argument a selector that the sortUsingSelector: method uses to compare two elements. Arrays can contain any type of objects in them, so the only way to implement a generic sorting method is to have you decide whether elements in the array are in order. To do this, you must add a method to compare two elements in the array.[4] The result returned from that method is to be of type NSComparisonResult. It should return NSOrderedAscending if you want the sorting method to place the first element before the second in the array, return NSOrderedSame if the two elements are considered equal, or return NSOrderedDescending if the first element should come after the second element in the sorted array.

First, here's the new sort method from your AddressBook class:

```
-(void) sort
{
    [book sortUsingSelector: @selector(compareNames:)];
}
```

As you learned in Chapter 9, "Polymorphism, Dynamic Typing, and Dynamic Binding," the expression

```
@selector (compareNames:)
```

creates a selector, which is of type SEL, from a specified method name; this is the method sortUsingSelector: uses to compare two elements in the array. When it needs to make such a comparison, it invokes the specified method, sending the message to the first element in the array (the receiver) to be compared against its argument. The returned value should be of type NSComparisonResult, as previously described.

Because the elements of your address book are AddressCard objects, the comparison method must be added to the AddressCard class. You must go back to your AddressCard class and add a compareNames: method to it. This is shown here:

```
// Compare the two names from the specified address cards
-(NSComparisonResult) compareNames: (id) element
{
    return [name compare: [element name]];
}
```

Because you are doing a string comparison of the two names from the address book, you can use the NSString compare: method to do the work for you.

---

[4] A method called sortUsingFunction:context: lets you use a function instead of a method to perform the comparison.

If you add the `sort` method to the `AddressBook` class and the `compareNames:` method to the `AddressCard` class, you can write a test program to test it (see Program 15.13).

Program 15.13 Test Program

```
#import "AddressBook.h"
#import <Foundation/NSAutoreleasePool.h>

int main (int argc, char *argv[])
{
    NSAutoreleasePool * pool = [[NSAutoreleasePool alloc] init];

    NSString *aName = @"Julia Kochan";
    NSString *aEmail = @"jewls337@axlc.com";
    NSString *bName = @"Tony Iannino";
    NSString *bEmail = @"tony.iannino@techfitness.com";
    NSString *cName = @"Stephen Kochan";
    NSString *cEmail = @"steve@kochan-wood.com";
    NSString *dName = @"Jamie Baker";
    NSString *dEmail = @"jbaker@kochan-wood.com";

    AddressCard *card1 = [[AddressCard alloc] init];
    AddressCard *card2 = [[AddressCard alloc] init];
    AddressCard *card3 = [[AddressCard alloc] init];
    AddressCard *card4 = [[AddressCard alloc] init];

    AddressBook *myBook = [AddressBook alloc];

    // First set up four address cards

    [card1 setName: aName andEmail: aEmail];
    [card2 setName: bName andEmail: bEmail];
    [card3 setName: cName andEmail: cEmail];
    [card4 setName: dName andEmail: dEmail];

    myBook = [myBook initWithName: @"Linda's Address Book"];

    // Add some cards to the address book

    [myBook addCard: card1];
    [myBook addCard: card2];
    [myBook addCard: card3];
    [myBook addCard: card4];

    // List the unsorted book

    [myBook list];

    // Sort it and list it again
```

```
    [myBook sort];
    [myBook list];

    [card1 release];
    [card2 release];
    [card3 release];
    [card4 release];
    [myBook release];
    [pool drain];
    return 0;
}
```

Program 15.13 Output

```
======== Contents of: Linda's Address Book =========
Julia Kochan          jewls337@axlc.com
Tony Iannino          tony.iannino@techfitness.com
Stephen Kochan        steve@kochan-wood.com
Jamie Baker           jbaker@kochan-wood.com
===================================================


======== Contents of: Linda's Address Book =========
Jamie Baker           jbaker@kochan-wood.com
Julia Kochan          jewls337@axlc.com
Stephen Kochan        steve@kochan-wood.com
Tony Iannino          tony.iannino@techfitness.com
===================================================
```

Note that the sort is an ascending one. However, you can easily perform a descending sort by modifying the compareNames: method in the AddressCard class to reverse the sense of the values that are returned.

More than 50 methods are available for working with array objects. Tables 15.4 and 15.5 list some commonly used methods for working with immutable and mutable arrays, respectively. Because NSMutableArray is a subclass of NSArray, the former inherits the methods of the latter.

In Tables 15.4 and 15.5, *obj*, *obj1*, and *obj2* are any objects; *i* is an NSUInteger integer representing a valid index number into the array; *selector* is a selector object of type SEL; and *size* is an NSUInteger integer.

Table 15.4   Common **NSArray** Methods

Method	Description
+(id) arrayWithObjects: *obj1*, *obj2*, ... nil	Creates a new array with *obj1*, *obj2*, ... as its elements
-(BOOL) containsObject: *obj*	Determines whether the array contains *obj* (uses the isEqual: method)
-(NSUInteger) *count*	Indicates the number of elements in the array
-(NSUInteger) indexOfObject: *obj*	Specifies the index number of the first element that contains *obj* (uses the isEqual: method)
-(id) objectAtIndex: *i*	Indicates the object stored in element *i*
-(void) makeObjectsPerform Selector: (SEL) *selector*	Sends the message indicated by *selector* to every element of the array
-(NSArray *) sortedArrayUsing Selector: (SEL) *selector*	Sorts the array according to the comparison method specified by *selector*
-(BOOL) writeToFile: *path* atomically: (BOOL) *flag*	Writes the array to the specified file, creating a temporary file first if *flag* is YES

Table 15.5   Common **NSMutableArray** Methods

Method	Description
+(id) array	Creates an empty array
+(id) arrayWithCapacity: *size*	Creates an array with a specified initial *size*
-(id) initWithCapacity: *size*	Initializes a newly allocated array with a specified initial *size*
-(void) addObject: *obj*	Adds *obj* to the end of the array
-(void) insertObject: *obj* atIndex: *i*	Inserts *obj* into element *i* of the array
-(void) replaceObjectAtIndex: *i* withObject: *obj*	Replaces element *i* of the array with *obj*
-(void) removeObject: *obj*	Removes all occurrences of *obj* from the array
-(void) removeObjectAtIndex: *i*	Removes element *i* from the array, moving down elements *i*+1 through the end of the array
-(void) sortUsingSelector: (SEL) *selector*	Sorts the array based on the comparison method indicated by *selector*

Dictionary Objects

A *dictionary* is a collection of data consisting of key-object pairs. Just as you would look up the definition of a word in a dictionary, you obtain the value (object) from an Objective-C dictionary by its key. The keys in a dictionary must be unique, and they can be of any object type, although they are typically strings. The value associated with the key can also be of any object type, but it cannot be nil.

Dictionaries can be mutable or immutable; mutable ones can have entries dynamically added and removed. Dictionaries can be searched based on a particular key, and their contents can be enumerated. Program 15.14 sets up a mutable dictionary to be used as a glossary of Objective-C terms and fills in the first three entries.

To use dictionaries in your programs, include the following line:

```
#import <Foundation/NSDictionary.h>
```

Program 15.14

```
#import <Foundation/NSObject.h>
#import <Foundation/NSString.h>
#import <Foundation/NSDictionary.h>
#import <Foundation/NSAutoreleasePool.h>

int main (int argc, char *argv[])
{
    NSAutoreleasePool  * pool = [[NSAutoreleasePool alloc] init];

    NSMutableDictionary *glossary = [NSMutableDictionary dictionary];

    // Store three entries in the glossary

    [glossary setObject: @"A class defined so other classes can inherit from it"
               forKey: @"abstract class" ];
    [glossary setObject: @"To implement all the methods defined in a protocol"
               forKey: @"adopt"];
    [glossary setObject: @"Storing an object for later use"
               forKey: @"archiving"];

    // Retrieve and display them

    NSLog (@"abstract class: %@", [glossary objectForKey: @"abstract class"]);
    NSLog (@"adopt: %@", [glossary objectForKey: @"adopt"]);
    NSLog (@"archiving: %@", [glossary objectForKey: @"archiving"]);
```

```
        [pool drain];
        return 0;
}
```

Program 15.14 Output

```
abstract class: A class defined so other classes can inherit from it
adopt: To implement all the methods defined in a protocol
archiving: Storing an object for later use
```

The expression

```
[NSMutableDictionary dictionary]
```

creates an empty mutable dictionary. You can add key-value pairs to the dictionary using the setObject:forKey: method. After the dictionary has been constructed, you can retrieve the value for a given key using the objectForKey: method. Program 15.14 shows how the three entries in the glossary were retrieved and displayed. In a more practical application, the user would type in the word to define and the program would search the glossary for its definition.

Enumerating a Dictionary

Program 15.15 illustrates how a dictionary can be defined with initial key-value pairs using the dictionaryWithObjectsAndKeys: method. An immutable dictionary is created, and the program also shows how a fast enumeration loop can be used to retrieve each element from a dictionary one key at a time. Unlike array objects, dictionary objects are not ordered, so the first key-object pair placed in a dictionary might not be the first key extracted when the dictionary is enumerated.

Program 15.15

```
#import <Foundation/NSObject.h>
#import <Foundation/NSString.h>
#import <Foundation/NSDictionary.h>
#import <Foundation/NSAutoreleasePool.h>

int main (int argc, char *argv[])
{
    NSAutoreleasePool  * pool = [[NSAutoreleasePool alloc] init];

    NSDictionary *glossary =
     [NSDictionary dictionaryWithObjectsAndKeys:
       @"A class defined so other classes can inherit from it",
       @"abstract class",
       @"To implement all the methods defined in a protocol",
       @"adopt",
       @"Storing an object for later use",
       @"archiving",
       nil
     ];
```

```
// Print all key-value pairs from the dictionary

    for ( NSString *key in glossary )
        NSLog (@"%@%@",  key, [glossary objectForKey: key]);

    [pool drain];
    return 0;
}
```

Program 15.15 Output

```
abstract class: A class defined so other classes can inherit from it
adopt: To implement all the methods defined in a protocol
archiving: Storing an object for later use
```

The argument to `dictionaryWithObjectsAndKeys:` is a list of object-key pairs (yes, in that order!), each separated by a comma. The list must be terminated with the special `nil` object.

After the program creates the dictionary, it sets up a loop to enumerate its contents. As noted, the keys are retrieved from the dictionary in turn, in no special order. If you wanted to display the contents of a dictionary in alphabetical order, you could retrieve all the keys from the dictionary, sort them, and then retrieve all the values for those sorted keys in order. The method `keysSortedByValueUsingSelector:` does half of the work for you, returning the sorted keys in an array based on your sorting criteria.

We have just shown some basic operations with dictionaries here. Tables 15.6 and 15.7 summarize some of the more commonly used methods for working with immutable and mutable dictionaries, respectively. Because `NSMutableDictionary` is a subset of `NSDictionary`, it inherits its methods.

In Tables 15.6 and 15.7, *key*, *key1*, *key2*, *obj*, *obj1*, and *obj2* are any objects, and *size* is an `NSUInteger` unsigned integer.

Table 15.6   **Common NSDictionary Methods**

Method	Description
+(id) dictionaryWithObjectsAndKeys: *obj1, key1, obj2, key2, ...,* nil	Creates a dictionary with key-object pairs {*key1, obj1*}, {*key2, obj2*}, ...
-(id) initWithObjectsAndKeys: *obj1, key1, obj2, key2,...,* nil	Initializes a newly allocated dictionary with key-object pairs {*key1, obj1*}, {*key2, obj2*}, ...
-(unsigned int) count	Returns the number of entries in the dictionary

Table 15.6 **Common NSDictionary Methods**

Method	Description
-(NSEnumerator *) keyEnumerator	Returns an NSEnumerator object for all the keys in the dictionary
-(NSArray *) keysSortedByValueUsingSelector: (SEL) *selector*	Returns an array of keys in the dictionary sorted according to the comparison method *selector* specifies
-(NSEnumerator *) objectEnumerator	Returns an NSEnumerator object for all the values in the dictionary
-(id) objectForKey: *key*	Returns the object for the specified *key*

Table 15.7 **Common NSMutableDictionary Methods**

Method	Description
+(id) dictionaryWithCapacity: *size*	Creates a mutable dictionary with an initial specified *size*
-(id) initWithCapacity: *size*	Initializes a newly allocated dictionary to be of an initial specified *size*
-(void) removeAllObjects	Removes all entries from the dictionary
-(void) removeObjectForKey: *key*	Removes the entry for the specified *key* from the dictionary
-(void) setObject: *obj* forKey: *key*	Adds *obj* to the dictionary for the key *key* and replaces the value if *key* already exists

Set Objects

A *set* is a collection of unique objects, and it can be mutable or immutable. Operations include searching, adding, and removing members (mutable sets); comparing two sets; and finding the intersection and union of two sets.

To work with sets in your program, include the following line:

```
#import <Foundation/NSSet.h>
```

Program 15.16 shows some basic operations on sets. Say you wanted to display the contents of your sets several times during execution of the program. You therefore have decided to create a new method called print. You add the print method to the NSSet class by creating a new category called Printing. NSMutableSet is a subclass of NSSet, so mutable sets can use the new print method as well.

Program 15.16

```objc
#import <Foundation/NSObject.h>
#import <Foundation/NSSet.h>
#import <Foundation/NSValue.h>
#import <Foundation/NSAutoreleasePool.h>
#import <Foundation/NSString.h>

// Create an integer object
#define INTOBJ(v) [NSNumber numberWithInteger: v]

// Add a print method to NSSet with the Printing category

@interface NSSet (Printing)
-(void) print;
@end

@implementation NSSet (Printing)
-(void) print {
    printf ("{");

    for (NSNumber *element in self)
        printf (" %li ", (long) [element integerValue]);

    printf ("}\n");
}
@end


int main (int argc, char *argv[])
{
    NSAutoreleasePool  * pool = [[NSAutoreleasePool alloc] init];

    NSMutableSet *set1 = [NSMutableSet setWithObjects:
        INTOBJ(1), INTOBJ(3), INTOBJ(5), INTOBJ(10), nil];
    NSSet *set2 = [NSSet setWithObjects:
        INTOBJ(-5), INTOBJ(100), INTOBJ(3), INTOBJ(5), nil];
    NSSet *set3 = [NSSet setWithObjects:
        INTOBJ(12), INTOBJ(200), INTOBJ(3), nil];
```

```
NSLog (@"set1: ");
[set1 print];
NSLog (@"set2: ");
[set2 print];

// Equality test
if ([set1 isEqualToSet: set2] == YES)
   NSLog (@"set1 equals set2");
else
   NSLog (@"set1 is not equal to set2");

// Membership test

if ([set1 containsObject: INTOBJ(10)] == YES)
   NSLog (@"set1 contains 10");
else
   NSLog (@"set1 does not contain 10");

if ([set2 containsObject: INTOBJ(10)] == YES)
   NSLog (@"set2 contains 10");
else
   NSLog (@"set2 does not contain 10");

// add and remove objects from mutable set set1

[set1 addObject: INTOBJ(4)];
[set1 removeObject: INTOBJ(10)];
NSLog (@"set1 after adding 4 and removing 10: ");
[set1 print];

// get intersection of two sets

[set1 intersectSet: set2];
NSLog (@"set1 intersect set2: ");
[set1 print];

// union of two sets

[set1 unionSet:set3];
NSLog (@"set1 union set3: ");
[set1 print];

[pool drain];
return 0;
}
```

Program 15.16 Output

```
set1:
{ 3 10 1 5 }
set2:
{ 100 3 -5 5 }
set1 is not equal to set2
set1 contains 10
set2 does not contain 10
set1 after adding 4 and removing 10:
{ 3 1 5 4 }
set1 intersect set2:
{ 3 5 }
set1 union set3:
{ 12 3 5 200 }
```

The `print` method uses the fast enumeration technique previously described to re-trieve each element from the set. You also defined a macro called `INTOBJ` to create an ob-ject from an integer value. This enables you to make your program more concise and saves some unnecessary typing. Of course, your `print` method is not that general because it works only with sets that have integer members in them. But it's a good reminder here of how to add methods to a class through a category.[5] (Note that the C library's `printf` rou-tine is used in the `print` method to display the elements of each set on a single line.)

`setWithObjects:` creates a new set from a `nil`-terminated list of objects. After creat-ing three sets, the program displays the first two using your new `print` method. The `isEqualToSet:` method then tests whether `set1` is equal to `set2`—it isn't.

The `containsObject:` method sees first whether the integer `10` is in `set1` and then whether it is in `set2`. The Boolean values the method returns verify that it is in the first set, not in the second.

The program next uses the `addObject:` and `removeObject:` methods to add and re-move `4` and `10` from `set1`, respectively. Displaying the contents of the set verifies that the operations were successful.

You can use the `intersect:` and `union:` methods to calculate the intersection and union of two sets. In both cases, the result of the operation replaces the receiver of the message.

The Foundation framework also provides a class called `NSCountedSet`. These sets can represent more than one occurrence of the same object; however, instead of the object appearing multiple times in the set, a count of the number of times is maintained. So the first time an object is added to the set, its count is `1`. Subsequently adding the object to

---

[5] A more general method could invoke each object's `description` method for displaying each mem-ber of the set. That would allow sets containing any types of objects to be displayed in a readable for-mat. Also note that you can display the contents of any collection with a single call to `NSLog`, using the "print object" format characters `"%@"`.

the set increments the count, whereas removing the object from the set decrements the count. If it reaches zero, the actual object itself is removed from the set. The `countForObject:` retrieves the count for a specified object in a set.

One application for a counted set might be a word counter application. Each time a word is found in some text, it can be added to the counted set. When the scan of the text is complete, each word can be retrieved from the set along with its count, which indicates the number of times the word appeared in the text.

We have just shown some basic operations with sets. Tables 15.8 and 15.9 summarize commonly used methods for working with immutable and mutable sets, respectively. Because `NSMutableSet` is a subclass of `NSSet`, it inherits its methods.

In Tables 15.8 and 15.9, *obj*, *obj1*, and *obj2* are any objects; nsset is an `NSSet` or `NSMutableSet` object; and *size* is an `NSUInteger` integer.

Table 15.8   **Common NSSet Methods**

Method	Description
+(id) setWithObjects: *obj1*, *obj2*, ..., nil	Creates a new set from the list of objects
-(id) initWithObjects: *obj1*, *obj2*, ..., nil	Initializes a newly allocated set with a list of objects
-(NSUInteger) count	Returns the number of members in the set
-(BOOL) containsObject: *obj*	Determines whether the set contains *obj*
-(BOOL) member: *obj*	Determines whether the set contains *obj* (using the isEqual: method)
-(NSEnumerator *) objectEnumerator	Returns an `NSEnumerator` object for all the objects in the set
-(BOOL) isSubsetOfSet: *nsset*	Determines whether every member of the receiver is present in *nsset*
-(BOOL) intersectsSet: *nsset*	Determines whether at least one member of the receiver appears in *nsset*
-(BOOL) isEqualToSet: *nsset*	Determines whether the two sets are equal

Table 15.9   **Common NSMutableSet Methods**

Method	Description
-(id) setWithCapacity: *size*	Creates a new set with an initial capacity to store *size* members
-(id) initWithCapacity: *size*	Sets the initial capacity of a newly allocated set to *size* members
-(void) addObject: *obj*	Adds *obj* to the set

-(void) removeObject: *obj*	Removes *obj* from the set
-(void) removeAllObjects	Removes all members of the receiver
-(void) unionSet: *nsset*	Adds each member of *nsset* to the receiver
-(void) minusSet: *nsset*	Removes all members of *nsset* from the receiver
-(void) intersectSet: *nsset*	Removes all members from the receiver that are not also in *nsset*

Exercises

1. Look up the NSCalendarDate class in your documentation. Then add a new category to NSCalendarDate called ElapsedDays. In that new category, add a method based on the following method declaration:

-(unsigned long) numberOfElapsedDays: (NSCalendarDate *) theDate;

Have the new method return the number of elapsed days between the receiver and the argument to the method. Write a test program to test your new method. (*Hint:* Look at the years:months:days:hours:minutes:seconds:sinceDate: method.)

2. Modify the lookup: method developed in this chapter for the AddressBook class so that partial matches of a name can be made. The message expression [myBook lookup: @"steve"] should match an entry that contains the string steve anywhere within the name.

3. Modify the lookup: method developed in this chapter for the AddressBook class to search the address book for all matches. Have the method return an array of all such matching address cards, or nil if no match is made.

4. Add new fields of your choice to the AddressCard class. Some suggestions are separating the name field into first and last name fields, and adding address (perhaps with separate state, city, zip, and country fields) and phone number fields. Write appropriate setter and getter methods, and ensure that the print and list methods properly display the fields.

5. After completing exercise 3, modify the lookup: method from exercise 2 to perform a search on all the fields of an address card. Can you think of a way to design your AddressCard and AddressBook classes so that the latter does not have to know all the fields stored in the former?

6. Add the method removeName: to the AddressBook class to remove someone from the address book given this declaration for the method:

-(BOOL) removeName: (NSString *) theName;

Use the lookup: method developed in exercise 2. If the name is not found or if multiple entries exist, have the method return NO. If the person is successfully removed, have it return YES.

7. Using the `Fraction` class defined in Part I, set up an array of fractions with some arbitrary values. Then write some code that finds the sum of all the fractions stored in the array.

8. Using the `Fraction` class defined in Part I, set up a mutable array of fractions with arbitrary values. Then sort the array using the `sortUsingSelector:` method from the `NSMutableArray` class. Add a `Comparison` category to the `Fraction` class and implement your comparison method in that category.

9. Define three new classes, called `Song`, `PlayList`, and `MusicCollection`. A `Song` object will contain information about a particular song, such as its title, artist, album, and playing time. A `PlayList` object will contain the name of the playlist and a collection of songs. A `MusicCollection` object will contain a collection of playlists, including a special master playlist called `library` that contains every song in the collection. Define these three classes and write methods to do the following:

   - Create a `Song` object and set its information.
   - Create a `Playlist` object, and add songs to and remove songs from a playlist. A new song should be added to the master playlist if it's not already there. Make sure that if a song is removed from the master playlist, it is removed from all playlists in the music collection as well.
   - Create a `MusicCollection` object, and add playlists to and remove playlists from the collection.
   - Search and display the information about any song, any playlist, or the entire music collection.

   Make sure all your classes do not leak memory!

10. Write a program that takes an `NSArray` of `NSNumber` objects (where each `NSNumber` represents an integer) and produces a frequency chart that lists each integer and how many times it occurs in the array. Use an `NSCountedSet` object to construct your frequency counts.

16

Working with Files

The Foundation framework enables you to get access to the file system to perform basic operations on files and directories. This is provided by NSFileManager, whose methods include the capability to

- Create a new file
- Read from an existing file
- Write data to a file
- Rename a file
- Remove (delete) a file
- Test for the existence of a file
- Determine the size of a file as well as other attributes
- Make a copy of a file
- Test two files to see whether their contents are equal

Many of these operations can also be performed on directories. For example, you can create a directory, read its contents, or delete it. Another feature is the ability to *link* files. That is, the ability to have the same file exist under two different names, perhaps even in different directories.

To open a file and perform multiple read-and-write operations on the file, you use the methods provided by NSFileHandle. The methods in this class enable you to

- Open a file for reading, writing, or updating (reading and writing)
- Seek to a specified position within a file
- Read or write a specified number of bytes from and to a file

The methods provided by NSFileHandle can also be applied to devices or sockets. However, we will focus only on dealing with ordinary files in this chapter.

Managing Files and Directories:
`NSFileManager`

A file or directory is uniquely identified to `NSFileManager` using a *pathname* to the file. A pathname is an `NSString` object that can either be a relative or full pathname. A *relative* pathname is one that is relative to the current directory. So, the filename `copy1.m` would mean the file `copy1.m` in the current directory. Slash characters separate a list of directories in a path. The filename `ch16/copy1.m` is also a relative pathname, identifying the file `copy1.m` stored in the directory `ch16`, which is contained in the current directory.

Full pathnames, also known as *absolute* pathnames, begin with a leading `/`. Slash is actually a directory, called the *root* directory. On my Mac, the full pathname to my home directory is `/Users/stevekochan`. This pathname specifies three directories: `/` (the root directory), `Users`, and `stevekochan`.

The special tilde character (~) is used as an abbreviation for a user's home directory. `~linda` would, therefore, be an abbreviation for the user `linda`'s home directory, which might be the path `/Users/linda`. A solitary tilde character indicates the current user's home directory, meaning the pathname `~/copy1.m` would reference the file `copy1.m` stored in the current user's home directory. Other special UNIX-style pathname characters, such as `.` for the current directory and `..` for the parent directory, should be removed from pathnames before they're used by any of the Foundation file-handling methods. An assortment of path utilities are available that you can use for this, and they're discussed later in this chapter.

You should try to avoid hard-coding pathnames into your programs. As you'll see in this chapter, methods and functions are available that enable you to obtain the pathname for the current directory, a user's home directory, and a directory that can be used for creating temporary files. You should avail yourself of these as much as possible. You'll see later in this chapter that Foundation has a function for obtaining a list of special directories, such as a user's `Documents` directory.

Table 16.1 summarizes some basic `NSFileManager` methods for working with files. In that table, *path*, *path1*, *path2*, *from*, and *to* are all `NSString` objects; *attr* is an `NSDictionary` object; and *handler* is a callback handler that you can provide to handle errors in your own way. If you specify `nil` for *handler*, the default action will be taken, which for methods that return a `BOOL` is to return `YES` if the operation succeeds and `NO` if it fails. We won't be getting into writing your own handler in this chapter.

Table 16.1   **Common NSFileManager File Methods**

Method	Description
`-(NSData *) contentsAtPath:` *path*	Reads data from a file
`-(BOOL) createFileAtPath:` *path* `contents: (BOOL)` *data* `attributes:` *attr*	Writes data to a file

Table 16.1   **Common NSFileManager File Methods**

Method	Description
-(BOOL) removeFileAtPath: *path* handler: *handler*	Removes a file
-(BOOL) movePath: *from* toPath: *to* handler: *handler*	Renames or moves a file (*to* cannot already exist)
-(BOOL) copyPath: *from* toPath: *to* handler: *handler*	Copies a file (*to* cannot already exist)
-(BOOL) contentsEqualAtPath: *path1* andPath: *path2*	Compares contents of two files
-(BOOL) fileExistsAtPath: *path*	Tests for file existence
-(BOOL) isReadableFileAtPath: *path*	Tests whether file exists and can be read
-(BOOL) isWritableFileAtPath: *path*	Tests whether file exists and can be written
-(NSDictionary *) fileAttributesAtPath: *path* traverseLink: (BOOL) *flag*	Gets attributes for file
-(BOOL) changeFileAttributes: *attr* atPath: *path*	Changes file attributes

Each of the file methods is invoked on an NSFileManager object that is created by sending a defaultManager message to the class, like so:

```
NSFileManager *fm;
    . . .
  fm = [NSFileManager defaultManager];
```

For example, to delete a file called todolist from the current directory, you would first create the NSFileManager object as shown previously and then invoke the removeFileAtPath: method, like so:

```
[fm removeFileAtPath: @"todolist" handler: nil];
```

You can test the result that is returned to ensure that the file removal succeeds:

```
if ([fm removeFileAtPath: @"todolist" handler: nil] == NO) {
   NSLog (@"Couldn't remove file todolist");
   return 1;
}
```

The attributes dictionary enables you to specify, among other things, the permissions for a file you are creating or to obtain or change information for an existing file. For file creation, if you specify nil for this parameter, the default permissions are set for the file. The fileAttributesAtPath:traverseLink: method returns a dictionary containing

the specified file's attributes. The `traverseLink:` parameter is YES or NO for symbolic
links. If the file is a symbolic link and YES is specified, the attributes of the linked-to file
are returned; if NO is specified, the attributes of the link itself are returned.

For preexisting files, the attributes dictionary includes information such as the file's
owner, its size, its creation date, and so on. Each attribute in the dictionary can be extracted based on its key, all of which are defined in `<Foundation/NSFileManager.h>`. For
example, `NSFileSize` is the key for a file's size.

Program 16.1 shows some basic operations with files. This example assumes you have a
file called `testfile` in your current directory with the following three lines of text:

```
This is a test file with some data in it.
Here's another line of data.
And a third.
```

Program 16.1

```
// Basic file operations
// Assumes the existence of a file called "testfile"
// in the current working directory

#import <Foundation/NSObject.h>
#import <Foundation/NSString.h>
#import <Foundation/NSFileManager.h>
#import <Foundation/NSAutoreleasePool.h>
#import <Foundation/NSDictionary.h>

int main (int argc, char *argv[])
{
    NSAutoreleasePool * pool = [[NSAutoreleasePool alloc] init];
    NSString           *fName = @"testfile";
    NSFileManager      *fm;
    NSDictionary       *attr;

    // Need to create an instance of the file manager

    fm = [NSFileManager defaultManager];

    // Let's make sure our test file exists first

    if ([fm fileExistsAtPath: fName] == NO) {
        NSLog (@"File doesn't exist!");
        return 1;
    }

    // Now let's make a copy
```

```
    if ([fm copyPath: fName toPath: @"newfile" handler: nil] == NO) {
        NSLog (@"File copy failed!");
        return 2;
    }

    // Let's test to see if the two files are identical

    if ([fm contentsEqualAtPath: fName andPath: @"newfile"] == NO) {
        NSLog (@"Files are not equal!");
        return 3;
    }

    // Now let's rename the copy

    if ([fm movePath: @"newfile" toPath: @"newfile2"
            handler: nil] == NO) {
        NSLog (@"File rename failed!");
        return 4;
    }
}

    // Get the size of newfile2

    if ((attr = [fm fileAttributesAtPath: @"newfile2"
                traverseLink: NO]) == nil) {
        NSLog (@"Couldn't get file attributes!");
        return 5;
    }
}

    NSLog (@"File size is %i bytes",
            [[attr objectForKey: NSFileSize] intValue]);

    // And finally, let's delete the original file

    if ([fm removeFileAtPath: fName handler: nil] == NO) {
        NSLog (@"File removal failed!");
        return 6;
    }

    NSLog (@"All operations were successful!");

    // Display the contents of the newly-created file

    NSLog(@"%@" [NSString stringWithContentsOfFile: @"newfile2" encoding:
            NSUTF8StringEncoding error: nil]);

    [pool drain];
    return 0;
}
```

Program 16.1 Output

```
File size is 84 bytes
All operations were successful!

This is a test file with some data in it.
Here's another line of data.
And a third.
```

The program first tests whether `testfile` exists. If it does, it makes a copy of it and then tests the two files for equality. Experienced UNIX users should note that you can't move or copy a file into a directory simply by specifying the destination directory for the `copyPath:toPath:` and `movePath:toPath:` methods; the filename within that directory must be explicitly specified.

> **Note**
>
> You can create `testfile` with Xcode by selecting New File... from the File menu. In the left pane that appears, highlight Other, and then select Empty File in the right pane. Enter `testfile` as the name of the file and be sure to create it in the same directory as your executable file. This will be in your project's Build/Debug folder.

The `movePath:toPath:` method can be used to move a file from one directory to another. (It can also be used to move entire directories.) If the two paths reference files in the same directory (as in our example), the effect is to simply rename the file. So, in Program 16.1, you use this method to rename the file `newfile` to `newfile2`.

As noted in Table 16.1, when performing copying, renaming, or moving operations, the destination file cannot already exist. If it does, the operation will fail.

The size of `newfile2` is determined by using the `fileAttributesAtPath:traverseLink:` method. You test to make sure a non–nil dictionary is returned and then use the `NSDictionary` method `objectForKey:` to get the file's size from the dictionary using the key `NSFileSize`. The integer value from the dictionary is then displayed.

The program uses the `removeFileAtPath:handler:` method to remove your original file `testfile`.

Finally, `NSString`'s `stringWithContentsOfFile:` method is used to read the contents of the file `newfile2` into a string object, which is then passed as an argument to `NSLog` to be displayed.

Each of the file operations is tested for success in Program 16.1. If any fails, an error is logged using `NSLog`, and the program exits by returning a nonzero exit status. Each nonzero value, which by convention indicates program failure, is unique based on the type of error. If you write command-line tools, this is a useful technique because another program can test the return value, such as from within a shell script.

Working with the `NSData` Class

When working with files, you frequently need to read data into a temporary storage area, often called a *buffer*. When collecting data for subsequent output to a file, a storage area is also often used. Foundation's `NSData` class provides an easy way to set up a buffer, read the contents of the file into it, or write the contents of a buffer out to a file. And just in case you're wondering, for a 32-bit application, an `NSDATA` buffer can store up to 2GB. For a 64-bit application, it can hold up to 8EB (that's exabytes) or 8 billion gigabytes of data!

As you would expect, you can define either immutable (`NSData`) or mutable (`NSMutableData`) storage areas. We introduce methods from this class in this chapter and in succeeding chapters as well.

Program 16.2 shows how easily you can read the contents of a file into a buffer in memory.

The program reads the contents of your file `newfile2` and writes it to a new file called `newfile3`. In a sense, it implements a file copy operation, although not in as straightforward a fashion as the `copyPath:toPath:handler:` method.

Program 16.2

```
// Make a copy of a file


#import <Foundation/NSObject.h>
#import <Foundation/NSString.h>
#import <Foundation/NSFileManager.h>
#import <Foundation/NSAutoreleasePool.h>
#import <Foundation/NSData.h>

int main (int argc, char *argv[])
{
   NSAutoreleasePool * pool = [[NSAutoreleasePool alloc] init];
   NSFileManager     *fm;
   NSData            *fileData;

   fm = [NSFileManager defaultManager];


   // Read the file newfile2

   fileData = [fm contentsAtPath: @"newfile2"];

   if (fileData == nil) {
        NSLog (@"File read failed!");
        return 1;
   }

   // Write the data to newfile3

   if ([fm createFileAtPath: @"newfile3" contents: fileData
              attributes: nil] == NO) {
        NSLog (@"Couldn't create the copy!");
        return 2;
```

```
    }

    NSLog (@"File copy was successful!");

    [pool drain];
    return 0;
}
```

Program 16.2 Output

> File copy was successful!

The `NSData` `contentsAtPath:` method simply takes a pathname and reads the contents of the specified file into a storage area that it creates, returning the storage area object as the result or `nil` if the read fails (for example, if the file doesn't exist or can't be read by you).

The `createFileAtPath:contents:attributes:` method creates a file with the specified attributes (or uses the default if `nil` is supplied for the `attributes` argument). The contents of the specified `NSData` object are then written to the file. In our example, this data area contains the contents of the previously read file.

Working with Directories

Table 16.2 summarizes some of the methods provided by `NSFileManager` for working with directories. Many of these methods are the same as those for ordinary files, as listed in Table 16.1.

Table 16.2   **Common** `NSFileManager` **Directory Methods**

Method	Description
`-(NSString *) currentDirectoryPath`	Gets the current directory
`-(BOOL) changeCurrentDirectoryPath: path`	Changes the current directory
`-(BOOL) copyPath: from toPath: to handler: handler`	Copies a directory structure; *to* cannot previously exist
`-(BOOL) createDirectoryAtPath: path attributes: attr`	Creates a new directory

Table 16.2   **Common** NSFileManager **Directory Methods**

Method	Description
-(BOOL) fileExistsAtPath: *path* isDirectory: (BOOL *) *flag*	Tests whether the file is a directory (YES/NO result is stored in flag)
-(NSArray *) directoryContentsAtPath: *path*	Lists the contents of the directory
-(NSDirectoryEnumerator *) enumeratorAtPath: *path*	Enumerates the contents of the directory
-(BOOL) removeFileAtPath: *path* handler: *handler*	Deletes an empty directory
-(BOOL) movePath: *from* toPath: *to* handler: *handler*	Renames or moves a directory; *to* cannot previously exist

Program 16.3 shows basic operations with directories.

Program 16.3

```
// Some basic directory operations


#import <Foundation/NSObject.h>
#import <Foundation/NSString.h>
#import <Foundation/NSFileManager.h>
#import <Foundation/NSAutoreleasePool.h>

int main (int argc, char *argv[])
{
  NSAutoreleasePool * pool = [[NSAutoreleasePool alloc] init];
  NSString          *dirName = @"testdir";
  NSString          *path;
  NSFileManager     *fm;

  // Need to create an instance of the file manager

  fm = [NSFileManager defaultManager];

  // Get current directory

  path = [fm currentDirectoryPath];
  NSLog (@"Current directory path is %@", path);

  // Create a new directory
```

```
    if ([fm createDirectoryAtPath: dirName attributes: nil] == NO) {
        NSLog (@"Couldn't create directory!");
        return 1;
    }

    // Rename the new directory

    if ([fm movePath: dirName toPath: @"newdir" handler: nil] == NO) {
        NSLog (@"Directory rename failed!");
        return 2;
    }

    // Change directory into the new directory

    if ([fm changeCurrentDirectoryPath: @"newdir"] == NO) {
        NSLog (@"Change directory failed!");
        return 3;
    }

    // Now get and display current working directory

    path = [fm currentDirectoryPath];
    NSLog (@"Current directory path is %@", path);

    NSLog (@"All operations were successful!");

    [pool drain];
    return 0;
}
```

Program 16.3 Output

```
Current directory path is /Users/stevekochan/progs/ch16
Current directory path is /Users/stevekochan/progs/ch16/newdir
All operations were successful!
```

Program 16.3 is relatively self-explanatory. The current directory path is first obtained for informative purposes. Next, a new directory called testdir is created in the current directory. The program then uses the movePath:toPath:handler: method to rename the new directory from testdir to newdir. Remember that this method can also be used to move an entire directory structure (that means including its contents) from one place in the file system to another.

After renaming the new directory, the program makes that new directory the current directory using the changeCurrentDirectoryPath: method. The current directory path is then displayed to verify that the change was successful.

Enumerating the Contents of a Directory

Sometimes you need to get a list of the contents of a directory. This enumeration process can be accomplished using either the enumeratorAtPath: or the directoryContentsAtPath: method. In the former case, each file in the specified directory is enumerated one at a time and, by default, if one of those files is a directory, its contents are also recursively enumerated. During this process you can dynamically prevent this recursion by sending a skipDescendants message to an enumeration object so that its contents will not be enumerated.

In the case of directoryContentsAtPath:, the contents of the specified directory are enumerated, and the file list is returned in an array by the method. If any of the files contained in a directory is itself a directory, its contents are not recursively enumerated by this method.

Program 16.4 shows how you can use either method in your programs.

Program 16.4

```
// Enumerate the contents of a directory


#import <Foundation/NSString.h>
#import <Foundation/NSFileManager.h>
#import <Foundation/NSAutoreleasePool.h>
#import <Foundation/NSArray.h>

int main (int argc, char *argv[])
{
    NSAutoreleasePool      * pool = [[NSAutoreleasePool alloc] init];
    NSString               *path;
    NSFileManager          *fm;
    NSDirectoryEnumerator  *dirEnum;
    NSArray                *dirArray;

    // Need to create an instance of the file manager

    fm = [NSFileManager defaultManager];

    // Get current working directory path

    path = [fm currentDirectoryPath];

    // Enumerate the directory

    dirEnum = [fm enumeratorAtPath: path];

    NSLog (@"Contents of %@:", path);
```

```
    while ((path = [dirEnum nextObject]) != nil)
        NSLog (@"%@", path);

    // Another way to enumerate a directory
    dirArray = [fm directoryContentsAtPath:
                            [fm currentDirectoryPath]];
    NSLog (@"Contents using directoryContentsAtPath:");


    for ( path in dirArray )
        NSLog (@"%@", path);

    [pool drain];
    return 0;
}
```

Program 16.4 Output

```
Contents of /Users/stevekochan/mysrc/ch16:
a.out
dir1.m
dir2.m
file1.m
newdir
newdir/file1.m
newdir/output
path1.m
testfile

Contents using directoryContentsAtPath:
a.out
dir1.m
dir2.m
file1.m
newdir
path1.m
testfile
```

Let's take a closer look at the following code sequence:

```
    dirEnum = [fm enumeratorAtPath: path];


    NSLog (@"Contents of %@:", path);


    while ((path = [dirEnum nextObject]) != nil)
        NSLog (@"%@", path);
```

You begin enumeration of a directory by sending an `enumerationAtPath:` message to a file manager object, in this case `fm`. An `NSDirectortyEnumerator` object gets returned by the `enumeratorAtPath:` method, which is stored inside `dirEnum`. Now, each time you send a `nextObject` message to this object, you get returned a path to the next file in the directory you are enumerating. When no more files are left to enumerate, you get nil returned.

You can see the difference between the two enumeration techniques from the output of Program 16.4. The `enumeratorAtPath:` method lists the contents of the `newdir` directory, whereas `directoryContentsAtPath:` does not. If `newdir` had contained subdirectories, they too would have been enumerated by `enumeratorAtPath:`.

As noted, during execution of the `while` loop in Program 16.4, you could have prevented enumeration of any subdirectories by making the following change to the code:

```
while ((path = [dirEnum nextObject]) != nil) {
    NSLog (@"%@", path);

    [fm fileExistsAtPath: path isDirectory: &flag];

    if (flag == YES)
        [dirEnum skipDescendents];
}
```

Here `flag` is a `BOOL` variable. The `fileExistsAtPath:` stores `YES` in `flag` if the specified path is a directory; otherwise, it stores `NO`.

Incidentally, as a reminder, you can display the entire `dirArray` contents with this single `NSLog` call

```
NSLog (@"%@", dirArray);
```

instead of using fast enumeration as was done in the program.

Working with Paths: `NSPathUtilities.h`

`NSPathUtilities.h` includes functions and category extensions to `NSString` to enable you to manipulate pathnames. You should use these whenever possible to make your program more independent of the structure of the file system and locations of particular files and directories. Program 16.5 shows how to use several of the functions and methods provided by `NSPathUtilities.h`.

Program 16.5

```
// Some basic path operations

#import <Foundation/NSString.h>
#import <Foundation/NSArray.h>
#import <Foundation/NSFileManager.h>
#import <Foundation/NSAutoreleasePool.h>
#import <Foundation/NSPathUtilities.h>
```

```objc
int main (int argc, char *argv[])
{
   NSAutoreleasePool  * pool = [[NSAutoreleasePool alloc] init];
   NSString           *fName = @"path.m";
   NSFileManager      *fm;
   NSString           *path, *tempdir, *extension, *homedir, *fullpath;
   NSString           *upath = @"~stevekochan/progs/../ch16/./path.m";

   NSArray            *components;

   fm = [NSFileManager defaultManager];

   // Get the temporary working directory

   tempdir = NSTemporaryDirectory ();

   NSLog (@"Temporary Directory is %@", tempdir);

   // Extract the base directory from current directory

   path = [fm currentDirectoryPath];
   NSLog (@"Base dir is %@", [path lastPathComponent]);

   // Create a full path to the file fName in current directory

   fullpath = [path stringByAppendingPathComponent: fName];
   NSLog (@"fullpath to %@ is %@", fName, fullpath);

   // Get the file name extension

   extension = [fullpath pathExtension];
   NSLog (@"extension for %@ is %@", fullpath, extension);

   // Get user's home directory

   homedir = NSHomeDirectory ();
   NSLog (@"Your home directory is %@", homedir);

   // Divide a path into its components

   components = [homedir pathComponents];

   for ( path in components)
```

```
    NSLog (@"%@", path);

  // "Standardize" a path

  NSLog (@"%@ => %@", upath ,
       [upath stringByStandardizingPath] );

  [pool drain];
  return 0;
}
```

Program 16.5 Output

```
Temporary Directory is /var/folders/HT/HTyGLvSNHTuNb6NrMuo7QE+++TI/-Tmp-/
Base dir is examples
fullpath to path.m is /Users/stevekochan/progs/examples/path.m
extension for /Users/stevekochan/progs/examples/path.m is m
Your home directory is /Users/stevekochan
/
Users
stevekochan
~stevekochan/progs/../ch16/./path.m => /Users/stevekochan/ch16/path.m
```

The function `NSTemporaryDirectory` returns the pathname of a directory on the system you can use for the creation of temporary files. If you create temporary files in this directory, be sure to remove them when you're done. Also, make sure that your filenames are unique, particularly if more than one instance of your application might be running at the same time. (See Exercise 5 at the end of this chapter.) This can easily happen if more than one user logged on to your system is running the same application.

The `lastPathComponent` method extracts the last file in a path. This is useful when you have an absolute pathname and just want to get the base filename from it.

The `stringByAppendingPathComponent:` is useful for tacking on a filename to the end of a path. If the pathname specified as the receiver doesn't end in a slash, the method inserts one in the pathname to separate it from the appended filename. By combining the `currentDirectory` method with the method `stringByAppendingPathComponent:`, you can create a full pathname to a file in the current directory. That technique is shown in Program 16.5.

The `pathExtension` method gives the file extension for the provided pathname. In the example, the extension for the file `path.m` is `m`, which is returned by the method. If the file does not have an extension, the method simply returns an empty string.

The `NSHomeDirectory` function returns the home directory for the current user. You can get the home directory for any particular user by using the `NSHomeDirectoryForUser` function instead, supplying the user's name as the argument to the function.

The `pathComponents` method returns an array containing each of the components of the specified path. Program 16.5 sequences through each element of the returned array and displays each path component on a separate line of output.

Finally, sometimes pathnames contain tilde (~) characters, as we've previously discussed. The `FileManager` methods accept ~ as an abbreviation for the user's home directory or *~user* for a specified user's home directory. If your pathnames might contain tilde characters, you can resolve them by using the `stringByStandardizingPath` method. This method returns a path with these special characters eliminated, or standardized. You can also use the `stringByExpandingTildeInPath` method to expand just a tilde character if it appears in a pathname.

Common Methods for Working with Paths

Table 16.3 summarizes many of the commonly used methods for working with paths. In this table, *components* is an `NSArray` object containing string objects for each component in a path; *path* is a string object specifying a path to a file; and *ext* is a string object indicating a path extension (for example, `@"mp4"`).

Table 16.3   **Common Path Utility Methods**

Method	Description
`+(NSString *) pathWithComponents:` *components*	Constructs a valid path from elements in *components*
`-(NSArray *) pathComponents`	Deconstructs a path into its constituent components
`-(NSString *) lastPathComponent`	Extracts the last component in a path
`-(NSString *) pathExtension`	Extracts the extension from the last component in a path
`-(NSString *)` `stringByAppendingPathComponent:` *path*	Adds *path* to the end of an existing path
`-(NSString *)` `stringByAppendingPathExtension:` *ext*	Adds the specified extension to the last component in the path
`-(NSString *)` `stringByDeletingLastPathComponent`	Removes the last path component
`-(NSString *)` `stringByDeletingPathExtension`	Removes the extension from the last path component
`-(NSString *)` `stringByExpandingTildeInPath`	Expands any tildes in the path to the user's home directory (~) or a specified user's home directory (*~user*)

Table 16.3   **Common Path Utility Methods**

Method	Description
-(NSString *) stringByResolvingSymlinksInPath	Attempts to resolve symbolic links in the path
-(NSString *) stringByStandardizingPath	Standardizes a path by attempting to resolve ~, ..(parent directory), .(current directory), and symbolic links

Table 16.4 presents the *functions* available to obtain information about a user, her home directory, and a directory for storing temporary files.

Table 16.4   **Common Path Utility Functions**

Function	Description
NSString *NSUserName (void)	Returns the current user's login name
NSString *NSFullUserName (void)	Returns the current user's full username
NSString *NSHomeDirectory (void)	Returns the path to the current user's home directory
NSString *NSHomeDirectoryForUser (NSString *user)	Returns the home directory for *user*
NSString *NSTemporaryDirectory (void)	Returns the path to a directory that can be used for creating a temporary file

You also might want to look at the Foundation function NSSearchPathForDirectories InDomains, which you can use to locate special directories on the system, such as the Application directory.

Copying Files and Using the NSProcessInfo Class

Program 16.6 illustrates a command-line tool to implement a simple file copy operation. Usage of this command is as follows:

copy *from-file to-file*

Unlike NSFileManager's copyPath:toPath:handler: method, your command-line tool enables *to-file* to be a directory name. In that case, the file is copied into the *to-file* directory under the name *from-file*. Also unlike the method, if *to-file* already exists, you allow its contents to be overwritten. This is more in line with the standard UNIX copy command cp.

You can get the filenames from the command line by using the `argc` and `argv` arguments to `main`. These two arguments are populated, respectively, with the number of arguments types on the command line (including the command name), and a pointer to an array of C-style character strings.

Instead of having to deal with C strings, which is what you have to do when you work with `argv`, use instead a Foundation class called `NSProcessInfo`. `NSProcessInfo` contains methods that allow you to set and retrieve various types of information about your running application (that is, your *process*). These methods are summarized in Table 16.5.

Table 16.5   **NSProcessInfo Methods**

Method	Description
`+(NSProcessInfo *) processInfo`	Returns information about the current process
`-(NSArray *) arguments`	Returns the arguments to the current process as an array of `NSString` objects
`-(NSDictionary *) environment`	Returns a dictionary of variable/value pairs representing the current environment variables (such as `PATH` and `HOME`) and their values
`-(int) processIdentifier`	Returns the process identifier, which is a unique number assigned by the operating system to identify each running process
`-(NSString *) processName`	Returns the name of the current executing process
`-(NSString *) globallyUniqueString`	Returns a different unique string each time it is invoked. This could be used for generating unique temporary filenames (see Exercise 5)
`-(NSString *) hostName`	Returns the name of the host system (returns `Steve-Kochans-Computer.local` on my Mac OS X system)
`-(NSUInteger) operatingSystem`	Returns a number indicating the operating system (returns the value `5` on my Mac)
`-(NSString *) operatingSystemName`	Returns the name of the operating system (returns the constant `NSMACHOperatingSystem` on my Mac, where the possible return values are defined in `NSProcessInfo.h`)
`-(NSString *) operatingSystemVersionString`	Returns the current version of the operating system (returns `Version 10.5.4 (Build 9E17` on my Mac OS X system)
`-(void) setProcessName: (NSString *) name`	Sets the name of the current process to *name*. Should be used with caution because some assumptions can be made about the name of your process (for example, by the user default settings)

Program 16.6

```
// Implement a basic copy utility


#import <Foundation/NSString.h>
#import <Foundation/NSArray.h>
#import <Foundation/NSFileManager.h>
#import <Foundation/NSAutoreleasePool.h>
#import <Foundation/NSPathUtilities.h>
#import <Foundation/NSProcessInfo.h>

int main (int argc, char *argv[])
{
   NSAutoreleasePool  * pool = [[NSAutoreleasePool alloc] init];
   NSFileManager      *fm;
   NSString           *source, *dest;
   BOOL               isDir;
   NSProcessInfo      *proc = [NSProcessInfo processInfo];
   NSArray            *args = [proc arguments];

   fm = [NSFileManager defaultManager];

   // Check for two arguments on the command line

   if ([args count] != 3) {
      NSLog (@"Usage: %@ src dest", [proc processName]);
      return 1;
   }

   source = [args objectAtIndex: 1];
   dest = [args objectAtIndex: 2];


   // Make sure the source file can be read

   if ([fm isReadableFileAtPath: source] == NO) {
      NSLog (@"Can't read %@", source);
      return 2;
   }

   // See if the destination file is a directory
   // if it is, add the source to the end of the destination

   [fm fileExistsAtPath: dest isDirectory: &isDir];

   if (isDir == YES)
      dest = [dest stringByAppendingPathComponent:
            [source lastPathComponent]];

   // Remove the destination file if it already exists

   [fm removeFileAtPath: dest handler: nil];

   // Okay, time to perform the copy
```

```
    if ([fm copyPath: source toPath: dest handler: nil] == NO) {
      NSLog (@"Copy failed!");
      return 3;
    }

    NSLog (@"Copy of %@ to %@ succeeded!", source, dest);

    [pool drain];
    return 0;
}
```

Program 16.6 Output

```
$ ls -l          see what files we have
total 96
-rwxr-xr-x 1 stevekoc staff 19956 Jul 24 14:33 copy
-rw-r--r-- 1 stevekoc staff 1484 Jul 24 14:32 copy.m
-rw-r--r-- 1 stevekoc staff 1403 Jul 24 13:00 file1.m
drwxr-xr-x 2 stevekoc staff   68 Jul 24 14:40 newdir
-rw-r--r-- 1 stevekoc staff 1567 Jul 24 14:12 path1.m
-rw-r--r-- 1 stevekoc staff   84 Jul 24 13:22 testfile
$ copy         try with no args
Usage: copy src dest
$ copy foo copy2
Can't read foo
$ copy copy.m backup.m
Copy of copy.m to backup.m succeeded!
$ diff copy.m backup.m    compare the files
$ copy copy.m newdir      try copy into directory
Copy of copy.m to newdir/copy.m succeeeded!
$ ls -l newdir
total 8
-rw-r--r-- 1 stevekoc staff 1484 Jul 24 14:44 copy.m
$
```

NSProcessInfo's arguments method returns an array of string objects. The first element of the array is the name of the process, and the remaining elements contain the arguments typed on the command line.

You first check to ensure that two arguments were typed on the command line. This is done by testing the size of the array args that is returned from the arguments method. If this test succeeds, the program then extracts the source and destination filenames from the args array, assigning their values to source and dest, respectively.

The program next checks to ensure that the source file can be read, issuing an error message and exiting if it can't.

The statement

```
[fm fileExistsAtPath: dest isDirectory: &isDir];
```

checks the file specified by dest to see whether it is a directory. As you've seen previously, the answer—YES or NO—is stored in the variable isDir.

If dest is a directory, you want to append the last path component of the source filename to the end of the directory's name. You use the path utility method stringByAppendingPathComponent: to do this. So, if the value of source is the string ch16/copy1.m and the value of dest is /Users/stevekochan/progs and the latter is a directory, you change the value of dest to /Users/stevekochan/progs/copy1.m.

The copyPath:ToPath:handler: method doesn't allow files to be overwritten. Thus, to avoid an error, the program tries to remove the destination file first by using the removeFileAtPath:handler: method. It doesn't really matter whether this method succeeds because it will fail anyway if the destination file doesn't exist.

Upon reaching the end of the program, you can assume all went well and issue a message to that effect.

Basic File Operations: **NSFileHandle**

The methods provided by NSFileHandle enable you to work more closely with files. At the beginning of this chapter, we listed some of the things you can do with these methods.

In general follow these three steps when working with a file:

1. Open the file and obtain an NSFileHandle object to reference the file in subsequent I/O operations.

2. Perform your I/O operations on the open file.

3. Close the file.

Table 16.6 summarizes some commonly used NSFileHandle methods. In this table *fh* is an NSFileHandle object, *data* is an NSData object, *path* is an NSString object, and *offset* is an unsigned long long.

Table 16.6   **Common** NSFileHandle **Methods**

Method	Description
+(NSFileHandle *) fileHandleForReadingAtPath: *path*	Opens a file for reading
+(NSFileHandle *) fileHandleForWritingAtPath: *path*	Opens a file for writing
+(NSFileHandle *) fileHandleForUpdatingAtPath: *path*	Opens a file for updating (reading and writing)
-(NSData *) availableData	Returns data available for reading from a device or channel

Table 16.6   **Common** NSFileHandle **Methods**

Method	Description
-(NSData *) readDataToEndOfFile	Reads the remaining data up to the end of the file (UINT_MAX) bytes max
-(NSData *) readDataOfLength: (NSUInteger) *bytes*	Reads a specified number of *bytes* from the file
-(void) writeData: *data*	Writes *data* to the file
-(unsigned long long) offsetInFile	Obtains the current file offset
-(void) seekToFileOffset: *offset*	Sets the current file offset
-(unsigned long long) seekToEndOfFile	Positions the current file offset at the end of the file
-(void) truncateFileAtOffset: *offset*	Sets the file size to *offset* bytes (pad if needed)
-(void) closeFile	Closes the file

Not shown here are methods for obtaining NSFileHandles for standard input, standard output, standard error, and the null device. These are of the form fileHandleWithDevice, where Device can be StandardInput, StandardOutput, StandardError, or NullDevice.

Also not shown here are methods for reading and writing data in the background, that is, asynchronously.

You should note that the FileHandle class does not provide for the creation of files. That has to be done with FileManager methods, as we've already described. So, both fileHandleForWritingAtPath: and fileHandleForUpdatingAtPath: assume the file exists and return nil if it doesn't. In both cases, the file offset is set to the beginning of the file, so writing (or reading for update mode) begins at the start of the file. Also, if you're used to programming under UNIX, you should note that opening a file for writing does not truncate the file. You have to do that yourself if that's your intention.

Program 16.7 opens the original testfile file you created at the start of this chapter, reads in its contents, and copies it to a file called testout.

Program 16.7

```
// Some basic file handle operations
// Assumes the existence of a file called "testfile"
// in the current working directory

#import <Foundation/NSObject.h>
#import <Foundation/NSString.h>
#import <Foundation/NSFileHandle.h>
#import <Foundation/NSFileManager.h>
```

```objc
#import <Foundation/NSAutoreleasePool.h>
#import <Foundation/NSData.h>

int main (int argc, char *argv[])
{
    NSAutoreleasePool * pool = [[NSAutoreleasePool alloc] init];
    NSFileHandle      *inFile, *outFile;
    NSData            *buffer;


    // Open the file testfile for reading

    inFile = [NSFileHandle fileHandleForReadingAtPath: @"testfile"];

    if (inFile == nil) {
        NSLog (@"Open of testfile for reading failed");
        return 1;
    }

    // Create the output file first if necessary

    [[NSFileManager defaultManager] createFileAtPath: @"testout"
        contents: nil attributes: nil];

    // Now open outfile for writing

    outFile = [NSFileHandle fileHandleForWritingAtPath: @"testout"];

    if (outFile == nil) {
        NSLog (@"Open of testout for writing failed");
        return 2;
    }

    // Truncate the output file since it may contain data

    [outFile truncateFileAtOffset: 0];

    // Read the data from inFile and write it to outFile

    buffer = [inFile readDataToEndOfFile];

    [outFile writeData: buffer];

    // Close the two files

    [inFile closeFile];
    [outFile closeFile];

    // Verify the file's contents

    NSLog(@"%@", [NSString StringWithContentsOfFile: @"testout" encoding:
            NSUTF8StringEncoding error: nil]);

    [pool drain];
    return 0;
}
```

Program 16.7 Output

```
This is a test file with some data in it.
Here's another line of data.
And a third.
```

The method `readDataToEndOfFile:` reads up to `UINT_MAX` bytes of data at a time, which is defined in `<limits.h>` and equal to $FFFFFFFF_{16}$. This will be large enough for any application you'll have to write. You can also break up the operation to perform smaller-sized reads and writes. You can even set up a loop to transfer a buffer full of bytes between the files at a time, using the `readDataOfLength:` method. Your buffer size might be 8,192 (8kb) or 131,072 (128kb) bytes, for example. A power of 2 is normally used because the underlying operating system typically performs its I/O operations in chunks of data of such sizes. You might want to experiment with different values on your system to see what works best.

If a read method reaches the end of the file without reading any data, it returns an empty `NSData` object (that is, a buffer with no bytes in it). You can apply the `length` method to the buffer and test for equality with zero to see whether any data remains to be read from the file.

If you open a file for updating, the file offset is set to the beginning of the file. You can change that offset by seeking within a file and then perform your read or write operations on the file. So, to seek to the 10th byte in a file whose handle is `databaseHandle`, you can write the following message expression:

```
[databaseHandle seekToFileOffset: 10];
```

Relative file positioning is done by obtaining the current file offset and then adding to or subtracting from it. So, to skip over the next 128 bytes in the file, write the following:

```
[databaseHandle seekToFileOffet:
       [databaseHandle offsetInFile] + 128];
```

And to move back the equivalent of five integers in the file, write this:

```
[databaseHandle seekToFileOffet:
       [databaseHandle offsetInFile] - 5 * sizeof (int)];
```

Program 16.8 appends the contents of one file to another. It does this by opening the second file for writing, seeking to the end of the file, and then writing the contents of the first file to the second.

Program 16.8

```
// Append the file "fileA" to the end of "fileB"


#import <Foundation/NSObject.h>
#import <Foundation/NSString.h>
```

```
#import <Foundation/NSFileHandle.h>
#import <Foundation/NSFileManager.h>
#import <Foundation/NSAutoreleasePool.h>
#import <Foundation/NSData.h>

int main (int argc, char *argv[])
{
    NSAutoreleasePool      * pool = [[NSAutoreleasePool alloc] init];
    NSFileHandle           *inFile, *outFile;
    NSData                 *buffer;


    // Open the file fileA for reading

    inFile = [NSFileHandle fileHandleForReadingAtPath: @"fileA"];

    if (inFile == nil) {
        NSLog (@"Open of fileA for reading failed");
        return 1;
    }

    // Open the file fileB for updating

    outFile = [NSFileHandle fileHandleForWritingAtPath: @"fileB"];

    if (outFile == nil) {
        NSLog (@"Open of fileB for writing failed");
        return 2;
    }

    // Seek to the end of outFile

    [outFile seekToEndOfFile];

    // Read inFile and write its contents to outFile

    buffer = [inFile readDataToEndOfFile];
    [outFile writeData: buffer];

    // Close the two files

    [inFile closeFile];
    [outFile closeFile];

    [pool drain];
    return 0;
}
```

Contents of FileA before running Program 16.8

This is line 1 in the first file.
This is line 2 in the first file.

Contents of FileB before running Program 16.8

```
This is line 1 in the second file.
This is line 2 in the second file.
```

Program 16.8 Output

Contents of fileB
```
This is line 1 in the second file.
This is line 2 in the second file.
This is line 1 in the first file.
This is line 2 in the first file.
```

You can see from the output that the contents of the first file were successfully appended to the end of the second file. Incidentally, `seekToEndOfFile` returns the current file offset after the seek is performed. We chose to ignore that value; you can use that information to obtain the size of a file in your program if you need it.

Exercises

1. Modify the copy program developed in Program 16.6 so that it can accept more than one source file to be copied into a directory, like the standard UNIX `cp` command. So, the command

   $ **copy copy1.m file1.m file2.m progs**

   should copy the three files `copy1.m`, `file1.m`, and `file2.m` into the directory `progs`. Be sure that when more than one source file is specified, the last argument is, in fact, an existing directory.

2. Write a command-line tool called `myfind` that takes two arguments. The first is a starting directory to begin the search, and the second is a filename to locate. So, the command line

   $ **myfind /Users proposal.doc**
   /Users/stevekochan/MyDocuments/proposals/proposal.doc
   $

   begins searching the file system from `/Users` to locate the file `proposal.doc`. Print either a full path to the file if it's found (as shown) or an appropriate message if it's not.

3. Write your own version of the standard UNIX tools basename and dirname.

4. Using NSProcessInfo, write a program to display all the information returned by each of its getter methods.

5. Given the NSPathUtilities.h function NSTemporaryDirectory and the NSProcessInfo method globallyUniqueString described in this chapter, add a category called TempFiles to NSString, and in it define a method called temporaryFileName that returns a different, unique filename every time it is invoked.

6. Modify Program 16.7 so that the file is read and written kBufSize bytes at a time, where kBufSize is defined at the beginning of your program. Be sure to test the program on large files (that is, files larger than kBufSize bytes).

7. Open a file, read its contents 128 bytes at a time, and write it to the terminal. Use FileHandle's fileHandleWithStandardOutput method to obtain a handle for the terminal's output.

Memory Management

We have focused on the topic of memory management throughout this book. You should understand by now when you are responsible for releasing objects and when you are not. Even though the examples in this book have all been small, we have emphasized the importance of paying attention to memory management, to teach good programming practice and to develop leak-free programs.

Depending on the type of application you're writing, judicious use of memory can be critical. For example, if you're writing an interactive drawing application that creates many objects during the execution of the program, you must take care that your program doesn't continue to consume more memory resources as it runs. In such cases, it becomes your responsibility to intelligently manage those resources and free them when they're no longer needed. This means freeing resources during the program's execution instead of just waiting until the end.

In this chapter, you will learn about Foundation's memory-allocation strategy in more detail. This involves a more thorough discussion of the autorelease pool and the idea of retaining objects. You will also learn about an object's reference count. Finally, we talk about a mechanism known as *garbage collection* that alleviates the burden of having to retain and subsequently release your objects when you're done using them. However, as you'll see, garbage collection cannot be used for iPhone applications, so you still must understand the techniques for memory management described throughout this book (and in more detail in this chapter).

The Autorelease Pool

You are familiar with the autorelease pool from previous program examples in this second part of the book. When dealing with Foundation programs, you must set up this pool to use the Foundation objects. This pool is where the system keeps track of your objects for later release. As you've seen, your application can set up the pool with a call like so:

```
NSAutoreleasePool * pool = [[NSAutoreleasePool alloc] init];
```

When the pool is set up, Foundation automatically adds certain arrays, strings, diction-aries, and other objects to this pool. When you're done using the pool, you can release the memory it uses by sending it a `drain` message:

```
[pool drain];
```

The autorelease pool gets its name from the fact that any objects that have been marked as autorelease and, therefore, added to the pool are automatically released when the pool itself is released. In fact, you can have more than one autorelease pool in your program, and they can be nested as well.

If your program generates a lot of temporary objects (which can easily happen when executing code inside a loop), you might need to create multiple autorelease pools in your program. For example, the following code fragment illustrates how you can set up autorelease pools to release the temporary objects created by each iteration of the `for` loop:

```
NSAutoreleasePool  *tempPool;
  ...
for (i = 0; i < n; ++i) {
  tempPool = [[NSAutoReleasePool alloc] init];
    ... // lots of work with temporary objects here
  [tempPool drain];
}
```

Note that the autorelease pool doesn't contain the actual objects themselves—only a reference to the objects that are to be released when the pool is drained.

You can add an object to the current autorelease pool for later release by sending it an `autorelease` message:

```
[myFraction autorelease];
```

The system then adds `myFraction` to the autorelease pool for automatic release later. As you'll see, the `autorelease` method is useful for marking objects from inside a method, for later disposal.

Reference Counting

When we talked about the basic Objective-C object class `NSObject`, we noted that mem-ory is allocated with the `alloc` method and can subsequently be released with a `release` message. Unfortunately, it's not always that simple. A running application can reference an object that you create in several places; an object also can be stored in an array or refer-enced by an instance variable someplace else, for example. You can't free up the memory an object uses until you are certain that everyone is done using that object.

Luckily, the Foundation framework provides an elegant solution for keeping track of the number of references to an object. It involves a fairly straightforward technique called *reference counting*. The concept is as follows: When an object is created, its reference count is set to 1. Each time you need to ensure that the object be kept around, you increment its reference count by 1 by sending it a `retain` message, like so:

```
[myFraction retain];
```

Some of the methods in the Foundation framework also increment this reference count, such as when an object is added to an array.

When you no longer need an object, you decrement its reference count by 1 by sending it a `release` message, like this:

```
[myFraction release];
```

When the reference count of an object reaches 0, the system knows that the object is no longer needed (because, in theory, it is no longer referenced), so it frees up (*deallocates*) its memory. This is done by sending the object a `dealloc` message.

Successful operation of this strategy requires diligence by you, the programmer, to ensure that the reference count is appropriately incremented and decremented during program execution. The system handles some, but not all, of this, as you'll see.

Let's take a look at reference counting in a little more detail. The `retainCount` message can be sent to an object to obtain its reference (or *retain*) count. You will normally never need to use this method, but it's useful here for illustrative purposes (see Program 17.1). Note that it returns an unsigned integer of type `NSUInteger`.

Program 17.1

```
// Introduction to reference counting


#import <Foundation/NSObject.h>
#import <Foundation/NSAutoreleasePool.h>
#import <Foundation/NSString.h>
#import <Foundation/NSArray.h>
#import <Foundation/NSValue.h>

int main (int argc, char *argv[])
{
    NSAutoreleasePool * pool = [[NSAutoreleasePool alloc] init];
    NSNumber          *myInt = [NSNumber numberWithInteger: 100];
    NSNumber          *myInt2;
    NSMutableArray    *myArr = [NSMutableArray array];

    NSLog (@"myInt retain count = %lx",
        (unsigned long) [myInt retainCount]);

    [myArr addObject: myInt];
    NSLog (@"after adding to array = %lx",
        (unsigned long) [myInt retainCount]);

    myInt2 = myInt;
    NSLog (@"after asssignment to myInt2 = %lx",
        (unsigned long) [myInt retainCount]);

    [myInt retain];
    NSLog (@"myInt after retain = %lx",
        (unsigned long) [myInt retainCount]);
```

```
    NSLog (@"myInt2 after retain = %lx",
        (unsigned long) [myInt2 retainCount]);

    [myInt release];
    NSLog (@"after release = %lx",
        (unsigned long) [myInt retainCount]);

    [myArr removeObjectAtIndex: 0];
    NSLog (@"after removal from array = %lx",
        (unsigned long) [myInt retainCount]);

    [pool drain];
    return 0;
}
```

Program 17.1 Output

```
myInt retain count = 1
after adding to array = 2
after asssignment to myInt2 = 2
myInt after retain = 3
myInt2 after retain = 3
after release = 2
after removal from array = 1
```

The NSNumber object myInt is set to the integer value 100, and the output shows that it has an initial retain count of 1. Next, the object is added to the array myArr using the addObject: method. Note that its reference count then goes to 2. The addObject: method does this automatically; if you check your documentation for the addObject: method, you will see this fact described there. Adding an object to any type of collection increments its reference count. That means if you subsequently release the object you've added, it will still have a valid reference from within the array and won't be deallocated.

Next, you assign myInt to myInt2. Note that this doesn't increment the reference count—this could mean potential trouble later. For example, if the reference count for myInt were decremented to 0 and its space were released, myInt2 would have an invalid object reference (remember that the assignment of myInt to myInt2 doesn't copy the actual object—only the pointer in memory to where the object is located).

Because myInt now has another reference (through myInt2), you increment its reference count by sending it a retain message. This is done in the next line of Program 17.1. As you can see, after sending it the retain message, its reference count becomes 3. The first reference is the actual object itself, the second is from the array, and the third is from the assignment. Although storing the element in the array creates an automatic increase in the reference count, assigning it to another variable does not, so you must do that your-self. Notice from the output that both `myInt` and `myInt2` have a reference count of 3; that's because they both reference the same object in memory.

Let's assume that you're finished using the `myInt` object in your program. You can tell the system that by sending a `release` message to the object. As you can see, its reference count then goes from 3 back down to 2. Because it's not 0, the other references to the object (from the array and through `myInt2`) remain valid. The system does not deallocate the memory the object used as long as it has a nonzero reference count.

If you remove the first element from the array `myArr` using the `removeObjectAtIndex:` method, you'll note that the reference count for `myInt` is auto-matically decremented to 1. In general, removing an object from any collection has the side effect of decrementing its reference count. This implies that the following code se-quence could lead to trouble:

```
myInt = [myArr ObjectAtIndex: 0];
  ...
[myArr removeObjectAtIndex: 0]
  ...
```

That's because, in this case, the object referenced by `myInt` can become invalid after the `removeObjectAtIndex:` method is invoked if its reference count is decremented to 0. The solution here, of course, is to retain `myInt` after it is retrieved from the array so that it won't matter what happens to its reference from other places.

Reference Counting and Strings

Program 17.2 shows how reference counting works for string objects.

Program 17.2

```
// Reference counting with string objects


#import <Foundation/NSObject.h>
#import <Foundation/NSAutoreleasePool.h>
#import <Foundation/NSString.h>
#import <Foundation/NSArray.h>

int main (int argc, char *argv[])
{
   NSAutoreleasePool * pool = [[NSAutoreleasePool alloc] init];
   NSString          *myStr1 = @"Constant string";
   NSString          *myStr2 = [NSString stringWithString: @"string 2"];
   NSMutableString   *myStr3 = [NSMutableString stringWithString: @"string 3"];
   NSMutableArray    *myArr = [NSMutableArray array];

   NSLog (@"Retain count: myStr1: %lx, myStr2: %lx, myStr3: %lx",
          (unsigned long) [myStr1 retainCount],
          (unsigned long) [myStr2 retainCount],
          (unsigned long) [myStr3 retainCount]);

   [myArr addObject: myStr1];
```

```
    [myArr addObject: myStr2];
    [myArr addObject: myStr3];

    NSLog (@"Retain count: myStr1: %lx, myStr2: %lx, myStr3: %lx",
          (unsigned long) [myStr1 retainCount],
          (unsigned long) [myStr2retainCount],
            (unsigned long) [myStr3 retainCount]);

    [myArr addObject: myStr1];
    [myArr addObject: myStr2];
    [myArr addObject: myStr3];

    NSLog (@"Retain count: myStr1: %lx, myStr2: %lx, myStr3: %lx",
          (unsigned long) [myStr1 retainCount],
          (unsigned long) [myStr2retainCount],
            (unsigned long) [myStr3 retainCount]);

    [myStr1 retain];
    [myStr2 retain];
    [myStr3 retain];

    NSLog (@"Retain count: myStr1: %lx, myStr2: %lx, myStr3: %lx",
          (unsigned long) [myStr1 retainCount],
          (unsigned long) [myStr2 retainCount],
            (unsigned long) [myStr3 retainCount]);

    // Bring the reference count of myStr3 back down to 2
    [myStr3 release];

    [pool drain];
    return 0;
}
```

Program 17.2 Output

```
Retain count: myStr1: ffffffff, myStr2: ffffffff, myStr3: 1
Retain count: myStr1: ffffffff, myStr2: ffffffff, myStr3: 2
Retain count: myStr1: ffffffff, myStr2: ffffffff, myStr3: 3
```

The NSString object myStr1 is assigned the NSConstantString @"Constant string". Space for constant strings is allocated differently in memory than for other objects. Constant strings have no reference-counting mechanism because they can never be released. This is why when the retainCount message is sent to myStr1, it returns a value of 0xffffffff. (This value is actually defined as the largest possible unsigned integer value, or UINT_MAX, in the standard header file <limits.h>.)

Note

Apparently, on some systems, the retain count that is returned for the constant strings in Program 17.2 is 0x7fffffff (and not 0xffffffff), which is the largest possible signed integer value, or INT_MAX.

Notice that the same applies to an immutable string object that is initialized with a constant string: It, too, has no retain count, as verified by the retain count displayed for myStr2.

> **Note**
>
> Here the system is clever and determines that the immutable string object is being initial-ized by a constant string object. Before the release of Leopard, this optimization was not done, and `mystr2` would have had a retain count.

In the statement

```
NSMutableString *myStr3 = [NSMutableString stringWithString: @"string 3"];
```

the variable `myStr3` is set to a string made from a copy of the constant character string `@"string 3"`. A copy of the string had to be made because the message `stringWithString:` was sent to the `NSMutableString` class, indicating that the string's contents might have changed during the course of the program's execution. And because constant character strings can't have their contents changed, the system can't just set the `myStr3` variable to point to the constant string `@"string 3"`, as was done with `myStr2`.

So the string object `myStr3` does have a reference count, as verified by the output. The reference count can be changed by adding this string to an array or by sending it a `retain` message, as verified by the output from the last two `NSLog` calls. Foundation's `stringWithString:` method added this object to the autorelease pool when it was cre-ated. Foundation's `array` method also added the array `myArr` to the pool.

Before the autorelease pool itself is released, `myStr3` is released. This brings its reference count down to 2. The release of the autorelease pool then decrements the reference count of this object to 0, which causes it to be deallocated. How does that happen? When the autorelease pool is released, each of the objects in the pool gets a `release` message sent to it for each time it was sent an `autorelease` message. Because the string object `myStr3` was added to the autorelease pool when the `stringWithString:` method created it, it is sent a `release` message. That brings its reference count down to 1. When an array in the autore-lease pool is released, each of its elements also is released. Therefore, when `myArr` is re-leased from the pool, each of its elements—which includes `myStr3`—is sent `release` messages. This brings its reference count down to 0, which then causes it to be deallocated.

You must be careful not to over-release an object. In Program 17.2, if you brought the reference count of `mystr3` below 2 before the pool was released, the pool would contain a reference to an invalid object. Then when the pool was released, the reference to the in-valid object would most likely cause the program to terminate abnormally with a segmen-tation fault error.

Reference Counting and Instance Variables

You also must pay attention to reference counts when you deal with instance variables. For example, recall the `setName:` method from your `AddressCard` class:

```
-(void) setName: (NSString *) theName
{
    [name release];
    name = [[NSString alloc] initWithString: theName];
}
```

Suppose we had defined `setName:` this way instead and did not have it take ownership of its name object:

```
-(void) setName: (NSString *) theName
{
    name = theName;
}
```

This version of the method takes a string representing the person's name and stores it in the `name` instance variable. It seems straightforward enough, but consider the following method call:

```
NSString  *newName;
    ...
[myCard setName: newName];
```

Suppose `newName` is a temporary storage space for the name of the person you want to add to the address card and that later you want to release it. What do you think would happen to the `name` instance variable in `myCard`? Its `name` field would no longer be valid because it would reference an object that had been destroyed. That's why your classes need to own their own member objects: You don't have to worry about those objects inadvertently being deallocated or modified.

The next few examples illustrate this point in more detail. Let's start by defining a new class called `ClassA` that has one instance variable: a string object called `str`. You'll just write setter and getter methods for this variable. We don't synthesize the methods here, but we write them ourselves so it's clear precisely what's going on.

Program 17.3

```
// Introduction to reference counting

#import <Foundation/NSObject.h>
#import <Foundation/NSAutoreleasePool.h>
#import <Foundation/NSString.h>

@interface ClassA: NSObject
{
    NSString *str;
}

-(void) setStr: (NSString *) s;
-(NSString *) str;
@end

@implementation ClassA
-(void) setStr: (NSString *) s
{
    str = s;
```

```
}

-(NSString *) str
{
   return str;
}
@end

int main (int argc, char *argv[])
{
   NSAutoreleasePool * pool = [[NSAutoreleasePool alloc] init];
   NSMutableString *myStr = [NSMutableString stringWithString: @"A string"];
   ClassA    *myA = [[ClassA alloc] init];

   NSLog (@"myStr retain count: %x", [myStr retainCount]);

   [myA setStr: myStr];
   NSLog (@"myStr retain count: %x", [myStr retainCount]);

   [myA release];
   [pool drain];
   return 0;
}
```

Program 17.3 Output

```
myStr retain count: 1
myStr retain count: 1
```

The program simply allocates a ClassA object called myA and then invokes the setter method to set it to the NSString object specified by myStr. The reference count for myStr is 1 both before and after the setStr method is invoked, as you would expect, because the method simply stores the value of its argument in its instance variable str. Once again, however, if the program released myStr after calling the setStr method, the value stored inside the str instance variable would become invalid because its reference count would be decremented to 0 and the memory space occupied by the object it references would be deallocated.

This happens in Progam 17.3 when the autorelease pool is released. Even though we didn't add it to that pool explicitly ourselves, when we created the string object myStr using the stringWithString: method, that method added it to the autorelease pool. When the pool was released, so was myStr. Any attempt to access it after the pool was released would therefore be invalid.

Program 17.4 makes a change to the setStr: method to retain the value of str. This protects you from someone else later releasing the object str references.

Program 17.4

```
// Retaining objects

#import <Foundation/NSObject.h>
#import <Foundation/NSAutoreleasePool.h>
#import <Foundation/NSString.h>
#import <Foundation/NSArray.h>

@interface ClassA: NSObject
{
  NSString *str;
}

-(void) setStr: (NSString *) s;
-(NSString *) str;
@end

@implementation ClassA
-(void) setStr: (NSString *) s
{
   str = s;
  [str retain];
}

-(NSString *) str
{
   return str;
}
@end

int main (int argc, char *argv[])
{
    NSAutoreleasePool * pool = [[NSAutoreleasePool alloc] init];
    NSString  *myStr = [NSMutableString stringWithString: @"A string"];
    ClassA    *myA = [[ClassA alloc] init];

    NSLog (@"myStr retain count: %x", [myStr retainCount]);

    [myA setStr: myStr];
    NSLog (@"myStr retain count: %x", [myStr retainCount]);

    [myStr release];
    NSLog (@"myStr retain count: %x", [myStr retainCount]);

    [myA release];
    [pool drain];
    return 0;
}
```

Program 17.4 Output

```
myStr retain count: 1
myStr retain count: 2
myStr retain count: 1
```

You can see that the reference count for `myStr` is bumped to 2 after the `setStr:` method is invoked, so this particular problem has been solved. Subsequently releasing `myStr` in the program makes its reference through the instance variable still valid because its reference count is still 1.

Because you allocated `myA` in the program using `alloc`, you are still responsible for releasing it yourself. Instead of having to worry about releasing it yourself, you could have added it to the autorelease pool by sending it an `autorelease` message:

```
[myA autorelease];
```

You can do this immediately after the object is allocated, if you want. Remember, adding an object to the autorelease pool doesn't release it or invalidate it; it just marks it for later release. You can continue to use the object until it is deallocated, which happens when the pool is released if the reference count of the object becomes 0 at that time.

You are still left with some potential problems that you might have spotted. Your `setStr:` method does its job of retaining the string object it gets as its argument, but when does *that* string object get released? Also, what about the old value of the instance variable `str` that you are overwriting? Shouldn't you release its value to free up its memory? Program 17.5 provides a solution to this problem.

Program 17.5

```
// Introduction to reference counting

#import <Foundation/NSObject.h>
#import <Foundation/NSAutoreleasePool.h>
#import <Foundation/NSString.h>
#import <Foundation/NSArray.h>

@interface ClassA: NSObject
{
    NSString *str;
}

-(void) setStr: (NSString *) s;
-(NSString *) str;
-(void) dealloc;
@end

@implementation ClassA
-(void) setStr: (NSString *) s
{
```

```
        // free up old object since we're done with it
        [str autorelease];

        // retain argument in case someone else releases it
        str = [s retain];
    }

-(NSString *) str
{
    return str;
}

-(void) dealloc {
    NSLog (@"ClassA dealloc");
    [str release];
    [super dealloc];
}
@end

int main (int argc, char *argv[])
{
    NSAutoreleasePool * pool = [[NSAutoreleasePool alloc] init];
    NSString  *myStr = [NSMutableString stringWithString: @"A string"];
    ClassA   *myA = [[ClassA alloc] init];

    NSLog (@"myStr retain count: %x", [myStr retainCount]);
    [myA autorelease];

    [myA setStr: myStr];
    NSLog (@"myStr retain count: %x", [myStr retainCount]);

    [pool drain];
    return 0;
}
```

Program 17.5 Output

```
myStr retain count: 1
myStr retain count: 2
ClassA dealloc
```

The setStr: method first takes whatever is currently stored in the str instance variable and autoreleases it. That is, it makes it available for later release. This is important if the method might be called many times throughout the execution of a program to set the same field to different values. Each time a new value is stored, the old value should be marked for release. After the old value is released, the new one is retained and stored in the `str` field. The message expression

```
str = [s retain];
```

takes advantage of the fact that the `retain` method returns its receiver.

> **Note**
>
> If the `str` variable is nil, that's not a problem. The Objective-C runtime initializes all instance variables to nil, and it's okay to send a message to nil.

The `dealloc` method is not new; you encountered it in Chapter 15, "Numbers, Strings, and Collections," with your `AddressBook` and `AddressCard` classes. Overriding `dealloc` provides a tidy way for you to dispose of the last object your `str` instance variable references when its memory is to be released (that is, when its reference count becomes 0). In such a case, the system calls the `dealloc` method, which is inherited from `NSObject` and which you normally don't want to override. In the case of objects you retain, allocate with `alloc`, or copy (with one of the copy methods discussed in the next chapter) inside your methods, you might need to override `dealloc` so that you get a chance to free them up. The statements

```
[str release];
[super dealloc];
```

first release the `str` instance variable and then call the parent's `dealloc` method to finish the job.

The `NSLog` call was placed inside the `dealloc` method to display a message when it is called. We did this just to verify that the `ClassA` object is deallocated properly when the autorelease pool is released.

You might have spotted one last pitfall with the setter method `setStr`. Take another look at Program 17.5. Suppose that `myStr` were a mutable string instead of an immutable one, and further suppose that one or more characters in `myStr` were changed after invoking `setStr`. Changes to the string referenced by `myStr` would also affect the string referenced by the instance variable because they reference the same object. Reread that last sentence to make sure you understand that point. Also realize that setting `myStr` to a completely new string object does not cause this problem. The problem occurs only if one or more characters of the string are modified in some way.

The solution to this particular problem is to make a new copy of the string inside the setter if you want to protect it and make it completely independent of the setter's argument. This is why you chose to make a copy of the `name` and `email` members in the `setName:` and `setEmail:` `AddressCard` methods in Chapter 15.

An Autorelease Example

Let's take a look at one last program example in this chapter to ensure that you really understand how reference counting, retaining, and releasing/autoreleasing objects work. Examine Program 17.6, which defines a dummy class called Foo with one instance variable and only inherited methods.

Program 17.6

```
#import <Foundation/NSObject.h>
#import <Foundation/NSAutoreleasePool.h>

@interface Foo: NSObject
{
    int x;
}
@end

@implementation Foo
@end

int main (int argc, char *argv[])
{
    NSAutoreleasePool * pool = [[NSAutoreleasePool alloc] init];
    Foo    *myFoo = [[Foo alloc] init];

    NSLog (@"myFoo retain count = %x", [myFoo retainCount]);

    [pool drain];
    NSLog (@"after pool drain = %x", [myFoo retainCount]);

    pool = [[NSAutoreleasePool alloc] init];
    [myFoo autorelease];
    NSLog (@"after autorelease = %x", [myFoo retainCount]);

    [myFoo retain];
    NSLog (@"after retain = %x", [myFoo retainCount]);

    [pool drain];
    NSLog (@"after second pool drain = %x", [myFoo retainCount]);

    [myFoo release];
    return 0;
}
```

Program 17.6 Output

```
myFoo retain count = 1
```

```
after pool drain = 1
after autorelease = 1
after retain = 2
after second pool drain = 1
```

The program allocates a new `Foo` object and assigns it to the variable `myFoo`. Its initial retain count is 1, as you've already seen. This object is not a part of the autorelease pool yet, so releasing the pool does not invalidate the object. A new pool is then allocated, and `myFoo` is added to the pool by sending it an `autorelease` message. Notice again that its reference count doesn't change, because adding an object to the autorelease pool does not affect its reference count—it only marks it for later release.

Next, you send `myFoo` a `retain` message. This changes its reference count to 2. When you subsequently release the pool the second time, the reference count for `myFoo` is decremented by 1 because it was previously sent an `autorelease` message and, therefore, is sent a `release` message when the pool is released.

Because `myFoo` was retained before the pool was released, its reference count after decrementing is still greater than 0. Therefore, `myFoo` survives the pool drain and is still a valid object. Of course, you must now release it yourself, which we do in Program 17.6 to properly clean up and avoid memory leaks.

Reread this explanation of the autorelease pool if it still seems a little fuzzy to you. When you understand Program 17.6, you will thoroughly understand the autorelease pool and how it works.

Summary of Memory-Management Rules

Let's summarize what you've learned about memory management in this chapter:

- Releasing an object can free up its memory, which can be a concern if you're creating many objects during the execution of a program. A good rule is to release objects you've created or retained when you're done with them.

- Sending a `release` message does not necessarily destroy an object. When an object's reference count is decremented to 0, the object is destroyed. The system does this by sending the `dealloc` message to the object to free its memory.

- The autorelease pool provides for the automatic release of objects when the pool itself is released. The system does this by sending a `release` message to each object in the pool for each time it was autoreleased. Each object in the autorelease pool whose reference count goes down to 0 is sent a `dealloc` message to destroy the object.

- If you no longer need an object from within a method but need to return it, send it an `autorelease` message to mark it for later release. The `autorelease` message does not affect the reference count of the object. So it enables the object to be used by the message sender but still be freed up later when the autorelease pool is released.

- When your application terminates, all the memory your objects take up is released, regardless of whether they were in the autorelease pool.

- When you develop more sophisticated applications (such as Cocoa applications), autorelease pools can be created and destroyed during execution of the program (for Cocoa applications, that happens each time an event occurs). In such cases, if you want to ensure that your object survives automatic deallocation when the autorelease pool itself is released, you need to explicitly retain it. All objects that have a reference count greater than the number of autorelease messages they have been sent will survive the release of the pool.

- If you directly create an object using the `new`, `alloc`, or `copy` methods (or with an `allocWithZone:`, `copyWithZone:`, or `mutableCopy` method), you are responsible for releasing it. For each time you `retain` an object, you should `release` or `autorelease` that object.

- You don't have to worry about releasing objects that are returned by methods other than those noted in the previous rule. It's not your responsibility; those methods should have autoreleased those objects. That's why you needed to create the autorelease pool in your program in the first place. Methods such as `stringWithString:` automatically add newly created string objects to the pool by sending them `autorelease` messages. If you don't have a pool set up, you get a message that you tried to autorelease an object without having a pool in place.

Garbage Collection

Up to this point in this book, you have been creating your programs to run in a *memory-managed* runtime environment. The memory-management rules summarized in the previous sections apply to such an environment, in which you deal with autorelease pools, issues related to retaining and releasing objects, and object ownership.

As of Objective C 2.0, an alternate form of memory management, known as *garbage collection,* became available. With garbage collection, you don't have to worry about retaining and releasing objects, autorelease pools, or retain counts. The system automatically keeps track of what objects own what other objects, automatically freeing up (or garbage-collecting) objects that are no longer referenced as space is needed during the program's execution.

If things can be that simple, why didn't we just take advantage of garbage collection throughout this book and skip all the discussions about memory management? There are three reasons: First, even in an environment that supports garbage collection, it's best to know who owns your objects and to keep track of when you don't need them anymore. This will make you more meticulous about writing your code because you will understand the relationships of your objects to each other and their lifespan in your program.

The second reason, as has been previously noted, is that the iPhone runtime environment doesn't support garbage collection, so you don't have a choice when developing programs for that platform.

The third reason applies to you if you plan on writing library routines, plugins, or shared code. Since that code might be loaded into a garbage-collected or non garbage-collected process, it has to be written to work in both environments. That means, you need to write your code using the memory management techniques described throughout this book. It also means you have to test your code with garbage-collection disabled and enabled.

If you decide to use garbage collection, you must turn it on when building programs with Xcode. You can do this through the Project, Edit Project Settings menu. Under the "GCC 4.0—Code Generation" settings, you'll see a setting called Objective-C Garbage Collection. Changing that from its default value of Unsupported to Required specifies that your program will be built with automatic garbage collection enabled (see Figure 17.1).

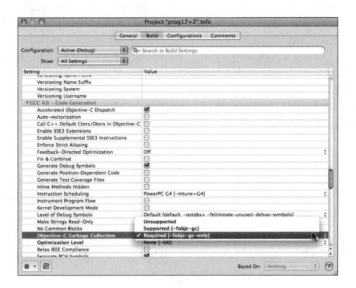

Figure 17.1   Enabling garbage collection.

When garbage collection is enabled, your program can still make its `retain`, `autorelease`, `release`, and `dealloc` method calls. However, they'll all be ignored. In that way, you can develop a program that can run in both memory-managed and garbage-collected environments. However, this also implies that if your code is to run in both environments, that you can't do any work in a `dealloc` method that you provide. That's because, as stated, `dealloc` calls are ignored when garbage-collection is enabled.

> **Note**
>
> The memory-management techniques described in this chapter will suffice for most applications. However, in more advanced cases, such as when writing multithreaded applications, you might need to do more. To learn more about these issues and others related to garbage collection, see Appendix D, "Resources."

Exercises

1. Write a program to test the effects of adding and removing entries in a dictionary on the reference count of the objects you add and remove.

2. What effect do you think the `NSArray`'s `replaceObjectAtIndex:withObject:` method will have on the reference count of the object that is replaced in the array? What effect will it have on the object placed into the array? Write a program to test it. Then consult your documentation on this method to verify your results.

3. Return to the `Fraction` class you worked with throughout Part I, "The Objective-C 2.0 Language." For your convenience, it is listed in Chapter 21, "Writing iPhone Applications." Modify that class to work under the Foundation framework. Then add messages as appropriate to the various `MathOps` category methods to add the fractions resulting from each operation to the autorelease pool. When that is done, can you write a statement like this:

   ```
   [[fractionA add: fractionB] print];
   ```

   without leaking memory? Explain your answer.

4. Return to your `AddressBook` and `AddressCard` examples from Chapter 15. Modify each `dealloc` method to print a message when the method is invoked. Then run some of the sample programs that use these classes, to ensure that a `dealloc` message is sent to every `AddressBook` and `AddressCard` object you use in the program before reaching the end of `main`.

5. Choose any two programs in this book and build and run them in Xcode with garbage collection turned on. Verify that when garbage collection is on, method calls such as `retain`, `autorelease`, and `release` are ignored.

18

Copying Objects

This chapter discusses some of the subtleties involved in copying objects. We introduce the concept of shallow versus deep copying and discuss how to make copies under the Foundation framework.

Chapter 8, "Inheritance," discussed what happens when you assign one object to another with a simple assignment statement, such as here:

```
origin = pt;
```

In this example, `origin` and `pt` are both `XYPoint` objects that we defined like this:

```
@interface XYPoint: NSObject
{
    int x;
    int y;
};
    ...
@end
```

Recall that the effect of the assignment is to simply copy the address of the object `pt` into `origin`. At the end of the assignment operation, both variables point to the same location in memory. Making changes to the instance variables with a message such as

```
[origin setX: 100 andY: 200];
```

changes the x, y coordinate of the `XYPoint` object referenced by both the `origin` and `pt` variables because they both reference the same object in memory.

The same applies to Foundation objects: Assigning one variable to another simply creates another reference to the object (but it does not increase the reference count, as discussed in Chapter 17, "Memory Management"). So if `dataArray` and `dataArray2` are both `NSMutableArray` objects, the following statements remove the first element from the same array that both variables reference:

```
dataArray2 = dataArray;
[dataArray2 removeObjectAtIndex: 0];
```

The copy and `mutableCopy` Methods

The Foundation classes implement methods known as `copy` and `mutableCopy` that you can use to create a copy of an object. This is done by implementing a method in conformance with the `<NSCopying>` protocol for making copies. If your class needs to distinguish between making mutable and immutable copies of an object, you must implement a method according to the `<NSMutableCopying>` protocol as well. You learn how to do that later in this section.

Getting back to the copy methods for the Foundation classes, given the two `NSMutableArray` objects `dataArray2` and `dataArray`, as described in the previous section, the statement

```
dataArray2 = [dataArray mutableCopy];
```

creates a new copy of `dataArray` in memory, duplicating all its elements. Subsequently, executing the statement

```
[dataArray2 removeObjectAtIndex: 0];
```

removes the first element from `dataArray2` but not from `dataArray`. Program 18.1 illustrates this.

Program 18.1

```
#import <Foundation/NSObject.h>
#import <Foundation/NSArray.h>
#import <Foundation/NSString.h>
#import <Foundation/NSAutoreleasePool.h>

int main (int argc, char *argv[])
{
   NSAutoreleasePool * pool = [[NSAutoreleasePool alloc] init];
   NSMutableArray    *dataArray = [NSMutableArray arrayWithObjects:
      @"one", @"two", @"three", @"four", nil];
   NSMutableArray    *dataArray2;

   // simple assignment

   dataArray2 = dataArray;
   [dataArray2 removeObjectAtIndex: 0];

   NSLog (@"dataArray:  ");
   for ( NSString *elem in dataArray )
      NSLog (@"    %@", elem);

   NSLog (@"dataArray2: ");

   for ( NSString *elem in dataArray2 )
      NSLog (@"    %@", elem);

   // try a Copy, then remove the first element from the copy
```

```
    dataArray2 = [dataArray mutableCopy];
    [dataArray2 removeObjectAtIndex: 0];

    NSLog (@"dataArray:   ");

    for ( NSString *elem in dataArray )
        NSLog (@"    %@", elem);

    NSLog (@"dataArray2: ");

    for ( NSString *elem in dataArray2 )
        NSLog (@"    %@", elem);

    [dataArray2 release];
    [pool drain];
    return 0;
}
```

Program 18.1 Output

```
dataArray:
    two
    three
    four
dataArray2:
    two
    three
    four
 dataArray:
    two
    three
    four
dataArray2:
    three
    four
```

The program defines the mutable array object `dataArray` and sets its elements to the string objects @"one", @"two", @"three", @"four", respectively

As we've discussed, the assignment

```
dataArray2 = dataArray;
```

simply creates another reference to the same array object in memory. When you remove the first object from `dataArray2` and subsequently print the elements from both array objects, it's no surprise that the first element (the string @"one") is gone from both array object references.

Next, you create a mutable copy of `dataArray` and assign the resulting copy to `dataArray2`. This creates two distinct mutable arrays in memory, both containing three elements. Now when you remove the first element from `dataArray2`, it has no effect on the contents of `dataArray`, as verified by the last two lines of the program's output.

Note that making a mutable copy of an object does not require that the object being copied be mutable. The same applies to immutable copies: You can make an immutable copy of a mutable object.

Also note when making a copy of an array that the copy operation automatically increments the retain count for each element in the array. Therefore, if you make a copy of an array and subsequently release the original array, the copy still contains valid elements.

Because a copy of `dataArray` was made in the program using the `mutableCopy` method, you are responsible for releasing its memory. The last chapter covered the rule stating that you are responsible for releasing objects you create with one of the copy methods. This explains the inclusion of this line toward the end of Program 18.1:

```
[dataArray2 release];
```

Shallow Versus Deep Copying

Program 18.1 fills the elements of `dataArray` with immutable strings (recall that constant string objects are immutable). In Program 18.2, you'll fill it with mutable strings instead so that you can change one of the strings in the array. Take a look at Program 18.2 and see whether you understand its output.

Program 18.2

```objc
#import <Foundation/NSObject.h>
#import <Foundation/NSArray.h>
#import <Foundation/NSString.h>
#import <Foundation/NSAutoreleasePool.h>

int main (int argc, char *argv[])
{
    NSAutoreleasePool * pool = [[NSAutoreleasePool alloc] init];
    NSMutableArray     *dataArray = [NSMutableArray arrayWithObjects:
       [NSMutableString stringWithString: @"one"],
       [NSMutableString stringWithString: @"two"],
       [NSMutableString stringWithString: @"three"],
       nil
    ];
    NSMutableArray     *dataArray2;
    NSMutableString    *mStr;

    NSLog (@"dataArray:  ");
    for ( NSString *elem in dataArray )
       NSLog (@"   %@", elem);
```

```
    // make a copy, then change one of the strings

    dataArray2 = [dataArray mutableCopy];


    mStr = [dataArray objectAtIndex: 0];
    [mStr appendString: @"ONE"];

    NSLog (@"dataArray:    ");
    for ( NSString *elem in dataArray )
       NSLog (@"    %@", elem);

    NSLog (@"dataArray2:   ");
    for ( NSString *elem in dataArray2 )
       NSLog (@"    %@", elem);

    [dataArray2 release];
    [pool drain];
    return 0;
}
```

Program 18.2 Output

```
dataArray:
    one
    two
    three
dataArray:
    oneONE
    two
    three
dataArray2:
    oneONE
    two
    three
```

You retrieved the first element of `dataArray` with the following statement:

```
mStr = [dataArray objectAtIndex: 0];
```

Then you appended the string `@"ONE"` to it with this statement:

```
[mStr appendString: @"ONE"];
```

Notice the value of the first element of both the original array and its copy: Both were modified. Perhaps you can understand why the first element of `dataArray` was changed but not why its copy was as well. When you get an element from a collection, you get a new reference to that element, but not a new copy. So when the `objectAtIndex:` method is invoked on `dataArray`, the returned object points to the same object in memory as the first element in `dataArray`. Subsequently modifying the string object `mStr` has the side effect of also changing the first element of `dataArray`, as you can see from the output.

But what about the copy you made? Why is its first element changed as well? This has to do with the fact that copies, by default, are *shallow* copies. Thus, when the array was copied with the `mutableCopy` method, space was allocated for a new array object in memory and the individual elements were copied into the new array. But copying each element in the array from the original to a new location meant just copying the reference from one element of the array to another. The net result was that the elements of both arrays referenced the same strings in memory. This is no different from assigning one object to another, which we covered at the beginning of this chapter.

To make distinct copies of each element of the array, you must perform a *deep* copy. This means making copies of the contents of each object in the array, not just copies of the references to the objects (and think about what that implies if an element of an array is itself an array object). But deep copies are not performed by default when you use the `copy` or `mutableCopy` methods with the Foundation classes. In Chapter 19, "Archiving," we show you how to use the Foundation's archiving capabilities to create a deep copy of an object.

When you copy an array, a dictionary, or a set, for example, you get a new copy of those collections. However, you might need to make your own copies of individual elements if you want to make changes to one collection but not to its copy. For example, if you wanted to change the first element of `dataArray2` but not `dataArray` in Program 18.2, you could make a new string (using a method such as `stringWithString:`) and store it into the first location of `dataArray2`, as follows:

```
mStr = [NSMutableString stringWithString: [dataArray2 objectAtIndex: 0]];
```

Then you could make the changes to `mStr` and add it to the array using the `replaceObject:atIndex:withObject:` method, as follows:

```
[mStr appendString @"ONE"];
[dataArray2 replaceObjectAtIndex: 0 withObject: mStr];
```

Hopefully you realize that even after replacing the object in the array, `mStr` and the first element of `dataArray2` refer to the same object in memory. Therefore, subsequent changes to `mStr` in your program will also change the first element of the array. If that's not what you want, you can always release `mStr` and allocate a new instance, because the `replaceObject:atIndex:withObject:` method automatically retains an object.

Implementing the `<NSCopying>` Protocol

If you try to use the `copy` method on one of your own classes—for example, on your address book, as follows

```
NewBook = [myBook mutableCopy];
```

you'll get an error message that looks something like this:

```
*** -[AddressBook copyWithZone:]:  selector not recognized
*** Uncaught exception:
*** -[AddressBook copyWithZone:]: selector not recognized
```

As noted, to implement copying with your own classes, you have to implement one or two methods according to the `<NSCopying>` protocol.

We now show how you can add a `copy` method to your `Fraction` class, which you used extensively in Part I, "The Objective-C 2.0 Language." Note that the techniques we describe here for copying strategies will work fine for your own classes. If those classes are subclasses of any of the Foundation classes, you might need to implement a more sophisticated copying strategy. You'll have to account for the fact that the superclass might have already implemented its own copying strategy.

Recall that your `Fraction` class contains two integer instance variables, called `numerator` and `denominator`. To make a copy of one of these objects, you must allocate space for a new fraction and then simply copy the values of the two integers into the new fraction.

When you implement the `<NSCopying>` protocol, your class must implement the `copyWithZone:` method to respond to a `copy` message. (The `copy` message just sends a `copyWithZone:` message to your class with an argument of `nil`.) If you want to make a distinction between mutable and immutable copies, as we noted, you'll also need to implement the `mutableCopyWithZone:` method according to the `<NSMutableCopying>` protocol. If you implement both methods, `copyWithZone:` should return an immutable copy and `mutableCopyWithZone:` should return a mutable one. Making a mutable copy of an object does not require that the object being copied also be mutable (and vice versa); it's perfectly reasonable to want to make a mutable copy of an immutable object (consider a string object, for example).

Here's what the `@interface` directive should look like:

```
@interface Fraction: NSObject <NSCopying>
```

`Fraction` is a subclass of `NSObject` and conforms to the `NSCopying` protocol.

In the implementation file `Fraction.m`, add the following definition for your new method:

```
-(id) copyWithZone: (NSZone *) zone
{
    Fraction *newFract = [[Fraction allocWithZone: zone] init];

    [newFract setTo: numerator over: denominator];
    return newFract;
}
```

The zone argument has to do with different memory zones that you can allocate and work with in your program. You need to deal with these only if you're writing applications that allocate a lot of memory and you want to optimize the allocation by grouping them into these zones. You can take the value passed to `copyWithZone:` and hand it off to a memory allocation method called `allocWithZone:`. This method allocates memory in a specified zone.

After allocating a new `Fraction` object, you copy the receiver's `numerator` and `denominator` variables into it. The `copyWithZone:` method is supposed to return the new copy of the object, which you do in your method.

Program 18.3 tests your new method.

Program 18.3

```
// Copying fractions

#import "Fraction.h"
#import <Foundation/NSAutoreleasePool.h>

int main (int argc, char *argv[])
{
    NSAutoreleasePool  * pool = [[NSAutoreleasePool alloc] init];
    Fraction *f1 = [[Fraction alloc] init];
    Fraction *f2;

    [f1 setTo: 2 over: 5];
    f2 = [f1 copy];

    [f2 setTo: 1 over: 3];

    [f1 print];
    [f2 print];

    [f1 release];
    [f2 release];
    [pool drain];
    return 0;
}
```

Program 18.3 Output

```
2/5
1/3
```

The program creates a `Fraction` object called `f1` and sets it to `2/5`. It then invokes the `copy` method to make a copy, which sends the `copyWithZone:` message to your object. That method makes a new `Fraction`, copies the values from `f1` into it, and returns the result. Back in `main`, you assign that result to `f2`. Subsequently setting the value in `f2` to the fraction `1/3` verifies that it had no effect on the original fraction `f1`. Change the line in the program that reads

```
f2 = [f1 copy];
```

to simply

```
f2 = f1;
```

and remove the `release` of `f2` at the end of the program to see the different results you will obtain.

If your class might be subclassed, your `copyWithZone:` method will be inherited. In that case, you should change the line in the method that reads

```
Fraction *newFract = [[Fraction allocWithZone: zone] init];
```

to read

```
Fraction *newFract = [[[self class] allocWithZone: zone] init];
```

That way, you allocate a new object from the class that is the receiver of the `copy`. (For example, if it has been subclassed to a class named `NewFraction`, be sure to allocate a new `NewFraction` object in the inherited method instead of a `Fraction` object.)

If you are writing a `copyWithZone:` method for a class whose superclass also implements the <NSCopying> protocol, you should first call the `copy` method on the superclass to copy the inherited instance variables and then include your own code to copy whatever additional instance variables (if any) you might have added to the class.

You must decide whether you want to implement a shallow or a deep copy in your class. Just document it for other users of your class so they know.

Copying Objects in Setter and Getter Methods

Whenever you implement a setter or getter method, you should think about what you're storing in the instance variables, what you're retrieving, and whether you need to protect these values. For example, consider this when you set the name of one of your `AddressCard` objects using the `setName:` method:

```
[newCard setName: newName];
```

Assume that `newName` is a string object containing the name for your new card. Assume that inside the setter routine you simply assigned the parameter to the corresponding instance variable:

```
-(void) setName: (NSString *) theName
{
    name = theName;


}
```

Now, what do you think would happen if the program later changed some of the characters contained in `newName` in the program? It would also unintentionally change the corresponding field in your address card because both would reference the same string object.

As you have already seen, a safer approach is to make a copy of the object in the setter routine, to prevent this inadvertent effect. We did this by using the `alloc` method to create a new string object and then using `initWithString:` to set it to the value of the parameter provided to the method.

You can also write a version of the `setName:` method to use `copy`, like this:

```
-(void) setName: (NSString *) theName
{
    name = [theName copy];
}
```

Of course, to make this setter routine memory management friendly, you should `autorelease` the old value first, like this:

```
-(void) setName: (NSString *) theName
{
    [name autorelease];
    name = [theName copy];
}
```

If you specify the `copy` attribute in a property declaration for an instance variable, the synthesized method will use the class's `copy` method (the one you wrote or the one you inherited). So the following `property` declaration

```
@property (nonatomic, copy) NSString *name;
```

will generate a synthesized method that behaves like this:

```
-(void) setName: (NSString *) theName
{
    if (theName != name) {
        [name release]
        name = [theName copy];
    }
}
```

Use of `nonatomic` here tells the system not to protect the property accessors with a *mutex* (*mut*ually *ex*clusive) lock. People writing threadsafe code use mutex locks to prevent two threads from executing in the same code at the same time, a situation that can often lead to dire problems. But these locks can slow programs down, and you can avoid using them if you know this code will only ever be running in a single thread.

If `nonatomic` is not specified or `atomic` is specified instead (which is the default), then your instance variable will be protected with a mutex lock. In addition, the synthesized getter method will retain and autorelease the instance variable before its value is returned. In a non–garbage collected environment, this protects the instance variable from possibly being overwritten by a setter method call that releases the instance variable's old value before setting its new value. The retain in the getter method ensures that old value is not deallocated.

Note

Even though the retain/autorelease issue is irrelevant in a garbage-collected environment (recall those method calls are ignored), the mutex lock issue is not. Therefore, consider using atomic accessor methods if your code will run in a multi-threaded environment.

The same discussion about protecting the value of your instance variables applies to the getter routines. If you return an object, you must ensure that changes to the returned value will not affect the value of your instance variables. In such a case, you can make a copy of the instance variable and return that instead.

Getting back to the implementation of a `copy` method, if you are copying instance variables that contain immutable objects (for example, immutable string objects), you might not need to make a new copy of the object's contents. It might suffice to simply make a new reference to the object by retaining it. For example, if you are implementing a copy method for the `AddressCard` class, which contains `name` and `email` members, the following implementation for `copyWithZone:` would suffice:

```
-(AddresssCard *) copyWithZone: (NSZone *) zone
{
    AddressCard *newCard = [[AddressCard allocWithZone: zone] init];
    [newCard retainName: name andEmail: email];
    return newCard;
}
```

```
-(void) retainName: (NSString *) theName andEmail: (NSString *) theEmail
{
   name = [theName retain];
   email = [theEmail retain];
}
```

The `setName:andEmail:` method isn't used here to copy the instance variables over because that method makes new copies of its arguments, which would defeat the whole purpose of this exercise. Instead, you just retained the two variables using a new method called `retainName:andEmail:`. (You could have set the two instance variables in `newCard` directly in the `copyWithZone:` method, but it involves pointer operations, which we've been able to avoid up to this point. Of course, the pointer operations would be more efficient and would not expose the user of this class to a method [`retainName:andEmail:`] that was not intended for public consumption, so at some point you might need to learn how to do that—just not right now!)

Realize that you can get away with retaining the instance variables here (instead of making complete copies of them) because the owner of the copied card can't affect the `name` and `email` members of the original. You might want to think about that for a second to verify that this is the case (hint: it has to do with the setter methods).

Exercises

1. Implement a `copy` method for the `AddressBook` class according to the `NSCopying` protocol. Would it make sense to also implement a `mutableCopy` method? Why or why not?

2. Modify the `Rectangle` and `XYPoint` classes defined in Chapter 8 to conform to the `<NSCopying>` protocol. Add a `copyWithZone:` method to both classes. Make sure that the `Rectangle` copies its `XYPoint` member `origin` using the `XYPoint`'s `copy` method. Does it make sense to implement both mutable and immutable copies for these classes? Explain.

3. Create an `NSDictionary` dictionary object and fill it with some key/object pairs. Then make both mutable and immutable copies. Are these deep copies or shallow copies that are made? Verify your answer.

4. Who is responsible for releasing the memory allocated for the new `AddressCard` in the `copyWithZone:` method as implemented in this chapter? Why?

19

Archiving

In Objective-C terms, archiving is the process of saving one or more objects in a format so that they can later be restored. Often this involves writing the object(s) to a file so it can subsequently be read back in. We discuss two methods for archiving data in this chapter: *property lists* and *key-valued coding*.

Archiving with XML Property Lists

Mac OS X applications use XML propertylists (or *plists*) for storing things such as your default preferences, application settings, and configuration information, so it's useful to know how to create them and read them back in. Their use for archiving purposes, however, is limited because when creating a property list for a data structure, specific object classes are not retained, multiple references to the same object are not stored, and the mutability of an object is not preserved.

> **Note**
>
> So-called "old-style" property lists store the data in a different format than XML property lists. Stick to using XML property lists in your program, if possible.

If your objects are of type `NSString`, `NSDictionary`, `NSArray`, `NSDate`, `NSData`, or `NSNumber`, you can use the `writeToFile:atomically:` method implemented in these classes to write your data to a file. In the case of writing out a dictionary or an array, this method writes the data to the file in the format of an XML property list. Program 19.1 shows how the dictionary you created as a simple glossary in Chapter 15, "Numbers, Strings, and Collections," can be written to a file as a property list.

Program 19.1

```
#import <Foundation/NSObject.h>
#import <Foundation/NSString.h>
#import <Foundation/NSDictionary.h>
#import <Foundation/NSAutoreleasePool.h>
int main (int argc, char *argv[])
```

```
{
    NSAutoreleasePool    * pool = [[NSAutoreleasePool alloc] init];
    NSDictionary *glossary =
    [NSDictionary  dictionaryWithObjectsAndKeys:
        @"A class defined so other classes can inherit from it.", @"abstract class",
        @"To implement all the methods defined in a protocol", @"adopt",
        @"Storing an object for later use. ",  @"archiving",
        nil
    ];
    if ([glossary writeToFile: @"glossary"  atomically: YES] == NO)
        NSLog (@"Save to file failed!");
    [pool drain];
    return 0;
}
```

The `writeToFile:atomically:encoding:error:` message is sent to your dictionary object `glossary`, causing the dictionary to be written to the file `glossary` in the form of a property list. The `atomically` parameter is set to `YES`, meaning that you want the write operation to be done to a temporary backup file first; once successful, the final data is to be moved to the specified file named `glossary`. This is a safeguard that protects the file from becoming corrupt if, for example, the system crashes in the middle of the write operation. In that case, the original `glossary` file (if it previously existed) isn't harmed.

If you examine the contents of the `glossary` file created by Program 19.1, it looks like this:

```
<?xml version="1.0" encoding="UTF-8"?>
<!DOCTYPE plist PUBLIC "-//Apple Computer//DTD PLIST 1.0//EN"
          "http://www.apple.com/DTDs/PropertyList-1.0.dtd">
<plist version="1.0">
<dict>
    <key>abstract class</key>
    <string>A class defined so other classes can inherit from it.</string>
    <key>adopt</key>
    <string>To implement all the methods defined in a protocol</string>
    <key>archiving</key>
    <string>Storing an object for later use. </string>
</dict>
</plist>
```

You can see from the XML file that was created that the dictionary is written to the file as a set of key (<key>...</key>) value (<string>...</string>) pairs.

When you create a property list from a dictionary, the keys in the dictionary must all be `NSString` objects. The elements of an array or the values in a dictionary can be `NSString`, `NSArray`, `NSDictionary`, `NSData`, `NSDate`, or `NSNumber` objects.

To read an XML property list from a file into your program, you use the `dictionaryWithContentsOfFile:` or `arrayWithContentsOfFile:` methods. To read

back data, use the `dataWithContentsOfFile:` method; to read back string objects, use
the `stringWithContentsOfFile:` method. Program 19.2 reads back the glossary written
in Program 19.1 and then displays its contents.

Program 19.2

```
#import <Foundation/NSObject.h>
#import <Foundation/NSString.h>
#import <Foundation/NSDictionary.h>
#import <Foundation/NSEnumerator.h>
#import <Foundation/NSAutoreleasePool.h>

int main (int argc, char *argv[])
{
   NSAutoreleasePool  * pool = [[NSAutoreleasePool alloc] init];
   NSDictionary *glossary;

   glossary = [NSDictionary dictionaryWithContentsOfFile: @"glossary"];

   for ( NSString *key in glossary )
      NSLog (@"%@: %@",  key, [glossary objectForKey: key]);

   [pool drain];
   return 0;
}
```

Program 19.2 Output

```
archiving: Storing an object for later use.
abstract class: A class defined so other classes can inherit from it.
adopt: To implement all the methods defined in a protocol
```

Your property lists don't need to be created from an Objective-C program; the property list can come from any source. You can make your own property lists using a simple
text editor, or you can use the Property List Editor program located in the
`/Developer/Applications/Utilities` directory on Mac OS X systems.

Archiving with NSKeyedArchiver

A more flexible approach enables you to save any type of objects to a file, not just strings,
arrays, and dictionaries. This is done by creating a *keyed* archive using the
`NSKeyedArchiver` class.

Mac OX X has supported keyed archives since version 10.2. Before that, *sequential*
archives were created with the `NSArchiver` class. Sequential archives require that the data
in the archive be read back in precisely the same order in which it was written.

A keyed archive is one in which each field of the archive has a name. When you
archive an object, you give it a name, or *key*. When you retrieve it from the archive, you
retrieve it by the same key. In that manner, objects can be written to the archive and re-

trieved in any order. Furthermore, if new instance variables are added or removed to a class, your program can account for it.

Note that NSArchiver is not available in the iPhone SDK. If you want to use archiving on the iPhone, you must use NSKeyedArchiver

To work with keyed archives you need to import <Foundation/NSKeyedArchiver.h>.

Program 19.3 shows that the glossary can be saved to a file on disk using the method archiveRootObject:toFile: from the NSKeyedArchiver class. To use this class, include the file

```
#import <Foundation/NSKeyedArchiver.h>
```

in your program.

Program 19.3

```
#import <Foundation/NSObject.h>
#import <Foundation/NSString.h>
#import <Foundation/NSDictionary.h>
#import <Foundation/NSKeyedArchiver.h>
#import <Foundation/NSAutoreleasePool.h>

int main (int argc, char *argv[])
{
    NSAutoreleasePool * pool = [[NSAutoreleasePool alloc] init];
    NSDictionary *glossary =
      [NSDictionary dictionaryWithObjectsAndKeys:
        @"A class defined so other classes can inherit from it",
        @"abstract class",
        @"To implement all the methods defined in a protocol",
        @"adopt",
        @"Storing an object for later use",
        @"archiving",
        nil
      ];

    [NSKeyedArchiver archiveRootObject: glossary toFile: @"glossary.archive"];

    [pool release];
    return 0;
}
```

Program 19.3 does not produce any output at the terminal. However, the statement

```
[NSKeyedArchiver archiveRootObject: glossary toFile: @"glossary.archive"];
```

writes the dictionary `glossary` to the file `glossary.archive`. Any pathname can be specified for the file. In this case, the file is written to the current directory.

The archive file created can later be read into your program by using `NSKeyedUnarchiver`'s `unArchiveObjectWithFile:` method, as is done in Program 19.4.

Program 19.4

```
#import <Foundation/NSObject.h>
#import <Foundation/NSString.h>
#import <Foundation/NSDictionary.h>
#import <Foundation/NSEnumerator.h>
#import <Foundation/NSKeyedArchiver.h>
#import <Foundation/NSAutoreleasePool.h>

int main (int argc, char *argv[])
{
   NSAutoreleasePool  * pool = [[NSAutoreleasePool alloc] init];
   NSDictionary *glossary;

   glossary = [NSKeyedUnarchiver unarchiveObjectWithFile:
                  @"glossary.archive"];


   for ( NSString *key in glossary )
           NSLog (@"%@: %@",  key, [glossary objectForKey: key]);

   [pool drain];
   return 0;
}
```

Program 19.4 Output

```
abstract class: A class defined so other classes can inherit from it.
adopt: To implement all the methods defined in a protocol
archiving: Storing an object for later use.
```

The statement

```
glossary = [NSKeyedUnarchiver unarchiveObjectWithFile: @"glossary.archive"];
```

causes the specified file to be opened and its contents to be read. This file must be the result of a previous archive operation. You can specify a full pathname for the file or a relative pathname, as in the example.

After the glossary has been restored, the program simply enumerates its contents to verify that the restore was successful.

Writing Encoding and Decoding Methods

Basic Objective-C class objects such as `NSString`, `NSArray`, `NSDictionary`, `NSSet`, `NSDate`, `NSNumber`, and `NSData` can be archived and restored in the manner just described. That includes nested objects as well, such as an array containing a string or even other array objects.

This implies that you can't directly archive your `AddressBook` using this technique because the Objective-C system doesn't know how to archive an `AddressBook` object. If you tried to archive it by inserting a line such as

```
[NSKeyedArchiver archiveRootObject: myAddressBook toFile: @"addrbook.arch"];
```

into your program, you'd get the following message displayed if you ran the program:

```
*** -[AddressBook encodeWithCoder:]: selector not recognized
*** Uncaught exception: <NSInvalidArgumentException>
*** -[AddressBook encodeWithCoder:]: selector not recognized
archiveTest: received signal: Trace/BPT trap
```

From the error messages, you can see that the system was looking for a method called `encodeWithCoder:` in the `AddressBook` class, but you never defined such a method.

To archive objects other than those listed, you must tell the system how to archive, or *encode*, your objects, and also how to unarchive, or *decode*, them. This is done by adding `encodeWithCoder:` and `initWithCoder:` methods to your class definitions, according to the `<NSCoding>` protocol. For our address book example, you'd have to add these methods to both the `AddressBook` and `AddressCard` classes.

The `encodeWithCoder:` method is invoked each time the archiver wants to encode an object from the specified class, and the method tells it how to do so. In a similar manner, the `initWithCoder:` method is invoked each time an object from the specified class is to be decoded.

In general, the encoder method should specify how to archive each instance variable in the object you want to save. Luckily, you have help doing this. For the basic Objective-C classes described previously, you can use the `encodeObject:forKey:` method. For basic underlying C data types (such as integers and floats), you use one of the methods listed in Table 19.1. The decoder method, `initWithCoder:`, works in reverse: You use `decodeObject:forKey:` to decode basic Objective-C classes and the appropriate decoder method shown in Table 19.1 for the basic data types.

Table 19.1   Encoding and Decoding Basic Data Types in Keyed Archives

Encoder	Decoder
encodeBool:forKey:	decodeBool:forKey:
encodeInt:forKey:	decodeInt:forKey:
encodeInt32:forKey:	decodeInt32:forKey:
encodeInt64: forKey:	decodeInt64:forKey:

Table 19.1   **Encoding and Decoding Basic Data Types in Keyed Archives**

Encoder	Decoder
encodeFloat:forKey:	decodeFloat:forKey:
encodeDouble:forKey:	decodeDouble:forKey:

Program 19.5 adds the two encoding and decoding methods to both the AddressCard and AddressBook classes.

Program 19.5 Addresscard.h Interface File

```
#import <Foundation/NSObject.h>
#import <Foundation/NSString.h>
#import <Foundation/NSKeyedArchiver.h>

@interface AddressCard: NSObject <NSCoding, NSCopying>
{
   NSString  *name;
   NSString  *email;
}

@property (copy, nonatomic) NSString *name, *email;

-(void) setName: (NSString *) theName andEmail: (NSString *) theEmail;
-(NSComparisonResult) compareNames: (id) element;
-(void) print;

// Additional methods for NSCopying protocol
-(AddressCard *) copyWithZone: (NSZone *) zone;
-(void) retainName: (NSString *) theName andEmail: (NSString *) theEmail;

@end
```

These are the two new methods used for your AddressCard class to be added to the implementation file:

```
-(void) encodeWithCoder: (NSCoder *) encoder
{
   [encoder encodeObject: name forKey: @"AddressCardName"];
   [encoder encodeObject: email forKey: @"AddressCardEmail"];
}


-(id) initWithCoder: (NSCoder *) decoder
{
   name = [[decoder decodeObjectforKey: @"AddressCardName"] retain];
   email = [[decoder decodeObjectforKey: @"AddressCardEmail"] retain];

   return self;
}
```

The encoding method `encodeWithCoder:` is passed an `NSCoder` object as its argument. Since your `AddressCard` class inherits directly from `NSObject,` you don't need to worry about encoding inherited instance variables. If you did, and if you knew the superclass of your class conformed to the `NSCoding` protocol, you should start your encoding method with a statement like the following to make sure your inherited instance variables are encoded:

```
[super encodeWithCoder: encoder];
```

Your address book has two instance variables, called `name` and `email`. Because these are both `NSString` objects, you can use the `encodeObject:forKey:` method to encode each of them in turn. These two instance variables are then added to the archive.

The `encodeObject:forKey:` method encodes an object and stores it under the specified key for later retrieval using that key. The key names are arbitrary, so as long you use the same name to retrieve (decode) the data as you did when you archived (encoded) it, you can specify any key you like. The only time a conflict might arise is if the same key is used for a subclass of an object being encoded. To prevent this from happening, you can insert the class name in front of the instance variable name when composing the key for the archive, as was done in Program 19.5.

Note that `encodeObject:forKey:` can be used for any object that has implemented a corresponding `encodeWithCoder:` method in its class.

The decoding process works in reverse. The argument passed to `initWithCoder:` is again an `NSCoder` object. You don't need to worry about this argument; just remember that it's the one that gets the messages for each object you want to extract from the archive.

Again, since our `AddressCard` class inherits directly from `NSObject`, you don't have to worry about decoding inherited instance variables. If you did, you would insert a line like this at the start of your decoder method (assuming the superclass of your class conformed to the `NSCoding` protocol):

```
self = [super initWithCoder: decoder];
```

Each instance variable is then decoded by invoking the `decodeObject:ForKey:` method and passing the same key that was used to encode the variable.

Similarly to your `AddressCard` class, you add encoding and decoding methods to your `AddressBook` class. The only line you need to change in your interface file is the `@interface` directive to declare that the `AddressBook` class now conforms to the `NSCoding` protocol. The change looks like this:

```
@interface AddressBook: NSObject <NSCoding, NSCopying>
```

Here are the method definitions for inclusion in the implementation file:

```
-(void) encodeWithCoder: (NSCoder *) encoder
{
```

```
    [encoder encodeObject: bookName forKey: @"AddressBookBookName"];
    [encoder encodeObject: book forKey: @"AddressBookBook"];
}


-(id) initWithCoder: (NSCoder *) decoder
{
    bookName = [[decoder decodeObjectForKey: @"AddressBookBookName"] retain];
    book = [[decoder decodeObjectForKey: @"AddressBookBook"] retain];

    return self;
}
```

The test program is shown next as Program 19.6.

Program 19.6 Test Program

```
#import "AddressBook.h"
#import <Foundation/NSAutoreleasePool.h>

int main (int argc, char *argv[])
{
    NSAutoreleasePool * pool = [[NSAutoreleasePool alloc] init];

    NSString   *aName = @"Julia Kochan";
    NSString   *aEmail = @"jewls337@axlc.com";
    NSString   *bName = @"Tony Iannino";
    NSString   *bEmail = @"tony.iannino@techfitness.com";
    NSString   *cName = @"Stephen Kochan";
    NSString   *cEmail = @"steve@steve_kochan.com";
    NSString   *dName = @"Jamie Baker";
    NSString   *dEmail = @"jbaker@hitmail.com";

    AddressCard *card1 = [[AddressCard alloc] init];
    AddressCard *card2 = [[AddressCard alloc] init];
    AddressCard *card3 = [[AddressCard alloc] init];
    AddressCard *card4 = [[AddressCard alloc] init];

    AddressBook  *myBook = [AddressBook alloc];

    // First set up four address cards

    [card1 setName: aName andEmail: aEmail];
    [card2 setName: bName andEmail: bEmail];
    [card3 setName: cName andEmail: cEmail];
    [card4 setName: dName andEmail: dEmail];

    myBook = [myBook initWithName: @"Steve's Address Book"];
```

```
   // Add some cards to the address book

   [myBook addCard: card1];
   [myBook addCard: card2];
   [myBook addCard: card3];
   [myBook addCard: card4];

   [myBook sort];

   if ([NSKeyedArchiver archiveRootObject: myBook toFile: @"addrbook.arch"] == NO)
      NSLog (@"archiving failed");

   [card1 release];
   [card2 release];
   [card3 release];
   [card4 release];
   [myBook release];

   [pool drain];
   return 0;
}
```

This program creates the address book and then archives it to the file addrbook.arch. In the process of creating the archive file, realize that the encoding methods from *both* the AddressBook and AddressCard classes were invoked. You can add some NSLog calls to these methods if you want proof.

Program 19.7 shows how you can read the archive into memory to set up the address book from a file.

Program 19.7

```
#import "AddressBook.h"
#import <Foundation/NSAutoreleasePool.h>

int main (int argc, char *argv[])
{
   AddressBook        *myBook;
   NSAutoreleasePool  * pool = [[NSAutoreleasePool alloc] init];

   myBook = [NSKeyedUnarchiver unarchiveObjectWithFile: @"addrbook.arch"];

   [myBook list];

   [pool drain];
   return 0;
}
```

Program 19.7 Output

```
======== Contents of: Steve's Address Book =========
Jamie Baker        jbaker@hitmail.com
Julia Kochan       jewls337@axlc.com
Stephen Kochan     steve@steve_kochan.com
Tony Iannino       tony.iannino@techfitness.com
====================================================
```

In the process of unarchiving the address book, the decoding methods added to your two classes were automatically invoked. Notice how easily you can read the address book back into the program.

As noted, the `encodeObject:forKey:` method works for built-in classes and classes for which you write your encoding and decoding methods according to the `NSCoding` protocol. If your instance contains some basic data types, such as integers or floats, you need to know how to encode and decode them (see Table 19.1).

Here's a simple definition for a class called `Foo` that contains three instance variables— one is an `NSString`, another is an `int`, and the third is a `float`. The class has one setter method, three getter methods, and two encoding/decoding methods to be used for archiving:

```
@interface Foo: NSObject <NSCoding>
{
   NSString *strVal;
   int      intVal;
   float    floatVal;
}

@property (copy, nonatomic) NSString *strVal;
@property int intVal;
@property float floatVal;
@end
```

The implementation file follows:

```
@implementation Foo

@synthesize strVal, intVal, floatVal;

-(void) encodeWithCoder: (NSCoder *) encoder
{
   [encoder encodeObject: strVal forKey: @"FoostrVal"];
   [encoder encodeInt: intVal forKey: @"FoointVal"];
   [encoder encodeFloat: floatVal forKey: @"FoofloatVal"];
}

-(id) initWithCoder: (NSCoder *) decoder
```

```
{
    strVal = [[decoder decodeObjectForKey: @"FoostrVal"] retain];
    intVal = [decoder decodeIntForKey: @"FoointVal"];
    floatVal = [decoder decodeFloatForKey: @"FoofloatVal"];

    return self;
}
@end
```

The encoding routine first encodes the string value strVal using the encodeObject:forKey: method, as was shown previously.

In Program 19.8, a Foo object is created, archived to a file, unarchived, and then displayed.

Program 19.8 Test Program

```
#import <Foundation/NSObject.h>
#import <Foundation/NSString.h>
#import <Foundation/NSKeyedArchiver.h>
#import <Foundation/NSAutoreleasePool.h>
#import "Foo.h"      // Definition for our Foo class

int main (int argc, char *argv[])
{
    NSAutoreleasePool * pool = [[NSAutoreleasePool alloc] init];
    Foo *myFoo1 = [[Foo alloc] init];
    Foo *myFoo2;

    [myFoo1 setStrVal: @"This is the string"];
    [myFoo1 setIntVal: 12345];
    [myFoo1 setFloatVal: 98.6];

    [NSKeyedArchiver archiveRootObject: myFoo1 toFile: @"foo.arch"];

    myFoo2 = [NSKeyedUnarchiver unarchiveObjectWithFile: @"foo.arch"];
    NSLog (@"%@\n%i\n%g", [myFoo2 strVal], [myFoo2 intVal], [myFoo2 floatVal]);
    [myFoo1 release];
    [pool drain];
    return 0;
}
```

Program 19.8 Output

```
This is the string
12345
98.6
```

The following messages archive the three instance variables from the object:

```
[encoder encodeObject: strVal forKey: @"FoostrVal"];
[encoder encodeInt: intVal forKey: @"FoointVal"];
[encoder encodeFloat: floatVal forKey: @"FoofloatVal"];
```

Some of the basic data types, such as char, short, long, and long long, are not listed in Table 19.1; you must determine the size of your data object and use the appropriate routine. For example, a short int is normally 16 bits, an int and long can be 32 or 64 bits, and a long long is 64 bits. (You can use the sizeof operator, described in Chapter 13, "Underlying C Language Features," to determine the size of any data type.) So to archive a short int, store it in an int first and then archive it with encodeIntForKey:. Reverse the process to get it back: Use decodeIntForKey: and then assign it to your short int variable.

Using NSData to Create Custom Archives

You might not want to write your object directly to a file using the archiveRootObject:ToFile: method, as was done in the previous program examples. For example, perhaps you want to collect some or all of your objects and store them in a single archive file. You can do this in Objective-C using the general data stream object class called NSData, which we briefly visited in Chapter 16, "Working with Files."

As mentioned in Chapter 16, an NSData object can be used to reserve an area of memory into which you can store data. Typical uses of this data area might be to provide temporary storage for data that will subsequently be written to a file or perhaps to hold the contents of a file read from the disk. The simplest way to create a mutable data area is with the data method:

```
dataArea = [NSMutableData data];
```

This creates an empty buffer space whose size expands as needed as the program executes.

As a simple example, let's assume that you want to archive your address book and one of your Foo objects in the same file. Assume for this example that you've added keyed archiving methods to the AddressBook and AddressCard classes (see Program 19.9).

Program 19.9

```
#import <Foundation/NSObject.h>
#import <Foundation/NSAutoreleasePool.h>
#import <Foundation/NSString.h>
#import <Foundation/NSKeyedArchiver.h>
#import <Foundation/NSCoder.h>
#import <Foundation/NSData.h>
#import "AddressBook.h"
#import "Foo.h"
```

```
int main (int argc, char *argv[])
{
   NSAutoreleasePool * pool = [[NSAutoreleasePool alloc] init];
   Foo             *myFoo1 = [[Foo alloc] init];
   Foo             *myFoo2;
   NSMutableData   *dataArea;
   NSKeyedArchiver *archiver;
   AddressBook     *myBook;

   // Insert code from Program 19.7 to create an Address Book
   // in myBook containing four address cards

   [myFoo1 setStrVal: @"This is the string"];
   [myFoo1 setIntVal: 12345];
   [myFoo1 setFloatVal: 98.6];


   // Set up a data area and connect it to an NSKeyedArchiver object
   dataArea = [NSMutableData data];

   archiver = [[NSKeyedArchiver alloc]
              initForWritingWithMutableData: dataArea];
   // Now we can begin to archive objects
   [archiver encodeObject: myBook forKey: @"myaddrbook"];
   [archiver encodeObject: myFoo1 forKey: @"myfoo1"];
   [archiver finishEncoding];

   // Write the archived data area to a file
   if ([dataArea writeToFile: @"myArchive" atomically: YES] == NO)
       NSLog (@"Archiving failed!");

   [archiver release];

   [myFoo1 release];
   [pool drain];
   return 0;
}
```

After allocating an NSKeyedArchiver object, the initForWritingWithMutableData: message is sent to specify the area in which to write the archived data; this is the NSMutabledata area dataArea that you previously created. The NSKeyedArchiver object stored in archiver can now be sent encoding messages to archive objects in your program. In fact, until it receives a finishEncoding message, it archives and stores all encoding messages in the specified data area.

You have two objects to encode here—the first is your address book and the second is your Foo object. You can use encodeObject:forKey: for these objects because you previously implemented encoder and decoder methods for the AddressBook, AddressCard, and Foo classes. (It's important to understand that concept.)

When you are finished archiving your two objects, you send the `archiver` object the `finishEncoding` message. No more objects can be encoded after that point, and you need to send this message to complete the archiving process.

The area you set aside and named `dataArea` now contains your archived objects in a form that you can write to a file. The message expression

```
[dataArea writeToFile: @"myArchive" atomically: YES
     encoding: NSUTF8Encoding error: nil]
```

sends the `writeToFile:atomically:encoding:error:` message to your data stream to ask it to write its data to the specified file, which you named `myArchive`.

As you can see from the `if` statement, the `writeToFile:atomically:encoding:error:` method returns a `BOOL` value: `YES` if the write operation succeeds and `NO` if it fails (perhaps an invalid pathname for the file was specified or the file system is full).

Restoring the data from your archive file is simple: You just do things in reverse. First, you need to allocate a data area like before. Next, you need to read your archive file into the data area; then you have to create an `NSKeyedUnarchiver` object and tell it to decode data from the specified area. You must invoke decode methods to extract and decode your archived objects. When you're finished, you send a `finishDecoding` message to the `NSKeyedUnarchiver` object.

This is all done in Program 19.10.

Program 19.10

```
#import <Foundation/NSObject.h>
#import <Foundation/NSAutoreleasePool.h>
#import <Foundation/NSString.h>
#import <Foundation/NSKeyedArchiver.h>
#import <Foundation/NSCoder.h>
#import <Foundation/NSData.h>
#import "AddressBook.h"
#import "Foo.h"

int main (int argc, char *argv[])
{
    NSAutoreleasePool * pool = [[NSAutoreleasePool alloc] init];
    NSData          *dataArea;
    NSKeyedUnarchiver *unarchiver;
    Foo             *myFoo1;
    AddressBook     *myBook;
    // Read in the archive and connect an
    // NSKeyedUnarchiver object to it

    dataArea = [NSData dataWithContentsOfFile: @"myArchive"];
```

```
    if (! dataArea) {
       NSLog (@"Can't read back archive file!");
       return 1;
    }

    unarchiver = [[NSKeyedUnarchiver alloc]
                         initForReadingWithData: dataArea];

    // Decode the objects we previously stored in the archive
    myBook = [unarchiver decodeObjectForKey: @"myaddrbook"];
    myFoo1 = [unarchiver decodeObjectForKey: @"myfoo1"];

    [unarchiver finishDecoding];

    [unarchiver release];

    // Verify that the restore was successful
    [myBook list];
    NSLog (@"%@\n%i\n%g", [myFoo1 strVal],
            [myFoo1 intVal], [myFoo1 floatVal]);

    [pool release];
    return 0;
}
```

Program 19.10 Output

```
======== Contents of: Steve's Address Book =========
Jamie Baker        jbaker@hitmail.com
Julia Kochan       jewls337@axlc.com
Stephen Kochan     steve@steve_kochan.com
Tony Iannino       tony.iannino@techfitness.com
===================================================

This is the string
12345
98.6
```

The output verifies that the address book and your `Foo` object were successfully re-stored from the archive file.

Using the Archiver to Copy Objects

In Program 18.2, you tried to make a copy of an array containing mutable string elements and you saw how a shallow copy of the array was made. That is, the actual strings themselves were not copied—only the references to them were.

You can use the Foundation's archiving capabilities to create a deep copy of an object. For example, Program 19.11 copies `dataArray` to `dataArray2` by archiving `dataArray` into a buffer and then unarchiving it, assigning the result to `dataArray2`. You don't need to use a file for this process; the archiving and unarchiving process can all take place in memory.

Program 19.11

```
#import <Foundation/NSObject.h>
#import <Foundation/NSAutoreleasePool.h>
#import <Foundation/NSString.h>
#import <Foundation/NSKeyedArchiver.h>
#import <Foundation/NSArray.h>

int main (int argc, char *argv[])
{
   NSAutoreleasePool *pool = [[NSAutoreleasePool alloc] init];
   NSData        *data;
   NSMutableArray  *dataArray = [NSMutableArray arrayWithObjects:
       [NSMutableString stringWithString: @"one"],
       [NSMutableString stringWithString: @"two"],
       [NSMutableString stringWithString: @"three"],
       nil
     ];

   NSMutableArray    *dataArray2;
   NSMutableString  *mStr;

   // Make a deep copy using the archiver

   data = [NSKeyedArchiver archivedDataWithRootObject: dataArray];
   dataArray2 = [NSKeyedUnarchiver unarchiveObjectWithData: data];

   mStr = [dataArray2 objectAtIndex: 0];
   [mStr appendString: @"ONE"];

   NSLog (@"dataArray: ");
   for ( NSString *elem in dataArray )
     NSLog (@"%@", elem);

   NSLog (@"\ndataArray2: ");
   for ( NSString *elem in dataArray2 )
     NSLog (@"%@", elem);

   [pool drain];
   return 0;
}
```

Program 19.11 Output

```
dataArray:
one
two
three

dataArray2:
oneONE
two
three
```

The output verifies that changing the first element of `dataArray2` had no effect on the first element of `dataArray`. That's because a new copy of the string was made through the archiving/unarchiving process.

The copy operation in Program 19.11 is performed with the following two lines:

```
data = [NSKeyedArchiver archivedDataWithRootObject: dataArray];
dataArray2 = [NSKeyedUnarchiver unarchiveObjectWithData: data];
```

You can even avoid the intermediate assignment and perform the copy with a single statement, like this:

```
dataArray2 = [NSKeyedUnarchiver unarchiveObjectWithData:
              [NSKeyedArchiver archivedDataWithRootObject: dataArray]];
```

This is a technique you might want to keep in mind next time you need to make a deep copy of an object or of an object that doesn't support the `NSCopying` protocol.

Exercises

1. In Chapter 15, Program 15.7 generated a table of prime numbers. Modify that program to write the resulting array as an XML property list to the file `primes.pl`. Then examine the contents of the file.

2. Write a program to read in the XML property list created in exercise 1 and store the values in an array object. Display all the elements of the array to verify that the restore operation was successful.

3. Modify Program 19.2 to display the contents of one of the XML property lists (.plist files) stored in the `/Library/Preferences` folder.

4. Write a program to read in an archived `AddressBook` and look up an entry based on a name supplied on the command line, like so:

   ```
   $ lookup gregory
   ```

Part III

Cocoa and the iPhone SDK

Introduction to Cocoa

Throughout this book you developed programs that had a simple user interface. You relied on the NSLog routine to display messages on the console. However, as useful as this routine is, it is very limited in its capabilities. Certainly, other programs you use on the Mac aren't as unfriendly. In fact, the Mac's reputation is based on its user-friendly dialogs and ease of use. Lucky for you, this is where XCode combined with the Interface Builder application come to the rescue. Not only does this combination offer a powerful environment for program development, consisting of editing and debugging tools, and convenient access to online documentation, but it also provides an environment for easily developing sophisticated graphical user interfaces (GUIs).

The frameworks that provide the support for your applications to provide a rich user experience are called Cocoa, which actually consists of two frameworks: the Foundation framework, with which you are already familiar, and the Application Kit (or AppKit) framework. This latter framework provides the classes associated with windows, buttons, lists, and so on.

Framework Layers

A diagram is often used to illustrate the different layers that separate the application at the topmost level from the underlying hardware. One such representation is depicted in Figure 20.1

The *kernel* provides the low-level communication to the hardware in the form of *device drivers*. It manages the system's resources, which includes scheduling programs for execution, managing memory and power, and performing basic I/O operations.

As its name implies, *Core Services* provides support at a lower or "core" level than that provided in the layers above it. For example, here you find support for collections, networking, debugging, file management, folders, memory management, threads, time, and power.

The *Application Services* layer includes support for printing and graphics rendering, including Quartz, OpenGL, and Quicktime.

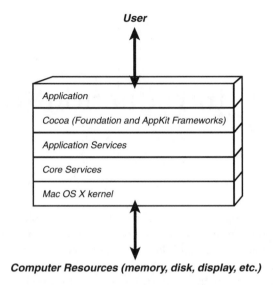

Figure 20.1   The application hierarchy

Directly below your application sits the Cocoa layer. As noted, *Cocoa* includes the Foundation and AppKit frameworks. Foundation offers classes for working with collections, strings, memory management, the file system, archiving, and so on. AppKit provides classes for managing views, windows, documents, and the rich user interface for which Mac OS X is well known.

From this description, there seems to be duplication of functionality between some of the layers. Collections exist in both the Cocoa and Core Services layers. However, the former builds on support of the latter. Also, in some cases, a layer can be bypassed. For example, some Foundation classes, such as those that deal with file system, rely directly on functionality in the Core Services layer and so bypass the Application Services layer. In many cases, the Foundation framework defines an object-oriented mapping of data structures defined in the lower-level Core Services layer (which is written primarily in the procedural C language).

Cocoa Touch

The iPhone contains a computer that runs a scaled-down version of Mac OS X. Some features in the iPhone's hardware, such as its accelerometer, are unique to the phone and are not found in other Mac OS X computers, such as MacBooks or iMacs.

> **Note**
> Actually, Mac notebooks contain an accelerometer so that the hard drive can be parked if the computer gets dropped; however, you can't access this accelerometer directly from your programs.

Whereas the Cocoa frameworks are designed for application development for Mac OS X desktop and notebook computers, the Cocoa Touch frameworks are for applications targeted for the iPhone and iPod Touch.

Both Cocoa and Cocoa Touch have the Foundation framework in common. However, the UIKit replaces the AppKit framework under Cocoa Touch, providing support for many of the same types of objects, such as windows, views, buttons, text fields, and so on. In addition, Cocoa Touch provides classes for working with the accelerometer, triangulating your location with GPS and WiFi signals, and the touch-driven interface, and also eliminates classes that aren't needed, such as those that support printing.

That concludes this brief overview of Cocoa. In the next chapter, you learn how to write an application for the iPhone, using the simulator that is part of the iPhone SDK.

Writing iPhone Applications

In this chapter, you'll develop two simple iPhone applications. The first illustrates some fundamental concepts to familiarize you with using Interface Builder, making connections, and understanding *delegates, outlets,* and *actions*. For the second iPhone application, you'll build a fraction calculator. It combines what you learned while developing the first application with what you learned throughout the rest of the book.

The iPhone SDK

To write an iPhone application, you have to install Xcode and the iPhone SDK. This SDK is available free of charge from Apple's Web site. To download the SDK, you'll need to first register to be an Apple Developer. That process is also free. To get the appropriate links, you can start at developer.apple.com and navigate to the appropriate point. It's a great idea to become familiar with that site. Appendix D, "Resources," lists some direct links to particular spots on this site that might be of interest to you.

The discussions in this chapter are based on Xcode 3.1.1 and the iPhone SDK for iPhone OS 2.1. Later versions of either should be compatible with what's described here.

Your First iPhone Application

The first application shows how you can put a black-colored window on the iPhone's screen, allow for the user to press a button, and then display some text in response to the pressing of that button.

> **Note**
>
> The second application is more fun! You use the knowledge gained from your first application to build a simple calculator that does operations with fractions. You can use your `Fraction` class that you worked with earlier in the book, as well as a modified `Calculator` class. This time, your calculator needs to know how to work with fractions.

Let's dive right into the first program. The pedagogy used in this chapter is not to cover all the details; as noted, there's simply not enough space to do that here. Instead, we walk you through the steps to give you the necessary foundation (no pun intended!) for you to explore and learn more concepts on your own with a separate Cocoa or iPhone programming text.

Figure 21.1 shows the first application you develop for the iPhone, running on the iPhone simulator (more about that shortly).

Figure 21.1   First iPhone application.

This application is designed so that when you press the button labeled "1" the corresponding digit appears in the display (see Figure 21.2). That's all it does! This simple application lays the groundwork for the second fraction calculator application.

You'll create you application using Xcode and your user interface using Interface Builder. By this point in the book, you should be quite comfortable using Xcode if you've been using it throughout to enter and test your programs. Interface Builder, as noted, is the tool that lets you design your user interface by placing UI elements such as tables, labels, and buttons in a window that resembles the iPhone's screen. Using Interface Builder, like any powerful development tool, takes some getting used to.

Apple distributes an iPhone simulator as part of the iPhone SDK. The simulator replicates much of your iPhone environment, including its home screen, Safari web browser,

Figure 21.2   iPhone application results.

Contacts application, and so on. The simulator makes it much easier to debug your applications; you don't have to download each iteration of your application to an actual iPhone device and then debug it there. This can save you a lot of time and effort.

To run applications on the iPhone device, you need to register for the iPhone developer program and pay a $99 fee (as of the time of this writing) to Apple. In turn, you will receive an activation code that will allow you to get an iPhone Development Certificate to enable you to test and install applications on your iPhone. Unfortunately, you cannot develop applications even for your own iPhone without going through this process. Note that the application we develop in this chapter will be loaded and tested on the iPhone simulator and not on an iPhone device.

Creating a New iPhone Application Project

Let's return to developing your first application. After you install the iPhone SDK, start up the Xcode application. Select New Project from the File menu. Under iPhone OS (and if you don't see this in the left pane, you haven't installed the iPhone SDK), click on Application. You should see a window, as shown in Figure 21.3.

Here you see templates that provide starting points for different types of applications, as summarized in the Table 21.1.

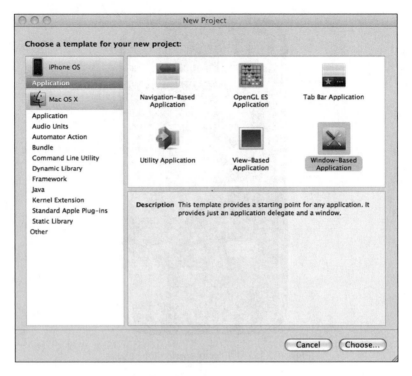

Figure 21.3   Starting a new iPhone project.

Table 21.1   **iPhone Application Templates**

Application Type	Description
Navigation-Based	For an application that uses a navigation controller. Contacts is a sample application of this type.
OpenGL ES	For OpenGL graphics-based applications such as games.
Tab Bar	For applications that use a tab bar. An example would be the iPod application.
Utility	For an application that has a flipside view. The Stock Quote application is an example of this type.
View-Based	For an application that has a single view. You draw into the view and then display that view in the window.
Window-Based	For an application that starts with just the main iPhone window. You can use this as the starting point for any application.

Returning to your New Project window, select Window-Based Application in the top rightmost pane and then click on the Choose button. When next prompted to enter the project name (in the Save As box), enter the text `iPhone_1` and click Save. This also becomes your application's name by default. As you know from previous projects you created with Xcode, a new project will now be created for you that contains templates for files you'll want to use. This is shown in Figure 21.4.

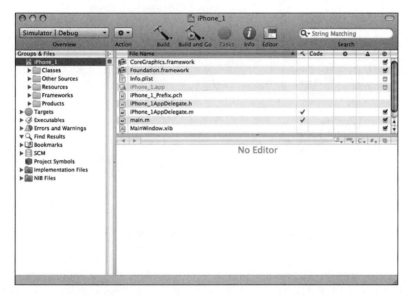

Figure 21.4   New iPhone project iPhone_1 is created.

Depending on your settings and previous uses of Xcode, your window might not appear precisely as depicted in Figure 21.4. You can choose to follow along with whatever your current layout resembles or else try to make it match the figure more closely.

In the top-left corner of your Xcode window, you see a drop-down labeled with your current selection of SDK and Active Configuration. Because we're not developing your application to run directly on the iPhone, you want the SDK set up to run with the iPhone simulator and the Configuration to be set to Debug. If the drop-down is not labeled Simulator | Debug, set the appropriate options as shown in Figure 21.5.

Entering Your Code

Now we're ready to modify some of your project files. Notice that a class called *project-name* AppDelegate.h and *project-name* AppDelegate.m were created for you, where in this example *project-name* is iPhone_1. The work of handling the various buttons and labels in the type of Window-based application you're creating gets *delegated* to a class called *project-name* AppDelegate, or in this case, `iPhone_1AppDelegate`. In this class we'll define meth-

Figure 21.5   iPhone_1 project with SDK
and Configuration options set.

ods to respond to *actions* that occur in the iPhone's window, such as the pressing of a button or the movement of a slider. As you'll see, it's in the Interface Builder application that you make the actual connection between these controls and the corresponding methods.

The class will also have instance variables whose values correspond to some control in your iPhone's window, such as the name on a label or the text displayed in an editable text box. These variables are known as *outlets*, and like your action routines, in Interface Builder you connect your instance variables to the actual control in the iPhone's window.

For our first application, we need a method that responds to the action of the pressing of the button labeled 1. We also need an outlet variable that contains (among other information) the text to be displayed in the label that we create at the top of the iPhone's window.

Edit the file `iPhone_1AppDelegate.h` to add a new `UILabel` variable called `display` and declare an action method called `click1:` to respond to the pressing of the button. Your interface file should look as shown in Program 21.1. (The comment lines automatically inserted at the head of the file are not shown here.)

Program 21.1 iPhone_1AppDelegate.h

```
#import <UIKit/UIKit.h>


@interface iPhone_1AppDelegate : NSObject <UIApplicationDelegate> {
    UIWindow *window;
```

```
    UILabel *display;
}

@property (nonatomic, retain) IBOutlet UIWindow *window;
@property (nonatomic, retain) IBOutlet UILabel *display;

- (IBAction) click1: (id) sender;

@end
```

Notice that iPhone applications import the header file `<UIKit/UIKit.h>`. This header file, in turn, imports other UIKit header files, in a similar way that the `Foundation.h` header file imported other header files you needed, such as `NSString.h` and `NSObject.h`. If you want to examine the contents of this file, you have to hunt a bit. Here's where it's installed on my system at the time of this writing:

`/Developer/Platforms/iPhoneSimulator.platform/Developer/SDKs/iPhoneSimulat or2.1.sdk/System/Library/Frameworks/UIKit.framework/Headers/UIKit.h`.

The `iPhone_1AppDelegate` class now has two instance variables. The first is a `UIWindow` object called `window`. That instance variable is created automatically when you create the project, and it references the iPhone's main window. You added another instance variable belonging to the `UILabel` class called `display`. This will be an outlet variable that will be connected to a label. When you set this variable's text field, it updates the corresponding text for the label in the window. Other methods defined for the `UILabel` class allow you to set and retrieve other attributes of a label, such as its color, the number of lines, and the size of the font.

You'll want to use other classes in your interface as you learn more about iPhone programming that we won't describe here. The names of some of these give you a clue as to their purpose: UITextField, UIFont, UIView, UITableView, UIImageView, UIImage, and UIButton.

Both the `window` and `display` instance variables are outlets, and in the property declarations for these two variables, note the use of `IBOutlet` identifier. `IBOutlet` is really `defined` as *nothing* in the UIKit header file `UINibDeclarations.h`. (That is, it is literally replaced by nothing in the source file by the preprocessor.) However, it's needed because Interface Builder looks for `IBOutlet` when it reads your header file to determine which of your variables can be used as outlets.

In the interface file, note that we declare a method called `click1:` that takes a single argument called `sender`. When the `click1:` method is called, the method will be passed information related to the event in this argument. For example, if you had a single action routine that you used to handle the pressing of different buttons, the argument can be queried to ascertain the particular button that was pressed.

The `click1:` method is defined to return a value of type `IBAction`. (This is defined as `void` in the `UINibDeclarations.h` header file.) Like `IBOutlet`, Interface Builder uses this identifier when it examines your header file to identify methods that can be used as actions.

Now it's time to modify the corresponding `iPhone_1AppDelegate.m` implementation file for your class. Here you synthesize the accessor methods for your `display` variable (the `window` access methods are already synthesized for you) and add the definition for your `click1:` method.

Edit your implementation file so that it resembles the one shown in Program 21.1.

Program 21.1 iPhone_1AppDelegate.m

```
#import ""iPhone_1AppDelegate.h""
@implementation iPhone_1AppDelegate

@synthesize window, display;

- (void) applicationDidFinishLaunching:(UIApplication *)application {

    // Override point for customization after application launch
    [window makeKeyAndVisible];
}

-(IBAction) click1: (id) sender
{
    [display setText: @"1"];
}

- (void) dealloc {
    [window release];
    [super dealloc];
}

@end
```

The `applicationDidFinishLaunching:` method is automatically called by the iPhone runtime system once; as its name implies, your application has finished launching. This is the place where you can initialize your instance variables, draw things on the screen, and make your window visible to display its contents. This last action is done by sending the `makeKeyAndVisible` message sent to your window at the end of the method.

The `click1:` method sets the outlet variable `display` to the string 1 by using `UILabel`'s `setText:` method. After you connect the pressing of the button to the invocation of this method, it can perform the desired action of putting a 1 into the display in the iPhone's window. To make the connection, you must now learn how to use Interface builder. Before you do that, build the program to remove any compiler warning or error messages.

Designing the Interface

In Figure 21.4, and in your Xcode main window, notice a file called `MainWindow.xib`. An `xib` file contains all the information about the user interface for your program, including information about its windows, buttons, labels, tab bars, text fields, and so on. Of course you don't have a user interface yet! That's the next step.

Double-click on the `MainWindow.xib` file. This causes another application, called Interface Builder, to launch. You can also access the XIB file from the Resources folder of your project.

When Interface Builder starts, you get a series of windows drawn on your screen, as depicted in Figures 21.6, 21.7, and 21.8. The actual windows that are opened might differ from the figures.

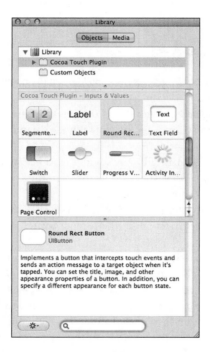

Figure 21.6   Interface Builder Library window.

The Library window provides a palette of controls that you can use for your interface. This window is depicted in Figure 21.6 in one of its display formats.

The `MainWindow.xib` window (Figure 21.7) is the controlling window for establishing connections between your application code and the interface, as you'll see shortly.

Figure 21.7   Interface Builder MainWindow.xib.

The window simply labeled Window shows the layout of the iPhone's main window. Because you haven't designed anything for your iPhone's window yet, it starts out empty, as shown in Figure 21.8.

The first thing we'll do is set the iPhone's window to black. To do this, first click inside the window labeled Window. Now, select Inspector from the Tools menu. This should bring up the Inspector window, as shown in Figure 21.9.

Make sure your Inspector window is labeled Window Attributes, as shown in Figure 21.9. If it isn't, click on the leftmost tab in the top tab bar to get the correct window displayed.

If you glance down to the View section of the window, you see an attribute labeled Background. If you double-click inside the white-filled rectangle next to Background, it brings up a color picker for you. Choose black from the picker, which changes the rectangle next to Background attribute in the Inspector from white to black (see Figure 21.10).

If you take a look at the window labeled Window, which represents the iPhone's display window, you see that it's been changed to black, as shown in Figure 21.11.

You can now close the Colors window.

You create new objects in your iPhone interface window by click-dragging an object from the Library window into your iPhone window. Click-drag a Label now. Release the mouse when the label is near the center of the window, close to the top, as shown in Figure 21.12.

Blue guide lines appear in your window as you move the label around inside your window. Sometimes they appear to help you align objects with other objects previously placed in the window. At other times, they appear to make sure your objects are spaced far enough apart from other objects and from the edges of the window, to be consistent with Apple's interface guidelines.

Figure 21.8   Interface Builder iPhone window.

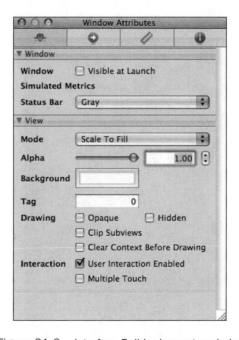

Figure 21.9   Interface Builder Inspector window.

Figure 21.10   Changing the window's background color.

Figure 21.11   Interface window changes to black.

Figure 21.12   Adding a label.

You can always reposition the label in the window at any time in the future by click-dragging it to another spot inside the window.

Let's now set some attributes for this label. In your window, if it's not currently selected, click the label you just created to select it. Notice that the Inspector window automatically changes to give you information about the currently selected object in your window. We don't want any text to appear by default for this label, so change the Text value to an empty string. (That is, delete the string Label from the text field shown in the Inspector's window.)

For the Layout attribute, select Right-justified for the alignment. Finally, change the background color for the label to blue (or any other color you choose), like you changed the window's background color to black. Your Inspector window should resemble Figure 21.13.

Now let's change the size of the label. Go back to Window and simply resize the label by pulling out along its corners and sides. Resize and reposition the label so that it looks like the one shown in Figure 21.14

Now we add a button to the interface. From the Library window, click-drag a Round Rect Button object into your interface window, placing it toward the lower-left corner of the window, as shown in Figure 21.15. You can change the label on the button in one of

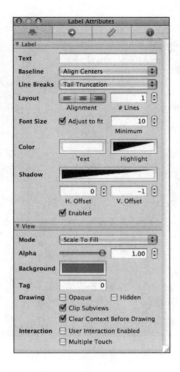

Figure 21.13   Changing the label's attributes.

two ways: by double-clicking on the button and then typing your text, or by setting the Title field in the Inspector window. Either way you choose, make you window match the one shown in Figure 21.15.

Now we have a label that we want to connect to our `display` instance variable in our program so that when we set the variable in our program the label's text will be changed.

We also have a button labeled 1 that we want to set to invoke our `click1:` method whenever it gets pressed. That method sets the value of `display`'s text field to 1. And because that variable will be connected to the label, the label will then be updated. As a recap, here's the sequence we want to set up:

1. The user presses the button labeled 1.

2. This event causes the `click1:` method to be invoked.

3. The `click1:` method changes the text of the instance variable `display` to the string 1.

4. Because the `UILabel` object `display` connects to the label in the iPhone's window, this label updates to the corresponding text value, or to the value 1.

Figure 21.14   Sizing and positioning a label.

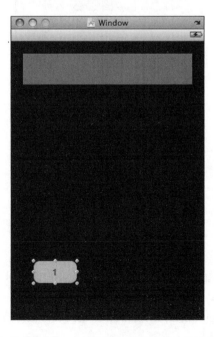

Figure 21.15   Adding a button to the interface.

For this sequence to work, we just need to make the two connections. Let's discuss how to do it.

First, let's connect the button to the IBAction method click1:. You do this by holding down the Control key while you click on the button and drag the blue line that appears on the screen to the application delegate in the MainWindow.xib window. This is shown in Figure 21.16.

When you release the mouse over the Delegate cube, a drop-down appears that allows you to select an IBAction method to connect to this button. In our case, we have only one such method called click1: so that appears in the drop down. Select that method to make the connection, as shown in Figure 21.17.

Now, let's connect the display variable to the label. Whereas pressing the button causes a method in the application to be executed (that is, the flow of action is from the interface to the application delegate), setting the value of an instance variable in the application causes the label in the iPhone's window to be updated. (Here the flow is from the application delegate to the interface.) So for this reason, you start by holding down the Control key while clicking on the application delegate icon and dragging the blue line that appears to the label in Window. This is shown in Figure 21.18.

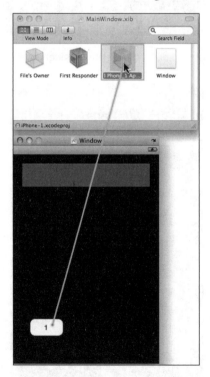

Figure 21.16   Adding an action for a button.

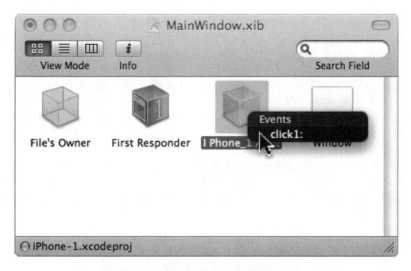

Figure 21.17   Connecting the event to the method.

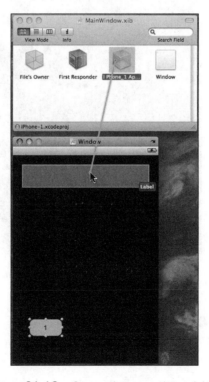

Figure 21.18   Connecting an outlet variable.

When you release the mouse, you get a list of IBOutlet variables of the corresponding class as the control (UILabel) to choose from. We have one such variable in our program, and it's called display. Choose this variable (as shown in Figure 21.19) and make the connection.

That's it; you're done! Select File->Save from Interface Builder's menu bar and then Build and Go from Xcode. (You can initiate this from Interface Builder as well.)

If all goes well, the program will successfully build and begin execution. When execution begins, your program will be loaded into the iPhone simulator, which will appear on your computer's display. The simulator window should appear as shown in Figure 21.1 at the start of this chapter. You simulate pressing a button with the simulator by simply clicking it. When you do that, the sequence of steps we outlined and the connections you made should result in the display of the string 1 in the label at the top of the display, as shown in Figure 21.2.

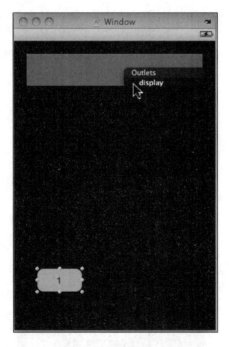

Figure 21.19   Finishing the connection.

An iPhone Fraction Calculator

The next example is a bit more involved, but the concepts from the previous example equally apply. We're not going to show all the steps to create this example, but rather give a summary of the steps and an overview of the design methodology. Of course, we'll also show all the code.

First, let's see how the application works. Figure 21.20 shows what the application looks like in the simulator just after launching.

The calculator application allows you to enter fractions by first keying in the numerator, pressing the key labeled Over, and then keying in the denominator. So to enter the fraction 2/5, you would press 2, followed by Over, followed by 5. You'll note that, unlike other calculators, this one actually shows the fraction in the display, so 2/5 is displayed as 2/5.

After keying in one fraction, you then choose an operation—addition, subtraction, multiplication, or division—by pressing the appropriately labeled key +, −, ×, or ÷, respectively.

After keying-in the second fraction, you then complete the operation by pressing the = key, just as you would with a standard calculator.

> **Note**
>
> This calculator is designed to perform just a single operation between two fractions. It's left as an exercise at the end of this chapter for you to remove this limitation.

Figure 21.20   Fraction calculator after launch.

The display is continuously updated as keys are pressed. Figure 21.21 shows the display after the fraction 4/6 has been entered and the multiplication key has been pressed.

Figure 21.22 shows the result of multiplying the fractions 4/6 and 2/8 together. You'll note that the result of 1/6 indicates that the result has first been reduced.

Starting the New `Fraction_Calculator` Project

The first iPhone program started from a Windows-based project template. Here you did your (minimal) UI work directly in the application controller (the AppDelegate class). This is not the recommended approach for developing UI-rich applications. The AppDelegate class typically just handles changes related to the state of the application itself, such as when the application finishes launching or when it is about to be deactivated.

Figure 21.21   Keying in an operation.

The view controller (implemented with the `UIViewController` class) is where you should perform your actions related to the UI. This might be displaying text, reacting to the pressing of a button, or putting an entirely new view on the iPhone's screen.

For this second program example, you'll start by creating a new project. This time, select View-Based Application from the New Project window. Call your new project `Fraction_Calculator`.

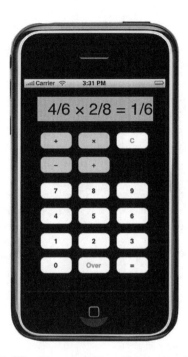

Figure 21.22   The result of multiplying two fractions.

When your project is created, this time you'll notice you get two class templates defined for you. Fraction_CalculatorAppDelegate.h and Fraction_CalculatorAppDelegate.m define the application's controller class for your project, while Fraction_CalculatorViewController.h and Fraction_CalculatorViewController.m define the view controller class for your project. As noted, it's in this latter class where you'll perform all your work.

We'll start first with the application controller class. It contains two instance variables: one for referencing the iPhone's window and another for the view controller. These have both been set up for you by Xcode. In fact, there are no changes you need to make to either the application controller's .h or .m files.

The Fraction_CalculatorAppDelegate interface file is shown in Program 21.2.

Program 21.2 Fraction_CalculatorAppDelegate.h Interface File

```
#import <UIKit/UIKit.h>


@class Fraction_CalculatorViewController;

@interface Fraction_CalculatorAppDelegate : NSObject <UIApplicationDelegate> {
    IBOutlet UIWindow *window;
    IBOutlet Fraction_CalculatorViewController *viewController;
}
```

```
@property (nonatomic, retain) UIWindow *window;
@property (nonatomic, retain) Fraction_CalculatorViewController *viewController;

@end
```

The `UIWindow` instance variable `window` serves the same purpose as in the first program example: it represents the iPhone's window. The `Fraction_CalculatorViewController` instance variable represents the view controller that will manage all the interaction with the user, as well as the display. In the implementation file for this class you will put all the work associated with these tasks.

Program 21.2 shows the implementation file for the application controller class. As noted, we're not doing any of the work in this file like we did in Program 21.1; that's all being delegated to the view controller. So this file appears untouched, exactly as it was generated by Xcode for you when you created the new project.

Program 21.2 Fraction_CalculatorAppDelegate.m Implementation File

```
#import "Fraction_CalculatorAppDelegate.h"
#import "Fraction_CalculatorViewController.h"

@implementation Fraction_CalculatorAppDelegate

@synthesize window;
@synthesize viewController;

- (void)applicationDidFinishLaunching:(UIApplication *)application {

    // Override point for customization after app launch
    [window addSubview:viewController.view];
    [window makeKeyAndVisible];
}

- (void)dealloc {
    [viewController release];
    [super dealloc];
}

@end
```

Defining the View Controller

Now let's write the code for the view controller class `Fraction_CalculatorViewController`. We'll start with the interface file. This is shown in Program 21.2.

Program 21.2 Fraction_CalculatorViewController.h Interface File

```
#import <UIKit/UIKit.h>
#import "Calculator.h"

@interface Fraction_CalculatorViewController : UIViewController {
    UILabel         *display;
    char            op;
```

```
    int             currentNumber;
    NSMutableString *displayString;
    BOOL            firstOperand, isNumerator;
    Calculator      *myCalculator;
}

@property (nonatomic, retain) IBOutlet UILabel *display;
@property (nonatomic, retain) NSMutableString *displayString;

-(void) processDigit: (int) digit;
-(void) processOp: (char) theOp;
-(void) storeFracPart;

// Numeric keys

-(IBAction) clickDigit: (id) sender;

// Arithmetic Operation keys

-(IBAction) clickPlus: (id) sender;
-(IBAction) clickMinus: (id) sender;
-(IBAction) clickMultiply: (id) sender;
-(IBAction) clickDivide: (id) sender;

// Misc. Keys

-(IBAction) clickOver: (id) sender;
-(IBAction) clickEquals: (id) sender;
-(IBAction) clickClear: (id) sender;

@end
```

There are housekeeping variables for building the fractions (`currentNumber`, `firstOperand`, and `isNumerator`), and for building the string for the display (`displayString`). There is also a `Calculator` object (`myCalculator`) that can perform the actual calculation between the two fractions. We will associate a single method called `clickDigit:` to handle the pressing of any of the digit keys 0-9. Finally, we define methods to handle storing the operation to be performed (`clickPlus:`, `clickMinus:`, `clickMultiply:`, `clickDivide:`), carrying out the actual calculation when the = key is pressed (`clickEquals:`), clearing the current operation (`clickClear:`), and separating the numerator from the denominator when the Over key is pressed (`clickOver:`). Several methods (`processDigit:`, `processOp:`, and `storeFracPart`) are defined to assist in the aforementioned chores.

Program 21.2 shows the implementation file for this controller class.

Program 21.2 Fraction_CalculatorViewController.m Implementation File

```
#import "Fraction_CalculatorViewController.h"
@implementation Fraction_CalculatorViewController

@synthesize display, displayString;

-(void) viewDidLoad {
```

```
    // Override point for customization after application launch

    firstOperand = YES;
    isNumerator = YES;
    self.displayString = [NSMutableString stringWithCapacity: 40];
    myCalculator = [[Calculator alloc] init];
}

-(void) processDigit: (int) digit
{
    currentNumber = currentNumber * 10 + digit;

    [displayString appendString: [NSString stringWithFormat: @"%i", digit]];
    [display setText: displayString];
}

- (IBAction) clickDigit:(id)sender
{
    int digit = [sender tag];

    [self processDigit:digit];
}

-(void) processOp: (char) theOp
{
    NSString *opStr;

    op = theOp;

    switch (theOp) {
        case '+':
            opStr = @" + ";
            break;
        case '-':
            opStr = @" — ";
            break;
        case '*':
            opStr = @" × ";
            break;
        case '/':
            opStr = @" ÷ ";
            break;
    }

    [self storeFracPart];
    firstOperand = NO;
    isNumerator = YES;

    [displayString appendString: opStr];
    [display setText: displayString];
}

-(void) storeFracPart
{
```

```
    if (firstOperand) {
        if (isNumerator) {
            myCalculator.operand1.numerator = currentNumber;
            myCalculator.operand1.denominator = 1; // e.g. 3 * 4/5 =
        }
        else
            myCalculator.operand1.denominator = currentNumber;
    }
    else if (isNumerator) {
        myCalculator.operand2.numerator = currentNumber;
        myCalculator.operand2.denominator = 1; // e.g. 3/2 * 4 =
    }
    else {
        myCalculator.operand2.denominator = currentNumber;
        firstOperand = YES;
    }

    currentNumber = 0;
}

-(IBAction) clickOver: (id) sender
{
    [self storeFracPart];
    isNumerator = NO;
    [displayString appendString: @"/"];
    [display setText: displayString];
}

// Arithmetic Operation keys

-(IBAction) clickPlus: (id) sender
{
    [self processOp: '+'];
}

-(IBAction) clickMinus: (id) sender
{
    [self processOp: '-'];
}

-(IBAction) clickMultiply: (id) sender
{
    [self processOp: '*'];
}

-(IBAction) clickDivide: (id) sender
{
    [self processOp: '/'];
}

// Misc. Keys

-(IBAction) clickEquals: (id) sender
{
    [self storeFracPart];
    [myCalculator performOperation: op];
```

```
    [displayString appendString: @" = "];
    [displayString appendString: [myCalculator.accumulator convertToString]];
    [display setText: displayString];

    currentNumber = 0;
    isNumerator = YES;
    firstOperand = YES;
    [displayString setString: @""];
}

-(IBAction) clickClear: (id) sender
{
    isNumerator = YES;
    firstOperand = YES;
    currentNumber = 0;
    [myCalculator clear];

    [displayString setString: @""];
    [display setText: displayString];
}

- (void)dealloc {
    [myCalculator release];
    [super dealloc];
}
```

@end

The calculator's window still contains just one label as in the previous application, and we still call it display. As the user enters a number digit-by-digit, we need to build the number along the way. The variable current_Number holds the number-in-progress, while the BOOL variables firstOperand and isNumerator keep track of whether this is the first or second operand entered and whether the user is currently keying in the numerator or the denominator of that operand.

When a digit button is pressed on the calculator, we set it up so that some identifying information will be passed to the clickDigit: method to identify which digit button was pressed. This is done by setting the button's attribute (using Interface Builder's Inspector) called tag to a unique value for each digit button. In this case, we want to set the tag to the corresponding digit number. So the tag for the button labeled 0 will be set to 0, the tag for the button labeled 1 to 1, and so on. By then sending the tag message to the sender parameter that is passed to the clickDigit: method, you can retrieve the value of the button's tag. This is done in the clickDigit: method as shown:

```
- (IBAction) clickDigit:(id)sender
{
    int digit = [sender tag];

    [self processDigit:digit];
}
```

There are a lot more buttons in Program 21.2 than in the first application. Most of the complexity in the view controller's implementation file revolves around building the fractions and displaying them. As noted, as a digit button 0–9 gets pressed, the action method `clickDigit:` gets executed. That method calls the `processDigit:` method to tack the digit onto the end of the number that's being built in the variable `currentNumber`. That method also adds the digit to the current display string that's kept in the variable `displayString`, and updates the display:

```
-(void) processDigit: (int) digit
{
    currentNumber = currentNumber * 10 + digit;

    [displayString appendString: [NSString stringWithFormat: @"%i", digit]];
    [display setText: displayString];
}
```

When the = key is pressed, the `clickEquals:` method gets invoked to perform the operation. The calculator performs the operation between the two fractions, storing the result in its accumulator. This accumulator is fetched inside the `clickEquals:` method, and the result is added to the display.

The Fraction Class

The `Fraction` class remains largely unchanged from earlier examples in this text. There is a new `convertToString` method that was added to convert a fraction to its equivalent string representation. Program 21.2 shows the `Fraction` interface file followed immediately by the corresponding implementation file.

Program 21.2 Fraction.h Interface File

```
#import <UIKit/UIKit.h>

@interface Fraction : NSObject {
    int numerator;
    int denominator;
}

@property int numerator, denominator;

-(void)      print;
-(void)      setTo: (int) n over: (int) d;
-(Fraction *)    add: (Fraction *) f;
-(Fraction *)    subtract: (Fraction *) f;
-(Fraction *)    multiply: (Fraction *) f;
-(Fraction *)    divide: (Fraction *) f;
-(void)       reduce;
-(double)      convertToNum;
-(NSString *) convertToString;

@end
```

Program 21.2 Fraction.m Implementation File

```
#import "Fraction.h"


@implementation Fraction

@synthesize numerator, denominator;


-(void) setTo: (int) n over: (int) d
{
    numerator = n;
    denominator = d;
}

-(void) print
{
    NSLog (@"%i/%i", numerator, denominator);
}

-(double) convertToNum
{
    if (denominator != 0)
        return (double) numerator / denominator;
    else
        return 1.0;
}

-(NSString *) convertToString
{
    if (numerator == denominator)
        if (numerator == 0)
            return @"0";
        else
            return @"1";
    else if (denominator == 1)
        return [NSString stringWithFormat: @"%i", numerator];
    else
        return [NSString stringWithFormat: @"%i/%i",
                numerator, denominator];
}

// add a Fraction to the receiver

-(Fraction *) add: (Fraction *) f
{
    // To add two fractions:
    // a/b + c/d = ((a*d) + (b*c)) / (b * d)

    // result will store the result of the addition
    Fraction    *result = [[Fraction alloc] init];
    int         resultNum, resultDenom;
```

```
    resultNum = numerator * f.denominator + denominator * f.numerator;
    resultDenom = denominator * f.denominator;

    [result setTo: resultNum over: resultDenom];
    [result reduce];

    return [result autorelease];
}

-(Fraction *) subtract: (Fraction *) f
{
    // To sub two fractions:
    // a/b - c/d = ((a*d) - (b*c)) / (b * d)

    Fraction *result = [[Fraction alloc] init];
    int    resultNum, resultDenom;

    resultNum = numerator * f.denominator - denominator * f.numerator;
    resultDenom = denominator * f.denominator;

    [result setTo: resultNum over: resultDenom];
    [result reduce];
    return [result autorelease];
}

-(Fraction *) multiply: (Fraction *) f
{
    Fraction *result = [[Fraction alloc] init];

    [result setTo: numerator * f.numerator over: denominator
            * f.denominator];
    [result reduce];

    return [result autorelease];
}

-(Fraction *) divide: (Fraction *) f
{
    Fraction *result = [[Fraction alloc] init];

    [result setTo: numerator * f.denominator over: denominator * f.numerator];
    [result reduce];

    return [result autorelease];
}

- (void) reduce
{
    int u = numerator;
    int v = denominator;
    int temp;

    if (u == 0)
        return;
    else if (u <0)
      u = -u;
```

```
    while (v != 0) {
       temp = u % v;
        u = v;
        v = temp;
    }

    numerator /= u;
    denominator /= u;
}

@end
```

The `convertToString:` method checks the numerator and denominator of the fraction to produce a more eye-pleasing result. If the numerator and denominator are equal (but not zero), we return `@"1"`. If the numerator is zero, the string `@"0"` is returned. If the denominator is 1, it's a whole number, so there's no need to show the denominator.

The `stringWithFormat:` method that's used inside `convertToString:` returns a string given a format string (akin to `NSLog`) and a comma-separated list of arguments. You pass arguments to a method that takes a variable number of arguments by separating them with commas, just like you did when passing the arguments to the `NSLog` function.

A Calculator Class That Deals with Fractions

Next, it's time to take a look at the `Calculator` class. The concept is similar to the class of the same name we developed earlier in this book. However, in this case, our calculator must know how to deal with fractions. Here are our new Calculator class interface and implementation files.

Program 21.2 Calculator.h Interface File

```
#import <UIKit/UIKit.h>
#import "Fraction.h"

@interface Calculator : NSObject {
    Fraction *operand1;
    Fraction *operand2;
    Fraction *accumulator;
}

@property (retain, nonatomic) Fraction *operand1, *operand2, *accumulator;

-(Fraction *) performOperation: (char) op;
-(void) clear;

@end
```

Program 21.2 Calculator.m Implementation File

```
#import "Calculator.h"


@implementation Calculator
```

```objc
@synthesize operand1, operand2, accumulator;

-(id) init
{
    self = [super init];

    operand1 = [[Fraction alloc] init];
    operand2 = [[Fraction alloc] init];
    accumulator = [[Fraction alloc] init];

    return self;
}


-(void) clear
{
    if (accumulator) {
        accumulator.numerator = 0;
        accumulator.denominator = 0;
    }
}


-(Fraction *) performOperation: (char) op
{
    Fraction *result;

    switch (op) {
        case '+':
            result = [operand1 add: operand2];
            break;
        case '-':
            result = [operand1 subtract: operand2];
            break;
        case '*':
            result = [operand1 multiply: operand2];
            break;
        case '/':
            result= [operand1 divide: operand2];
            break;
    }

    accumulator.numerator = result.numerator;
    accumulator.denominator = result.denominator;

    return accumulator;
}

-(void) dealloc
{
    [operand1 release];
    [operand2 release];
    [accumulator release];
    [super dealloc];
}

@end
```

Designing the UI

You may have noticed that you have two xib files in your project's Resources folder: one called `MainWindow.xib` and the other called `Fraction_CalculatorViewController.xib`. You don't need to work with the former file at all, so open up the latter by double-clicking on its file name. When Interface Builder starts up, you'll see that you have an icon labeled 'View' displayed in the window labeled `Fraction_CalculatorViewController.xib`. This is shown in Figure 21.23

If the View window isn't already open, double-click on the icon and open it. Inside this View window is where you will design your calculator's UI. Make the connections between each digit button and the `clickDigit:` method. Do this by Control-click-dragging each button in turn to the File's Owner icon in the `Fraction_CalculatorViewController.xib` window and selecting `clickDigit:` from the Events drop-down. Also, for each digit button, in the Inspector window set the Tag value to the number that corresponds to the button's title. So for the digit button labeled 0 set the Tag value to 0, for the digit button labeled 1, set the Tag value to 1, and so on.

Draw the remaining buttons in the View window and make the corresponding connections. Don't forget to insert a label for the calculator's display and Control-click-drag from the File's Owner to the label. Select `display` from the Outlets dropdown that appears.

That's it! Your interface design is done and your fraction calculator application is ready to be put into action.

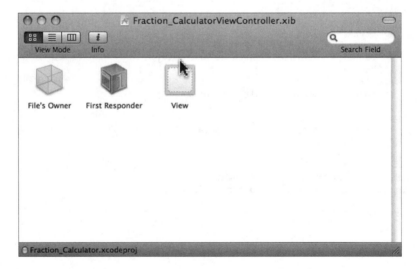

Figure 21.23   Fraction_CalculatorViewController.xib window.

Summary

Figure 21.24 shows the Xcode project window so that you can see all the files related to the Fraction calculator project.

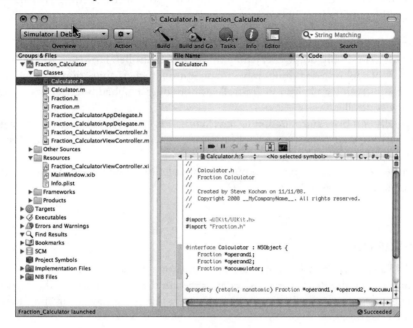

Figure 21.24   Fraction calculator project files.

The following summarizes the steps you followed to create you iPhone fraction calculator application:

1. Created a new View-based Application.

2. Entered your UI code into the `Fraction_CalculatorViewController` .h and .m files.

3. Added the Fraction and Calculator classes to the project.

4. Opened `Fraction_CalculatorViewController.xib` in Interface Builder to create the UI.

5. Made the `View` window's background black.

6. Created a label and buttons and positioned them inside the View window.

7. Control-click-dragged from `File's Owner` to the label you created in the View window and set that to 'display'.

8. Control-click-dragged from each button in the View window to the `File's Owner` and made the connection to the appropriate action method. For each digit button, you selected the `clickDigit:` method. Also, for each digit button, you set the `tag` button attribute to the corresponding digit 0-9 so that the `clickDigit:` method could identify which button was pressed.

It was a worthwhile exercise learning how to use a view controller, even though it was more work than simply doing everything in the app controller. However, if you want to do any sort of sophisticated things in your application, such as animation, responding to screen rotation, using a navigation controller, or building a tabbed interface, you'll need to use a view controller.

Hopefully this brief introduction to developing iPhone applications gives you a good start for writing your own iPhone applications. As noted earlier, there are many features offered in UIKit and lots for you to explore!

There are several limitations with our fraction calculator application. Many of these are addressed in the exercises that follow.

Exercises

1. Add a Convert button to the fraction calculator application. When the button is pressed, use the `Fraction` class's `convertToNum` method to produce the numeric representation of the fractional result. Convert that result to a string and show it in the calculator's display.

2. Modify the fraction calculator application so that a negative fraction can be entered if the − key gets pressed before a numerator is entered.

3. If the value of zero is keyed in for a denominator for either the first or second operand, display the string `Error` in the fraction calculator's display.

4. Modify the fraction calculator application so that calculations can be chained. For example, allow for the following operation to be keyed:

   $1/5 + 2/7 − 3/8 =$

5. You can add an icon to your application that will appear on the iPhone's home screen. This can be done by adding an image to be used as the icon (.png file) to your application's Resources folder and setting the value of the "Icon file" key in your information property list (Info.plist file in your Resources folder) to this image file, as shown in the Figure 21.25.

   Find a suitable calculator image on the Internet that you can use and set up the fraction calculator to use this image as its application icon.

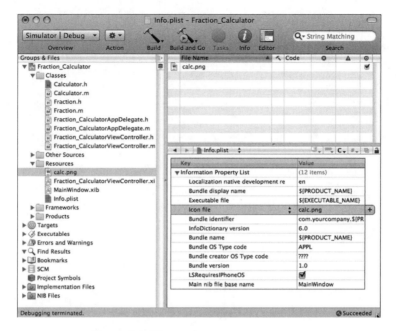

Figure 21.25   Adding an application icon.

Part IV

Appendixes

Glossary

This appendix contains informal definitions for many of the terms you will encounter. Some of these terms have to do directly with the Objective-C language itself, whereas others gain their etymology from the discipline of object-oriented programming. In the latter case, I provide the meaning of the term as it specifically applies to the Objective-C language.

abstract class   A class defined to make creating subclasses easier. Instances are created from the subclass, not of the abstract class. *See also* concrete subclass.

accessor method   A method that gets or sets the value of an instance variable. Using accessor methods to set and retrieve the values of instance variables is consistent with the methodology of data encapsulation.

Application Kit   A framework for developing an application's user interface, which includes objects such as menus, toolbars, and windows. Part of Cocoa and more commonly called AppKit.

archiving   Translating the representation of an object's data into a format that can later be restored (unarchived).

array   An ordered collection of values. Arrays can be defined as a basic Objective-C type and are implemented as objects under Foundation through the `NSArray` and `NSMutableArray` classes.

automatic variable   A variable that is automatically allocated and released when a statement block is entered and exited. Automatic variables have scope that is limited to the block in which they are defined and have no default initial value. They are optionally preceded by the keyword `auto`.

autorelease pool   An object defined in the Foundation framework that keeps track of objects that are to be released when the pool itself is released. Objects are added to the pool by sending them `autorelease` messages.

bitfield   A structure containing one or more integer fields of a specified bit width. Bitfields can be accessed and manipulated the same way other structure members can.

category   A set of methods grouped together under a specified name. Categories can modularize the method definitions for a class and can be used to add new methods to an existing class.

character string   A null-terminated sequence of characters.

class   A set of instance variables and methods that have access to those variables. After a class is defined, instances of the class (that is, objects) can be created.

class method   A method (defined with a leading + sign) that is invoked on class objects. *See also* instance method.

class object   An object that identifies a particular class. The class name can be used as the receiver of a message to invoke a class method. In other places, the `class` method can be invoked on the class to create a class object.

cluster   An abstract class that groups a set of private concrete subclasses, providing a simplified interface to the user through the abstract class.

Cocoa   A development environment that consists of the Foundation and Application Kit frameworks.

Cocoa Touch   A development environment that consists of the Foundation and UIKit frameworks.

collection   A Foundation framework object that is an array, a dictionary, or a set used for grouping and manipulating related objects.

compile time   The time during which the source code is analyzed and converted into a lower-level format known as object code.

composite class   A class that is composed of objects from other classes; often it's used as an alternative to subclassing.

concrete subclass   A subclass of an abstract class. Instances can be created from a concrete subclass.

conform   A class conforms to a protocol if it adopts all the required methods in the protocol, either directly through implementation or indirectly through inheritance.

constant character string   A sequence of characters enclosed inside a pair of double quotation marks. If preceded by an @ character, it defines a constant character string object of type `NSConstantString`.

data encapsulation   The notion that the data for an object is stored in its instance variables and is accessed only by the object's methods. This maintains the integrity of the data.

delegate   An object directed to carry out an action by another object.

designated initializer   The method that all other initialization methods in the class, or in subclasses (through messages to `super`), will invoke.

dictionary   A collection of key/value pairs implemented under Foundation with the `NSDictionary` and `NSMutableDictionary` classes.

directive   In Objective-C, a special construct that begins with an at sign (`@`). `@interface`, `@implementation`, `@end`, and `@class` are examples of directives.

Distributed Objects   The capability of Foundation objects in one application to communicate with Foundation objects in another application, possibly running on another machine.

dynamic binding   Determining the method to invoke with an object at runtime instead of at compile time.

dynamic typing   Determining the class to which an object belongs at runtime instead of at compile time. *See also* static typing.

encapsulation   *See* data encapsulation.

extern variable   *See* global variable.

factory method   *See* class method.

factory object   *See* class object.

formal protocol   A set of related methods grouped together under a name declared with the `@protocol` directive. Different classes (not necessarily related) can adopt a formal protocol by implementing (or inheriting) all its required methods. *See also* informal protocol.

forwarding   The process of sending a message and its associated argument(s) to another method for execution.

Foundation framework   A collection of classes, functions, and protocols that form the foundation for application development, providing basic facilities such as memory management, file and URL access, the tasks of archiving and working with collections, strings, and number and date objects.

framework   A collection of classes, functions, protocols, documentation, and header files and other resources that are all related. For example, the Cocoa framework is used in developing interactive graphical applications under Mac OS X.

function   A block of statements identified by a name that can accept one or more arguments passed to it by value and can optionally return a value. Functions can be either local (static) to the file in which they're defined or global, in which case they can be called from functions or methods defined in other files.

garbage collection   A memory-management system that automatically releases the memory used by unreferenced objects. Garbage collection is not supported in the iPhone runtime environment.

gcc   The name of the compiler developed by the Free Software Foundation (FSF). gcc supports many programming languages, including C, Objective-C, and C++. gcc is the standard compiler used in Mac OS X for compiling Objective-C programs.

gdb   The standard debugging tool for programs compiled with gcc.

getter method   An accessor method that retrieves the value of an instance variable. *See also* setter method.

global variable   A variable defined outside any method or function that can be accessed by any method or function in the same source file or from other source files that declare the variable as `extern`.

header file   A file that contains common definitions, macros, and variable declarations that is included in a program using either an `#import` or an `#include` statement.

id   The generic object type that can hold a pointer to any type of object.

immutable object   An object whose value cannot be modified. Examples from the Foundation framework include `NSString`, `NSDictionary`, and `NSArray` objects. *See also* mutable object.

implementation section   The section of a class definition that contains the actual code (that is, implementation) for the methods declared in the corresponding interface section (or as specified by a protocol definition).

informal protocol   A logically related set of methods declared as a category, often as a category of the root class. Unlike formal protocols, all the methods in an informal protocol do not have to be implemented. *See also* formal protocol.

inheritance   The process of passing methods and instance variables from a class, starting with the root object, down to subclasses.

instance   A concrete representation of a class. Instances are objects that are typically created by sending an `alloc` or `new` message to a class object.

instance method   A method that can be invoked by an instance of a class. *See also* class method.

instance variable   A variable declared in the interface section (or inherited from a parent) that is contained in every instance of the object. Instance methods have direct access to their instance variables.

Interface Builder   A tool under Mac OS X for building a graphical user interface for an application.

interface section   The section for declaring a class, its superclass, instance variables, and methods. For each method, the argument types and return type are also declared. *See also* implementation section.

internationalization   *See* localization.

isa   A special instance variable defined in the root object that all objects inherit. The `isa` variable is used to identify the class to which an object belongs at run-time.

linking   The process of converting one or more object files into a program that can be executed.

local variable   A variable whose scope is limited to the block in which it is defined. Variables can be local to a method, function, or statement block.

localization   The process of making a program suitable for execution within a particular geographic region, typically by translating messages to the local language and handling things such as local time zones, currency symbols, date formats, and so on. Sometimes *localization* is used just to refer to the language translation, and the term *internationalization* is used to refer to the rest of the process.

message   The method and its associated arguments that are sent to an object (the receiver).

message expression   An expression enclosed in square brackets that specifies an object (the receiver) and the message to send to the object.

method   A procedure that belongs to a class and can be executed by sending a message to a class object or to instances from the class. *See also* class method and instance method.

mutable object   An object whose value can be changed. The Foundation framework supports mutable and immutable arrays, sets, strings, and dictionaries. *See also* immutable object.

nil   An object of type `id`, which is used to represent an invalid object. Its value is defined as `0`. nil can be sent messages.

notification   The process of sending a message to objects that have registered to be alerted (notified) when a specific event occurs.

NSObject   The root object under the Foundation framework.

null character   A character whose value is `0`. A null character constant is denoted by `'\0'`.

null pointer   An invalid pointer value, normally defined as 0.

object   A set of variables and associated methods. An object can be sent messages to cause one of its methods to be executed.

object-oriented programming   A method of programming based on classes and objects, and performing actions on those objects.

parent class   A class from which another class inherits. Also referred to as the *super class.*

pointer   A value that references another object or data type. A pointer is implemented as the address of a particular object or value in memory. An instance of a class is a pointer to the location of the object's data in memory.

polymorphism   The capability of objects from different classes to accept the same message.

preprocessor   A program that makes a first pass through the source code processing lines that begin with a #, which presumably contain special preprocessor statements. Common uses are for defining macros with `#define`, including other source files with `#import` and `#include`, and conditionally including source lines with `#if`, `#ifdef`, and `#ifndef`.

procedural programming language   A language in which programs are defined by procedures and functions that operate on a set of data.

property declaration   A way to specify attributes for instance variables that enables the compiler to generate leak-free and thread-safe accessor methods for instance variables. Property declarations can also be used to declare attributes for accessor methods that will be dynamically loaded at runtime.

property list   A representation of different types of objects in a standardized format. Property lists are typically stored in XML format.

protocol   A list of methods that a class must implement to conform to or adopt the protocol. Protocols provide a way to standardize an interface across classes. *See also* formal protocol and informal protocol.

receiver   The object to which a message is sent. The receiver can be referred to as `self` from inside the method that is invoked.

reference count   *See* retain count.

retain count   A count of the number of times an object is referenced. It's incremented by sending a `retain` message to the object, and it's decremented by sending a `release` message to it.

root object   The topmost object in the inheritance hierarchy that has no parent.

runtime   The time when a program is executing; also the mechanism responsible for executing a program's instructions.

selector   The name used to select the method to execute for an object. Compiled selectors are of type `SEL` and can be generated using the `@selector` directive.

self   A variable used inside a method to refer to the receiver of the message.

set   An unordered collection of unique objects implemented under Foundation with the `NSSet`, `NSMutableSet`, and `NSCountedSet` classes.

setter method   An accessor method that sets the value of an instance variable. *See also* getter method.

statement   One or more expressions terminated by a semicolon.

statement block   One or more statements enclosed in a set of curly braces. Local variables can be declared within a statement block, and their scope is limited to that block.

static function   A function declared with the `static` keyword that can be called only by other functions or methods defined in the same source file.

static typing   Explicitly identifying the class to which an object belongs at compile time. *See also* dynamic typing.

static variable   A variable whose scope is limited to the block or module in which it is defined. Static variables have default initial values of 0 and retain their values through method or function invocations.

structure   An aggregate data type that can contain members of varying types. Structures can be assigned to other structures, passed as arguments to functions and methods, and returned by them as well.

subclass   Also known as a *child class*, a subclass inherits the methods and instance variables from its parent or superclass.

super A keyword used in a method to refer to the parent class of the receiver.

super class The parent class of a particular class. *See also* **super**.

synthesized method A setter or getter method that the compiler automatically creates for you. It was added to the Objective C 2.0 language.

UIKit A framework for developing applications on the iPhone and iTouch. In addition to providing classes for working with usual UI elements such as windows, button, and labels, it defines classes for dealing with device-specific features such as the accelerometer and the touch interface. UIKit is part of Cocoa Touch.

Unicode character A standard for representing characters from sets containing up to millions of characters. The `NSString` and `NSMutableString` classes work with strings containing Unicode characters.

union An aggregate data type, such as a structure containing members that share the same storage area. Only one of those members can occupy the storage area at any point in time.

Xcode A compiling and debugging tool for program development with Mac OS X.

XML Extensible Markup Language. The default format for property lists generated on Mac OS X.

zone A designated area of memory for allocating data and objects. A program can work with multiple zones to more efficiently manage memory.

Appendix B

Objective-C 2.0 Language Summary

This appendix summarizes the Objective-C language in a format suitable for quick reference. It is not intended to be a complete definition of the language, but rather a more informal description of its features. You should thoroughly read the material in this appendix after you have completed the text. Doing so will not only reinforce the material you learned, but also provide you with a better global understanding of Objective-C.

This summary is based on the ANSI C99 (ISO/IEC 9899:1999) standard with Objective-C 2.0 language extensions. As of this writing, the latest version of the GNU gcc compiler used on my Mac OS X v10.5.5 system is version 4.0.1.

Digraphs and Identifiers

Digraph Characters

The following special two-character sequences (*digraphs*) are equivalent to the listed single-character punctuators:

Digraph	Meaning
< :	[
: >	]
< %	{
% >	}
% :	#
% : % :	##

Identifiers

An *identifier* in Objective-C consists of a sequence of letters (upper- or lowercase), universal character names (1.2.1), digits, or underscore characters. The first character of an identifier must be a letter, an underscore, or a universal character name. The first 31 characters of an identifier are guaranteed to be significant in an external name, and the first 63 characters are guaranteed to be significant for an internal identifier or macro name.

Universal Character Names

A universal character name is formed by the characters \u followed by four hexadecimal numbers or the characters \U followed by eight hexadecimal numbers. If the first character of an identifier is specified by a universal character, its value cannot be that of a digit character. Universal characters, when used in identifier names, can also not specify a character whose value is less than $A0_{16}$ (other than 24_{16}, 40_{16}, or 60_{16}) or a character in the range $D800_{16}$ through $DFFF_{16}$, inclusive.

Universal character names can be used in identifier names, character constants, and character strings.

Keywords

The identifiers listed here are keywords that have special meanings to the Objective-C compiler:
```
_Bool
_Complex
_Imaginary
auto
break
bycopy
byref
case
char
const
continue
default
do
double
else
enum
extern
float
for
goto
if
in
inline
inout
int
long
oneway
out
```

```
register
restrict
return
self
short
signed
sizeof
static
struct
super
switch
typedef
union
unsigned
void
volatile
while
```

Directives

Compiler directives begin with an @ sign and are used specifically for working with classes and objects, as summarized in Table B.1.

Table B.1   **Compiler Directives**

Directive	Meaning	Example
@"chars"	Defines a constant NSSTRING character string object (Adjacent strings are concatenated.)	NSString *url = @"http://www.kochan-wood.com";
@class c1, c2,...	Declares c1, c2, ... as classes.	@class Point, Rectangle;
@defs (*class*)	Returns a list of the structure variables for *class*.	struct Fract { @defs(Fraction); } *fractPtr; fractPtr = (struct Fract *) [[Fraction alloc] init];
@dynamic *names*	Accessor methods for *names* may be provided dynamically	@dynamic drawRect;
@encode (*type*)	String encoding for *type*.	@encode (int *)
@end	Ends an interface section, an implementation section, or a protocol section.	@end
@implementation	Begins an implementation section.	@implementation Fraction

Table B.1   **Compiler Directives**

Directive	Meaning	Example
`@interface`	Begins an interface section.	`@interface Fraction: NSObject <Copying>`
`@private`	Defines the scope of one or more instance variables.	*See "Instance Variables."*
`@protected`	Defines the scope of one or more instance variables	
`@public`	Defines the scope of one or more instance variables	
`@property (list) names`	Declares properties in *list* for *names*.	`property (retain, nonatomic) NSSTRING *name;`
`@protocol`	Creates a Protocol object for a specified `protocol`.	`@protocol (Copying)]){...}` `if ([myObj conformsTo: (protocol)]`
`@protocol name`	Begins a protocol definition for `name`.	`@protocol Copying`
`@selector (method)`	SEL object for specified *method*.	`if ([myObj respondsTo: @selector (allocF)]) {...}`
`@synchronized (object)`	Begins a block to be executed by a single thread. *Object* is known as the mutual exclusion (mutex) semaphore.	
`@synthesize names`	Generates accessor methods for *names* if not provided.	`@synthesize name, email;` *See also "Instance Variables."*
`@try`	Begins a block to catch exceptions.	*See "Exception Handling."*
`@catch (exception)`	Begins a block to process *exception*.	
`@finally`	Begins a block that gets executed whether an exception is thrown in the previous `@try` block.	
`@throw`	Throws an exception.	

Predefined Identifiers

Table B.2 lists identifiers that have special meanings in Objective-C programs.

Table B.2   **Special Predefined Identifiers**

Identifier	Meaning
_cmd	A local variable automatically defined in a method that contains the selector for the method
__func__	A local character string variable automatically defined in a function or method containing the name of the function or method
BOOL	Boolean value, typically used with YES and NO
Class	Class object type
id	Generic object type
IMP	Pointer to a method returning the value of type id
nil	Null object
Nil	Null class object
NO	Defined as (BOOL) 0
NSObject	Root Foundation object defined in <Foundation/NSObject.h>
Protocol	Name of class for storing information about protocols
SEL	A compiled selector
self	A local variable automatically defined in a method that references the receiver of the message
super	The parent of the receiver of the message
YES	Defined as (BOOL) 1

Comments

There are two ways to insert comments into program. A comment can begin with the two characters //, in which case any characters that follow on the line are ignored by the compiler.

A comment can also begin with the two characters /* and end when the characters */ are encountered. Any characters can be included inside the comment, which can extend over multiple lines of the program. A comment can be used anywhere in the program where a blank space is allowed. Comments, however, cannot be nested, which means that the first */ characters encountered end the comment, no matter how many /* characters you use.

Constants

Integer Constants

An integer constant is a sequence of digits, optionally preceded by a plus or minus sign. If the first digit is 0, the integer is taken as an octal constant, in which case all digits that follow must be 0–7. If the first digit is 0 and is immediately followed by the letter x (or X), the integer is taken as a hexadecimal constant, and the digits that follow can be in the range 0–9 or a–f (or A–F).

The suffix letter l or L can be added to the end of a decimal integer constant to make it a long int constant. If the value can't fit into a long int, it's treated as a long long int. If the suffix letter l or L is added to the end of an octal or a hexadecimal constant, it is taken as a long int if it can fit; if it can't fit there, it is taken as a long long int. Finally, if it can't fit in a long long int, it is taken as an unsigned long long int constant.

The suffix letters ll or LL can be added to the end of a decimal integer constant to make it a long long int. When added to the end of an octal or a hexadecimal constant, it is taken as a long long int first, and if it can't fit there, it is taken as an unsigned long long int constant.

The suffix u or U can be added to the end of an integer constant to make it unsigned. If the constant is too large to fit inside an unsigned int, it's taken as an unsigned long int. If it's too large for an unsigned long int, it's taken as an unsigned long long int.

Both an unsigned and long suffix can be added to an integer constant to make it an unsigned long int. If the constant is too large to fit in an unsigned long int, it's taken as an unsigned long long int.

Both an unsigned and a long-long suffix can be added to an integer constant to make it an unsigned long long int.

If an unsuffixed decimal integer constant is too large to fit into a signed int, it is treated as a long int. If it's too large to fit into a long int, it's treated as a long long int.

If an unsuffixed octal or hexadecimal integer constant is too large to fit into a signed int, it is treated as an unsigned int. If it's too large to fit into an unsigned int, it's treated as a long int, and if it's too large to fit into a long int, it's treated as an unsigned long int. If it's too large for an unsigned long int, it's taken as a long long int. Finally, if it's too large to fit into a long long int, the constant is treated as an unsigned long long int.

Floating-Point Constants

A floating-point constant consists of a sequence of decimal digits, a decimal point, and another sequence of decimal digits. A minus sign can precede the value to denote a negative value. In addition, either the sequence of digits before the decimal point or after the decimal point can be omitted, but not both.

If the floating-point constant is immediately followed by the letter e (or E) and an optionally signed integer, the constant is expressed in scientific notation. This integer (the *exponent*) represents the power of 10 by which the value preceding the letter `e` (the *mantissa*) is multiplied (for example, `1.5e-2` represents 1.5×10^{-2} or .015).

A *hexadecimal* floating constant consists of a leading `0x` or `0X`, followed by one or more decimal or hexadecimal digits, followed by a `p` or `P`, followed by an optionally signed binary exponent. For example, `0x3p10` represents the value 3×2^{10}. Floating-point constants are treated as `double` precision values by the compiler. The suffix letter `f` or `F` can be added to specify a `float` constant instead of a `double` one, and the suffix letter `l` or `L` can be added to specify a `long double` constant.

Character Constants

A character enclosed within single quotation marks is a *character* constant. How the inclusion of more than one character inside the single quotation marks is handled is implementation-defined. A universal character can be used in a character constant to specify a character not included in the standard character set.

Escape Sequences

Special escape sequences are recognized and are introduced by the backslash character. These escape sequences are listed here:

Character	Meaning
\a	Audible alert
\b	Backspace
\f	Form feed
\n	Newline
\r	Carriage return
\t	Horizontal tab
\v	Vertical tab
\\	Backslash
\"	Double quote
\'	Single quote
\?	Question mark
nnn	Octal character value
\u*nnnn*	Universal character name
\U*nnnnnnnn*	Universal character name
\x*nn*	Hexadecimal character value

In the octal character case, from one to three octal digits can be specified. In the last three cases, hexadecimal digits are used.

Wide Character Constants

A *wide character constant* is written as L'*x*'. The type of such a constant is wchar_t, as defined in the standard header file <stddef.h>. Wide character constants provide a way to express a character from a character set that cannot be fully represented with the normal char type.

Character String Constants

A sequence of zero or more characters enclosed within double quotation marks represents a character string constant. Any valid character can be included in the string, including any of the escape characters listed previously. The compiler automatically inserts a null character ('\0') at the end of the string.

Normally, the compiler produces a pointer to the first character in the string and the type is "pointer to char." However, when the string constant is used with the sizeof operator to initialize a character array, or with the & operator, the type of the string constant is "array of char."

Character string constants cannot be modified by the program.

Character String Concatenation

The preprocessor automatically concatenates adjacent character string constants together. The strings can be separated by zero or more whitespace characters. So, the three strings

```
"a" " character "
  "string"
```

are equivalent to the single string

```
"a character string"
```

after concatenation.

Multibyte Characters

Implementation-defined sequences of characters can be used to shift between different states in a character string so that multibyte characters can be included.

Wide Character String Constants

Character string constants from an extended character set are expressed using the format `L'...'`. The type of such a constant is "pointer to `wchar_t`," where `wchar_t` is defined in `<stddef.h>`.

Constant Character String Objects

A constant character string *object* can be created by placing an `@` character in front of a constant character string. The type of the object is `NSConstantString`.

Adjacent constant string objects are concatenated together. So the three string objects

```
@"a" @" character "
  @"string"
```

are equivalent to the single string object

```
@"a character string"
```

Enumeration Constants

An identifier that has been declared as a value for an enumerated type is taken as a constant of that particular type and is otherwise treated as type `int` by the compiler.

Data Types and Declarations

This section summarizes the basic data types, derived data types, enumerated data types, and `typedef`. Also summarized in this section is the format for declaring variables.

Declarations

When defining a particular structure, union, enumerated data type, or `typedef`, the compiler does not automatically reserve any storage. The definition merely tells the compiler about the particular data type and (optionally) associates a name with it. Such a definition can be made either inside or outside a function or method. In the former case, only the function or method knows of its existence; in the latter case, it is known throughout the remainder of the file.

After the definition has been made, variables can be declared to be of that particular data type. A variable that is declared to be of any data type will have storage reserved for it, unless it is an `extern` declaration, in which case it might or might not have storage allocated (see the section "Storage Classes and Scope").

The language also enables storage to be allocated at the same time that a particular structure, union, or enumerated data type is defined. This is done by simply listing the variables before the terminating semicolon of the definition.

Basic Data Types

The basic Objective-C data types are summarized in Table B.3. A variable can be declared to be of a particular basic data type using the following format:

```
type name = initial_value;
```

The assignment of an initial value to the variable is optional and is subject to the rules summarized in the section "Variables." More than one variable can be declared simultaneously using the following general format:

```
type name = initial_value, name = initial_value, .. ;
```

Before the type declaration, an optional storage class can also be specified, as summarized in the section "Variables." If a storage class is specified and the type of the variable is int, then int can be omitted. For example

```
static counter;
```

declares counter to be a static int variable.

Table B.3   **Summary of Basic Data Types**

Type	Meaning
int	Integer value; that is, a value that contains no decimal point; guaranteed to contain at least 32 bits of accuracy
short int	Integer value of reduced accuracy; takes half as much memory as an int on some machines; guaranteed to contain at least 16 bits of accuracy
long int	Integer value of extended accuracy; guaranteed to contain at least 32 bits of accuracy
long long int	Integer value of extra-extended accuracy; guaranteed to contain at least 64 bits of accuracy
unsigned int	Positive integer value; can store positive values up to twice as large as an int; guaranteed to contain at least 32 bits of accuracy

Table B.3   **Summary of Basic Data Types**

Type	Meaning
float	Floating-point value; that is, a value that can contain decimal places; guaranteed to contain at least six digits of precision
double	Extended accuracy floating-point value; guaranteed to contain at least 10 digits of precision
long double	Extra-extended accuracy floating-point value; guaranteed to contain at least 10 digits of precision
char	Single character value; on some systems, sign extension can occur when used in an expression
unsigned char	Same as char, except it ensures that sign extension will not occur as a result of integral promotion
signed char	Same as char, except it ensures that sign extension will occur as a result of integral promotion
_Bool	Boolean type; large enough to store the value 0 or 1
float _Complex	Complex number
double _Complex	Extended accuracy complex number
long double _Complex	Extra-extended accuracy complex number
void	No type; used to ensure that a function or method that does not return a value is not used as if it does return one, or to explicitly discard the results of an expression; also used as a generic pointer type (void *)

Note that the signed modifier can also be placed in front of the short int, int, long int, and long long int types. Because these types are signed by default anyway, this has no effect.

_Complex and _Imaginary data types enable complex and imaginary numbers to be declared and manipulated, with functions in the library for supporting arithmetic on these types. Normally, you should include the file <complex.h> in your program, which defines macros and declares functions for working with complex and imaginary numbers. For example, a double _Complex variable c1 can be declared and initialized to the value 5 + 10.5i with a statement such as follows:

```
double _Complex c1 = 5 + 10.5 * I;
```

Library routines such as `creal` and `cimag` can then be used to extract the real and imaginary parts of `c1`, respectively.

An implementation is not required to support types `_Complex` and `_Imaginary`, and it can optionally support one but not the other.

Derived Data Types

A *derived* data type is one that is built up from one or more of the basic data types. Derived data types are arrays, structures, unions, and pointers (which include objects). A function or method that returns a value of a specified type is also considered a derived data type. Each of these, with the exception of functions and methods, is summarized in the following paragraphs. Functions and methods are separately covered in the sections "Functions" and "Classes," respectively.

Arrays
Single-Dimensional Arrays

Arrays can be defined to contain any basic data type or any derived data type. Arrays of functions are not permitted (although arrays of function pointers are).

The declaration of an array has the following basic format:

```
type name[n]  = { initExpression, initExpression, .. };
```

The expression *n* determines the number of elements in the array name and can be omitted, provided a list of initial values is specified. In such a case, the size of the array is determined based on the number of initial values listed or on the largest index element referenced if designated initializers are used.

Each initial value must be a constant expression if a global array is defined. Fewer values can exist in the initialization list than there are elements in the array, but more cannot exist. If fewer values are specified, only that many elements of the array are initialized— the remaining elements are set to 0.

A special case of array initialization occurs in the case of character arrays, which can be initialized by a constant character string. For example

```
char today[] = "Monday";
```

declares `today` as an array of characters. This array is initialized to the characters 'M', 'o', 'n', 'd', 'a', 'y', and '\0', respectively.

If you explicitly dimension the character array and don't leave room for the terminating null, the compiler doesn't place a null at the end of the array:

```
char today[6] = "Monday";
```

This declares `today` as an array of six characters and sets its elements to the characters 'M', 'o', 'n', 'd', 'a', and 'y', respectively.

By enclosing an element number in a pair of brackets, specific array elements can be initialized in any order. For example

```
int    x = 1233;
int    a[] = { [9] = x + 1, [2] = 3, [1] = 2, [0] = 1 };
```

defines a 10-element array called a (based on the highest index into the array) and initializes the last element to the value of x + 1 (1234) and the first three elements to 1, 2, and 3, respectively.

Variable-Length Arrays

Inside a function, method, or block, you can dimension an array using an expression containing variables. In that case, the size is calculated at runtime. For example, the function

```
int makeVals (int n)
{
  int valArray[n];
 ...
}
```

defines an automatic array called valArray with a size of n elements, where n is evaluated at runtime and can vary between function calls. Variable-length arrays cannot be initialized.

Multidimensional Arrays

The general format for declaring a multidimensional array follows:

```
type name[d1] [d2]...[dn] = initializationList;
```

The array name is defined to contain *d1* x *d2* x...x *dn* elements of the specified type. For example

```
int three_d [5] [2] [20];
```

defines a three-dimensional array, three_d, containing 200 integers.
A particular element is referenced from a multidimensional array by enclosing the desired subscript for each dimension in its own set of brackets. For example, the statement

```
three_d [4] [0] [15] = 100;
```

stores 100 into the indicated element of the array three_d.

Multidimensional arrays can be initialized in the same manner as one-dimensional arrays. Nested pairs of braces can be used to control the assignment of values to the elements in the array.

The following declares matrix to be a two-dimensional array containing four rows and three columns:

```
int matrix[4] [3] =
      { { 1, 2, 3 },
        { 4, 5, 6 },
        { 7, 8, 9 } };
```

Elements in the first row of matrix are set to the values 1, 2, and 3, respectively; in the second row they are set to 4, 5, and 6, respectively; and in the third row they are set to 7, 8, and 9, respectively. The elements in the fourth row are set to 0 because no values are specified for that row. The declaration

```
int matrix[4][3] =
    { 1, 2, 3, 4, 5, 6, 7, 8, 9 };
```

initializes matrix to the same values because the elements of a multidimensional array are initialized in *dimension order*—that is, from leftmost to rightmost dimension.

The declaration

```
int matrix[4][3] =
    { { 1 },
      { 4 },
      { 7 } };
```

sets the first element of the first row of matrix to 1, the first element of the second row to 4, and the first element of the third row to 7. All remaining elements are set to 0 by default.

Finally, the declaration

```
int matrix[4][3] = { [0][0] = 1, [1][1] = 5, [2][2] = 9 };
```

initializes the indicated elements of the matrix to the specified values.

Structures

General Format:

```
struct name
{
    memberDeclaration
    memberDeclaration
    ...
} variableList;
```

The structure *name* is defined to contain the members as specified by each *memberDeclaration*. Each such declaration consists of a type specification followed by a list of one or more member names.

Variables can be declared at the time that the structure is defined simply by listing them before the terminating semicolon, or they can subsequently be declared using the following format:

```
struct name variableList;
```

This format cannot be used if *name* is omitted when the structure is defined. In that case, all variables of that structure type must be declared with the definition.

The format for initializing a structure variable is similar to that for arrays. Its members can be initialized by enclosing the list of initial values in a pair of curly braces. Each value in the list must be a constant expression if a global structure is initialized.

The declaration

```
struct point
{
    float x;
    float y;
} start = {100.0, 200.0};
```

defines a structure called `point` and a `struct point` variable called `start` with initial values as specified. Specific members can be designated for initialization in any order with the notation

```
.member = value
```

in the initialization list, as in

```
struct point end = { .y = 500, .x = 200 };
```

The declaration

```
struct entry
{
  char *word;
  char *def;
} dictionary[1000] = {
    { "a",     "first letter of the alphabet" },
    { "aardvark", "a burrowing African mammal" },
    { "aback",    "to startle"          }
};
```

declares `dictionary` to contain 1,000 `entry` structures, with the first 3 elements initialized to the specified character string pointers. Using designated initializers, you could have also written it like this:

```
struct entry
{
  char *word;
  char *def;
} dictionary[1000] = {
    [0].word = "a",     [0].def = "first letter of the alphabet",
    [1].word = "aardvark", [1].def = "a burrowing African mammal",
    [2].word = "aback",   [2].def = "to startle"
};
```

or equivalently like this:

```
struct entry
{
   char *word;
   char *def;
} dictionary[1000] = {
   {  {.word = "a",      .def = "first letter of the alphabet" },
      {.word = "aardvark", .def = "a burrowing African mammal"} ,
      {.word = "aback",   .def = "to startle"}
};
```

An automatic structure variable can be initialized to another structure of the same type like this:

```
struct date tomorrow = today;
```

This declares the date structure variable tomorrow and assigns to it the contents of the (previously declared) date structure variable today.

A *memberDeclaration* that has the format

type fieldName : n

defines a *field* that is *n* bits wide inside the structure, where *n* is an integer value. Fields can be packed from left to right on some machines and right to left on others. If *fieldName* is omitted, the specified number of bits is reserved but cannot be referenced. If *fieldName* is omitted and *n* is 0, the field that follows is aligned on the next storage *unit* boundary, where a *unit* is implementation-defined. The type of a field can be int, signed int, or unsigned int. It is implementation-defined whether an int field is treated as signed or unsigned. The address operator (&) cannot be applied to a field, and arrays of fields cannot be defined.

Unions

General Format:

```
union name
{
   memberDeclaration
   memberDeclaration
   ...
} variableList;
```

This defines a union called *name* with members as specified by each *memberDeclaration*. Each member of the union shares overlapping storage space, and the compiler ensures that enough space is reserved to contain the largest member of the union.

Variables can be declared at the time that the union is defined, or they can be subsequently declared using the notation

```
union name variableList;
```

provided the union was given a name when it was defined.

It is the programmer's responsibility to ensure that the value retrieved from a union is consistent with the last value stored inside the union. The first member of a union can be initialized by enclosing the initial value, which, in the case of a global union variable, must be a constant expression, inside a pair of curly braces:

```
union shared
{
   long long int l;
   long int    w[2];
} swap = { 0xffffffff };
```

A different member can be initialized instead by specifying the member name, as in

```
union shared swap2 = {.w[0] = 0x0, .w[1] = 0xffffffff};
```

This declares the union variable swap and sets the l member to hexadecimal ffffffff.

An automatic union variable can also be initialized to a union of the same type, as in

```
union shared swap2 = swap;
```

Pointers

The basic format for declaring a pointer variable is as follows:

```
type *name;
```

The identifier *name* is declared to be of type "pointer to *type*," which can be a basic data type or a derived data type. For example

```
int *ip;
```

declares ip to be a pointer to an int, and the declaration

```
struct entry *ep;
```

declares ep to be a pointer to an entry structure. If Fraction is defined as a class, the declaration

```
Fraction *myFract;
```

declares myFract to be an object of type Fraction—or more explicitly, myFract is used to hold a pointer to the object's data structure after an instance of the object is created and assigned to the variable.

Pointers that point to elements in an array are declared to point to the type of element contained in the array. For example, the previous declaration of ip would also be used to declare a pointer into an array of integers.

More advanced forms of pointer declarations are also permitted. For example, the declaration

```
char *tp[100];
```

declares tp to be an array of 100 character pointers, and the declaration

```
struct entry (*fnPtr) (int);
```

declares fnPtr to be a pointer to a function that returns an entry structure and takes a single int argument.

A pointer can be tested to see whether it's null by comparing it against a constant expression whose value is 0. The implementation can choose to internally represent a null pointer with a value other than 0. However, a comparison between such an internally represented null pointer and a constant value of 0 must prove equal.

The manner in which pointers are converted to integers and integers are converted to pointers is machine-dependent, as is the size of the integer required to hold a pointer.

The type "pointer to void" is the generic pointer type. The language guarantees that a pointer of any type can be assigned to a void pointer and back again without changing its value.

The type id is a generic object pointer. Any object from any class can be assigned to an id variable, and vice versa.

Other than these two special cases, assignment of different pointer types is not permitted and typically results in a warning message from the compiler if attempted.

Enumerated Data Types

General Format:

```
enum name { enum_1, enum_2, .. } variableList;
```

The enumerated type name is defined with enumeration values enum_1, enum_2,..., each of which is an identifier or an identifier followed by an equals sign and a constant expression. variableList is an optional list of variables (with optional initial values) declared to be of type enum name.

The compiler assigns sequential integers to the enumeration identifiers starting at 0. If an identifier is followed by = and a constant expression, the value of that expression is assigned to the identifier. Subsequent identifiers are assigned values beginning with that constant expression plus one. Enumeration identifiers are treated as constant integer values by the compiler.

If you want to declare variables to be of a previously defined (and named) enumeration type, you can use the following construct:

```
enum name variableList;
```

A variable declared to be of a particular enumerated type can be assigned only a value of the same data type, although the compiler might not flag this as an error.

typedef

The typedef statement is used to assign a new name to a basic or derived data type. The typedef does not define a new type but simply a new name for an existing type. Therefore, variables declared to be of the newly named type are treated by the compiler exactly as if they were declared to be of the type associated with the new name.

In forming a typedef definition, proceed as though a normal variable declaration were being made. Then, place the new type name where the variable name would normally appear. Finally, in front of everything, place the keyword typedef.

As an example,

```
typedef struct
{
    float x;
    float y;
} POINT;
```

associates the name POINT with a structure containing two floating-point members called x and y. Variables can subsequently be declared to be of type POINT, like so:

```
POINT origin = { 0.0, 0.0 };
```

Type Modifiers: const, volatile, and restrict

The keyword const can be placed before a type declaration to tell the compiler the value cannot be modified. So, the declaration

```
const int x5 = 100;
```

declares x5 to be a constant integer. (That is, it won't be set to anything else during the program's execution.) The compiler is not required to flag attempts to change the value of a const variable.

The volatile modifier explicitly tells the compiler that the value changes (usually dynamically). When a volatile variable is used in an expression, its value is accessed each place it appears.

To declare port17 to be of type "volatile pointer to char," you would write this line:

```
char *volatile port17;
```

The `restrict` keyword can be used with pointers. It is a hint to the compiler for optimization (similar to the `register` keyword for variables). The `restrict` keyword specifies to the compiler that the pointer will be the only reference to a particular object—that is, it will not be referenced by any other pointer within the same scope. The lines

```
int * restrict intPtrA;
int * restrict intPtrB;
```

tell the compiler that, for the duration of the scope in which `intPtrA` and `intPtrB` are defined, they will never access the same value. Their use for pointing to integers (in an array, for example) is mutually exclusive.

Expressions

Variable names, function names, message expressions, array names, constants, function calls, array references, and structure and union references are all considered expressions. Applying a unary operator (where appropriate) to one of these expressions is also an expression, as is combining two or more of these expressions with a binary or ternary operator. Finally, an expression enclosed within parentheses is also an expression.

An expression of any type other than `void` that identifies a data object is called an *lvalue*. If it can be assigned a value, it is known as a *modifiable lvalue*.

Modifiable lvalue expressions are required in certain places. The expression on the left side of an assignment operator must be a modifiable lvalue. The unary address operator can be applied only to a modifiable `lvalue` or a function name. Finally, the increment and decrement operators can be applied only to modifiable lvalues.

Summary of Objective-C Operators

Table B.4 summarizes the various operators in the Objective-C language. These operators are listed in order of decreasing precedence, and operators grouped together have the same precedence.

As an example of how to use Table B.4, consider the following expression:

```
b | c & d * e
```

The multiplication operator has higher precedence than both the bitwise OR and bitwise AND operators because it appears above both of these in Table B.4. Similarly, the bitwise AND operator has higher precedence than the bitwise OR operator because the former appears above the latter in the table. Therefore, this expression would be evaluated as

```
b | ( c & ( d * e ) )
```

Now, consider the following expression:

```
b % c * d
```

Table B.4 **Summary of Objective-C Operators**

Operator	Description	Associativity
()	Function call	
[]	Array element reference or message expression	
->	Pointer to structure member reference	Left to right
.	Structure member reference or method call	
-	Unary minus	
+	Unary plus	
++	Increment	
--	Decrement	
!	Logical negation	
~	Ones complement	Right to left
*	Pointer reference (indirection)	
&	Address	
sizeof	Size of an object	
(type)	Type cast (conversion)	
*	Multiplication	
/	Division	Left to right
%	Modulus	
+	Addition	Left to right
-	Subtraction	
<<	Left shift	Left to right
>>	Right shift	
<	Less than	
<=	Less than or equal to	Left to right
>	Greater than	
>=	Greater than or equal to	
==	Equality	Left to right
!=	Inequality	
&	Bitwise AND	Left to right

Table B.4   **Summary of Objective-C Operators**

Operator	Description	Associativity
^	Bitwise XOR	Left to right
|	Bitwise OR	Left to right
&&	Logical AND	Left to right
||	Logical OR	Left to right
? :	Conditional	Right to left
= *= /= %= += -= &= ^= |= <<= >>=	Assignment operators	Right to left
,	Comma operator	Right to left

Because the modulus and multiplication operators appear in the same grouping in Table B.4, they have the same precedence. The associativity listed for these operators is left to right, indicating that the expression would be evaluated as follows:

```
( b % c ) * d
```

As another example, the expression

```
++a->b
```

would be evaluated as

```
++(a->b)
```

because the -> operator has higher precedence than the ++ operator.

Finally, because the assignment operators group from right to left, the statement

```
a = b = 0;
```

would be evaluated as

```
a = (b = 0);
```

which would have the net result of setting the values of a and b to 0. In the case of the expression

```
x[i] + ++i
```

it is not defined whether the compiler will evaluate the left side of the plus operator or the right side first. Here, the way that it's done affects the result because the value of i might be incremented before x[i] is evaluated.

Another case in which the order of evaluation is not defined is in the expression shown here:

```
x[i] = ++i
```

In this situation, it is not defined whether the value of i will be incremented before or after its value is used to index into x.

The order of evaluation of function and method arguments is also undefined. Therefore, in the function call

```
f (i, ++i);
```

or in the message expression

```
[myFract setTo: i over: ++i];
```

i might be incremented first, thereby causing the same value to be sent as the two arguments to the function or method.

The Objective-C language guarantees that the && and || operators will be evaluated from left to right. Furthermore, in the case of &&, it is guaranteed that the second operand will not be evaluated if the first is 0; in the case of ||, it is guaranteed that the second operand will not be evaluated if the first is nonzero. This fact is worth considering when forming expressions such as

```
if ( dataFlag || [myData checkData] )
  . . .
```

because, in this case, checkData is invoked only if the value of dataFlag is 0. As another example, if the array object a is defined to contain n elements, the statement that begins

```
if (index >= 0 && index < n && ([a objectAtIndex: index] == 0))
  . . .
```

references the element contained in the array only if index is a valid subscript into the array.

Constant Expressions

A *constant* expression is an expression in which each of the terms is a constant value. Constant expressions are required in the following situations:

1. As the value after a case in a `switch` statement

2. For specifying the size of an array

3. For assigning a value to an enumeration identifier

4. For specifying the bit field size in a structure definition

5. For assigning initial values to external or static variables

6. For specifying initial values to global variables

7. As the expression following the `#if` in a `#if` preprocessor statement

In the first four cases, the constant expression must consist of integer constants, character constants, enumeration constants, and `sizeof` expressions. The only operators that can be used are the arithmetic operators, bitwise operators, relational operators, conditional expression operator, and type cast operator.

In the fifth and sixth cases, in addition to the rules cited earlier, the address operator can be implicitly or explicitly used. However, it can be applied only to external or static variables or functions. So, for example, the expression

```
&x + 10
```

would be a valid constant expression, provided that x is an external or static variable. Furthermore, the expression

```
&a[10] - 5
```

is a valid constant expression if a is an external or static array. Finally, because &a[0] is equivalent to the expression a

```
a + sizeof (char) * 100
```

is also a valid constant expression.

For the last situation that requires a constant expression (after the `#if`), the rules are the same as for the first four cases, except the `sizeof` operator, enumeration constants, and type cast operator cannot be used. However, the special `defined` operator is permitted (see the section "The #if Directive").

Arithmetic Operators

Given that

a, b	are expressions of any basic data type except void;
i, j	are expressions of any integer data type;

the expression

-a	negates the value of a;
+a	gives the value of a;
a + b	adds a with b;
a - b	subtracts b from a;
a * b	multiplies a by b;
a / b	divides a by b;
i % j	gives the remainder of i divided by j.

In each expression, the usual arithmetic conversions are performed on the operands (see the section "Conversion of Basic Data Types"). If a is unsigned, -a is calculated by first applying integral promotion to it, subtracting it from the largest value of the promoted type, and adding 1 to the result.

If two integral values are divided, the result is truncated. If either operand is negative, the direction of the truncation is not defined (that is, −3 / 2 can produce −1 on some machines and −2 on others); otherwise, truncation is always toward 0 (3 / 2 always produces 1). See the section "Basic Operations with Pointers" for a summary of arithmetic operations with pointers.

Logical Operators

Given that

a, b	are expressions of any basic data type except void, or are both pointers;

the expression

a && b	has the value 1 if both a and b are nonzero and 0 otherwise (and b is evaluated only if a is nonzero);
a || b	has the value 1 if either a or b is nonzero and 0 otherwise (and b is evaluated only if a is 0);
! a	has the value 1 if a is 0, and 0 otherwise.

The usual arithmetic conversions are applied to a and b (see the section "Conversion of Basic Data Types"). The type of the result in all cases is int.

Relational Operators

Given that

a, b   are expressions of any basic data type except void, or are both pointers;

the expression

a < b   has the value 1 if a is less than b, and 0 otherwise;

a <= b   has the value 1 if a is less than or equal to b, and 0 otherwise;

a > b   has the value 1 if a is greater than b, and 0 otherwise;

a >= b   has the value 1 if a is greater than or equal to b, and 0 otherwise;

a == b   has the value 1 if a is equal to b, and 0 otherwise;

a != b   has the value 1 if a is not equal to b, and 0 otherwise.

The usual arithmetic conversions are performed on a and b (see the section "Conversion of Basic Data Types"). The first four relational tests are meaningful for pointers only if they both point into the same array or to members of the same structure or union. The type of the result in each case is int.

Bitwise Operators

Given that

i, j, n   are expressions of any integer data type; the expression

the expression

i & j   performs a bitwise AND of i and j;

i | j   performs a bitwise OR of i and j;

i ^ j   performs a bitwise XOR of i and j;

~i   takes the ones complement of i;

i << n   shifts i to the left n bits;

i >> n   shifts i to the right n bits.

The usual arithmetic conversions are performed on the operands, except with << and >>, in which case just integral promotion is performed on each operand (see the section "Conversion of Basic Data Types"). If the shift count is negative or is greater than or equal to the number of bits contained in the object being shifted, the result of the shift is undefined. On some machines, a right shift is arithmetic (sign fill) and on others logical (zero fill). The type of the result of a shift operation is that of the promoted left operand.

Increment and Decrement Operators

Given that

l   is a modifiable lvalue expression, whose type is not qualified as const;

the expression

++l   increments l and then uses its value as the value of the expression;

l++   uses l as the value of the expression and then increments l;

--l   decrements l and then uses its value as the value of the expression;

l--   uses l as the value of the expression and then decrements l.

The section "Basic Operations with Pointers" describes these operations on pointers.

Assignment Operators

Given that

l   is a modifiable lvalue expression, whose type is not qualified as const;

op   is any operator that can be used as an assignment operator (see Table B.4);

a   is an expression;

the expression

l = a   stores the value of a into l;

l op= a   applies op to l and a, storing the result into l.

In the first expression, if a is one of the basic data types (except void), it is converted to match the type of l. If l is a pointer, a must be a pointer to the same type as l, a void pointer, or the null pointer.

If l is a void pointer, a can be of any pointer type. The second expression is treated as if it were written l = l *op* (a), except l is evaluated only once (consider x[i++] += 10).

Conditional Operator

Given that

a, b, c   are expressions;

the expression

a ? b : c   has as its value b if a is nonzero, and c otherwise. Only expression b or c is evaluated.

Expressions b and c must be of the same data type. If they are not, but are both arithmetic data types, the usual arithmetic conversions are applied to make their types the same. If one is a pointer and the other is 0, the latter is taken as a null pointer of the same type as the former. If one is a pointer to void and the other is a pointer to another type, the latter is converted to be a pointer to void and is the resulting type.

Type Cast Operator

Given that

type   is the name of a basic data type, an enumerated data type (preceded by the keyword enum), or a typedef-defined type, or is a derived data type;

a   is an expression;

the expression

(*type*)   converts a to the specified type.

Note that the use of a parenthesized type in a method declaration or definition is not an example of the use of the type cast operator.

sizeof Operator

Given that

type   is as described previously;

a   is an expression;

the expression

sizeof   has as its value the number of bytes needed to contain a value of the
(type)   specified type;

sizeof a   has as its value the number of bytes required to hold the result of the evalua-
           tion of a.

If type is char, the result is defined to be 1. If a is the name of an array that has been dimensioned (either explicitly or implicitly through initialization) and is not a formal parameter or undimensioned extern array, sizeof a gives the number of bytes required to store the elements in a.

If a is the name of a class, sizeof (a) gives the size of the data structure needed to hold an instance of a.

The type of the integer produced by the sizeof operator is size_t, which is defined in the standard header file <stddef.h>.

If a is a variable length array, then the expression is evaluated at runtime; otherwise, it is evaluated at compile time and can be used in constant expressions (refer to the section "Constant Expressions").

Comma Operator

Given that

a, b   are expressions;

the expression

a, b   causes a to be evaluated and then b to be evaluated. The type and value of the
          expression are that of b.

Basic Operations with Arrays

Given that

a   is declared as an array of *n* elements;

i   is an expression of any integer data type;

v   is an expression;

the expression

a[0]   references the first element of a;

a[n - 1]   references the last element of a;

a[i]   references element number i of a;

a[i] = v   stores the value of v into a[i].

In each case, the type of the result is the type of the elements contained in a. See the section "Basic Operations with Pointers" for a summary of operations with pointers and arrays.

Basic Operations with Structures

> **Note**
>
> This also applies to unions.

Given that

x   is a modifiable lvalue expression of type struct *s*;

y   is an expression of type struct *s*;

m   is the name of one of the members of the structure *s*;

obj   is any object;

M   is any method;

v   is an expression;

the expression

x   references the entire structure and is of type struct *s*;

y.m   references the member m of the structure y and is of the type declared for the member m;

`x.m = v`	assigns v to the member m of x and is of the type declared for the member m;
`x = y`	assigns y to x and is of type struct *s*;
`f (y)`	calls the function f, passing contents of the structure y as the argument (inside f, the formal parameter must be declared to be of type `struct` *s*);
`[obj M: y]`	invokes the method M on the object obj, passing the contents of the structure y as the argument (inside the method, the parameter must be declared to be of type `struct` *s*);
`return y;`	returns the structure y (the return type declared for the function or method must be `struct` *s*).

Basic Operations with Pointers

Given that

x	is an lvalue expression of type t;
pt	is a modifiable lvalue expression of type "pointer to *t*";
v	is an expression;

the expression

`&x`	produces a pointer to x and has type "pointer to *t*";
`pt = &x`	sets pt pointing to x and has type "pointer to *t*";
`pt = 0`	assigns the null pointer to pt;
`pt == 0`	tests whether pt is null;
`*pt`	references the value pointed to by pt and has type *t*;
`*pt = v`	stores the value of v into the location pointed to by pt and has type t.

Pointers to Arrays

Given that

a	is an array of elements of type *t;*
pa1	is a modifiable lvalue expression of type "pointer to *t*" that points to an element in a;
pa2	is an lvalue expression of type "pointer to *t*" that points to an element in a, or to one past the last element in *a;*
v	is an expression;
n	is an integral expression;

the expression

a, &a, &a[0]	each produces a pointer to the first element;
&a[n]	produces a pointer to element number n of a and has type "pointer to *t*";
*pa1	references the element of a that pa1 points to and has type *t;*
*pa1 = v	stores the value of v into the element pointed to by pa1 and has type *t;*
++pa1	sets pa1 pointing to the next element of a, no matter which type of elements is contained in a, and has type "pointer to *t*";
--pa1	sets pa1 pointing to the previous element of a, no matter which type of elements is contained in a, and has type "pointer to *t*";
*++pa1	increments pa1 and then references the value in a that pa1 points to and has type *t;*
*pa1++	references the value in a that pa1 points to before incrementing pa1 and has type *t;*
pa1 + n	produces a pointer that points n elements further into a than pa1 and has type "pointer to *t*";
pa1 - n	produces a pointer to a that points n elements previous to that pointed to by pa1 and has type "pointer to *t*";
*(pa1 + n)	stores the value of v into the element pointed to by pa1 + n and has = v type *t;*
pa1 < pa2	tests whether pa1 is pointing to an earlier element in a than is pa2 and has type int (any relational operators can be used to compare two pointers);

`pa2 - pa1`   produces the number of elements in a contained between the pointers `pa2` and `pa1` (assuming that `pa2` points to an element further in `a` than `pa1`) and has integer type;

`a + n`   produces a pointer to element number n of `a`, has type "pointer to t," and is in all ways equivalent to the expression `&a[n]`;

`*(a + n)`   references element number n of `a`, has type t, and is in all ways equivalent to the expression `a[n]`.

The actual type of the integer produced by subtracting two pointers is specified by `ptrdiff_t`, which is defined in the standard header file <stddef.h>.

Pointers to Structures

Given that

`x`   is an lvalue expression of type `struct s`;

`ps`   is a modifiable lvalue expression of type "pointer to `struct s`";

`m`   is the name of a member of the structure s and is of type t;

`v`   is an expression;

the expression

`&x`   produces a pointer to x and is of type "pointer to `struct s`";

`ps = &x`   sets ps pointing to x and is of type "pointer to `struct s`";

`ps->m`   references member `m` of the structure pointed to by `ps` and is of type t;

`(*ps).m`   also references this member and is in all ways equivalent to the expression `ps->m`;

`ps->m = v`   stores the value of v into the member `m` of the structure pointed to by `ps` and is of type t

Compound Literals

A *compound literal* is a type name enclosed in parentheses followed by an initialization list. It creates an unnamed value of the specified type, which has scope limited to the block in which it is created, or global scope if defined outside of any block. In the latter case, the initializers must all be constant expressions.

As an example,

```
(struct point) {.x = 0, .y = 0}
```

is an expression that produces a structure of type `struct point` with the specified initial values. This can be assigned to another `struct point` structure, like so:

```
origin = (struct point) {.x = 0, .y = 0};
```

Or it can be passed to a function or method expecting an argument of `struct point`, like so:

```
moveToPoint ((struct point) {.x = 0, .y = 0});
```

Types other than structures can be defined as well—for example, if `intPtr` is of type `int *`, the statement

```
intPtr = (int [100]) {[0] = 1, [50] = 50, [99] = 99 };
```

(which can appear anywhere in the program) sets `intptr` pointing to an array of 100 integers, whose 3 elements are initialized as specified.

If the size of the array is not specified, it is determined by the initializer list.

Conversion of Basic Data Types

The Objective-C language converts operands in arithmetic expressions in a predefined order, known as the *usual arithmetic conversions*:

1. If either operand is of type `long double`, the other is converted to `long double` and that is the type of the result.

2. If either operand is of type `double`, the other is converted to `double` and that is the type of the result.

3. If either operand is of type `float`, the other is converted to `float` and that is the type of the result.

4. If either operand is of type `_Bool`, `char`, `short int`, `int` bit field, or an enumerated data type, it is converted to `int`, if an `int` can fully represent its range of values; otherwise, it is converted to `unsigned int`. If both operands are of the same type, that is the type of the result.

5. If both operands are signed or both are unsigned, the smaller integer type is converted to the larger integer type and that is the type of the result.

6. If the unsigned operand is equal in size or larger than the signed operand, the signed operand is converted to the type of the unsigned operand, and that is the type of the result.

7. If the signed operand can represent all the values in the unsigned operand, the latter is converted to the type of the former if it can fully represent its range of values, and that is the type of the result.

8. If this step is reached, both operands are converted to the unsigned type corresponding to the type of the signed type.

Step 4 is known more formally as *integral promotion*.

Conversion of operands is well behaved in most situations, although the following points should be noted:

1. Conversion of a `char` to an `int` can involve sign extension on some machines, unless the `char` is declared as `unsigned`.

2. Conversion of a signed integer to a longer integer results in extension of the sign to the left; conversion of an unsigned integer to a longer integer results in zero fill to the left.

3. Conversion of any value to a `_Bool` results in `0` if the value is zero and `1` otherwise.

4. Conversion of a longer integer to a shorter one results in truncation of the integer on the left.

5. Conversion of a floating-point value to an integer results in truncation of the decimal portion of the value. If the integer is not large enough to contain the converted floating-point value, the result is not defined, as is the result of converting a negative floating-point value to an unsigned integer.

6. Conversion of a longer floating-point value to a shorter one might or might not result in rounding before the truncation occurs.

Storage Classes and Scope

The term *storage class* refers to the manner in which memory is allocated by the compiler in the case of variables and to the scope of a particular function or method definition. Storage classes are `auto`, `static`, `extern`, and `register`. A storage class can be omitted in a declaration, and a default storage class will be assigned, as discussed next.

The term *scope* refers to the extent of the meaning of a particular identifier within a program. An identifier defined outside any function, method, or statement block (herein referred to as a *BLOCK*) can be referenced anywhere subsequent in the file. Identifiers defined within a BLOCK are local to that BLOCK and can locally redefine an identifier defined outside it. Label names are known throughout the BLOCK, as are formal parameter names. Labels, instance variables, structure and structure member names, union and union member names, and enumerated type names do not have to be distinct from each other or from variable, function, or method names. However, enumeration identifiers do have to be distinct from variable names and from other enumeration identifiers defined within the same scope. Class names have global scope and must be distinct from other variables and type names with the same scope.

Functions

If a storage class is specified when a function is defined, it must be either `static` or `extern`. Functions that are declared `static` can be referenced only from within the same file that contains the function. Functions specified as `extern` (or that have no class specified) can be called by functions or methods from other files.

Variables

Table B.5 summarizes the various storage classes that can be used in declaring variables as well as their scopes and methods of initialization.

Table B.5   **Variables: Summary of Storage Classes, Scope, and Initialization.**

If storage class is	And variable is declared	Then it can be referenced	And be initialized with	Comments
static	Outside any BLOCK	Anywhere within the file	Constant expression only	Variables are initialized only once at the start of program execution; values are retained through BLOCKS; the default value is 0
	Inside a Block	Within the Block		
extern	Outside any BLOCK	Anywhere within the file	Constant expression only	Variable must be declared in at least one place without the `extern` keyword, or in one place using the keyword `extern` and assigned an initial value
	Inside a BLOCK	Within the BLOCK		
auto	Inside a BLOCK	Within the BLOCK	Any valid expression	Variable is initialized each time the BLOCK is entered; no default value

Table B.5   **Variables: Summary of Storage Classes, Scope, and Initialization.**

If storage class is	And variable is declared	Then it can be referenced	And be initialized with	Comments
`register`	Inside a BLOCK	Within the BLOCK	Any valid expression	Assignment `register` not guaranteed; varying restrictions on types of variables that can be declared; cannot take the address of a `register` variable; initialized each time BLOCK is entered; no default value
`omitted`	Outside any BLOCK	Anywhere within the file or by other files that contain appropriate declarations	Constant expressions only	This declaration can appear in only one place; the variable is initialized at the start of program execution; the default value is `0`; it defaults to `auto`
	Inside a BLOCK	(See `auto`)	(See `auto`)	

Instance Variables

Instance variables can be accessed by any instance method defined for the class, either in the `interface` section that explicitly defines the variable or in categories created for the class. Inherited instance variables can also be accessed directly without any special declarations. Class methods do not have access to instance variables.

The special directives `@private`, `@protected`, and `@public` can be used to control the scope of an instance variable. After these directives appear, they remain in effect until the closing curly brace ending the declaration of the instance variables is encountered or until another of the three listed directives is used. For example, the following begins an interface declaration for a class called `Point` containing four instance variables:

```
@interface  Point: NSObject
{
@private
    int internalID;
@protected
    float x;
    float y;
@public
    BOOL valid;
}
```

The `internalID` variable is `private`, the `x` and `y` variables are `protected` (the default), and the `valid` variable is public.

These directives are summarized in Table B.6.

Table B.6   **Scope of Instance Variables**

If variable is declared after this directive...	...then it can be referenced...	Comments
`@protected`	By instance methods in the class, instance methods in subclasses, and instance methods in category extensions to the class	This is the default.
`@private`	By instance methods in the class and instance methods in any category extensions to the class, but not by any subclasses	This restricts access to the class itself.
`@public`	By instance methods in the class, instance methods in subclasses, and instance methods in category extensions to the class; it can also be accessed from other functions or methods by applying the structure pointer indirection operator (`->`) to an instance of the class followed by the name of the instance variable (as in `myFract->numerator`)	This should not be used unless necessary; it defeats the notion of data encapsulation.

Functions

This section summarizes the syntax and operation of functions.

Function Definition

General Format:

```
returnType  name ( type1 param1, type2 param2, .. )
{
    variableDeclarations

    programStatement
    programStatement
    . . .
    return expression;
}
```

The function called *name* is defined, which returns a value of type *returnType* and has formal parameters *param1, param2, ... param1* is declared to be of type *type1, param2* of type *type2,* and so on.

Local variables are typically declared at the beginning of the function, but that's not required. They can be declared anywhere, in which case their access is limited to statements appearing after their declaration in the function.

If the function does not return a value, *returnType* is specified as void.

If just void is specified inside the parentheses, the function takes no arguments. If .. is used as the last (or only) parameter in the list, the function takes a variable number of arguments, as in the following:

```
int printf (char *format, ...)
{
    . . .
}
```

Declarations for single-dimensional array arguments do not have to specify the number of elements in the array. For multidimensional arrays, the size of each dimension except the first must be specified.

See the section "The return Statement" for a discussion of the return statement.

An older way of defining functions is still supported. The general format is

```
returnType  name (param1, param2, .. )
param_declarations
{
    variableDeclarations
    programStatement
    programStatement
    . . .
    return expression;
}
```

Here, just the parameter names are listed inside the parentheses. If no arguments are expected, nothing appears between the left and right parentheses. The type of each parameter is declared outside the parentheses and before the opening curly brace of the function definition. For example, the following defines a function called `rotate` that takes two arguments called `value` and n:

```
unsigned int rotate (value, n)
unsigned int value;
int n;
{
    ...
}
```

The first argument is an `unsigned int`, and the second is an `int`.

The keyword `inline` can be placed in front of a function definition as a hint to the compiler. Some compilers replace the function call with the actual code for the function itself, thus providing for faster execution. An example is shown here:

```
inline int min (int a, int b)
{
    return ( a < b ? a : b);
}
```

Function Call

General Format:

name (*arg1*, *arg2*, ..)

The function called *name* is called and the values *arg1*, *arg2*, ... are passed as arguments to the function. If the function takes no arguments, just the open and closed parentheses are specified (as in `initialize ()`).

If you are calling a function that is defined after the call, or in another file, you should include a prototype declaration for the function, which has the following general format:

returnType name (*type1 param1*, *type2 param2*, ..) ;

This tells the compiler the function's return type, the number of arguments it takes, and the type of each argument. As an example, the line

```
long double power (double x, int n);
```

declares `power` to be a function that returns a `long double` and that takes two arguments—the first of which is a `double` and the second of which is an `int`. The argument names inside the parentheses are actually dummy names and can be omitted if desired, so

```
long double power (double, int);
```

works just as well.

If the compiler has previously encountered the function definition or a prototype declaration for the function, the type of each argument is automatically converted (where possible) to match the type expected by the function when the function is called.

If neither the function's definition nor a prototype declaration has been encountered, the compiler assumes the function returns a value of type `int` and automatically converts all `float` arguments to type `double` and performs integral promotion on any integer arguments as outlined in the section *Conversion of Basic Data Types*. Other function arguments are passed without conversion.

Functions that take a variable number of arguments must be declared as such. Otherwise, the compiler is at liberty to assume the function takes a fixed number of arguments based on the number actually used in the call.

If the function were defined with the old-style format (refer to the section "Function Definition"), a declaration for the function takes the following format:

```
returnType name ();
```

Arguments to such functions are converted, as described in the previous paragraph.

A function whose return type is declared as `void` causes the compiler to flag any calls to that function that try to make use of a returned value.

All arguments to a function are passed by value; therefore, their values cannot be changed by the function. If, however, a pointer is passed to a function, the function can change values referenced by the pointer, but it still cannot change the value of the pointer variable itself.

Function Pointers

A function name, without a following set of parentheses, produces a pointer to that function. The address operator can also be applied to a function name to produce a pointer to it.

If `fp` is a pointer to a function, the corresponding function can be called either by writing

```
fp ()
```

or

```
(*fp) ()
```

If the function takes arguments, they can be listed inside the parentheses.

Classes

This section summarizes the syntax and semantics associated with classes.

Class Definition

A class definition consists of declaring the instance variables and methods in an interface section and defining the code for each method in an implementation section.

Interface Section
General Format:

```
@interface className : parentClass <protocol, ...>
{
    instanceVariableDeclarations
}
methodDeclaration
methodDeclaration
    ...
@end
```

The class *className* is declared with the parent class *parentClass*. If *className* also adopts one or more formal protocols, the protocol names are listed inside a pair of angular brackets after *parentClass*. In that case, the corresponding implementation section must contain definitions for all such methods in the listed protocols.

If the colon and *parentClass* are omitted, a new root class is declared.

Instance Variable Declarations

The optional *instanceVariableDeclarations* section lists the type and name of each instance variable for the class. Each instance of *className* gets its own set of these variables, plus any variables inherited from *parentClass*. All such variables can be referenced directly by name either by instance methods defined in *className* or by any subclasses of *className*. If access has been restricted with an @private directive, subclasses cannot access the variables declared as such (refer to the section "Instance Variables").

Class methods do not have access to instance variables.

Property Declarations
General Format:

```
@property (attributes) nameList;
```

This declares properties with the specified comma-separated list of attributes. *nameList* is a comma-separated list of property names of a declared type:

```
(type) propertyName1, propertyName2, propertyName3,...
```

An @property directive can appear anywhere inside the method declaration section for a class, protocol, or category.

Table B.7   **Property Attributes**

Attribute	Meaning
assign	Use simple assignment to set the value of the instance variable in the setter method. (This is a default attribute.)
copy	Use the `copy` method to set the value of the instance variable.
getter=*name*	Use *name* for the name of the getter method instead of *propertyName*, which is the default for the synthesized getter method.
nonatomic	The value from a synthesized getter method can be returned directly. If this attribute is not declared, then the accessor methods are atomic—meaning access to the instance variables is mutex-locked. This provides protection in a multithreaded environment by ensuring the get or set operation runs in a single thread. Further, by default, in a nongarbage-collected environment, the synthesized getter method retains and autoreleases the property before its value is returned.
readonly	The property's value cannot be set. No setter method is expected from the compiler, nor will one be synthesized. (This is a default attribute.)
readwrite	The property's value can be retrieved and set. The compiler expects you to provide both getter and setter methods or will synthesize both methods if `@synthesize` is used.
retain	The property should be retained on assignment. This can only be specified for Objective-C types.
setter=*name*	Use *name* for the name of the setter method instead of *setPropertyName*, which is the default for the synthesized accessor method.

You can only specify one of the attributes `assign`, `copy`, or `retain`. If you don't use garbage collection, then one of these attributes should be explicitly used; otherwise you will get a warning from the compiler. If you use garbage collection and you don't specify one of these three attributes, the default attribute, `assign`, will be used. In that case, the compiler gives a warning only if the class conforms to the NSCopying protocol (in which case you might want to copy and not assign the property).

If you use the `copy` attribute, the object's `copy` method will be used by the synthesized setter method. This results in an immutable copy. You must supply your own setter method if you need a mutable copy instead.

Method Declaration
General Format:

$mType$ $(returnType)$ $name_1$: $(type1)$ $param1$ $name_2$: $(type2)$ $param2$, ...;

The method $name_1$:$name_2$:.. is declared, which returns a value of type $returnType$ and has formal parameters $param1$, $param2$, ... $param1$ is declared to be of type $type1$, $param2$ is declared to be of type $type2$, and so on.

Any of the names after $name_1$ (meaning $name_2$, ...) can be omitted, in which case a colon is still used as a placeholder and becomes part of the method name (see the following example).

If $mType$ is +, a class method is declared, but if $mType$ is -, an instance method is declared.

If the declared method is inherited from a parent class, the parent's definition is overridden by the new definition. In such a case, the method from the parent class can still be accessed by sending a message to super.

Class methods are invoked when a corresponding message is sent to a class object, whereas instance methods are invoked when a corresponding message is sent to an instance of the class. Class methods and instance methods can have the same name.

The same method name can also be used by different classes. The capability of objects from different classes to respond to the same named method is known as *polymorphism*.

If the method does not return a value, $returnType$ is void. If the function returns an id value, $returnType$ can be omitted, although specifying id as the return type is better programming practice.

If , ... is used as the last (or only) parameter in the list, the method takes a variable number of arguments, as in

```
-(void) print: (NSSTRING *) format, ...
{
  ...
}
```

As an example of a class declaration, the following interface declaration section declares a class called Fraction whose parent is NSObject:

```
@interface Fraction: NSObject
{
  int numerator, denominator;
}
+(Fraction *) newFract;
-(void) setTo: (int) n : (int) d;
-(void) setNumerator: (int) n andDenominator: (int) d;
-(int)  numerator;
-(int)  denominator;
@end
```

The Fraction class has two integer instance variables called numerator and denominator. It also has one class method called newFract, which returns a Fraction

object. It has two instance methods called `setTo::` and
`setNumerator:andDenominator:`, each of which takes two arguments and does not return a value. It also has two instance methods called `numerator` and `denominator` that
take no arguments and return an `int`.

Implementation Section
General Format:

```
@implementation className;
    methodDefinition
    methodDefinition
    ...
@end
```

The class called *className* is defined. The parent class and instance variables are not
typically redeclared in the implementation section (although they can be) because they
have been previously declared in the interface section.

Unless the methods for a category are being implemented (see the section "Category
Definition"), all the methods declared in the interface section must be defined in the implementation section. If one or more protocols were listed in the interface section, all the
protocols' methods must be defined—either implicitly through inheritance or explicitly
by definition in the implementation section.

Each *methodDefinition* contains the code that will be executed when the method is
invoked.

Method Definition
General Format:

```
mType (returnType)  name₁ : (type1) param1 : name₂ (type2) param2, ...
{
    variableDeclarations

    programStatement
    programStatement
    ...
    return expression;
}
```

The method $name_1$:$name_2$: ... is defined, which returns a value of type *returnType*
and has formal parameters *param1, param2, ... param1* is declared to be of type *type1*,
param2 is declared to be of type *type2*, and so on. If *mType* is +, a class method is defined;
if *mType* is -, an instance method is defined. This method declaration must be consistent
with the corresponding method declaration from the interface section or from a previously defined protocol definition.

An instance method can reference the class's instance variables and any variables it has inherited directly by name. If a class method is being defined, it cannot reference any instance variables.

The identifier `self` can be used inside a method to reference the object on which the method was invoked—that is, the *receiver* of the message.

The identifier `super` can be used inside a method to reference the parent class of the object on which the method was invoked.

If *returnType* is not void, one or more `return` statements with expressions of type *returnType* must appear in the method definition. If *returnType* is void, use of a return statement is optional, and if used, it cannot contain a value to return.

As an example of a method definition, the following defines a `setNumerator:andDenominator:` method in accordance with its declaration (refer to the section "Method Declaration"):

```
-(void) setNumerator: (int) n andDenominator: (int) d
{
    numerator = n;
    denominator = d;
}
```

The method sets its two instance variables to the supplied arguments and does not execute a return (although it could) because the method is declared to return no value.

Declarations for single-dimensional array arguments do not have to specify the number of elements in the array. For multidimensional arrays, the size of each dimension except the first must be specified.

Local variables can be declared inside a method and are typically declared at the start of the method definition. Automatic local variables are allocated when the method is invoked and deallocated when the method is exited.

See the section "The `return` Statement" for a discussion of the `return` statement.

Synthesized Accessor Methods
General Format:

```
@synthesize property_1, property_2, ...
```

This specifies that methods should be synthesized for the listed properties *property_1*, *property_2*, ...

The notation

```
property=instance_var
```

can be used in the list to specify that *property* will be associated with the instance variable *instance_var*. The synthesized methods will have characteristics based on attributes declared for the property through a prior `@property` directive.

Category Definition

General Format:

```
@interface className (categoryName) <protocol,...>
 methodDeclaration
 methodDeclaration
    ...
@end
```

This defines the category *categoryName* for the class specified by *className* with the associated listed methods. If one or more protocols are listed, the category adopts the listed protocols.

The compiler must know about *className* through a previous @interface section declaration for the class.

You can define as many categories as you want in as many different source files as you want. The listed methods become part of the class and are inherited by subclasses.

Categories are uniquely defined by *className/categoryName* pairs. For example, in a given program there can be only one NSArray (Private) category. However, individual category names can be reused. So, a given program can include an NSArray (Private) category and an NSString (Private) category, and both categories will be distinct from each other.

You do not need to implement the methods defined in a category that you do not intend to use.

A category can only extend the definition of a class with additional methods, or it can override existing methods in the class. It cannot define any new instance variables for the class.

If more than one category declares a method with the same name for the same class, it does not define which method will be executed when invoked.

As an example, the following defines a category for the Complex class called ComplexOps, with four instance methods:

```
#import "Complex.h"
@interface Complex (ComplexOps)
-(Complex *) abs;
-(Complex *) exp;
-(Complex *) log;
-(Complex *) sqrt;
@end
```

Presumably, a corresponding implementation section appears somewhere that implements one or more of these methods:

```
#import "ComplexOps.h"
@implementation Complex (ComplexOps)
-(Complex *) abs
{
    ...
```

```
}
-(Complex *) exp
{
   ...
}
-(Complex *) log
{
   ...
}
-(Complex *) sqrt
{
   ...
}
@end
```

A category that defines methods meant for other subclasses to implement is known as an *informal* protocol or *abstract* category. Unlike formal protocols, the compiler does not perform any checks for conformance to an informal protocol. At runtime, an object might or might not test for conformance to an informal protocol on an individual method basis. For example, one method might be required at runtime, whereas another method in the same protocol might not.

Protocol Definition

General Format:

```
@protocol protocolName <protocol, ...>
    methodDeclarations
@optional
    methodDeclarations
@required
    methodDeclarations
...
@end
```

The protocol called *protocolName* is defined with associated methods. If other protocols are listed, *protocolName* also adopts the listed protocols.

This definition is known as a formal protocol definition.

A class conforms to the *protocolName* protocol if it defines or inherits all the required methods declared in the protocol plus all the methods of any other listed protocols. The compiler checks for conformance and generates a warning if a class does not conform to a declared formal protocol. Objects might or might not be tested for conformance to a formal protocol at runtime.

The @optional directive can precede a list of methods whose implementation is optional. An @required directive can subsequently be used to resume the list of required methods that must be implemented for conformance to the protocol.

Protocols are often not associated with any particular class but provide a way to define a common interface that is shared among classes.

Special Type Modifiers

The method parameters and return type declared in protocols can use the type qualifiers listed in Table B.8. These qualifiers are used for distributed object applications.

Table B.8   **Special Protocol Type Modifiers**

Qualifier	Meaning
in	The argument references an object whose value will be changed by the sender and sent (that is, copied) back to the receiver.
out	The argument references an object whose value will be changed by the receiver and sent back to the sender.
inout	The argument references an object whose value will be set by both the sender and the receiver and will be sent back and forth; this is the default.
oneway	It's used for return type declarations; typically (one way void) is used to specify that the invoker of this method does not have to wait for a return value—that is, the method can execute asynchronously.
bycopy	The argument or return value is to be copied.
byref	The argument or return value is passed by reference and not copied.

Object Declaration

General Format:

className *var1, *var2, ...;

This defines *var1*, *var2*, ... to be objects from the class *className*. Note that this declares pointer variables and does not reserve space for the actual data contained in each object. The declaration

```
Fraction *myFract;
```

defines myFract as a Fraction object or, technically, as a pointer to one. To allocate the actual space for the data structure of a Fraction, the alloc or new method is typically invoked on the class, like so:

```
myFract = [Fraction alloc];
```

This causes enough space to be reserved for a Fraction object and a pointer to it to be returned and assigned to myFract. The variable myFract is often referred to as an object or as an *instance* of the Fraction class. As the alloc method in the root object is defined, a newly allocated object has all its instance variables set to 0. However, that does not mean the object has been properly initialized and an initialization method (like init) should be invoked on the object before it is used.

Because the myFract variable has been explicitly declared as an object from the Fraction class, the variable is said to be *statically* typed. The compiler can check the use of statically typed variables for consistency by consulting the class definition for proper use of methods and their arguments and return types.

id Object Declaration

General Format:

id <*protocol,...*> *var1*, *var2*, ...;

This declares *var1*, *var2*, ... to be objects from an indeterminate class that conform to the protocols listed in the angular brackets. The protocol list is optional.

Objects from any class can be assigned to id variables, and vice versa. If one or more protocols is listed, the compiler checks that methods used from the listed protocols on any of the declared variables are used in a consistent manner—that is, consistent with respect to argument and return types for the methods declared in the formal protocol.

For example, in the statements

```
id <MathOps> number;
    ...
result = [number add: number2];
```

the compiler checks whether the MathOps protocol defines an add: method. If it does, it then checks for consistency with respect to the argument and return types for that method. So, if the `add:` method takes an integer argument and you are passing it a `Fraction` object above, the compiler complains.

The system keeps track of the class to which each object belongs; therefore, at runtime it can determine the class of an object and then select the correct method to invoke. These two processes are known as *dynamic typing* and *dynamic binding*, respectively.

Message Expressions

Format 1:

`[receiver name_1: arg1 name_2: arg2, name_3: arg3 .. ]`

The method $name_1:name_2:name_3$ ... from the class specified by `receiver` is invoked and the values `arg1, arg2`, ... are passed as arguments. This is called a *message expression*. The value of the expression is the value returned by the method, or `void` if the method is declared as such and returns no value. The type of the expression is that of the type declared for the method invoked.

Format 2:

`[receiver name];`

If a method takes no arguments, this format is used to invoked the method name from the class specified by receiver.

If `receiver` is an `id` type, the compiler looks among the declared classes for a definition or inherited definition of the specified method. If no such definition is found, the compiler issues a warning that the receiver might not respond to the specified message. It further assumes the method returns a value of type id and converts any float arguments to type double and performs integral promotion on any integer arguments as outlined earlier in the section "Conversion of Basic Data Types." Other method arguments are passed without conversion.

If `receiver` is a `class` object (which can be created by simply specifying the class name), the specified `class` method is invoked. Otherwise, `receiver` is an instance of a class, and the corresponding instance method is invoked.

If `receiver` is a statically typed variable or expression, the compiler looks in the class definition for the method (or for any inherited methods) and converts any arguments (where possible) to match the expected arguments for the method. So, a method expecting a floating value that is passed an integer has that argument automatically converted when the method is invoked.

If `receiver` is a null object pointer—that is, `nil`—it can be sent messages. If the method associated with the message returns an object, the value of the message expression is `nil`. If the method does not return an object, the value of the expression is not defined.

If the same method is defined in more than one class (either by explicit definition or from inheritance), the compiler checks for consistency for argument and return types among the classes.

All arguments to a method are passed by value; therefore, their values cannot be changed by the method. If a pointer is passed to a method, the method can change values referenced by the pointer, but it still cannot change the value of the pointer itself.

Format 3:

```
receiver.property
```

This calls the getter method (by default *property*) for *receiver*, unless this expression is used as an lvalue (see Format 4). The getter method name can be changed with an @property directive, in which case that will be the method that gets called.

If the default getter method name is used, then the previous expression is equivalent to the following:

```
[receiver property]
```

Format 4:

```
receiver.property = expression
```

This calls the setter method associated with the property *property*, passing as its argument the value of *expression*. By default, the setter method set*Property*: gets called, unless another setter method name was assigned to the property using a prior @property directive.

If the default setter property name is used, the previous expression is equivalent to writing the following:

```
[receiver setProperty: expression]
```

Statements

A program statement is any valid expression (usually an assignment or a function call) that is immediately followed by a semicolon, or it is one of the special statements described in the following. A *label* can optionally precede any statement and consists of an identifier followed immediately by a colon (see the goto statement).

Compound Statements

Program statements contained within a pair of braces are known collectively as a *compound* statement or *block* and can appear anywhere in the program that a single statement is permitted. A block can have its own set of variable declarations, which override any similarly named variables defined outside the block. The scope of such local variables is the block in which they are defined.

The break Statement

General Format:

```
break;
```

Execution of a `break` statement from within a `for`, `while`, `do`, or `switch` statement causes execution of that statement to be immediately terminated. Execution continues with the statement that immediately follows the loop or `switch`.

The `continue` Statement

General Format:

```
continue;
```

Execution of the `continue` statement from within a loop causes any statements that follow the `continue` in the loop to be skipped. Execution of the loop otherwise continues as normal.

The `do` Statement

General Format:

```
do
    programStatement
while ( expression );
```

programStatement is executed as long as *expression* evaluates to nonzero. Note that, because *expression* is evaluated each time after the execution of *programStatement*, it is guaranteed that *programStatement* will be executed at least once.

The `for` Statement

Format 1:

```
for ( expression_1; expression_2; expression_3 )
    programStatement
```

expression_1 is evaluated once when execution of the loop begins. Next, *expression_2* is evaluated. If its value is nonzero, *programStatement* is executed and then *expression_3* is evaluated. Execution of *programStatement* and the subsequent evaluation of *expression_3* continue as long as the value of *expression_2* is nonzero. Because *expression_2* is evaluated each time before *programStatement* is executed, *programStatement* might never be executed if the value of *expression_2* is 0 when the loop is first entered.

Variables local to the `for` loop can be declared in *expression_1*. The scope of such variables is the scope of the `for` loop. For example

```
for ( int i = 0; i < 100; ++i )
    ...
```

declares the integer variable `i` and sets its initial value to 0 when the loop begins. The variable can be accessed by any statements inside the loop, but it is not accessible after the loop is terminated.

Format 2:

```
for ( var in expression )
    programStatement
```

This variant of the `for` loop sets up a *fast enumeration*. *var* is a variable whose type can also be declared, making its scope local to the `for` loop. *expression* is an expression that produces a result that conforms to the `NSFastEnumeration` protocol. Typically, *expression* is a collection, such as an array or a dictionary.

Each time through the `for` loop, the next object produced by the initial evaluation of *expression* is assigned to *var* and the body of the loop, represented by *programStatenent*, is executed. Execution terminates when all objects in *expression* have been enumerated.

Note that the `for` loop cannot change the contents of the collection. If it does, an exception is raised.

An array has each of its elements enumerated in order. Enumerating a dictionary object results in each key being enumerated, in no particular order. Enumeration of a set results in each member of the set being enumerated, in no particular order.

The `goto` Statement

General Format:

```
goto identifier;
```

Execution of the `goto` causes control to be sent directly to the statement labeled *identifier*. The labeled statement must be located in the same function or method as the `goto`.

The `if` Statement

Format 1:

```
if ( expression )
    programStatement
```

If the result of evaluating *expression* is nonzero, *programStatement* is executed; otherwise, it is skipped.

Format 2:

```
if ( expression )
    programStatement_1
else
    programStatement_2
```

If the value of *expression* is nonzero, *programStatement_1* is executed; otherwise, *programStatement_2* is executed. If *programStatement_2* is another `if` statement, an `if`-`else` `if` chain is affected, like so:

```
if ( expression_1 )
```

```
    programStatement_1
else if ( expression_2 )
    programStatement_2
    . . .
else
    programStatement_n
```

An `else` clause is always associated with the last `if` statement that does not contain an `else`. Braces can be used to change this association if necessary.

The `null` Statement

General Format:

```
;
```

Execution of a null statement has no effect and is used primarily to satisfy the requirement of a program statement in a `for`, `do`, or `while` loop. The following statement copies a character string pointed to by `from` to one pointed to by `to`:

```
while ( *to++ = *from++ )
    ;
```

In this statement, the null statement is used to satisfy the requirement that a program statement appear after the looping expression of the `while`.

The `return` Statement

Format 1:

```
return;
```

Execution of the `return` statement causes program execution to be immediately returned to the calling function or method. This format can be used only to return from a function or method that does not return a value.

If execution proceeds to the end of a function or method and a `return` statement is not encountered, it returns as if a `return` statement of this form had been executed. Therefore, in such a case, no value is returned.

Format 2:

```
return expression;
```

The value of `expression` is returned to the calling function or method. If the type of `expression` does not agree with the return type declared in the function or method declaration, its value is automatically converted to the declared type before it is returned.

The `switch` Statement

General Format:

```
switch ( expression )
{
  case constant_1:
     programStatement
     programStatement
      . . .
     break;
  case constant_2:
     programStatement
     programStatement
      . . .
     break;
  . . .
  case constant_n:
     programStatement
     programStatement
      . . .
     break;
  default:
     programStatement
     programStatement
      . . .
     break;
}
```

expression is evaluated and compared against the constant expression values
constant_1, constant_2, ..., constant_n. If the value of *expression* matches one of
these case values, the program statements that immediately follow are executed. If no case
value matches the value of *expression*, the `default` case, if included, is executed. If the
`default` case is not included, no statements contained in the `switch` are executed.

The result of the evaluation of *expression* must be of integral type, and no two cases
can have the same value. Omitting the `break` statement from a particular case causes execution to continue into the next case.

The `while` Statement

General Format:

```
while ( expression )
     programStatement
```

programStatement is executed as long as the value of *expression* is nonzero. Because
expression is evaluated each time before the execution of *programStatement*,
programStatement might never be executed.

Exception Handling

Exceptions can be handled at runtime by enclosing statements that might generate an exception inside an @try block, whose general format is as follows:

```
@try
    programStatement 1
@catch (exception)
    programStatement 2
@catch (exception)
    ...
@finally
    programStatement n
```

If an exception is thrown by *programStatement 1*, the @catch blocks that follow will be tested (in order) to see if the corresponding *exception* matches the one that was thrown. If it does, the corresponding *programStatement* will be executed. Whether or not an exception is thrown and caught, the @finally block, if supplied, will be executed.

Preprocessor

The preprocessor analyzes the source file before the compiler proper sees the code. Here is what the preprocessor does:

1. It replaces trigraph sequences by their equivalents (refer to the section "Compound Statements").

2. It joins any lines that end with a backslash character (\) together into a single line.

3. It divides the program into a stream of tokens.

4. It removes comments, replacing them by a single space.

5. It processes preprocessor directives (see the section "Preprocessor Directives") and expands macros.

Trigraph Sequences

To handle non-ASCII character sets, the following three-character sequences (called *trigraphs*) are recognized and treated specially wherever they occur inside a program (as well as inside character strings):

Trigraph	Meaning
??=	#
??(	[
??)	]

??<	{
??>	}
??/	\
??'	^
??!	|
??-	~

Preprocessor Directives

All preprocessor directives begin with the character #, which must be the first nonwhite-space character on the line. The # can be optionally followed by one or more space or tab characters.

The #define Directive

Format 1:

```
#define name text
```

This defines the identifier name to the preprocessor and associates with it whatever *text* appears after the first blank space after *name* to the end of the line. Subsequent use of *name* in the program causes *text* to be substituted directly into the program at that point.

Format 2:

```
#define name(param_1, param_2, ..., param_n) text
```

The macro *name* is defined to take arguments as specified by *param_1*, *param_2*, ..., *param_n*, each of which is an identifier. Subsequent use of *name* in the program with an argument list causes *text* to be substituted directly into the program at that point, with the arguments of the macro call replacing all occurrences of the corresponding parameters inside *text*.

If the macro takes a variable number of arguments, three dots are used at the end of the argument list. The remaining arguments in the list are collectively referenced in the macro definition by the special identifier __VA_ARGS__. As an example, the following defines a macro called myPrintf to take a variable number of arguments:

```
#define myPrintf(...)  printf ("DEBUG: " __VA_ARGS__);
```

Legitimate macro uses would include

```
myPrintf ("Hello world!\n");
```

as well as

```
myPrintf ("i = %i, j = %i\n", i, j);
```

If a definition requires more than one line, each line to be continued must end with a backslash character. After a name has been defined, it can be used anywhere in the file.

The # operator is permitted in #define directives that take arguments and is followed by the name of an argument to the macro. The preprocessor puts double quotation marks around the actual value passed to the macro when it's invoked. That is, it turns it into a character string. For example, the definition

```
#define printint(x) printf (# x " = %d\n", x)
```

with the call

```
printint (count);
```

is expanded by the preprocessor into

```
printf ("count" " = %i\n", count);
```

or equivalently

```
printf ("count = %i\n", count);
```

The preprocessor puts a \ character in front of any " or \ characters when performing this stringizing operation. So, with the definition

```
#define str(x) # x
```

the call

```
str (The string "\t" contains a tab)
```

expands to the following:

```
"The string \"\\t\" contains a tab"
```

The ## operator is also allowed in #define directives that take arguments. It is preceded (or followed) by the name of an argument to the macro. The preprocessor takes the value passed when the macro is invoked and creates a single token from the argument to the macro and the token that follows (or precedes) it. For example, the macro definition

```
#define printx(n) printf ("%i\n", x ## n );
```

with the call

```
printx (5)
```

produces the following:

```
printf ("%i\n", x5);
```

The definition

```
#define printx(n) printf ("x" # n " = %i\n", x ## n );
```

with the call

```
printx(10)
```

produces

```
printf ("x10 = %i\n", x10);
```

after substitution and concatenation of the character strings.

Spaces are not required around the # and ## operators.

The #error Directive

General Format:

```
#error text
 . . .
```

The specified *text* is written as an error message by the preprocessor.

The #if Directive

Format 1:

```
#if constant_expression
 . . .
#endif
```

The value of *constant_expression* is evaluated. If the result is nonzero, all program lines up until the #endif directives are processed; otherwise, they are automatically skipped and are not processed by the preprocessor or the compiler.

Format 2:

```
#if constant_expression_1
 . . .
#elif constant_expression_2
 . . .
#elif constant_expression_n
 . . .
#else
 . . .
#endif
```

If *constant_expression_1* is nonzero, all program lines up until the #elif are processed and the remaining lines up to the #endif are skipped. Otherwise, if *constant_expression_2* is nonzero, all program lines up until the next #elif are processed and the remaining lines up to the #endif are skipped. If none of the constant expressions evaluates to nonzero, the lines after the #else (if included) are processed.

The special operator defined can be used as part of the constant expression, so

```
#if defined (DEBUG)
```

```
   ...
#endif
```

causes the code between the `#if` and `#endif` to be processed if the identifier DEBUG has been previously defined (see also `#ifdef` in the next section). The parentheses are not necessary around the identifier, so

```
#if defined DEBUG
```

works just as well.

The `#ifdef` Directive

General Format:

```
#ifdef identifier
   ...
#endif
```

If the value of *identifier* has been previously defined (either through a `#define` or with the `-D` command-line option when the program was compiled), all program lines up until the `#endif` are processed; otherwise, they are skipped. As with the `#if` directive, `#elif` and `#else` directives can be used with a `#ifdef` directive.

The `#ifndef` Directive

General Format:

```
#ifndef identifier
   ...
#endif
```

If the value of *identifier* has not been previously defined, all program lines up until the `#endif` are processed; otherwise, they are skipped. As with the `#if` directive, `#elif` and `#else` directives can be used with a `#ifndef` directive.

The `#import` Directive[4]

Format 1:

```
#import "fileName"
```

If the file specified by *fileName* has been previously included in the program, this statement is skipped. Otherwise, the preprocessor searches an implementation-defined directory or directories first for the file *fileName*. Typically, the same directory that contains the source file is searched first, and if the file is not found there, a sequence of implementation-defined standard places is searched. After it's found, the contents of the file are included in the program at the precise point that the `#import` directive appears. Preprocessor directives contained within the included file are analyzed; therefore, an included file can itself contain other `#import` or `#include` directives.

Format 2:

```
#import <fileName>
```

If the file has not been previously included, the preprocessor searches for the specified file only in the standard places. Specifically, the current source directory is omitted from the search. The action taken after the file is found is otherwise identical to that described previously.

In either format, a previously defined name can be supplied and expansion will occur. So, the following sequence works:

```
#define ROOTOBJECT  <NSObject.h>
  ...
#import ROOTOBJECT
```

The #include Directive

This behaves the same way as #import except no check is made for previous inclusion of the specified header file.

The #line Directive

General Format:

```
#line constant "fileName"
```

This directive causes the compiler to treat subsequent lines in the program as if the name of the source file were *fileName* and as if the line number of all subsequent lines began at *constant*. If *fileName* is not specified, the filename specified by the last #line directive, or the name of the source file (if no filename was previously specified), is used.

The #line directive is primarily used to control the filename and line number that are displayed whenever an error message is issued by the compiler.

The #pragma Directive

General Format:

```
#pragma text
```

This causes the preprocessor to perform some implementation-defined action. For example, under the pragma

```
#pragma loop_opt(on)
```

causes special loop optimization to be performed on a particular compiler. If this pragma is encountered by a compiler that doesn't recognize the loop_opt pragma, it is ignored.

The #undef Directive

General Format:

#undef *identifier*

The specified *identifier* becomes undefined to the preprocessor. Subsequent #ifdef or #ifndef directives behave as if the identifier were never defined.

The # Directive

This is a null directive and is ignored by the preprocessor.

Predefined Identifiers

The following identifiers are defined by the preprocessor:

Identifier	Meaning
__LINE__	Current line number being compiled
__FILE__	Name of the current source file being compiled
__DATE__	Date the file is being compiled, in the format "*Mmm dd yyyy*"
__TIME__	Time the file is being compiled, in the format "*hh:mm:ss*"
__STDC__	Defined as 1 if the compiler conforms to the ANSI standard and 0 if not
__STDC_HOSTED__	Defined as 1 if the implementation is hosted and 0 if not
__STDC_VERSION__	Defined as 199901L

Appendix C

Address Book Source Code

For your reference purposes, here are the complete interface and implementation files for the address book example you worked with throughout Part II, "The Foundation Framework." This includes the definitions for the `AddressCard`, and `AddressBook` classes. You should implement these classes on your system; then extend the class definitions to make them more practical and powerful. This is an excellent way for you to learn the language and become familiar with building programs, working with classes and objects, and working with the Foundation framework.

AddressCard Interface File

```
#import <Foundation/Foundation.h>


@interface AddressCard   : NSObject <NSCopying, NSCoding> {
    NSString    *name;
    NSString    *email;
}

@property (nonatomic, copy) NSString *name, *email;

-(void) setName: (NSString *) theName andEmail: (NSString *) theEmail;
-(void) retainName: (NSString *) theName andEmail: (NSString *) theEmail;
-(NSComparisonResult) compareNames: (id) element;

-(void) print;

@end
```

AddressBook Interface File

```
#import <Foundation/Foundation.h>
#import "AddressCard.h"

@interface AddressBook: NSObject <NSCopying, NSCoding>
{
    NSString        *bookName;
    NSMutableArray  *book;
}

@property (nonatomic, copy) NSString *bookName;
@property (nonatomic, copy) NSMutableArray *book;

-(id)   initWithName: (NSString *) name;
-(void) sort;
-(void) addCard: (AddressCard *) theCard;
-(void) removeCard: (AddressCard *) theCard;
-(int)  entries;
-(void) list;
-(AddressCard *) lookup: (NSString *) theName;

-(void) dealloc;

@end
```

AddressCard Implementation File

```
#import "AddressCard.h"

@implementation AddressCard

@synthesize name, email;

-(void) setName: (NSString *) theName andEmail: (NSString *) theEmail
{
    [self setName: theName];
    [self setEmail: theEmail];
}


// Compare the two names from the specified address cards
-(NSComparisonResult) compareNames: (id) element
{
    return [name  compare: [element name]];
```

```
}

-(void) print
{
    NSLog (@"===================================");
    NSLog (@"|                                 |");
    NSLog (@"|  %-31s |", [name  UTF8String]);
    NSLog (@"|  %-31s |", [email UTF8String]);
    NSLog (@"|                                 |");
    NSLog (@"|                                 |");
    NSLog (@"|                                 |");
    NSLog (@"|         O             O         |");
    NSLog (@"===================================");

}

-(AddressCard *) copyWithZone: (NSZone *) zone
{
    AddressCard *newCard = [[AddressCard allocWithZone: zone] init];

    [newCard retainName: name andEmail: email];
    return newCard;
}

-(void) retainName: (NSString *) theName andEmail: (NSString *) theEmail
{
    name = [theName retain];
    email = [theEmail retain];
}

-(void) encodeWithCoder: (NSCoder *) encoder
{
    [encoder encodeObject: name forKey: @"AddressCardName"];
    [encoder encodeObject: email forKey: @"AddressCardEmail"];
}

-(id) initWithCoder: (NSCoder *) decoder
{
    name = [[decoder decodeObjectForKey: @"AddressCardName"] retain];
    email = [[decoder decodeObjectForKey: @"AddressCardEmail"] retain];

    return self;
}

-(void) dealloc
{
```

```
    [name release];
    [email release];
    [super dealloc];
}
@end
```

AddressBook Implementation File

```
#import "AddressBook.h"

@implementation AddressBook

@synthesize book, bookName;

// set up the AddressBook's name and an empty book

-(id) initWithName: (NSString *) name{
    self = [super init];

    if (self) {
        bookName = [[NSString alloc] initWithString: name];
        book = [[NSMutableArray alloc] init];
    }

    return self;
}

-(void) sort
{
    [book sortUsingSelector: @selector(compareNames:)];
}

-(void) addCard: (AddressCard *) theCard
{
    [book addObject: theCard];
}

-(void) removeCard: (AddressCard *) theCard
{
    [book removeObjectIdenticalTo: theCard];
}

-(int) entries
{
    return [book count];
```

```objc
}

-(void) list
{
    NSLog (@"========= Contents of: %@ =========", bookName);

    for ( AddressCard *theCard in book )
        NSLog (@"%-20s     %-32s", [theCard.name UTF8String],
                [theCard.email UTF8String]);

    NSLog (@"=================================================");
}

// lookup address card by name — assumes an exact match

-(AddressCard *) lookup: (NSString *) theName
{
    for ( AddressCard *nextCard in book )
        if ( [[nextCard name] caseInsensitiveCompare: theName] == NSOrderedSame )
            return nextCard;

    return nil;
}

-(void) dealloc
{
    [bookName release];
    [book release];
    [super dealloc];
}

-(void) encodeWithCoder: (NSCoder *) encoder
{
    [encoder encodeObject:bookName forKey: @"AddressBookBookName"];
    [encoder encodeObject:book forKey: @"AddressBookBook"];
}

-(id) initWithCoder: (NSCoder *) decoder
{
    bookName = [[decoder decodeObjectForKey: @"AddressBookBookName"] retain];
    book = [[decoder decodeObjectForKey: @"AddressBookBook"] retain];

    return self;
}
```

```
// Method for NSCopying protocol

-(id) copyWithZone: (NSZone *) zone
{
    AddressBook *newBook = [[self class] allocWithZone: zone];

    [newBook initWithName: bookName];
    [newBook setBook: book];

    return newBook;
}
@end
```

Appendix D

Resources

This appendix contains a selective list of resources you can turn to for more information. Some of the information might be on your system, online at a Web site, or available from a book. We've compiled resources for C language, Objective-C, Cocoa, and iPhone/iTouch programming. This list gives you a good starting point to help you locate whatever it is you're looking for.

Answers to Exercises, Errata, and Such

You can visit the publisher's Web site www.informit.com/register to get answers to exercises and errata for this book.

Objective-C Language

Following is a list of resources you can turn to for more information about the Objective-C language.

Books

- The Objective-C 2.0 Programming Language. Apple Computer, Inc., 2008—This is the best reference available on Objective-C language and is a good book for you to read after completing this one. You can get to this text either through Xcode's Help->Documentation window or directly online from Apple's Web site. Here is the online link for the pdf version of this text: http://developer.apple.com/documentation/Cocoa/Conceptual/ObjectiveC/ObjC.pdf.

- Object-Oriented Programming: An Evolutionary Approach, Second Edition. Brad Cox and Andy Novobilski. Addison-Wesley, 1991—This is the original book about Objective-C, coauthored by Brad Cox, the designer of the language.

- Objective-C Pocket Reference. Andrew M. Duncan. O'Reilly Associates Inc., 2003—This is a terse reference for the Objective-C language.

Websites

- http://developer.apple.com/documentation/Cocoa/ObjectiveCLanguage-date.html—The part of the Apple Web site devoted to Objective-C language. Contains, among other things, online documentation, sample code, and technical notes.

C Programming Language

Because C is the underlying programming language, you might want to study it in more depth. The language has been around for more than 25 years, so there's certainly no dearth of information on the subject.

Books

- Programming in C, Third Edition. Stephen Kochan. Sams Publishing, 2004—This is the first book I wrote (way back when), revised several times along the way. This is a tutorial, but it covers in greater detail many of the language features that were lumped together in Chapter 13, "Underlying C Language Features."

- The C Programming Language, Second Edition. Brian W. Kernighan and Dennis M. Ritchie. Prentice Hall, Inc., 1988—This has always been the bible as far as a reference for the language. It was the first book written about C and was cowritten by Dennis Ritchie, who created the language.

- C: A Reference Manual, Fifth Edition. Samuel P. Harbison, III and Guy L. Steele, Jr. Prentice Hall, 2002—Another excellent reference book for C programmers.

Cocoa

If you are serious about application development under Mac OS X, you need to learn how to program with Cocoa. Many books are available on Cocoa, with new ones being published all the time. You can type in "Cocoa" in amazon.com's search window to see what pops up. The following are just a few of the books available.

Books

- Introduction to Cocoa Fundamentals Guide. Apple Computer, Inc., 2007—This is an excellent text covering application development with Cocoa. You can access it from Xcode's Documentation window. You can access it online and get a pdf version from here: http://developer.apple.com/documentation/Cocoa/Conceptual/CocoaFundamentals/CocoaFundamentals.pdf.
- Cocoa Programming for Mac OS X, Third Edition. Aaron Hillegass. Addison-Wesley, 2008—A good introduction to Cocoa written in an easy-to-read style.
- Cocoa in a Nutshell. Michael Beam and James Duncan Davidson. O'Reilly & Associates, Inc., 2003—This is a reference resource for the many different classes and methods that are part of the Cocoa development system.
- Learning Cocoa with Objective-C, Second Edition. James Duncan Davidson and Apple Computer, Inc. O'Reilly & Associates, Inc., 2002—This is an introductory book on Cocoa programming.

Websites

- http://developer.apple.com/cocoa/—Apple's main Web site for Cocoa developers includes documentation, sample code, technical notes, and a wealth of information.
- http://www.cocoadevcentral.com/—This is a Web site designed to help people learn how to program in Cocoa with Objective-C.
- http://www.cocoadev.com/—This is an open Web site that can be edited by anyone. There's a lot of good information to be found here.

iPhone and iTouch Application Development

The popularity of the iPhone will surely result in a stream of titles related to application development for this device. Here are a few of the titles that were published or announced at the time this book went to press.

Books

- iPhone OS Programming Guide.Apple Computer, Inc., 2008—This is an excellent text covering application development for the iPhone.You can access it from Xcode's Documentation window.You can access it online and get a pdf version from here: http://developer.apple.com/iphone/library/documentation/iPhone/Conceptual/iPhoneOSProgrammingGuide/iPhoneAppProgrammingGuide.pdf.
- The iPhone Developer's Cookbook: Building Applications with the iPhone SDK.Erica Sadun. Addison-Wesley Professional, 2008—Offers recipes for writing different types of iPhone applications.
- Beginning iPhone Development: Exploring the iPhone SDK.Dave Mark. Apress, 2008—An introductory text on writing applications for the iPhone and iTouch.
- iPhone Application Development: Building Applications for the AppStore.Jonathan Zdziarski, 2009, O'Reilly Media, Inc., 2002—Not yet published at the time this book went to press.

Websites

- http://developer.apple.com/iphone/—Apple's main Web site for iPhone developers (known as the iPhone DevCenter). Here you can find documentation, tutorial videos, sample code, technical notes, and a wealth of information.You can also download the iPhone SDK from here.

- http://www.iphonedevcentral.org/—This is a Web site offering free tutorials and a forum for exchanging ideas and asking questions.

Index

D

T

Join the Community for
Programming in Objective-C 2.0

Over 3,000 members at ClassroomM.com

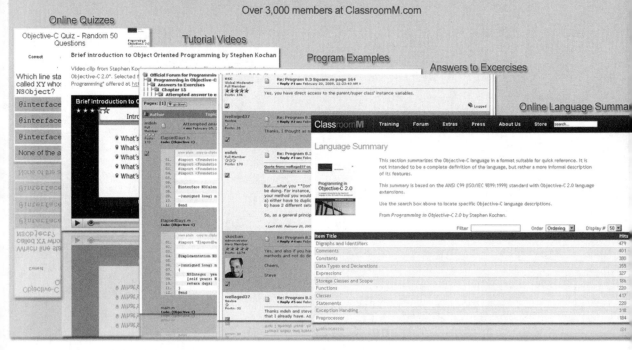

At ClassroomM.com You Will Find

1. Answers to Exercises

2. Program Examples

3. Online Quizzes

4. Tutorial Videos

5. Online Language Summary

6. Answers to your questions from the author and other forum members

There's More!

At ClassroomM.com you can sign up for live webcasts that are given by the author!

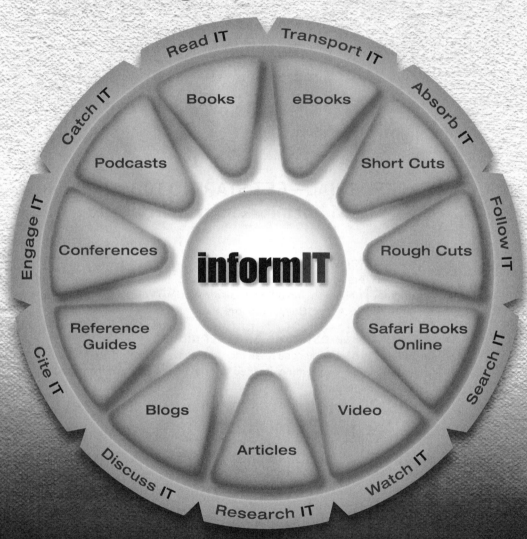

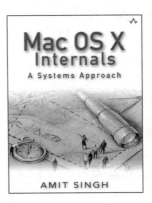

FREE Online Edition

Your purchase of **Programming in Objective-C 2.0** includes access to a free online edition for 45 days through the Safari Books Online subscription service. Nearly every Addison-Wesley Professional book is available online through Safari Books Online, along with more than 5,000 other technical books and videos from publishers such as Cisco Press, Exam Cram, IBM Press, O'Reilly, Prentice Hall, Que, and Sams.

SAFARI BOOKS ONLINE allows you to search for a specific answer, cut and paste code, download chapters, and stay current with emerging technologies.

Activate your FREE Online Edition at www.informit.com/safarifree

> **STEP 1:** Enter the coupon code: AFASLZG.

> **STEP 2:** New Safari users, complete the brief registration form. Safari subscribers, just log in.

If you have difficulty registering on Safari or accessing the online edition, please e-mail customer-service@safaribooksonline.com